THE SEDUCTION OF VENUS

Artists and Models

FRANCE BOREL

THE SEDUCTION OF VENUS

Artists and Models

SKIRA
RIZZOLI
NEW YORK

Published in the United States of America in 1990 by
RIZZOLI INTERNATIONAL PUBLICATIONS, INC.
300 Park Avenue South/New York 10010

Translated from the French by Jean-Marie Clarke

Library of Congress Cataloging-in-Publication Data

Borel, France.
[Le modèle ou l'artiste séduit. English]
The seduction of Venus: artists and models / by France Borel.
p. cm.
Translation of: Le modèle ou l'artiste séduit.
Includes bibliographical references.
ISBN 0-8478-1217-0: $45.00
1. Models, Artists'. 2. Artists — Psychology. 3. Artists — Relationship with women. I. Title.
N7574.B6713 1990
702'.8 – dc20 89-43608
CIP

Printed in Switzerland

Contents

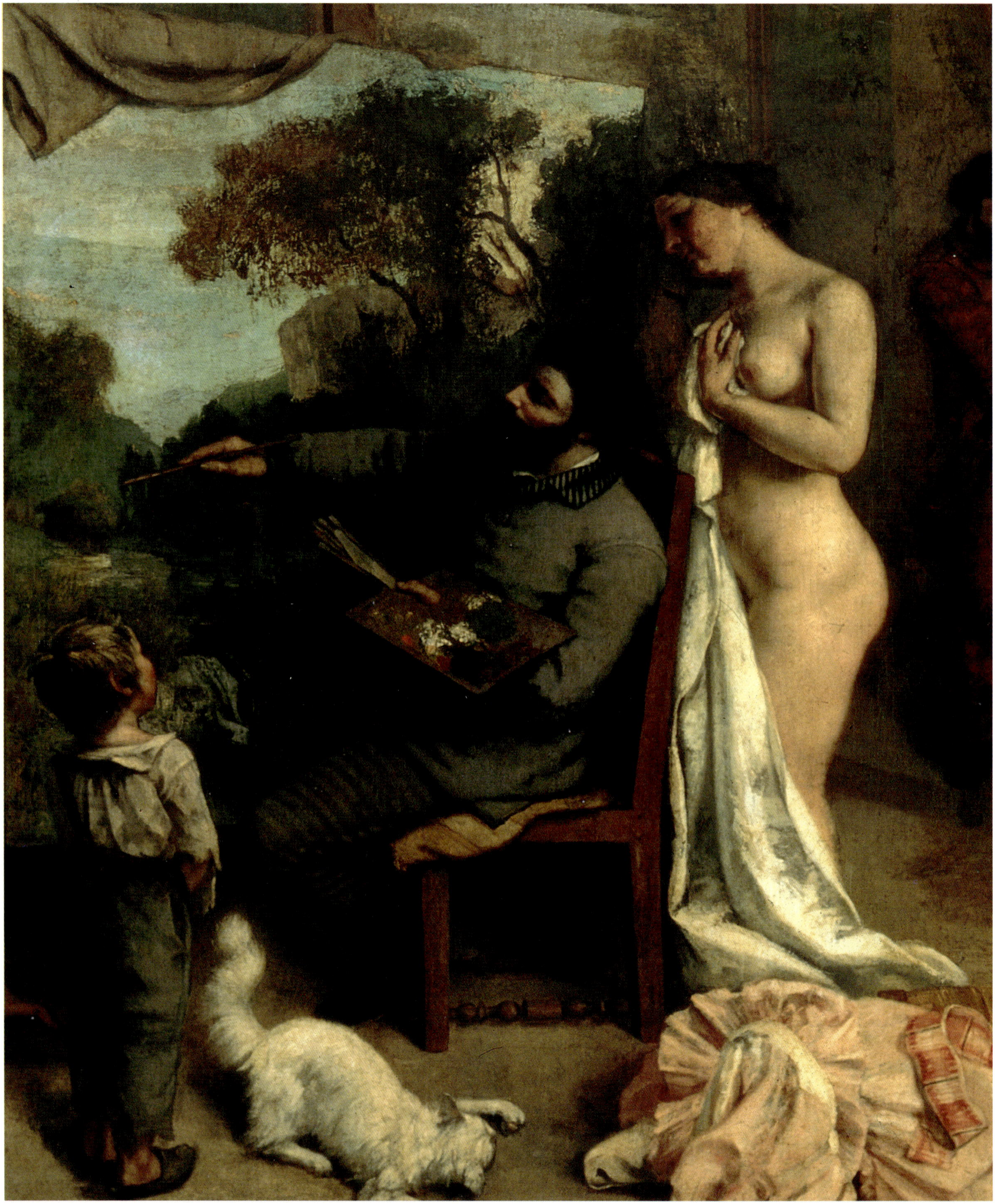

Introducing the Model

What takes place within that strange relationship between the artist and his model? Why has the artist been driven throughout the centuries to work from a live model who displays her nudity to his gaze? The instruction of the academies and studios revolved around the presence of live anatomies taking poses dictated by the fiat of the painter or of the sculptor. Nudity was offered to the eye in order to produce the nude, an inevitable and perennial theme of the visual arts. Artists replenished themselves in the presence of flesh. It was their inspiration, and they tried to capture its every vibration in order to transpose it into marble or paint. In a constant and ambiguous oscillation, the eye and the spirit, or the hand and the mind, moved back and forth between mental images, fantasies, ideals, cultural canons and the living presence of a human body.

The artist chose his models according to a "type" that haunted him. And yet he often seems to have been unsatisfied, ever searching for a more adequate subject, one corresponding more closely to his imagination. Unless, like a Narcissus in disguise, he was looking for a model resembling himself.

Out of weariness sometimes, he dispensed with the presence of a model in his everyday practice and worked from memory. Or, flirting with medicine, he turned to anatomy, with its cadavers, flayed bodies, skeletons and other still lifes.

Gustave Courbet:
The Painter's Studio, detail, 1855.

Henri Matisse:
The Painter and His Model, 1936.

Voluptuous Illusions

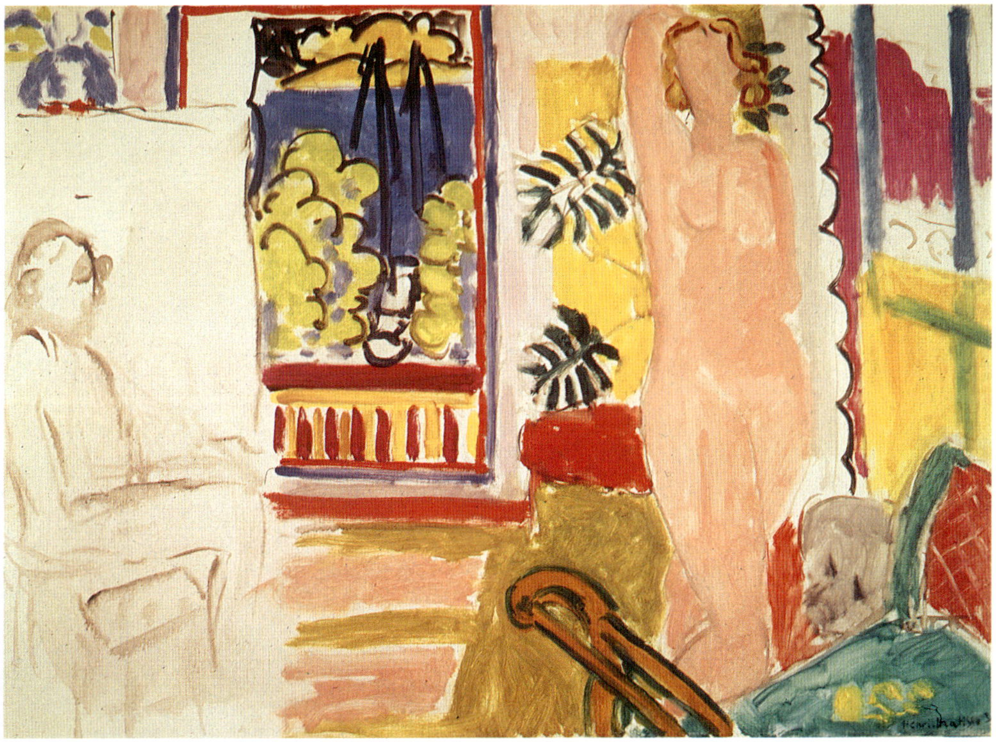

Pablo Picasso:
The Shadow, 1953.

The ubiquity of the body

The representation of the human body is omnipresent in the visual arts. It is majestically enthroned at the heart of Western iconography between Venus and Odalisque, Apollo and Cupid. There it sits, draped or undraped, offering endless avatars to the eye, disguised in its many masks. Its metamorphoses are without number; they reveal it or hide it, or by multiplying its appearances, render it impossible to grasp. Its presence is manifest, evident, seems palpable, and yet it is ever elusive. No sooner do we try to approach it than it is already somewhere else. Undoubtedly, because the human body never entirely falls within the grasp of the artist, he must return to it continually and approach it with the aid of all kinds of references, artifices and settings. Indefatigably, he attempts to bring it into being with his chisel or brush.

He represents it in various attitudes, drapes it, undrapes it, peels off its skin in order to know its muscles better, removes the muscles in order to know its skeleton. For it, he creates mythological or other kinds of decors favorable to the expression of its sensuality. He constructs and reconstructs it through the intermediary of more or less abstract systems. He measures it, calculates its ideal proportions, strives to domesticate it in every possible way.

The body attracts the artist inevitably, like a magnet, yet it also frightens him. Nevertheless, he uses it everywhere and in all of its states and forms: whole, in parts, fragmented, exploded, in pieces, asleep or active, sad or sated.

Over the figure officially represented on the canvas or in the marble, hovers the shadow of the body of its creator, interwoven in filigree. Insidiously and transparently, it projects or superimposes itself onto it. Being at the center of the work, it is its prime mover, but it acts secretly, almost clandestinely. The work of art is woven out of the substance of its creator ("a double of flesh," Sartre wrote of literature[1]), it is the extension of sensations in their physical state, and it incarnates his fears and his joys. The surface of the model's body offers itself to the traces of pleasure and anxiety.

Without the ferment of these ambiguities, art would be a bloodless, sterile, frigid affair. The work of art feeds on the desires of the artist; desire for the other, for his model, for the naked woman posing in front of him, as well as the narcissistic desire for himself. The act of creation is above all an act of love. Painting and sculpture are composed of erogenous zones, of tactile materials. By essence, they take on a human form. They are like a fetish, both a substitute and a support for the body's projections. Coming into being out of the body and mind of their creator, they become independent of him, they become means for the joy of the beholder.

The artist is omnipresent: in the subject he chooses, but also in the brushwork which characterizes him and constitutes his style. And yet he can disappear as an individual, his creation can function beyond him. Like a child coming of age, the fetish which he created for himself becomes autonomous, stands alone, without a support, and becomes a great reservoir of fantasies for those who contemplate and penetrate it.

By projecting himself "body and soul" into his work, the artist stimulates in turn the projections of the spectator. From the independent object it is at first, the fetish grows, extends itself, gives pleasure to more or less people. The pleasure of the creator is amplified, gives of itself, radiates outward. When this element is missing, art becomes mere stereotype, repetition, a hollow shell, empty appearance deprived of substance, a surface devoid of interest and fixed in its shortcomings, an utterly useless or banal imitation. The stereotype, as

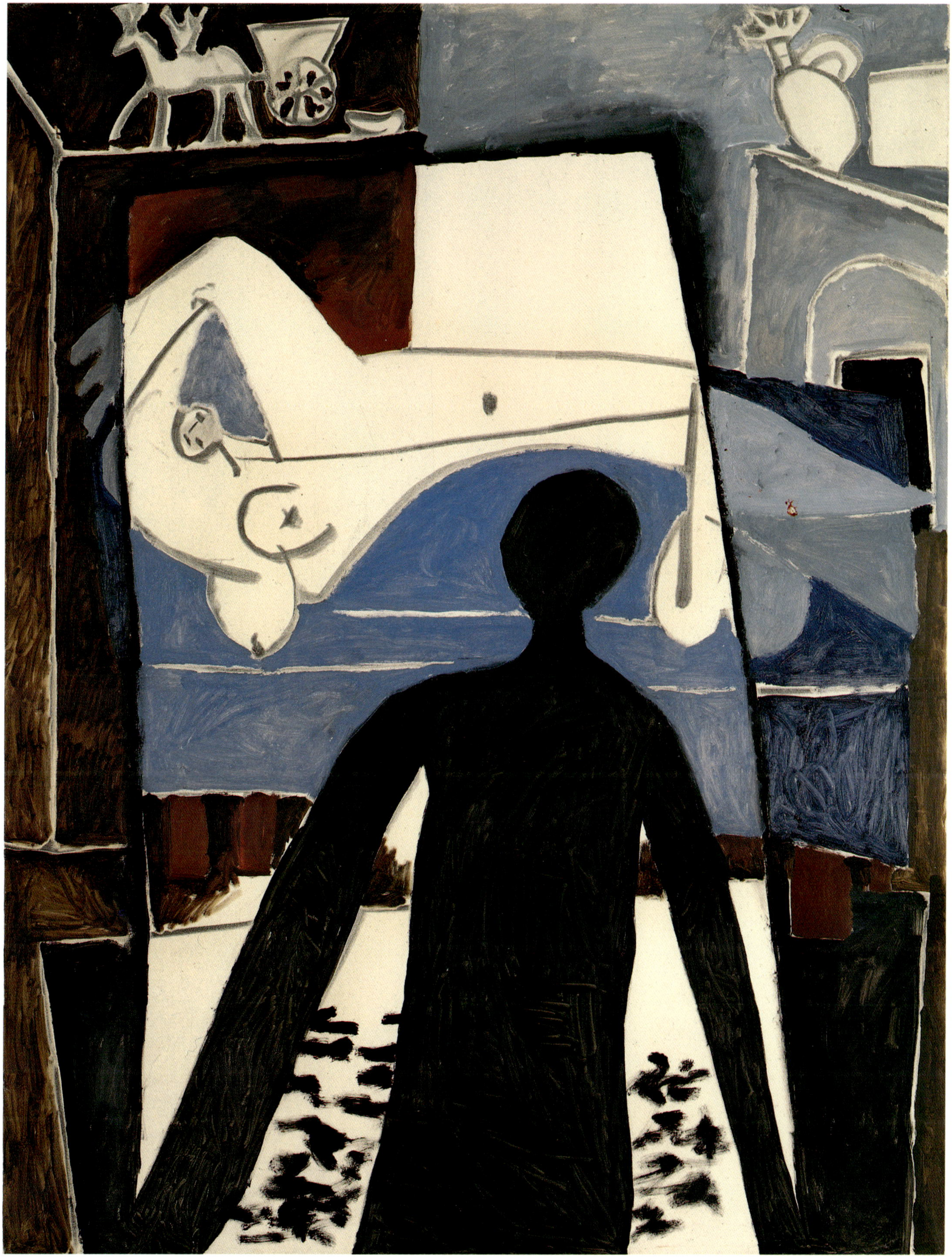

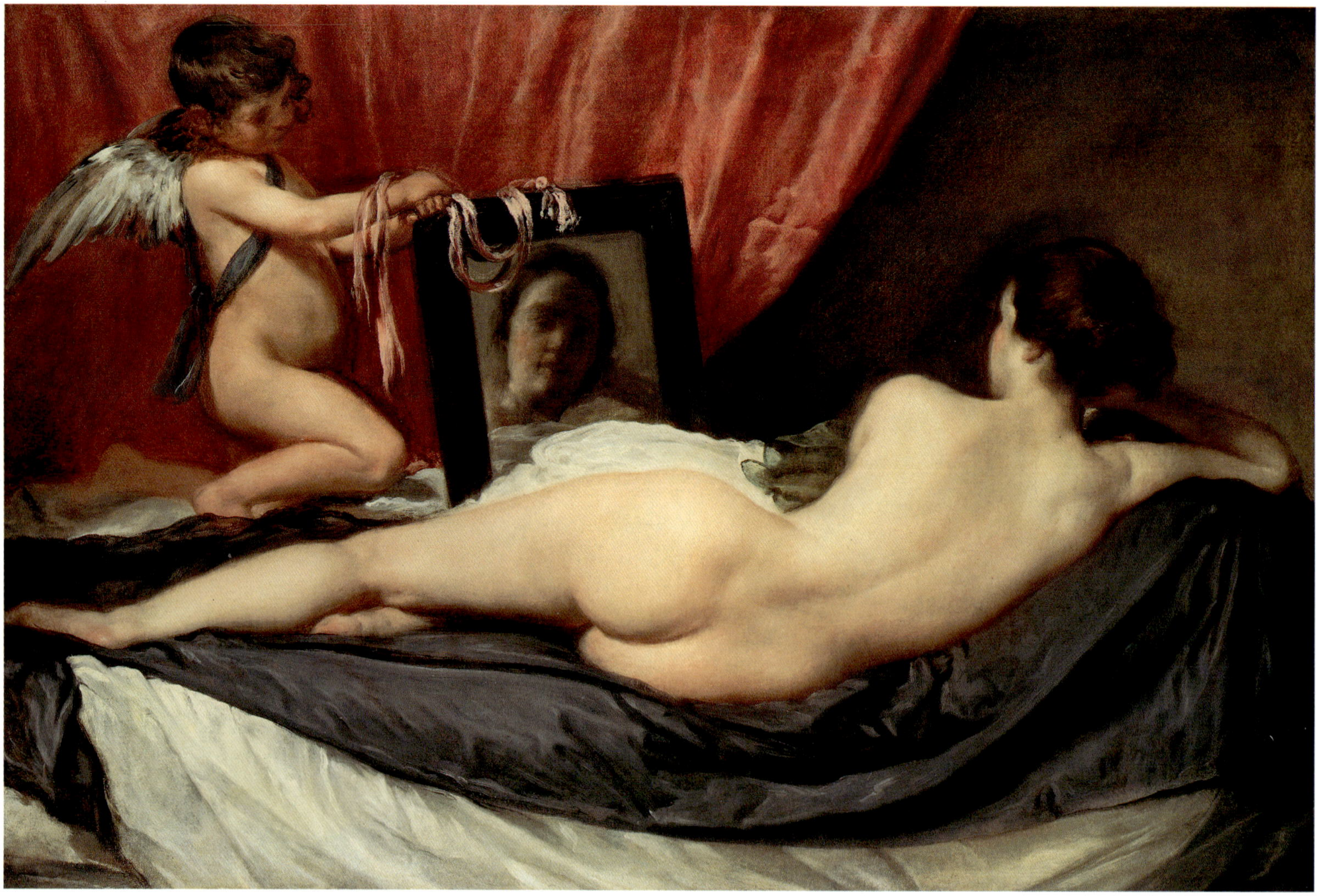

Diego Velázquez:
Venus with Mirror, c. 1650.

Roland Barthes defined it in literature, "is that place in discourse in which the body is absent, where we may be certain that it is not."[2] The same definition could be applied to painting. Art, like thought, should be a "flush of pleasure."[3]

The physical implication of the artist can take on quite different disguises; it can hide behind many layers of make-up, and then show itself where it is least expected. There can be something erotic in the way that greens and pinks are mixed in order to obtain the color of flesh. Not to mention the way of laying on coats of oil paint with brushes made of pig's bristles or of marten, polecat, or badger hair. The very gestures of the painter are so many ways of touching; like caresses they can be either rough or gentle, full of violence or tenderness. Beyond figuration, the sensual body is the very essence of the work. Any esthetic production worthy of the name is an intermingling of desires. It is subtended by the omnipresence of the body. The work of art blends with life, but without being contingent to it.

It comes into being through it and frees itself immediately afterwards, immortalizing the most subtle pulsations of pleasure and fear.

Art and the body are composed of a similar flesh, they reflect each other.[4] Through perception, the body establishes itself as the measure and reference of all things; artistic production extends the body and detaches itself from it, all the while keeping its imprint.

The phenomenon of creative work is usually described in terms of corporeal metaphors. Statements by artists are full of images of childbirth or expulsion, like defecation, or vomiting. The vocabulary of creation is often linked to the realm of physical processes, as we can see in the use of terms like inspiration, conception, gestation, procreation, etc.

Didier Anzieu remarks: "Creation is not just a matter of getting down to work. It is letting oneself be worked on by conscious, preconscious and unconscious thoughts, affected as well in one's body, or at least in the physical Ego; it is to work in turn on their ever-problematic conjunction, dissociation and reunification. The body of the artist, his actual body, his imaginary body, his fantasized body, are present throughout his work and he weaves their traces, their places, and their figures into the fabric of his work."[5] To create is also to claim a portion of immortality, and so to hope for a protection, a shield for the living flesh, as well as a life beyond that of the physical body. Artistic creation tries to free itself from fears and frontiers, all the while playing dangerously close to the brink. As in eroticism, it transgresses the taboos of death at its own risk, like the moth that singes its wings when it flies too close to the flame.

The work of art in its fullness avenges the human condition. The artistic creator brings the universe into being by a hand to hand struggle that is both a strain and a joy. "The canvas of the painter, the blank page of the poet, the ruled sheets of the composer, the stage or area used by the dancer or architect, and of course the surface of the film, the screen of the filmmaker, all materialize, symbolize and revitalize the experience of the frontier between two bodies as a symbiotic surface of inscription—with its paradoxical character, as in the work of art, which is both a surface of separation and of contacts."[6] The artist, like Pygmalion, gives body to the work, gives a concrete existence to a mental image. He models, animates, breathes life into imaginary forms.

The body of the work of art is extracted from the artist's own body (as lived and fantasized); it is as if, possessed of a strange power, he could turn his skin inside out like a glove by projecting onto it his dreams, his fantasies and his sensations. Because

Piero Manzoni:
Living Sculptures, 1961.

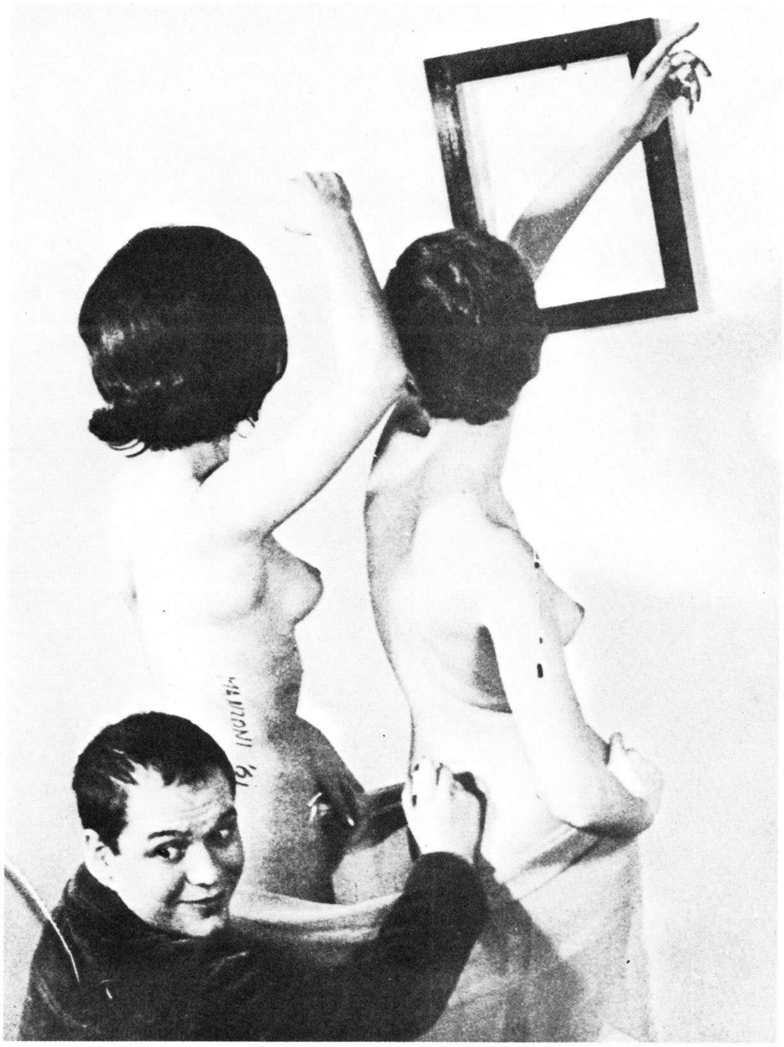

of its obvious availability, the artist uses his own body first of all, it is his first model, the true and essential archetype, the inevitable prototype which will very likely guide him, sometimes imperatively, if indirectly, in the choice of his later models. The obstinate search by painters and sculptors for certain types of "live" models is a symptom of this.

Starting with the sensations of his own body, the desire for the body of the other, and his mental images, the artist searches for the ideal body around which his imagination has somehow or other crystallized. It is in the body that the work of art originates; there it finds its basic structure, its language and its logic.

In its elaboration, the work of art constructs a new body for its author, a new skin, a sort of double which contains him and sustains itself with his most essential energies and his most physical sensations.[7] This metaphorical body, which is an open receptacle for fantasies, constitutes a place of liberty. The artist can "invent" his ideal figures beyond material constraints. Ingres added an extra vertebra to the neck of his Odalisque. Modigliani drew the faces of his women in an almond shape. El Greco shredded the contours of his figures into strident colors. Giacometti dissolved them into a thin metallic wire, etc. In the work of art, anatomy can be represented in all forms: smooth, torn, fragmented, exploded, elongated, stocky, or stout. The limits to the forms possible are those of the imagination itself. With his fingertips or with his whole hand, the artist engenders himself as he engenders his models. He turns regularly to reality to find the best subjects, sensing all the while that no living model will ever correspond exactly to his mental images.

The artistic creator has a dual existence: in his flesh and in his work. He turns himself inside out like the tunic of Nessus[8] and gives birth to himself in the image of a new maternal body. His blood and sperm spread into his work and fecundate it to such

Yves Klein:
Anthropometry 82, 1960.

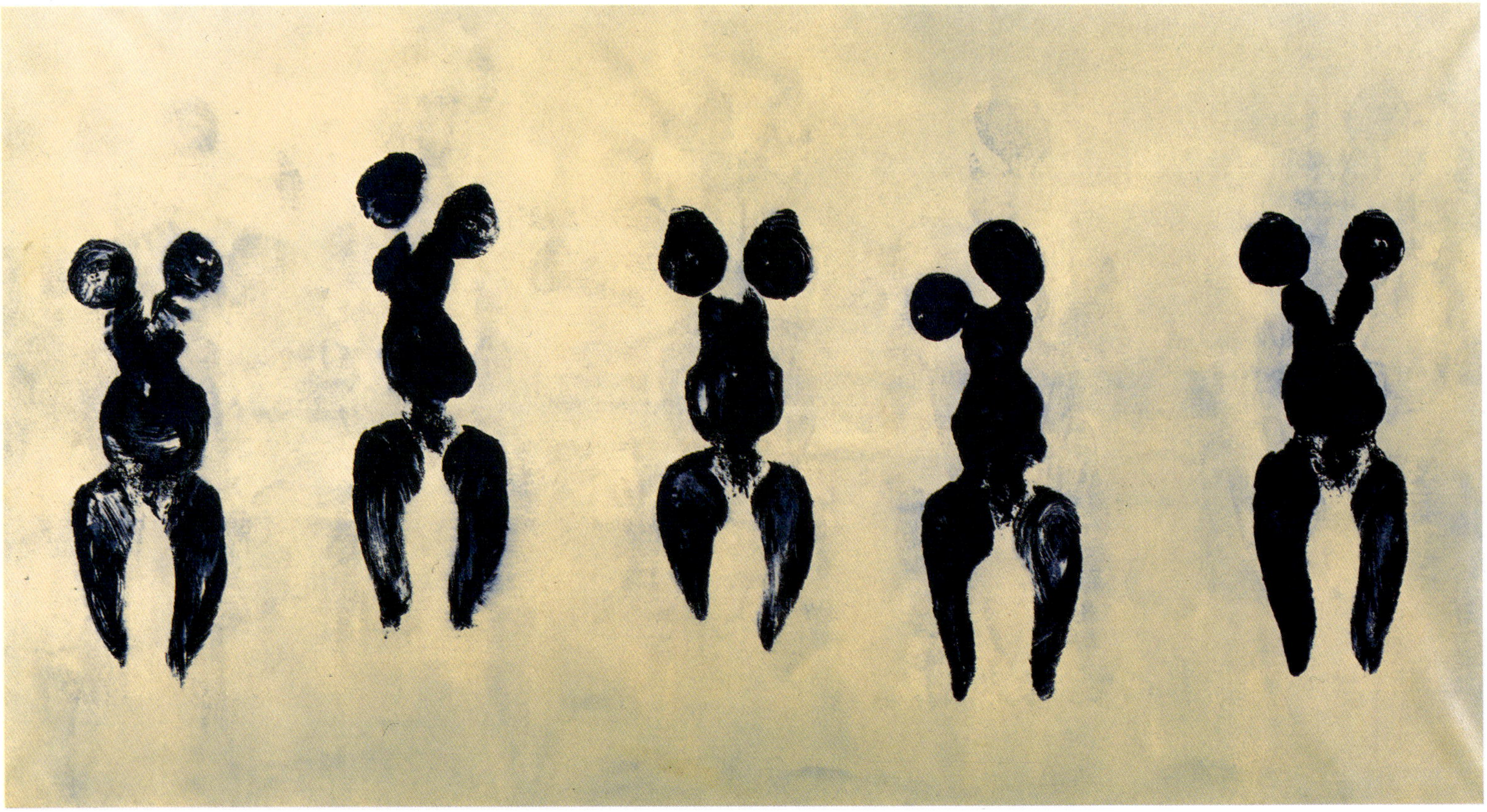

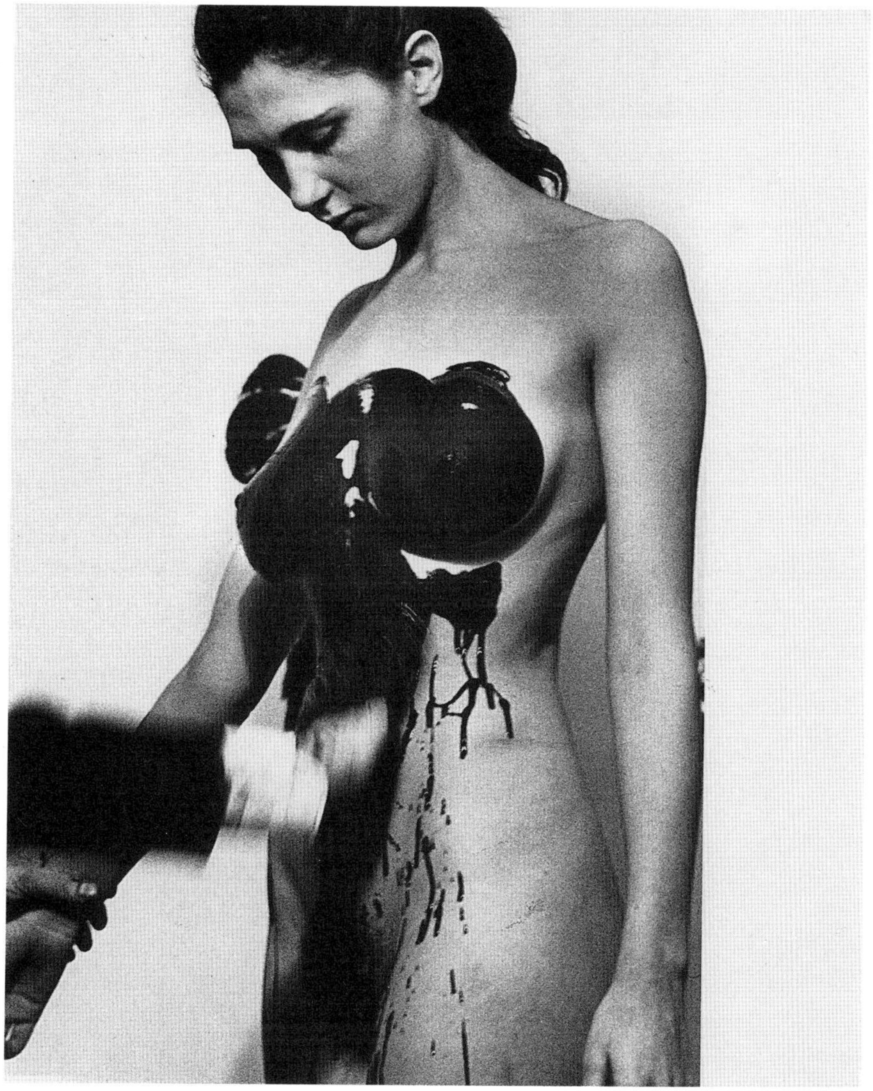

Yves Klein preparing his model for Anthropometry (ANT 15), *1960.*

an extent that some old masters famed for the exceptional quality of their flesh tints (like Titian, for example) were suspected of actually mixing blood or sperm with their pigments, that is to say, the vital substances of their being. The mystery of well-rendered flesh color has always been surrounded by speculations on alchemical means and highly elaborate rituals. The artist, however, keeps his recipes and the contents of his secrets to himself. It is in fact the body which dictates the first model, the original model.

The artist's relationship to his work establishes itself by his eminently sensual choice of tools and by his way of using them. Scraping, rubbing, brushing, coating, are all operations charged with sensuality, in which the body is implied directly as it impresses itself on a material support, be it canvas, marble, clay or metal. Often, the materials of the artist, canvas, cardboard, paper, or stone, are associated with the natural surfaces used for inscriptions.

Through his gestures, the artist incarnates and reincarnates himself in a great diversity and with

Edvard Munch:
Weeping Girl, 1907.

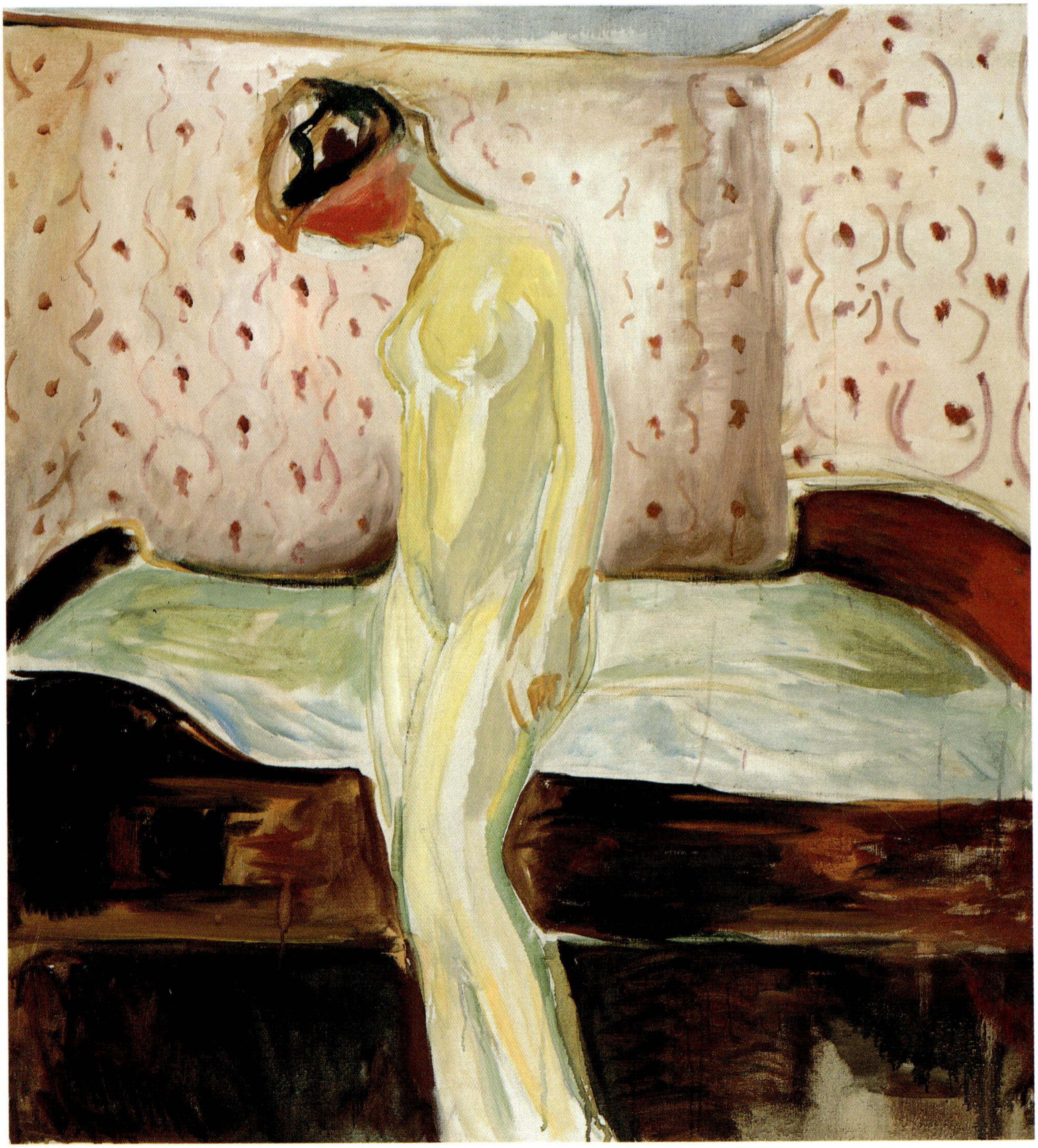

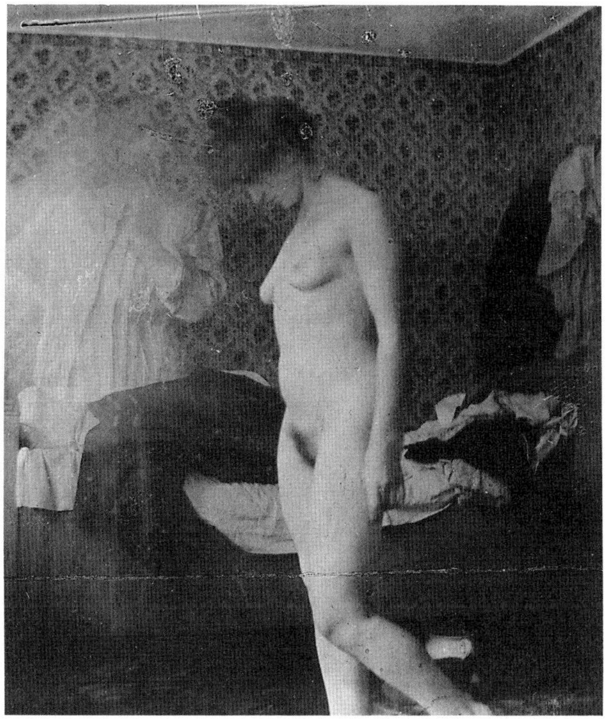

Edvard Munch:
The Model Rosa Meissner
at the Rohne Hotel, 1907.

great freedom. Through his gestures, he can recompose himself out of his many facets, like a writer creating his characters. It is as if the artist's skin (and its attendant visceral contents) were turned inside out in order to present a favorable surface, a support sensitive to the imagination.

"Thus the canvas," writes Max Loreau, "is secretly for the painter the double of his own body. When he manipulates it, experimenting with the play of its surfaces, it is his own body that he is inventing, that he is letting produce and make itself. Without knowing it, it is he whom he brings into being through it, he whom he discovers without seeing it, witnessing the formation of his physique, of his appearance, as if he were modeling his own flesh and giving a figure to his own being... The body is like a canvas, the canvas is like a body. In the hands of the painter, it is an artifice to make him understand his own body, to formulate it in his thought; and, more than that, it is a simulacrum offered to his practice and to his anxieties, the treatment of which permits him to have constantly within reach of his gaze a living body, a body in gestation and in activity which never ceases to emerge, and so an eternally elusive being because eternally at work—in short, a body exactly like his own which, because it has a nature that is like the silvering of a mirror, is condemned once and for all to be inaccessible to the gaze."[9] As he manipulates the canvas, it is indirectly his own body that the painter manipulates. The protagonist is a hidden actor who reveals himself only through traces and who creates a double of flesh.

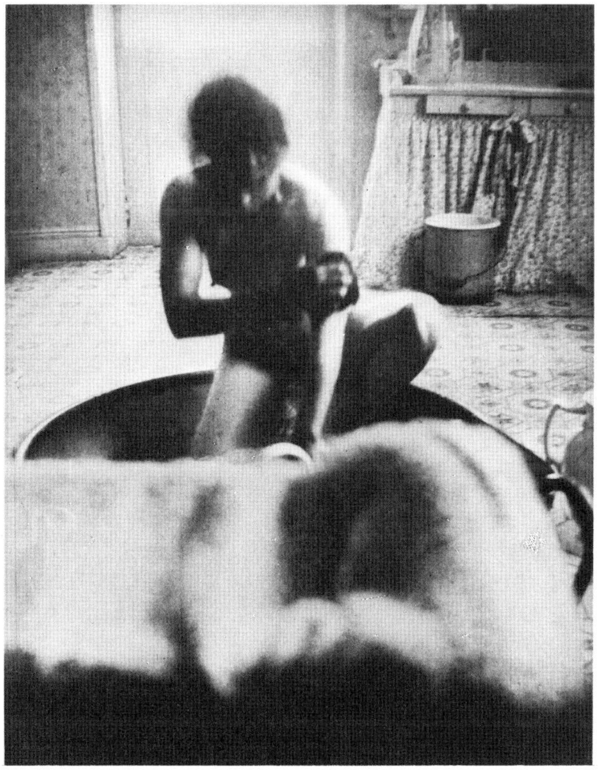

Pierre Bonnard:
Model in a Tub, undated.

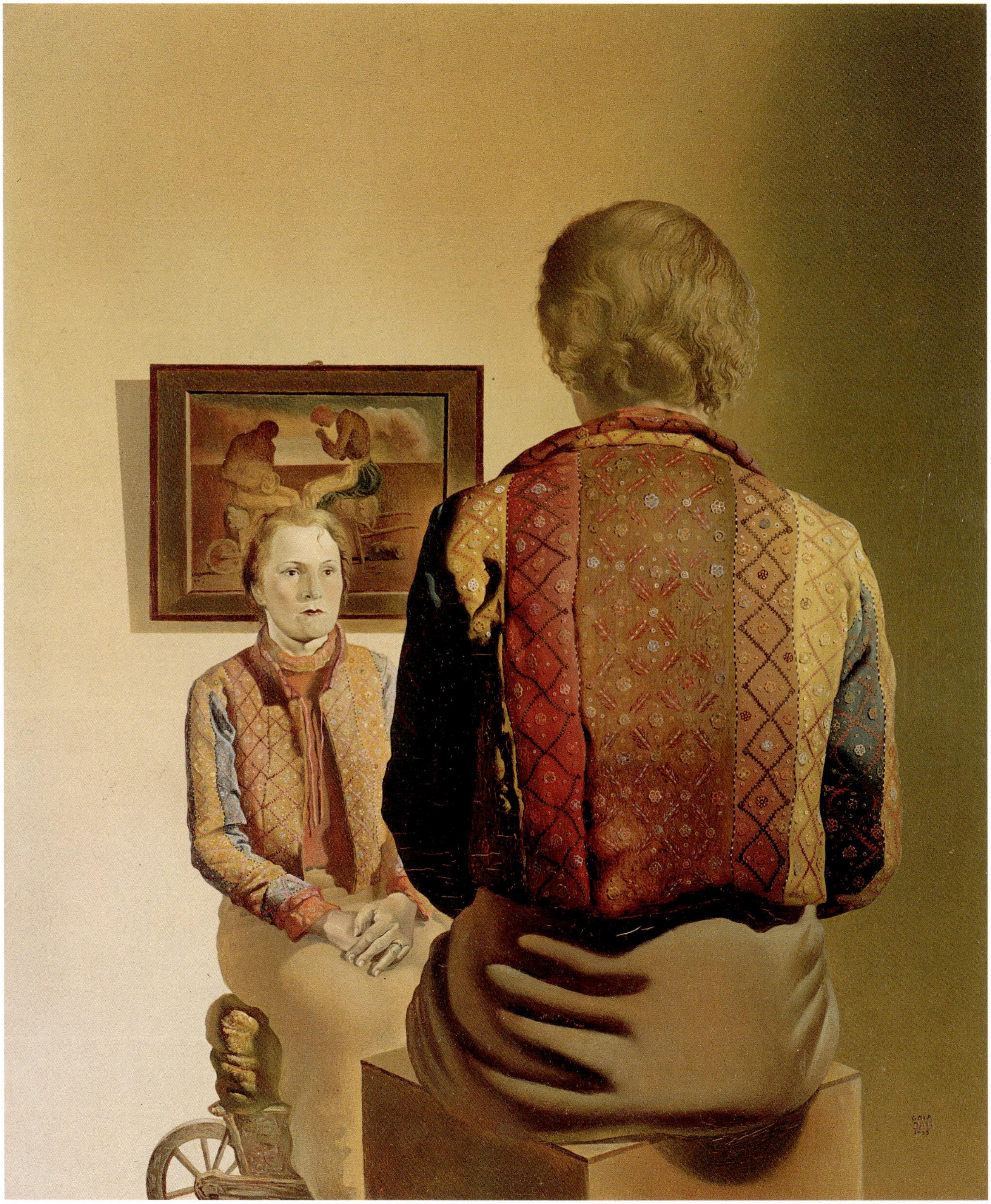

The double and its multiples

The artistic creator plays many roles; he is both subject and model, he splits into two, divides himself. For centuries, literature has explicitly recounted the adventures of doubles. Guy de Maupassant's *Le Horla* is about an ideal being, abstract like a work of art. "A new being? Why not? Surely he had to come! Why should we be the last? We do not see him, no more than we see those who were created before us! This is because his nature is more perfect, his body finer and more finished than ours, because ours is so weak, so awkwardly conceived, so encumbered with tired organs, always under pressure like over-complicated springs, because our body lives like a plant and a beast, painstakingly feeding itself with air, grass and meat; an animal machine that is prone to disease, deformations, putrefaction, that is short-winded, poorly regulated, bizarre and naive, ingeniously misshapen, a delicate and gross work, the rough draft of a being who could become intelligent and superb."[10]

In the tales of Hoffmann, the *Story of the Lost Reflection* tells of the misadventures of a man who falls in love with a diabolical woman who captures his reflection by kissing him in front of a mirror. In Hans Christian Andersen, it is the shadow which is captured. Shadows and reflections are images connected to a protagonist. The double resembles the hero, but it gets in his way, and even puts him in danger. More often than not, it is a female character that brings about the catastrophe.[11] Love creates a splitting up of the personality, it is a threat to its integrity, a part of the being dissociates itself and becomes autonomous. The resemblance is as evident as it is frightening. The individual loses control of a portion of himself. A diabolical power struggle begins between himself and himself. Jacob Pietrovich Goliadkin, the hero of Dostoyevsky's novel *The Double*,[12] engages in a cruel battle with a strange, new and unknown being whose characteristics have a disquieting resemblance with his own: he has the same

Salvador Dalí:
Gala's Angelus, 1935.

Giacomo Manzù:
Self-Portrait with Model in Bergamo, 1942.

Giorgio Vasari:
Apelles' Studio at Ephesus, detail, 1542.

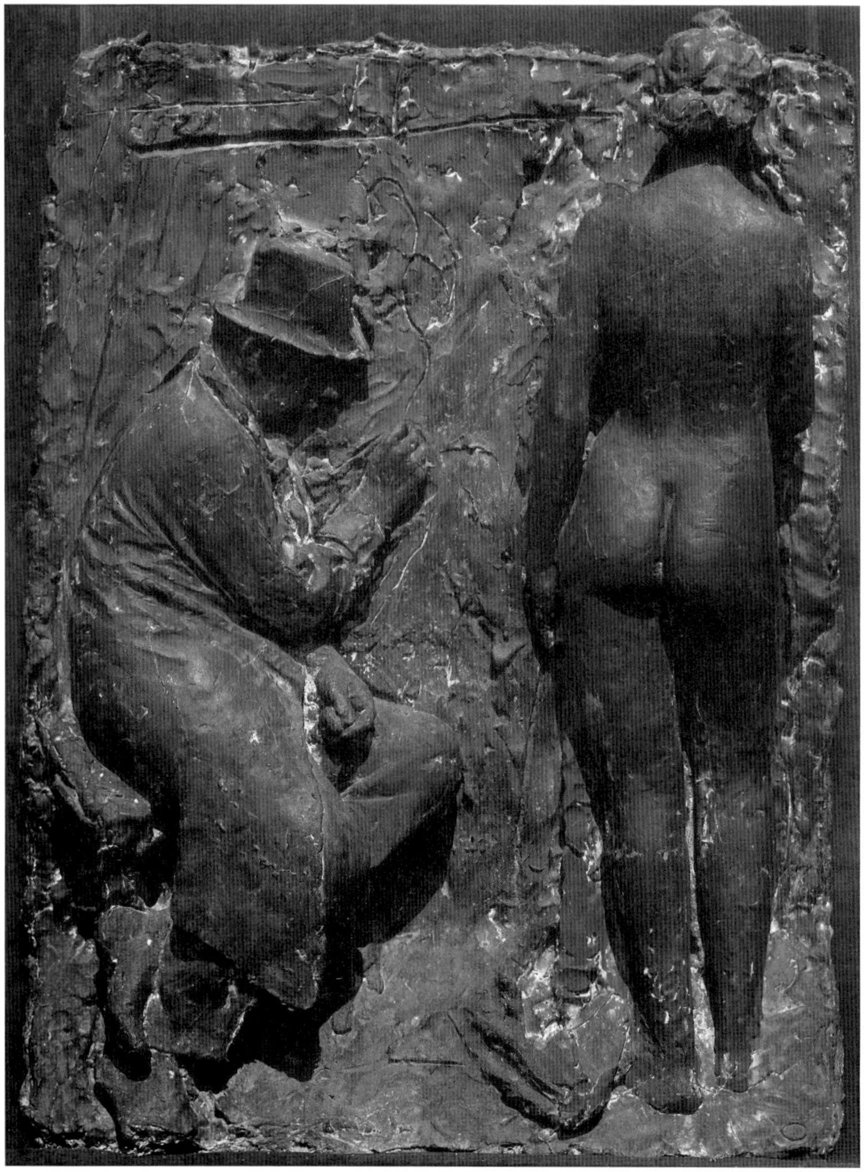

clothes, the same hat, etc. The fantastic aspect of the novel is all the more effective as it does not rely on any supernatural phenomenon. His colleagues and servants express no surprise. Goliadkin is alone with his double. The creator may be said to be in the same situation when he is faced with his own work.

The double, this extra life, continually flirts with death. The realm of the shades is like that of the dead, but it can also be a place of rebirth or immortality. The person without a shadow is suspect. The devil, it is said, has no shadow, and, according to certain traditional cultures, the loss of one's shadow is associated with impotence, infertility or the extreme imminence of death.

Shadows and reflections haunt the imagination of man. Folklore, literature and dreams abound with stories inspired by an indissociable blend of attraction and fear. In the image of all creation, the double transmits a memory, the memory of the past. It sometimes even opposes itself to the present personality, highlighting a part of the former personality. This play with time is inherent in the nature of the particular type of double linked with the obsession with immortality, whether in an abstract or general way, or in a more anecdotal way, as in stories of rejuvenation.

Thus, the double is not just a look-alike, an ordinary duplicate; it exists as something out of phase, similar yet different. In the reflected image, in the shadow, reality slips away, transfigures itself according to the same processes as the work of art.

Around the obession with immortality hovers the obsession with beauty. Many doubles are idealized portraits, disturbing by the very fact that they introduce too perfect, too absolute an image (even if it is found within the realm of evil!), and so there is the danger that they may lead to murder or suicide. The ingredients for the literature of the double are the same as those for painting: mirrors, shadow portraits, beauty, a fascination with woman and death.

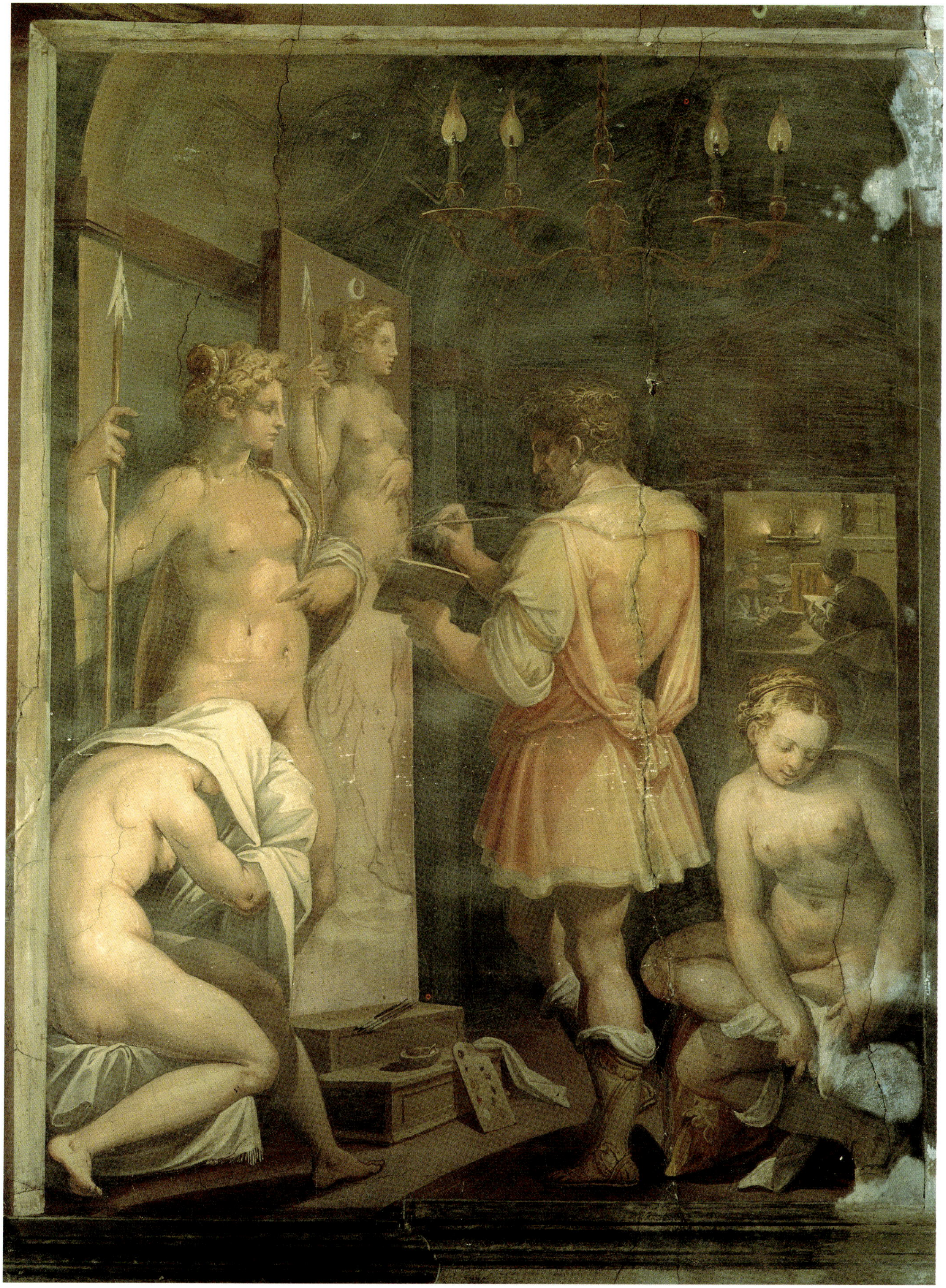

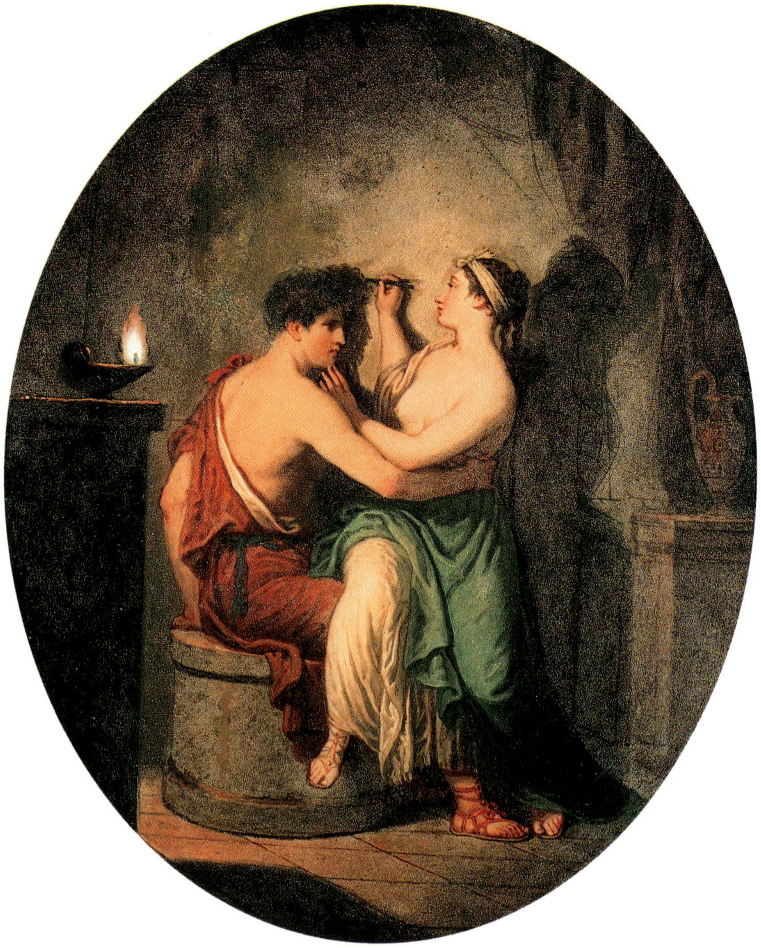

David Allan:
The Origin of Painting, 1773.

It is highly significant that Pliny the Elder, in his *Natural History*, associated the origins of art with the story of a body, a shadow and—love. Pliny writes that a potter from Sicyonia was the first man who "invented in Corinth the art of making portraits from the very same earth with which he worked, but it was thanks to his daughter: she was in love with a young man who was leaving for a long voyage, and so she drew a line around the shadow of his face projected by a lamp onto the wall; her father applied clay to the form and made a model which he fired along with his other pots. It is said that this first model was preserved in the Nymphaeum until the destruction of Corinth by Mummius."[13] This very dense text concentrates a number of elements. First, art came into being through a loving gesture which consisted in preserving the image of a loved one who is going far away. This outline, by enclosing and rendering a memory tangible, is a substitute which attempts to compensate for an absence. Love, the moving force of imagination—the Surrealists, and especially André Breton,[14] considered it such—compels one to find means to make a lack more bearable by supplying a new presence: the image of the beloved. The shadow, a mobile yet specific element of the individual is preserved, fixed, and serves as the starting point for a likeness of the absent person. This "guiding line" enables the father of the sorrowful young woman to make a model which he then submits to a trial by fire through which it will become solid and durable, in other words, eternal.

Progressively, Pliny says, the invention spread and artists modeled figures and ornaments, so well in fact that they soon became preoccupied with resemblance. "The first to make the portrait of a man with a plaster cast of the face itself and to restore this first image with the help of wax poured into the plaster, was Lysistratus of Sicyonia the brother of Lysippus; it was also he who strove to achieve a resemblance; before him, they only tried to make the most beautiful heads possible. The same artist had the idea of making models for statues; this idea became so popular that no figure or statue was made without a clay model; this would mean that marble statuary preceded the art of casting in bronze." Indeed, what better technique to capture a likeness than that of making a mold, the most direct way of taking an imprint of the model.

This very rich legend (and other, fairly similar ones repeated by Quintilian and Isidore of Seville) claimed the attention of artists and historiographers, especially during the Renaissance, a period that was particularly concerned with illusion. "The first painting," Leonardo da Vinci peremptorily declared, "was the linear contour of the shadow of a man cast on a wall by the sun." For Leonardo also, shadows were a sort of "company, joined to the body." Vasari, in his *Lives*, went even further by appropriating this affirmation and using it to stress the importance of drawing, the "foundation" and "soul of all the arts." "In my opinion," he wrote, "drawing is the foundation of sculpture and of painting, and even the soul, which conceives and nourishes within it all of the parts of intelligence, came fully into the world at the time of the origin of all things when the Lord, after having created the world and adorned the heavens with sparkling lights, descended through the transparent ether onto the earth and modeled man, and so revealed the first form of sculpture and of painting in the admirable invention of all things. Who can deny that from man, as from a living example, took form the ideas of sculpted statues and of all that which concerns contour and attitude."[15]

The imagination of the biographer warmed up to his subject and Vasari embellished the legend with

Edouard Dantan:
Moulding, 1887.

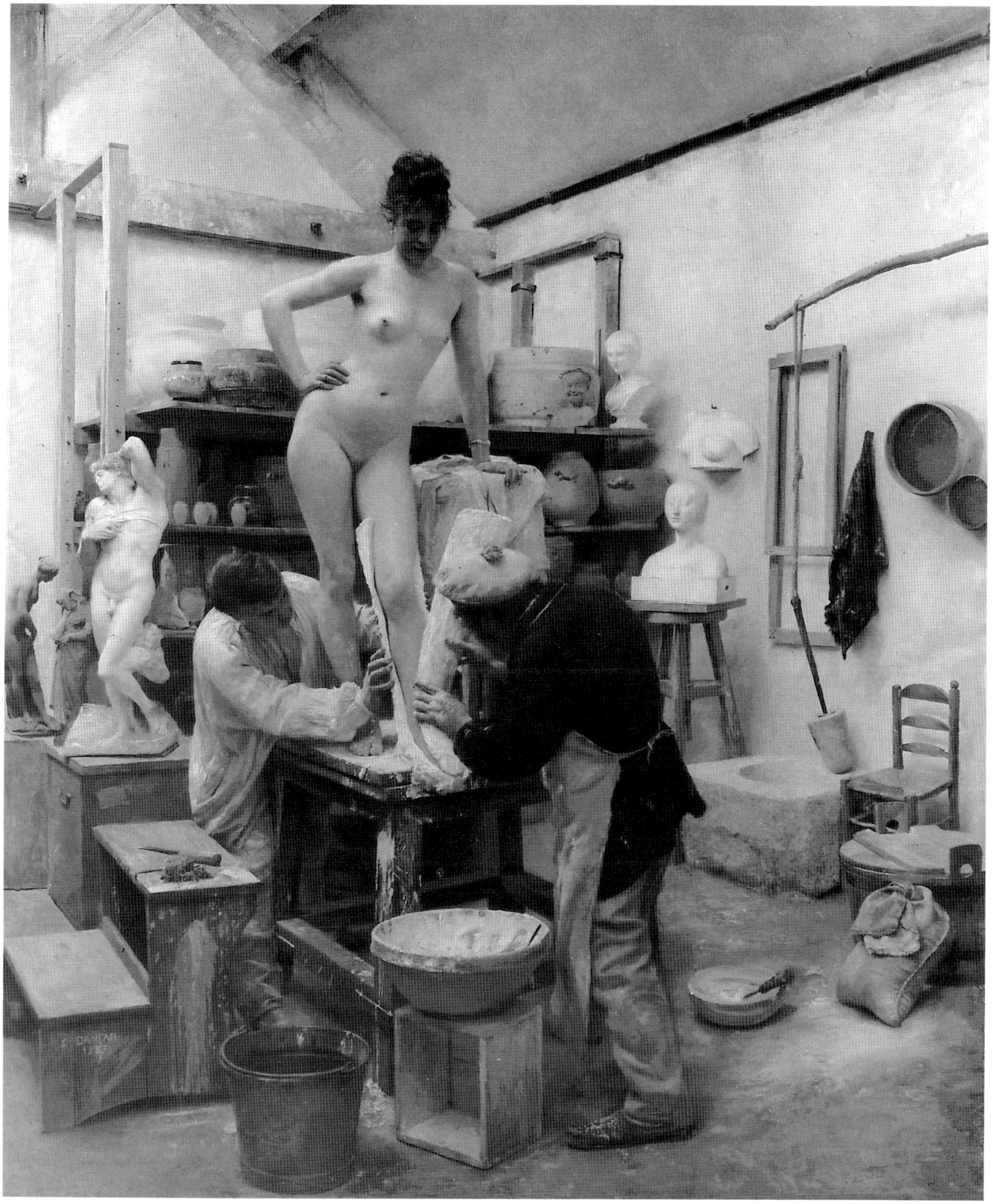

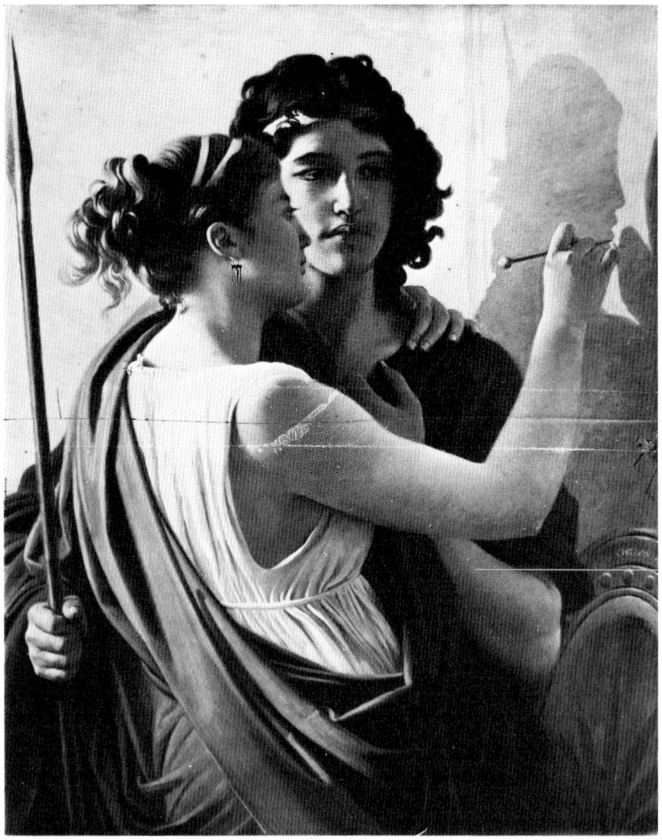

A. de Curzon:
The Portrait, undated.

Michael Sweerts:
A Painter's Studio, undated.

an anecdote of his own invention: according to his version, the credit for the first painting went to Gyges of Lydia who, sitting near a fireplace once, took a piece of charcoal to outline his own shadow on the wall—the prototype of the self-portrait, so to speak. In 1548 the painter-biographer depicted this scene in his house in Arezzo, and around 1570 he represented it again in his house in Florence.

Four years later, Gérard de Jode, in a book of engraved emblems, invented the figure of a shepherd using his staff to trace on the ground the shadow of one of his sheep. An illuminator from Rouen illustrated one of the finest letters in Ovid's *Heroides*, from Laodamia to Protesilaus, in which the Latin author describes Penelope dreaming at night of her husband away at war in Troy, and kissing his image during the day. A French translator, taking a few liberties with the text, transformed Laodamia into a woman-painter representing a portrait of her husband "as real as life." Leon Battista Alberti, an ardent protagonist of illusionism, was among those who emphasized the fact that painting had a major role in transmitting to posterity the image of the absent and in particular those who were absent forever—i.e. the dead.

We would observe in passing that this legend readily satisfied the desiderata of those who exploited it in the name of sculpture, painting or drawing. Furthermore, depending on the storyteller's mood, the first work of art could be the portrait of a lover, a self-portrait, or that of a friend.

The seventeenth century opted for the third formula. Murillo used it as the subject for the painting which he contributed to the chapel of the Painters' Guild at St. Andrew's in Seville on the occasion of his election to the head of the academy of this city; probably an elegant token of thanks to his electors in the form of an homage to friendship.

The following century, libertine through and through, represented this episode as a gallant scene in which the beautiful Dibutade and her charms are unveiled by Labor. With an outstretched arm, she points to the shadow, her hand assisted by Love, her guide and inspiration. This slight dramatization shows the stamp of Neoplatonic ideas, according to which love was the source of creation itself. In the century of Marivaux and Casanova, painters and theorists were necessarily seduced by this legend, which they elaborated upon in an atmosphere of genteel coquetry. Love was the prime mover, the source of all means of expression. Casanova traveled the length and breadth of Europe to make conquests which, although not military, were nonetheless planned according to elaborate strategies. And Marivaux's heroine, Marianne, lived solely in the hope of being able to seduce.

Having gotten off to such a good start, the legend survived in the nineteenth century in a variety of versions in which Cupid always plays a major role. He guides the young woman's hand, places the candle or lamp so that the outline of the shadow can be well traced. Sometimes, he even lends her an arrow to use as a stylus.

In fact, Cupid is the origin of painting. The lover becomes a specific and intermediary link between art and love. The following lines were dedicated to the glory of Cupid, the star figure:

> Yes, it was he in ancient Argolis
> Who guided the hand of a shy young beauty.

or:

> The soft Dibutade instructed by Love,
> Traced the contour of a fleeting shade...[16]

At the same time began the interminable debate on appearance and fidelity to the model. For Winckelmann, the pioneer of archaeology and an ardent defender of antiquity, "the first drawn figures represented men as they were and not as they seemed: they gave the form of the shadow and not the aspect of the body."[17] Pliny had already

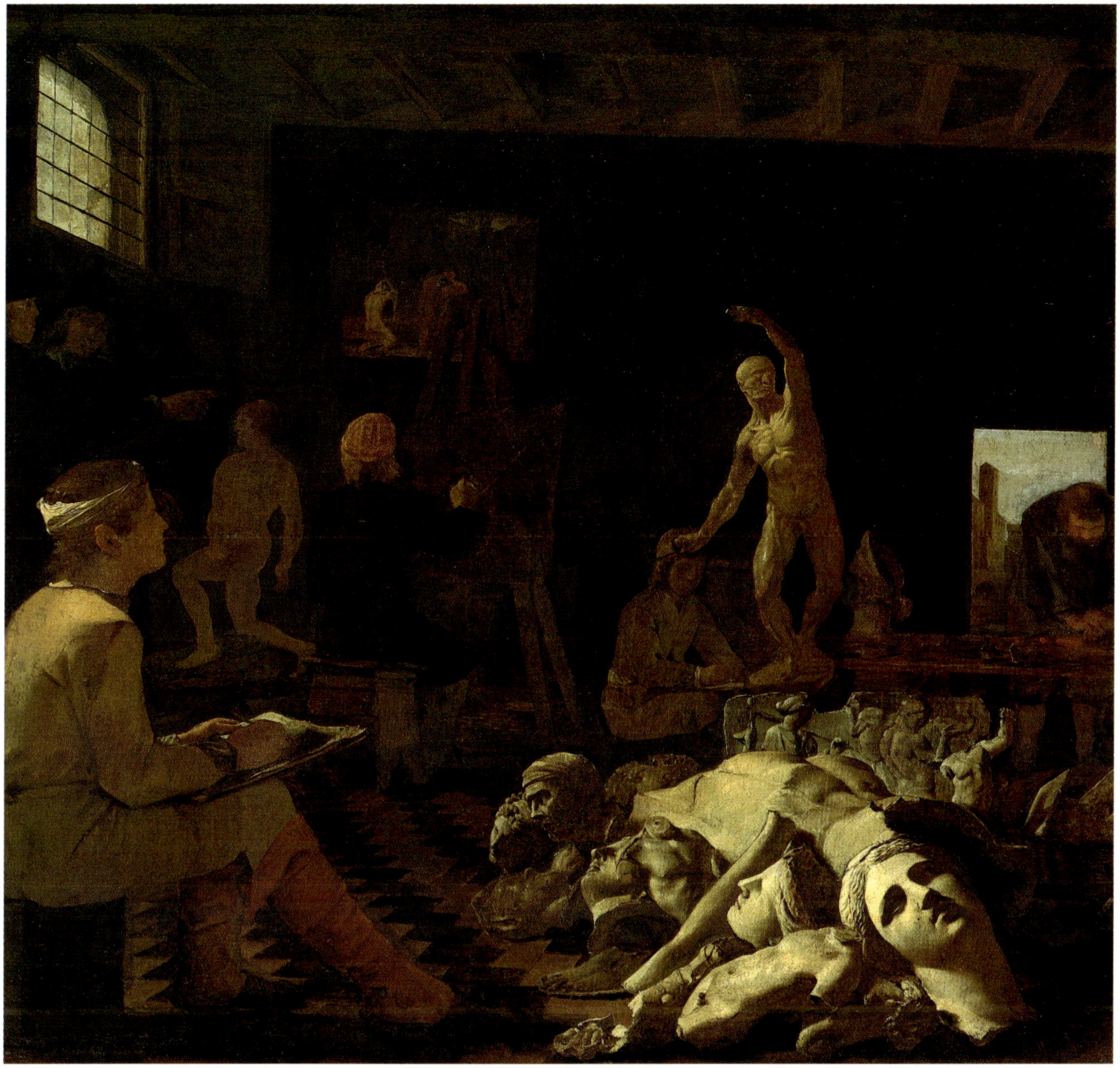

remarked that the origins of painting were obscure; to say that they remained in the shadows would be too tempting a play on words.

The recent reuse of the ancient legend by the world of photography further reveals the extent of the richness of these texts.

Often there are references to shadows, light, instants that are immobilized, immortalized and "fixed." The theorists of photography could not ignore the story of Dibutade. In spite of the technological differences between the action of the potter's daughter and that of the photographer, the process remains the same. For a simple proof of this, one need only observe how much love stories (so called) are consigned to film: official wedding pictures, nude photos (more private), or portable icons in wallets. These documents—fetishes and talismans—record moments that are charged with affectivity. In such little pieces of paper yellowed by time did Roland Barthes try to recapture his deceased mother.[18] Family albums are filled with haphazard collections of elusive instants.

Doubles accumulate, always more or less similar, more or less different. They refer to a portion of a being without ever managing to contain, or even to reflect him in his entirety. Ever frustrating, ever dissatisfying, they lead to an infernal multiplication that often becomes completely kitsch. Cheap doubles are produced in increasing numbers for lack of being perfectly exact look-alikes.

Rembrandt and others preferred trying to capture their images in self-portraits. In this way they immortalized themselves in youth and in old age, displaying all manner of expressions, from laughing to sulking, luxuriously attired in precious silks or wearing their everyday clothes, with or without hats of one kind or another.

It is certainly no coincidence that one of the most representative stories in the literature of the double takes place through the intervention of a painter. We are referring of course to Oscar Wilde's *The Picture of Dorian Gray*. The irresistible Dorian Gray is granted his wish to keep his youthful appearance intact, but his portrait, painted by an artist enthralled by his beauty, Basil Hallward, begins to display not only the marks of his true age, but also those of his sordid misdeeds. Although Basil Hallward realized that "every portrait that is painted with feeling is a portrait of the artist, not of the sitter" and that the "sitter is merely the accident, the occasion,"[19] he nevertheless had the distinct impression, when he met the elegant Dorian Gray, of being face to face with perfection itself. It is true that he executed the portrait in a state of mystical admiration for his sitter. In fact, the artist was completely subjugated by, and possibly in love with, his model. He would encounter him everywhere, even when he was not painting him. For Basil, Dorian was "more than a model or a sitter." The painter's confession to his sitter is a confession of love: "From the moment that I met you, Dorian, your personality had the most extraordinary influence on me. I was dominated, soul, brain, and power by you. You became to me the visible incarnation of that unseen ideal whose memory haunts us artists like an exquisite dream. I worshipped you. I grew jealous of every one to whom you spoke. I wanted to have you all to myself. I was only happy when I was with you. When you were away from me you were still present in my art."[20]

On seeing this portrait of himself charged with such passion, Dorian Gray is seduced by his own image, like Narcissus, and is prepared to exchange his soul for eternal youth. The work of art then parasitizes its model. "I am jealous of everything whose beauty does not die," Dorian tells the painter. "I am jealous of the portrait you have painted of me. Why should it keep what I must lose? Every moment that passes takes something from me, and gives something to it. Oh, if it were only the other way! If the picture could change, and I could be always what I am now! Why did you paint it? It will mock me some day—mock me horribly!"[21]

The portrait-double, charged with visible consequences of age and vice, is a secret and intolerable witness (Dorian keeps it carefully hidden from others). The aging dandy is constantly reminded of what he has become, although this is not directly observable on his own body and face, whose uncommon beauty has remained perfectly intact.

A young actress who has fallen desperately in love with him commits suicide when he ruthlessly abandons her; after this indirect murder takes place, the portrait displays a cruel smile. "Yet it was watching him, with its beautiful marred face and its cruel smile. Its bright hair gleamed in the early sunlight. Its blue eyes met his own. A sense of infinite pity, not for himself, but for the painted image of himself, came over him. It had altered already, and would alter more. Its gold would wither into grey. Its red and white roses would die. For every sin that he committed, a stain would fleck and wreck its fairness."[22]

Thus, over the years, the portrait records his decadence. Basil Hallward, the apparently innocent author of this satanic picture, does not believe his eyes when he discovers the metamorphosis on his own canvas. In despair, he tries to blame the quality of the colors which perhaps contain "some wretched mineral poison" or the dampness of the room. No longer able to stand the idea of his tragic mystery being revealed, even if only to the painter, Dorian Gray kills Basil Hallward and, simultaneously, a drop of blood stains the portrait, "a loathsome red dew that gleamed, wet and glistening, on one of the hands as though the canvas had sweated blood."[23]

By taking illusion as a foundation, the painting transposed the source of the evil, or rather its visible consequences. Dorian Gray wanted to think himself invulnerable, but his portrait knew the truth and it recorded the traces of his depravations, tormenting the sitter with a reminder of his actual physical and moral state.

The idle dandy, whose only art was his life, manages to "save face" by hiding his portrait until the day when, weary and enraged by this unbearable "living" witness of his acts, he decides to destroy the image. But because of the magic power of the double, he succeeds only in killing himself. He is discovered lying on the floor with a knife in his heart, his face withered, wrinkled and repulsive. Only by his rings could he be identified.

Oscar Wilde's novel is a remarkable homage to painting. In a famous aphorism, the writer declared that "nature imitates art," and also that "one should look neither at things nor at people. One should look only at mirrors, for they show us only masks."[24]

With Dorian Gray, the reflection became flesh, the mask became more real than life. The painted likeness captured the soul and a horrible split

René Magritte:
The Attempt of the Impossible, 1928.

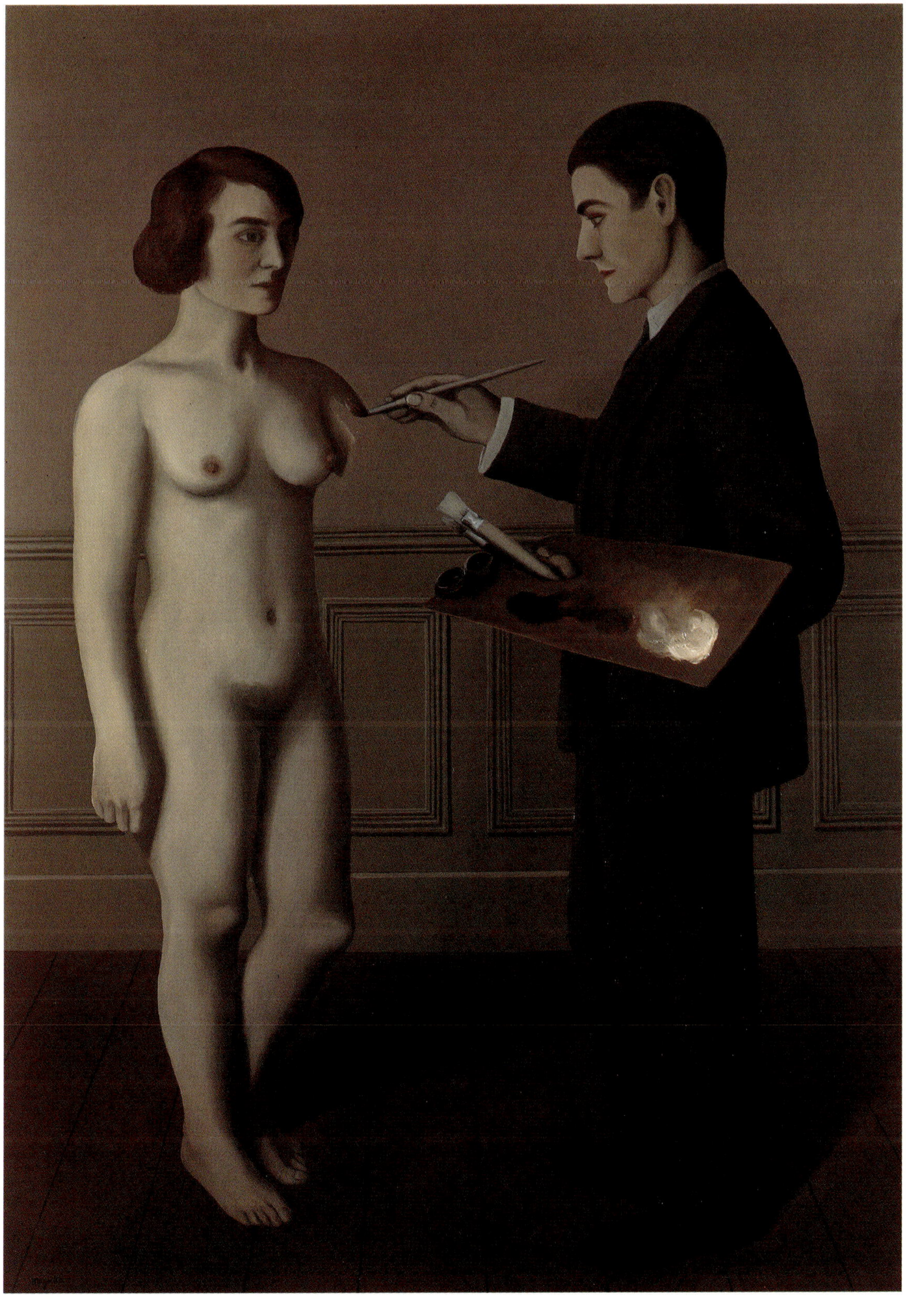

established itself between the changing appearance of the painting and the immutable features of Dorian. Being dissociated, the hero could only die, and in a theatrical way, that is, through an artifice, since he was a dandy and an esthete. His death was not a direct one, which would have been "vulgar," but a staged drama. The knife that he used to "kill" the monstrous picture was the same weapon with which he murdered the painter. His iconoclastic gesture, however, immediately became a suicide. Simultaneously, the picture was restored to its original appearance, while Dorian's remains were tainted with the marks of his vices. Illusion cruelly confused the relationship between art and life, between the visible and the invisible.

Edgar Allan Poe succumbed more than once to the fascination of the double. William Wilson's entire life,[25] from his schooldays to his deathbed, is spoiled by his double. Even more telling in this connection is the short story called *The Oval Portrait*, for it directly involves a painting. A wounded man seeks shelter at nightfall in a castle which seems to have been recently abandoned. He takes refuge in a remote tower room whose walls are hung with a great number of paintings. Unable to sleep, the hero contemplates the pictures by candlelight and studies a little book ("found on the pillow") which contains critiques and analyses of the paintings.

As he moves his candle closer to see them better, he discovers the portrait of a young woman, a portrait whose "charm" comes from a "vital expression that is absolutely equal to life itself." Horrified, the hero finds in the little book the story of the sitter: a young woman of rare beauty who reluctantly gave in to her husband's overwhelming desire to paint. As he painted her portrait, she gradually weakened and languished. "And he *would* not see that the tints which he spread upon the canvas were drawn from the cheeks of her who sat beside him. And when many weeks had passed, and but little remained to do, save one brush upon the mouth and one tint upon the eye, the spirit of the lady again flickered up as the flame within the socket of the lamp. And then the brush was given, and then the tint was placed; and, for one moment, the painter stood entranced before the work which he had wrought; but in the next, while he yet gazed, he grew tremulous and very pallid, and aghast, and crying with a loud voice, 'This is indeed *Life* itself!' turned suddenly to regard his beloved:—*She was dead!*"[26]

Here too, the painter "vampirized" his sitter, nourishing his art with her vital substance. The double fed upon the subject until it was completely drained. But in this way, did she not gain immortal life?

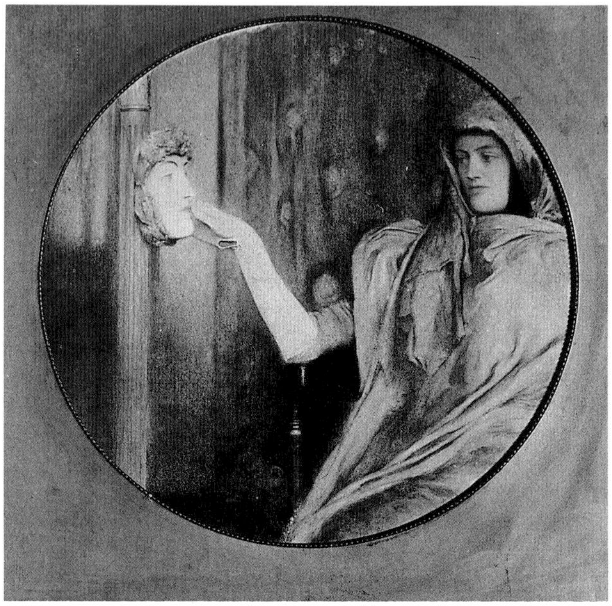

Fernand Khnopff:
The Secret and the Reflection, detail, c. 1910.

The reflections of Narcissus

Dorian Gray was the narcissistic individual par excellence. Wilde's novel revolves around this central figure which becomes the focus of a series of intrigues that lead eventually to the elegant aristocrat's tragic demise. Dorian's portrait is presented to the reader before the "original," and it is plainly titled "Narcissus." What could be more explicit? Narcissus was known for his great beauty, a beauty of a form even higher than genius, for it had no need of proving itself, it only had to show itself, display itself like a "reflection on the dark waters of that silver shell we call the moon."

This pure beauty was Basil Hallward's undoing. Freud would later remark upon the attraction exercised by narcissistic personalities and figures: women, children, cats, the great predatory beasts, criminals and humorists compel our interest. The dandy is another figure which could be added to the Viennese doctor's long, but not exhaustive list.

Dorian Gray exhibits the charm of the monster.[27] Behind his features radiant with beauty and innocence, crime leaves its stamp. What is more, he thinks only of himself, he alone exists. To the great misfortune of Dorian Gray, the painter gave shape to his soul. The appearance of the "original" Dorian Gray becomes like an empty and unchanging shell over which events no longer have any hold. In sitting for Basil, Dorian has no concern for the painter, he is interested only in his own image. He lets himself be dispossessed the better to be "possessed."[28]

Dorian, however, is not fooled by his adoration of himself. One day, he mimicks Narcissus and kisses, or pretends to kiss, the handsome, but cruel red lips of the smiling portrait. For a time, he sits each morning in front of the painting, enamored of his own beauty. He considers himself the criterium of beauty and judges the beauty of others through his own. His portrait sharpens his faculty of judgement to the point that he can no longer love anyone. Like Narcissus, he turns men and women away, and the nymph Echo is left to speak of love all alone.

It is interesting in the light of this novel to return again to the account of this mythological epic in Ovid's *Metamorphoses*.[29] The Roman poet tells the story of the birth of Narcissus, the son of the azure-haired Liriope and the river Cephisus, who

Caravaggio:
Narcissus, 1594-1596.

encircled her in his winding stream and violated her. Being a great beauty herself, Liriope could bring into the world only a child worthy of being loved by the nymphs. She consults the soothsayer Tiresias to find out if her son would have a long life. He announces enigmatically that he would live to a great old age if only "he did not recognize himself," obscure words which she long considers devoid of sense.

At the age of sixteen, the handsome Narcissus attracts young men and young women alike, but he remains indifferent, and does not let himself be approached by either. One day, as he was stag hunting, he enconters the nymph Echo, who still had her bodily form then, but who had been condemned by Juno to repeat only the last sounds uttered by the speaker. Full of desire for the youth, she secretly follows him, but her nature prevents her from approaching him and engaging him in a tender dialogue. By a happy chance which only mythology could invent, the amorous "dialogue" takes place solely through the repetition of the ends of Narcissus's sentences. But as soon as she rushes forward to embrace the youth, he pushes her away, saying that he perfers to die than to abandon himself to her.

Stricken with shame and sorrow, Echo's body withers and dries, leaving only her bones and her voice intact. Another of Narcissus's victims, also disdained, raises his hands heavenward and cries out: "May he fall in love too and never enjoy what he loves." The prayer is granted, for when the Narcissus goes to a spring to quench his thirst, he becomes enamored of his reflection and falls in love with an illusion. In the version told by Pausanias, it is the image of his beloved twin sister, who has just died, which he believes he sees in the reflection. There is a confusion here between incestuous love and self-love. "In any case, he falls in love with a thing that has no substance; and he thinks that to be a body which is but a shadow. He is astonished at himself, and remains unmoved with the same countenance, like a statue formed of Parian marble. Lying on the ground, he gazes on his eyes like two stars, and fingers worthy of Bacchus, and hair worthy of Apollo, and his youthful cheeks and ivory neck, and the comeliness of his mouth, and his blushing complexion mingled with the whiteness of snow; and everything he admires, for which he himself is worthy to be admired. In his ignorance, he covets himself; and he that approves, is himself the thing approved. While he pursues he is pursued, and at the same moment he inflames and burns. How often does he give vain kisses to the deceitful spring!"

Realizing his mistake, seeing that he burns for love of himself, he wastes away, longing to separate himself from his own body, tearing his clothing, beating his breast with "hands as white as marble," and dies. Being possessed of such an ideal, inhuman beauty, Narcissus can only die physically and be immortalized in myth. As Rainer Maria Rilke wrote in a poem:

> Narcissus lay perishing. From his beauty rose,
> Incessantly, close by, his essence,
> Concentrated like the perfume of the heliotrope.
> But his fate was to see himself.
>
> His love drank back what he was losing,
> No more was he contained in the open wind,
> Enchanted, he closed the circle of figures,
> Annihilated himself and could no longer be.[30]

In the literature of antiquity, beauty was closely associated with the notion of plastic creation, as we can see in the many metaphors of marble and wax used to describe the physical appearance of Narcissus. Accordingly, he would later be credited with the invention of painting. In his treatise *On Painting*, Leon Battista Alberti categorically asserted this origin: "I am wont to tell my friends, in accordance with the poets, that Narcissus, who was transformed into a flower, was the inventor of all art, and the entire story of Narcissus confirms this. Would you say indeed that painting is anything else but a way of kissing with art this surface of the spring."[31]

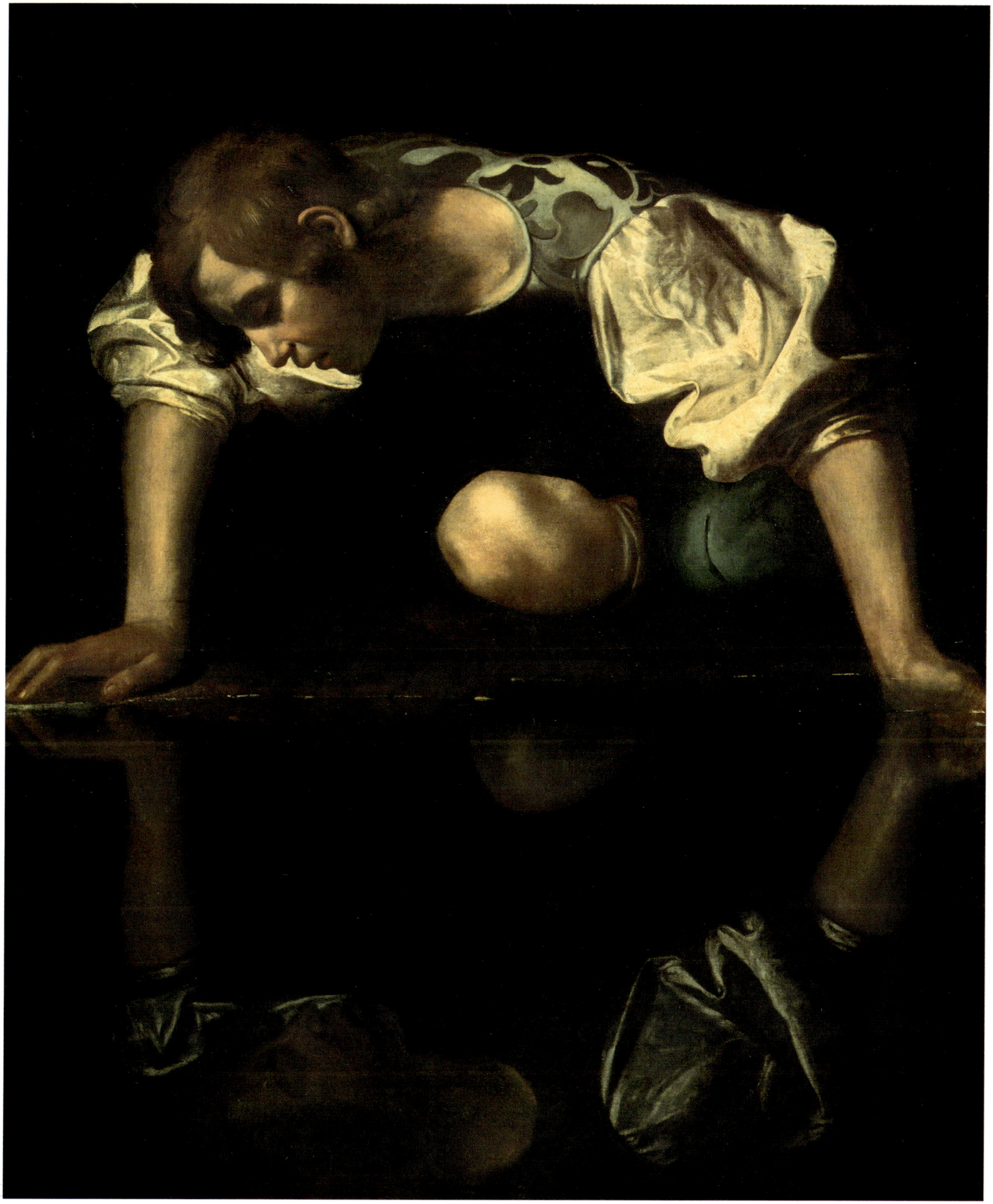

Once again, painting is presented as an act of physical love; to paint is to kiss oneself and to kiss a surface: that of water, of a mirror, of a canvas or of a stone.

For over twenty-five years, Freud elaborated the concept of narcissism and linked it with the phenomenon of artistic creation. Taking his own body as a love object, the painter gives birth to himself; it is through the "orgasm of the ego" that he brings other bodies into being. While psychoanalysis, like any other approach turned into a system, went astray in its pronouncements on the work of art in general and on the representation of the body in particular, it nevertheless could not resist the appeal of esthetics.

By venturing to interpret the childhood memories and fantasies of Leonardo da Vinci[32] and the *Moses* of Michelangelo,[33] the father of psychoanalysis flirted with artistic creation, just as he flirted with literary creation in turning his attention to Goethe, Jensen's *Gradiva*, Dostoyevsky and Poe.[34] The relationship between art and narcissism seems to be a fundamental one. The narcissistic structure seems to provide one of the keys to artistic activity which applies not only to the artist, but also to the spectator.

Like a god, the artist rebuilds the world in his own image. Leonardo would not have disowned this view; in his own writings, he puts artists on guard against a too immediate projection of their own bodies into their works, especially if the author is ugly, which, as the misanthropic genius points out, is often the case! "The painter who has shapely hands will give similar ones to his figures and he will do the same for all the other limbs unless he has come to awareness of this through long study... If you are brutish, your figures will appear likewise and will lack spirit; in this way, all that is good or bad in you will become apparent in some way in your figures... observe well the finer parts of many handsome faces, the beauty of which will have been confirmed by general opinion rather than by your own judgement, for you may be deluded by choosing faces similar to your own. It so happens that we like what resembles us... The greatest error of painters is to repeat in a composition the same movements and the same faces and drapery, and to make most of the faces resemble that of their author... each peculiarity of the painting matches a peculiarity of the painter himself. Having often reflected on the causes of this error, it seems to me that one should think that the soul, which governs the body, also determines our judgement, even before we have adopted it; it is the soul that has shaped the entire form of the man as it saw fit; with a long, short or pug nose, and, in the same way, it has fixed his size and the man as a whole; and this judgement is so strong that it moves the arm of the painter and obliges him to copy himself, for it seems to the soul that this is the true way to paint a man and that, whoever does otherwise, is wrong. And if it finds someone who resembles the body it has formed for itself, it loves it and often falls in love; and this is why many people come to love and marry women who resemble them, and often the children which they bring into the world resemble their parents."[35]

Narcissus putting himself on guard against Narcissus! Like a dream, the work of art is a projection that permits the hallucinatory satisfaction of desires. The artist draws his psychic games out of his self-sufficiency and gives them a body through illusion. "In only a single field of our civilization," says Freud, "has the omnipotence of thoughts been retained, and that is in the field of art. Only in art does it still happen that a man who is consumed by desires performs something resembling the

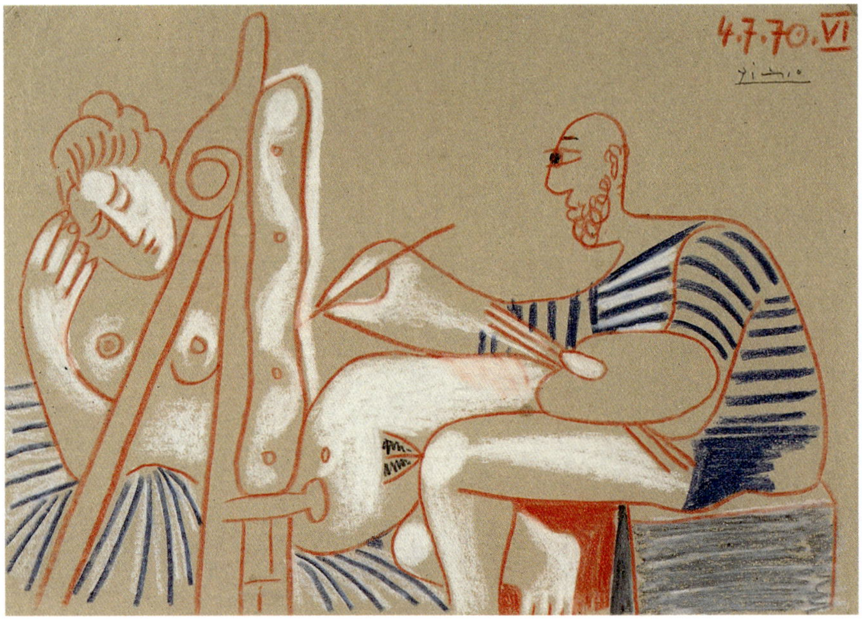

Pablo Picasso:
The Painter and His Model, 1970.

Jean-Dominique Ingres:
Raphael and the Fornarina, 1814.

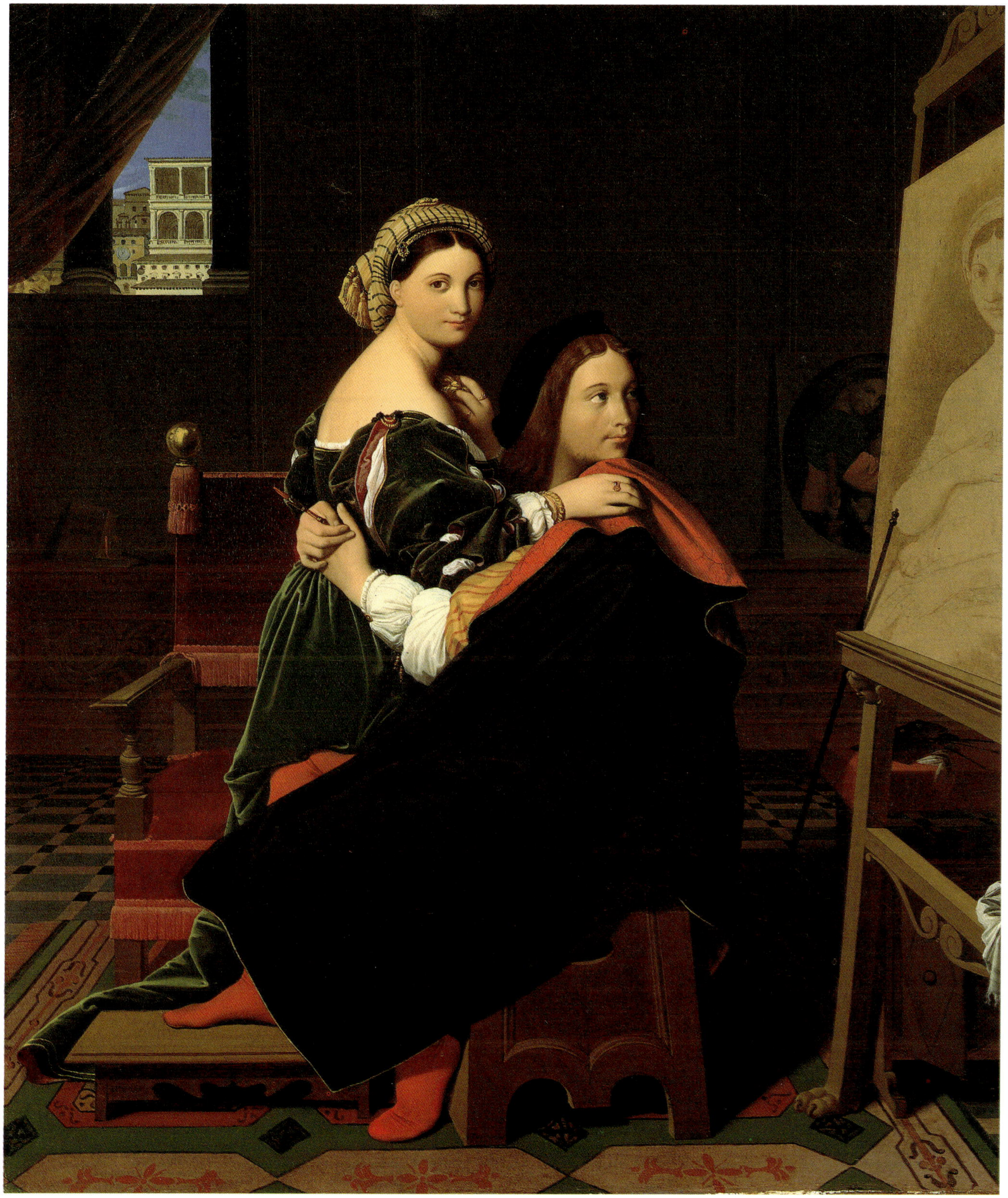

Christian Schad:
Self-Portrait with Model, 1927.

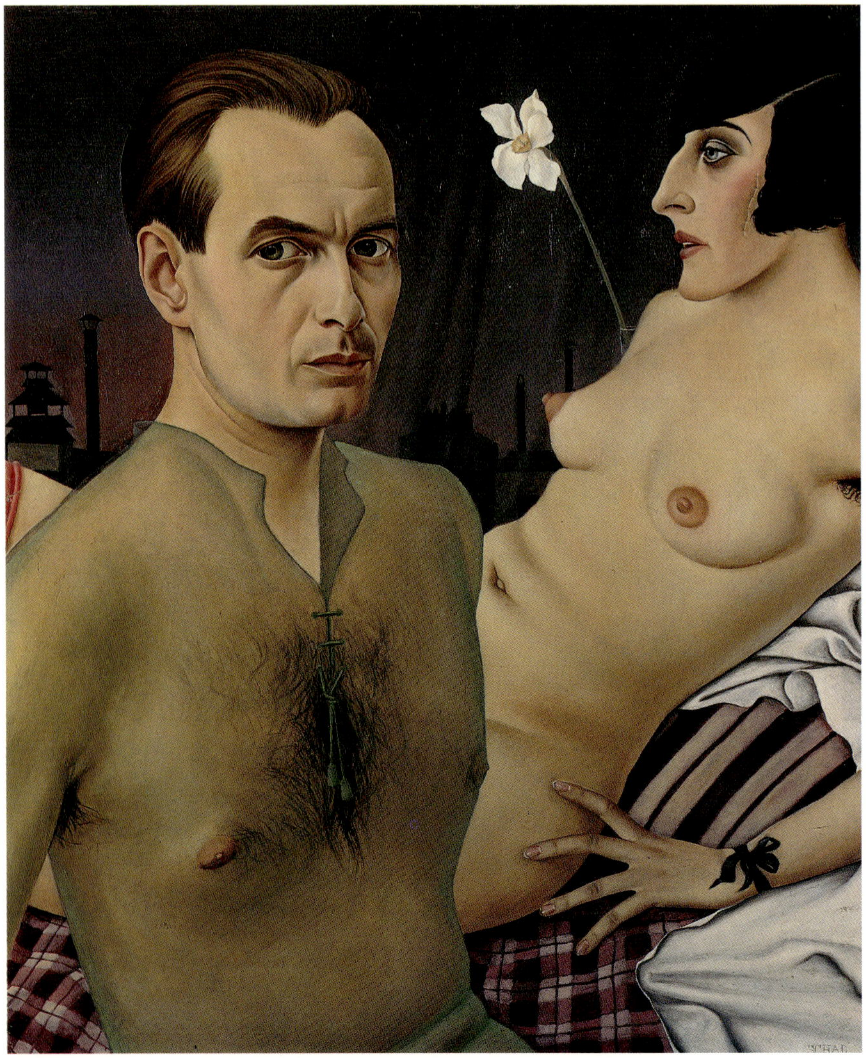

accomplishment of those desires and that what he does in play produces emotional effects—thanks to artistic illusion—just as though it were something real. People speak with justice of the 'magic of art' and compare artists to magicians. But the comparison is perhaps more significant than it claims to be. There can be no doubt that art did not begin as art for art's sake. It worked originally in the service of impulses which are for the most part extinct today. And among them we may suspect the presence of many magical purposes." [36]

Art is made in a zone between reality and imagination. The artist is the "hero" who has succeeded in "killing the father" in order to conquer his own immortality, and this often through the mediation of a beauty which hopes to be eternal and universal. The artist becomes the father of his works, he brings bodies into being which progressively gain autonomy by becoming works of art, but he is also brought into being by them, for they constitute his identity. The work "says" more than the artist himself, it reaches beyond him. The double is erected to conquer death. As Sarah Kofman observed, "it does not duplicate a presence, it is a substitute for it," thus it produces "an effect of uncanny strangeness."[37]

Inhabited by Eros and Thanatos, the double permits the artist to construct himself by using simultaneously the past, the present and the future. Memories, present desires, and the wish for immortality dwell in the work. Around the sacrosanct, but ineffable notion of beauty, pleasure gravitates.

The artist elaborates a "grandiose ego" through the intermediary of a fusional relationship with his work and also with his model. Anton Ehrenzweig, in *The Hidden Order of Art*, judiciously described this fusional stage inherent in artistic production. The creator is then "in his work; outer world and

Otto Müller:
Seated Couple, c. 1922.

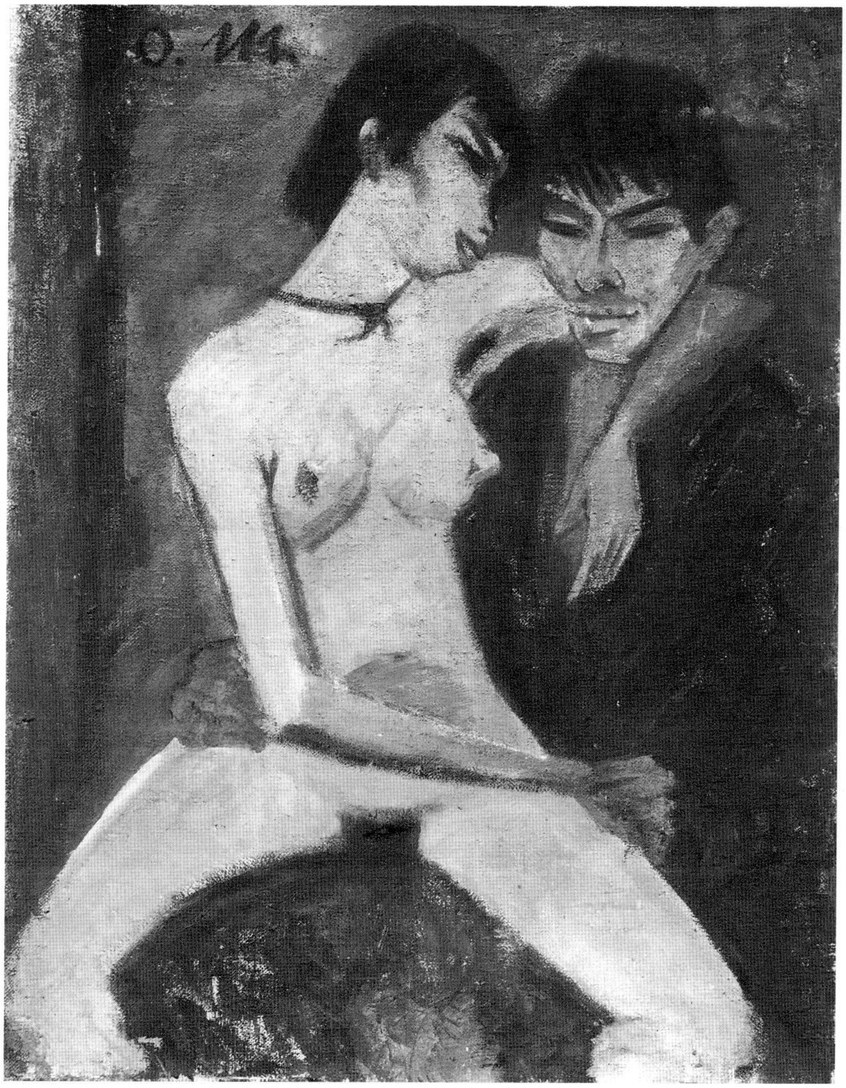

inner world become one. He does not look at the model, he is the model or rather, 'in' the model. He fiercely protects this 'oceanic feeling' in the warm and womblike atmosphere of the studio. Separations are abolished in favor of a privileged union, as in a love relationship."[38]

Beauty is brought into being by a hand to hand struggle. The work of art is never merely a reflection of the life of the artist, it is that which in his life transcends him. While he is bringing it into being, the creator, moved by his feeling of power, believes in unity and immortality.

"Creation," wrote Lou Andreas-Salomé, "be it of a philosophical, artistic, practical or other nature, is it not always also a method of restoring the primal unity of the world and of the subject—the latter being opposed to the former in the development of the ego—to unite oneself with the world?"[39] Desire is at the heart of the creative act. The share of Eros is a major one, and the sovereign body is omnipresent.

Less mathematically economical than Freud, the great lover that Lou Andreas-Salomé was "felt" that works of art exuded life and sexuality and that this was not necessarily to their detriment. Creation is thus the solemn and joyful theater in which the drama of reunification is staged. The artist (re)makes the world, he wants to make explicit and tangible the fact that the "other" and the "outside" are driven by the pulse of life and that together they are one with him.

"It is evident that, in what a creative spirit mediates through his work, we find an abundance of eroticism which enriches all who truly assimilate it. What benefited the work, the mysterious transformation of human warmth into a creation of the spirit, was for the creator himself not only a kind of release, but also a prodigality of himself which can make him lose the harmonious contact with his own basic nature. There is no path that leads from sublimation to sublimation, no more than from summit to summit, without the earthly detours through the abysses which separate them."[40] She then makes a somewhat ironic distinction between creators and "sublimators" who lack a joyful affirmation of the ego, who sadly direct their fecundity towards asexual goals.

It is through Eros that narcissism puts itself in the service of art. The Promethean artist makes of existence and of his body a second reality, a sublime and an ideal one, the ferment for which is love.

Rétif de La Bretonne:
Plate XXXVII in Le Paysan perverti*:*
Edmond Drawing a Nude, 1784.

Delights and Deliriums of the Voyeur

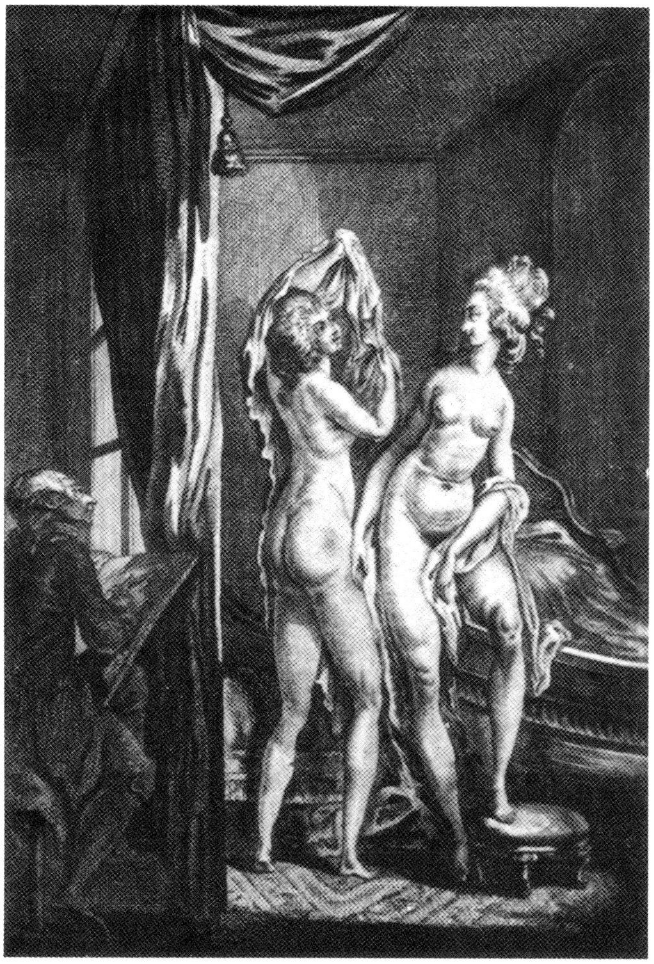

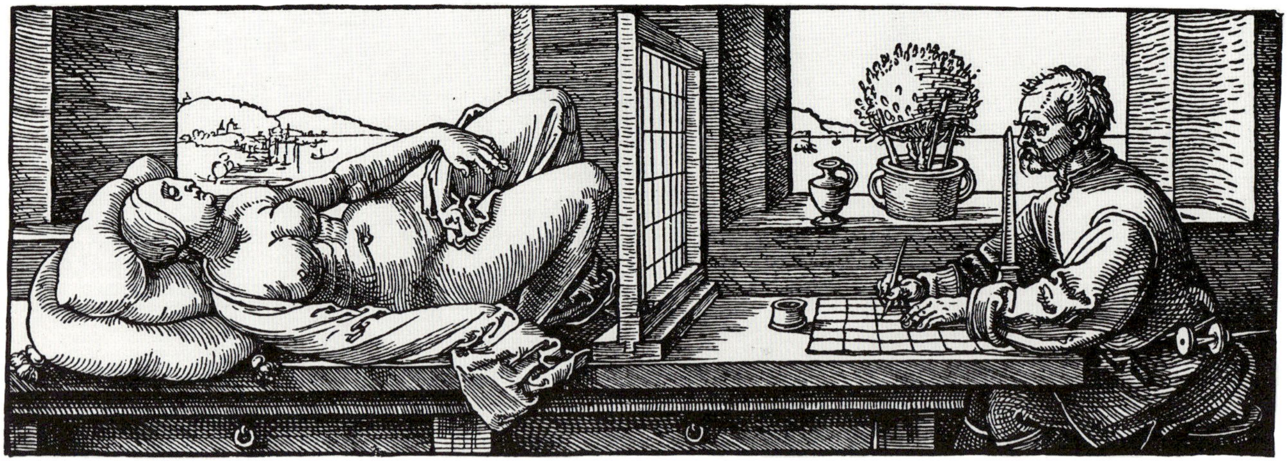

Albrecht Dürer:
Artist Drawing a Reclining Nude
Through a Grid Frame. c. 1525.

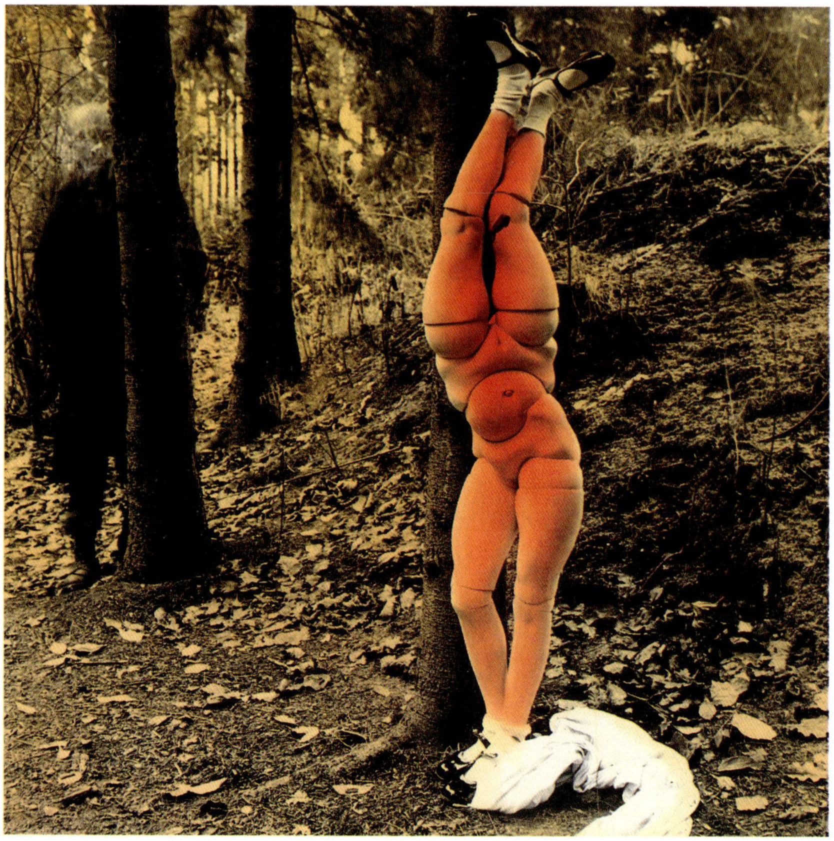

Hans Bellmer:
The Doll, 1949.

Pablo Picasso:
The Painter and His Model, 1914.

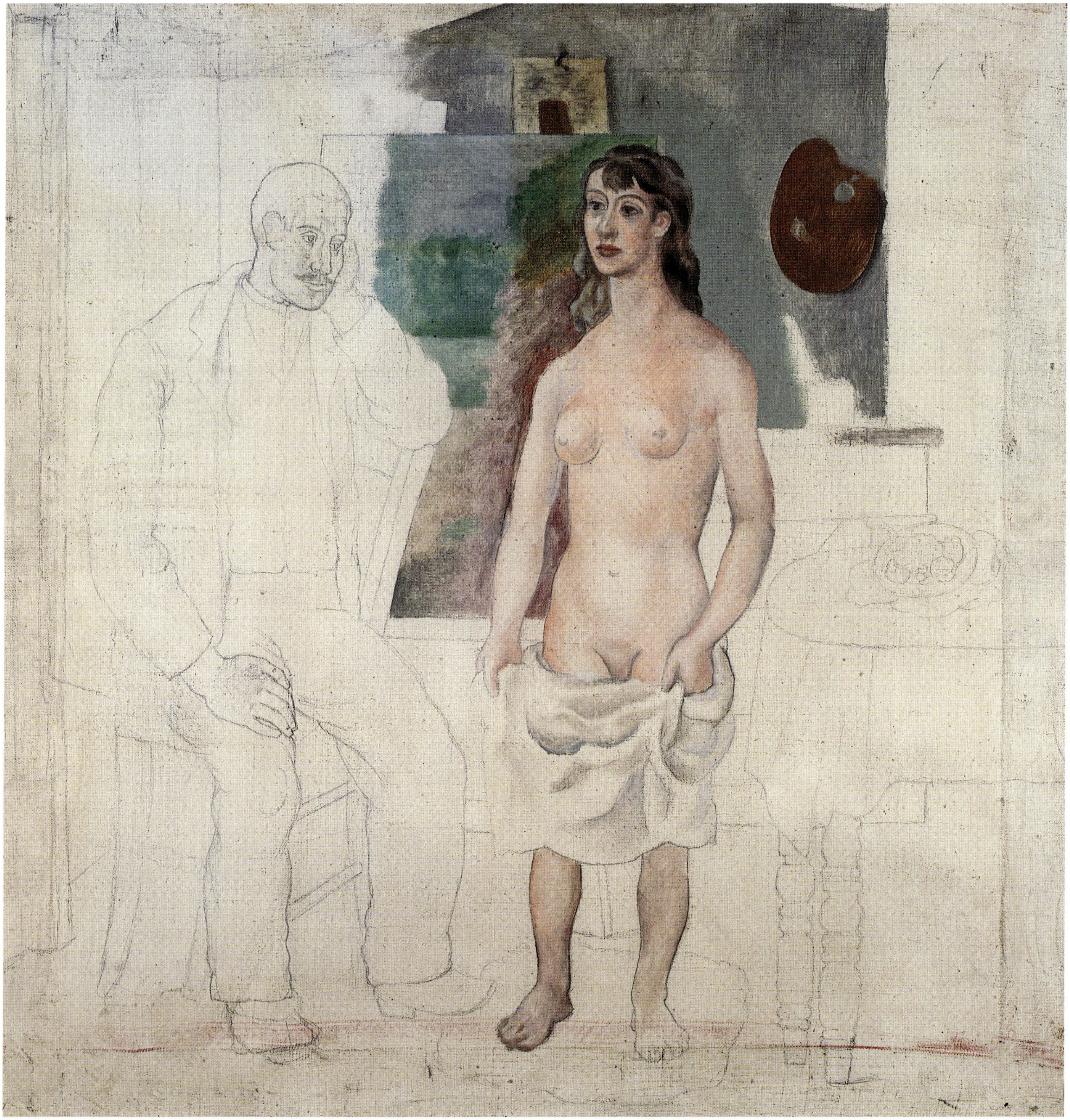

The charms and joys of the self-portrait

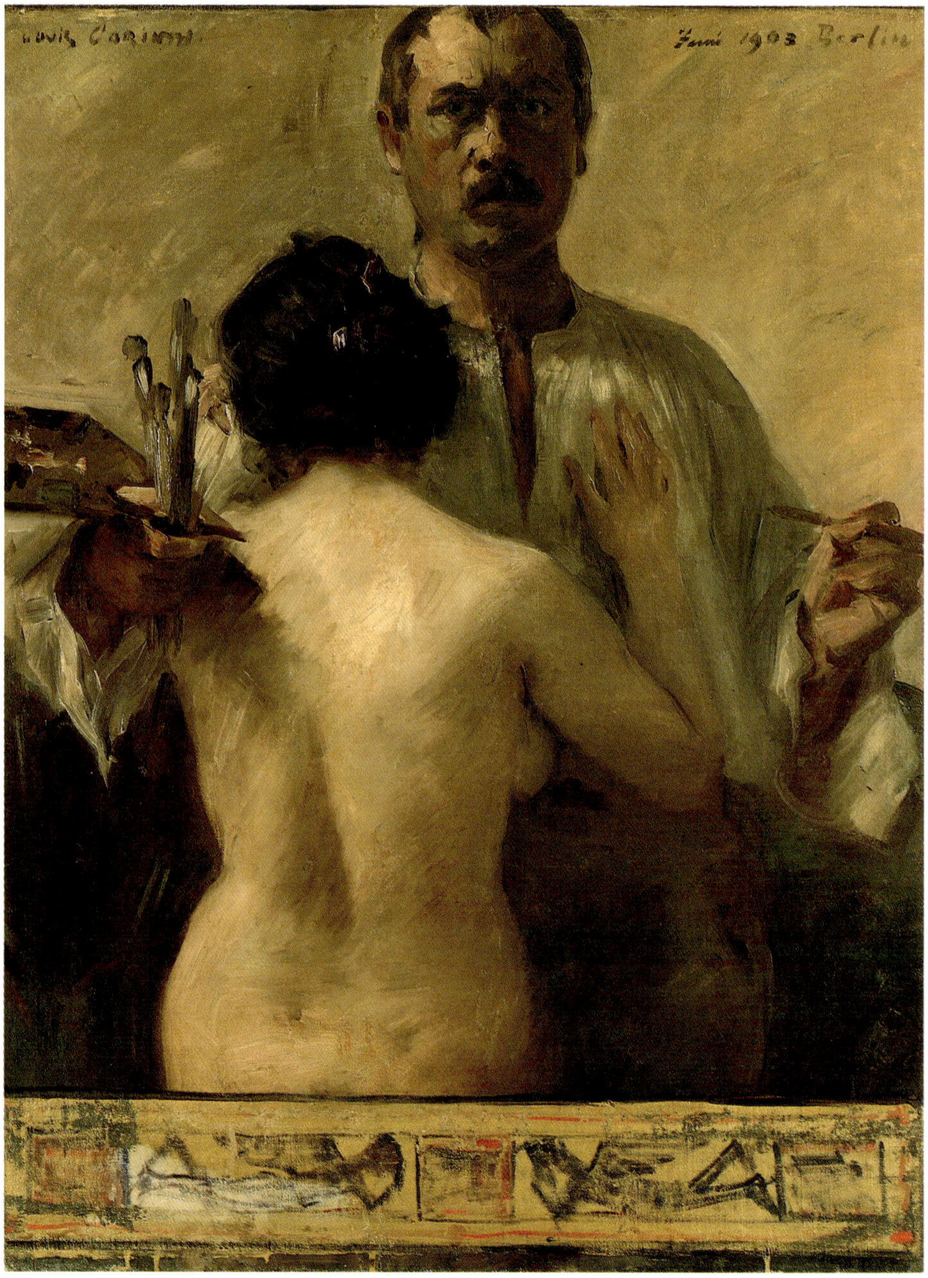

Lovis Corinth: Self-Portrait with Model, 1903.

Michelangelo:
Fragment of the Last Judgment:
St Bartholomew's Skin, 1537-1541.

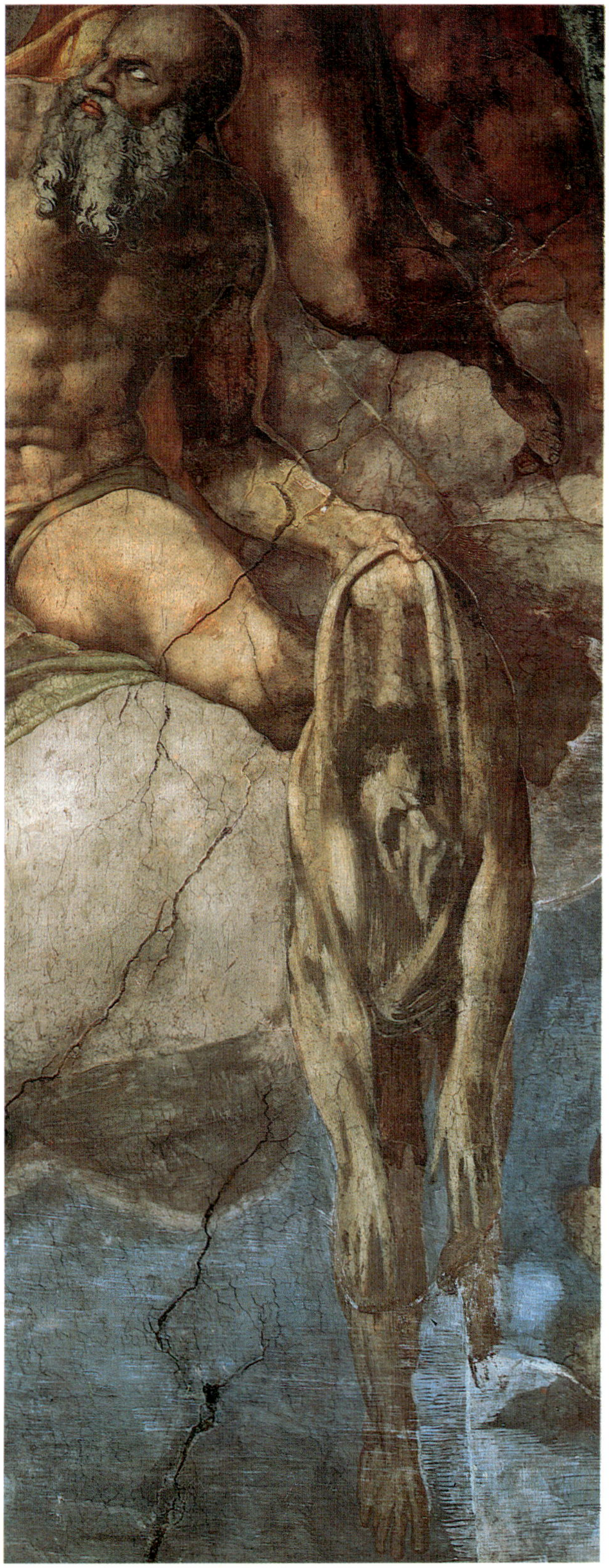

It is also through the intercession of the mirror that the artist accedes to the self-portrait and uses himself, in a fusional autarchy, as a model. The self-portrait could develop only in conjunction with the rise of individualism. Although self-portraits may be found in the margins of illuminated manuscripts as early as the thirteenth century, this was a rare—and marginal—occurrence.[1] When the painter asserted his identity, it was first of all by his gaze: he would include himself in a composition and distinguish himself by directing his gaze toward the spectator, beckoning to him or challenging him. It was only later that the painter represented himself with his attributes, brush and palette, and proclaimed his difference from his surroundings. The objects around him and his pose were full of meaning, like a code to be deciphered.

The self-portrait, in a striking condensation, makes a statement about the body of the painter and about painting itself. The painter shows himself at work, in the midst of his family, as a member of the social body or as an eccentric, if not as an outcast making a conspicuous display of his misery.

"When they did their portraits, they did so by looking in a mirror, without thinking that they themselves were a mirror," wrote Paul Eluard.[2] The painters were also the mirrors of their own fantasies. Caravaggio depicted himself as Goliath decapitated by David and as a Gorgon's head framed by writhing snakes. Michelangelo, in the Sistine Chapel, represented himself as the flayed skin of St. Bartholomew. A painter and martyr, Ensor showed himself crucified and decapitated by critics. Dürer assigned himself a more glorious role and lent his features to an image of Christ. Paul Gauguin followed his example in his *Christ in the Garden of Gethsemane*. Raphael, apparently more discreet, nevertheless slipped into the assembly of philosophers and thinkers of the *School of Athens* in the Vatican. To go from the mirror, or "speculum" in Latin, to speculation, there is but one step to take, and it is facilitated by the dual meaning of the verb "to reflect."

Rembrandt represented his own likeness throughout his career, from youth to old age, wearing all sorts of hats, trying out every kind of expression, from sadness to exultation. He portrayed himself with the women in his life, brandishing a glass or a sword. He posed, he loved to pose, and donned a great variety of costumes. He repeated his self-observation and did so without making any concessions to vanity: his swollen and red-veined nose, his double chin, his puffy face, the furrows of his skin, were consigned by the brush onto the canvas, suffused with light, amber and gold. On several occasions he holds his brushes,

Pablo Picasso:
In the Studio, 1954.

palette and mahlstick, on others, disguises himself as St. Paul. In most cases, we see him to the midsection, his body wrapped in velvets, silks and furs. He must have liked hats, for he sported a large variety of them: plumed, broad-rimmed, berets, caps, helmets, and even Turkish turbans did not intimidate him. Often, he wore a small earring. Sometimes, to pose, he did not dress up, but disguised himself, as if to accentuate the metamorphoses. And yet, over the decades, there is always the same gaze directed towards the mirror, towards the spectator and towards time, which Rembrandt caught in its flight.

There is an omnipresence of the gaze also in Vincent van Gogh, but a gaze which is always elsewhere and nowhere. The painter was concerned with the human figure, whose representation could only be consolidated through study. In his letters to his brother Theo, this preoccupation stands out as a leitmotif: "I am now trying to make

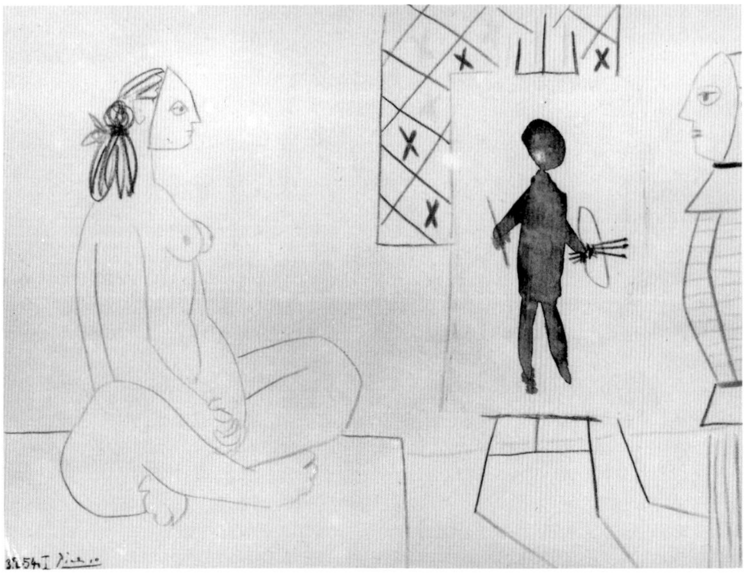

portraits. And I must say that I do not paint any the worse for it." "I think that I am going to give in to a furious desire to paint the figure; it is around this that I turn all the time as if it had no importance; but in reality, that is exactly my goal." "The figure I make is almost always detestable in my own eyes, and all the more so in the eyes of others; and yet it is the study of the figure which strengthens the most." "The change that I am going to try to make in my paintings will be to make more figures. It is the only thing that moves me to the depths in painting and that makes me feel the other things more." "There is no better or shorter path to improve the work than by doing figures." "I want to do figures, figures and more figures." "I would like to paint men and women with that ineffable portion of eternity which was once symbolized by the nimbus, which we seek in the very radiance, in the vibrations of our colors. Ah, the portrait, the portrait with the mind, the soul of the sitter, this seems to me so much like what should come."

However, on the pretext that he had no models and that he hated photographs, he not only took himself as a model but also as a sort of prototype, judging that if he succeeded in painting himself, he would be able to paint others. From the particular to the general. From the self to others. From the one to the many.

"I always find my best capacities frustrated because of the lack of models. I know this, that if I went to the models and implored them: but please pose for me, I beg of you, I would do like the good painter in Zola's novel *The Work.*" "I intentionally bought a mirror good enough to work after myself for lack of a model, for if I manage to paint the coloring of my own head, a task which is not without difficulty, I will just as well be able to paint the heads of other good men and women." "And so I am working on two portraits of myself at the moment—for lack of a model—because it is time I did some figures." "They say—and I believe it readily—that it is difficult to know oneself, but it is not easy to paint oneself either."[3]

Nothing is simple, even if the mirror tries to compensate for the absence of the other. Picasso, like Alice in Wonderland, would have liked to go through the looking-glass, to pierce it and combine it with a camera. "On waking up and seeing myself in the mirror with my dishevelled hair, do you know what idea I had? Well, I regretted not being a photographer! It is completely different, the way others see you and the way you see yourself in a mirror at certain moments. Several times in my life, I happened to catch an expression on my face which I have never been able to find in any of my portraits. And these were perhaps the most truthful expressions. We should make a hole in the mirror so that a camera lens could capture our most intimate face unawares."[4] But in November 1918, while shaving in front of a mirror in the Hotel Lutetia, Picasso learned of the death of Guillaume Apollinaire. Afterwards, he could no longer stand mirrors, so much did he associate them with the shock of this news.

The mirror is also an abyss, but the artist, in his creative omnipotence, acts like Dionysos observing himself in the mirror made by Hephaistos: he lets himself be seduced by his reflection and

Otto Dix:
Self-Portrait with Model, 1924.

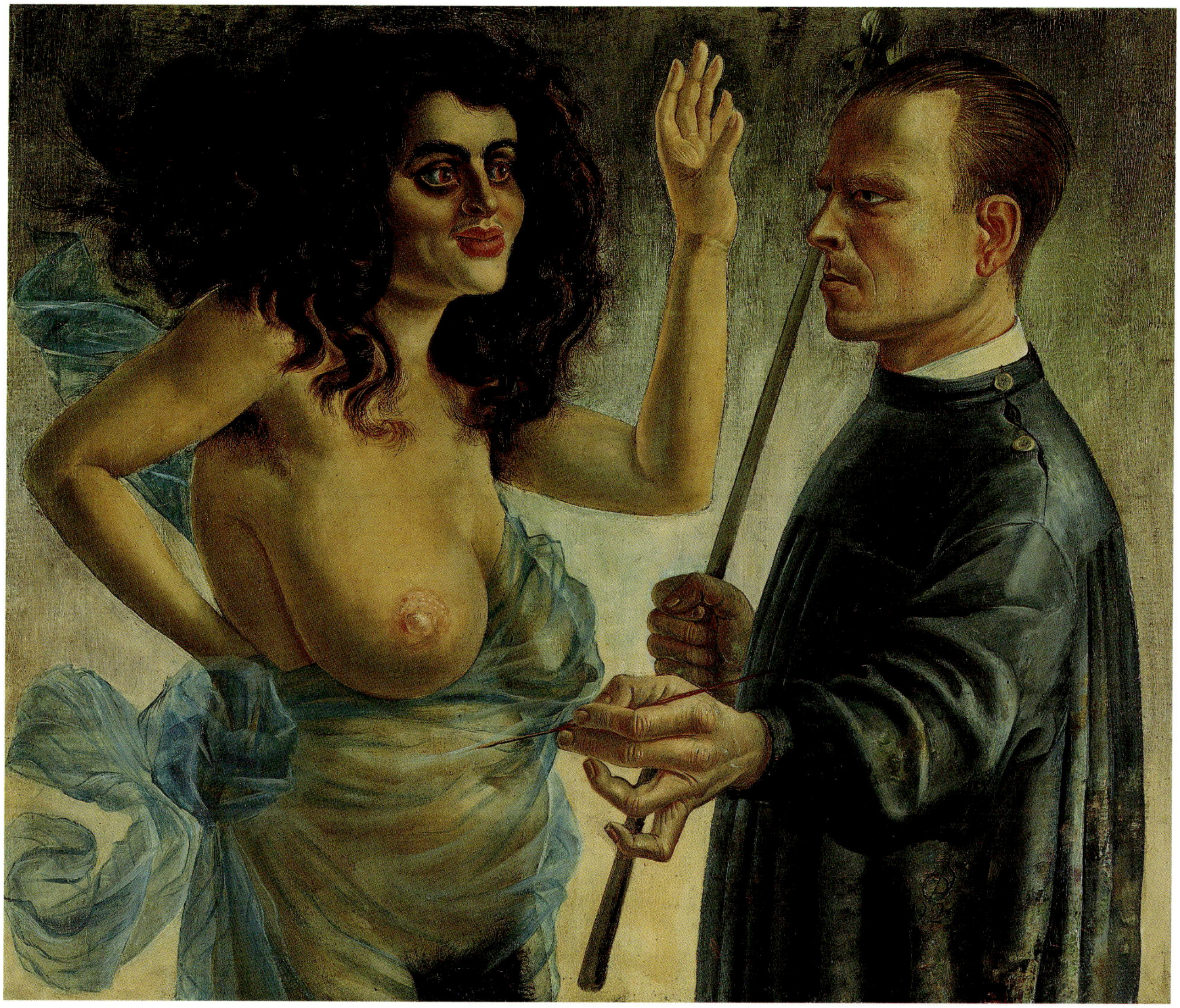

creates things in his own image. "And the portrait of the painter by himself is at the same time a metaphor of painting itself and of the specifics by which painting identifies itself. Painting and painter can nowhere else be more interwoven: the painter paints himself as a painter and the painting that he becomes is of his own making. The painter, the model and the work, bear the same name; and Narcissus looking at himself in the waters of a spring invented painting. Every painter who looks in the mirror at the model he is, the metaphor of Narcissus all over again, and in this way reinvents painting."[5]

It is in the self-portrait also that the painter struggles the most with death. This recalls the story of Géricault lying on his deathbed, drawing the image of his left hand with his right hand, using himself as his last model.

Iconographically, the self-portrait,[6] is often associated with the model, and we can see the painter with the attributes of his profession in the company of nude figures posing for him. The artist represents himself either in a state of tension, in action or in lascivious repose. Playing on the contrast between clothed and unclothed, as in a certain *Déjeuner sur l'herbe* by Manet, he is also the active

Brassaï:
Matisse and His Model, 1939.

factor in relation to the passive offering of nudity. The model is at the disposal of his gaze. In some cases, rare ones, it is true, the model is an ogress. Otto Dix portrays himself wrapped from head to toe in his painter's smock. He is armed with a mahlstick which he brandishes like a spear to fend off a menacing woman with a gluttonous mouth and superlative breasts, whom he daintily paints with the tip of his brush, at the risk, it would seem, of a real peril! The painter's fingers clutch his instruments like a shield. The painting is the stage of dramatic strategies, power struggles, attempts at keeping a distance.

Equally strange is the mise-en-scène created by Lovis Corinth: the painter shows himself frontally, with an anxious, feverish gaze, his chest puffed like a bull, his arms spread open, his palette and a bouquet of brushes in his right hand. A model resplendent in her nudity presses against him, showing her naked back in a gesture of tender familiarity which seems to disorient the painter completely. Surprised, lost, he wonders what is happening to him. Will the model abuse him, expose him?

There are also gentler relationships between the model and the self-portrait. Matisse was a master at this alchemy: he represented himself bespectacled, in a three-piece suit with tie, to introduce himself into a confused space in which the model reigns with her sovereign, but intimate beauty. The serenity of the model lying down in her languorous pose radiates through the drawing, making us forget the complexity of the composition. In fact, the model is lying down in front of a mirror, she is doubled, and it is the mirror which shows us the figure of Matisse studiously absorbed in his work. The presence of the looking-glass is not explicit, and yet it is the cause of the spatial confusion by which the self-portrait and model are interwoven and fused. Matisse depicts his model twice, once directly, and the second time in a reflection, sharing with him the same space, on the same level.

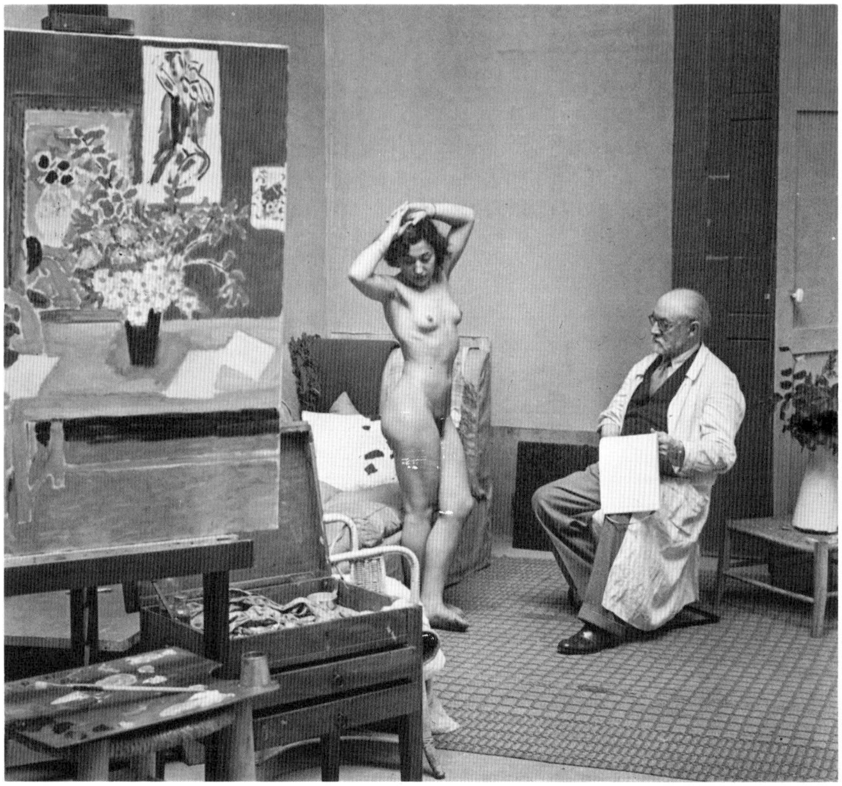

Beyond the active-passive, clothed-unclothed duality, the two figures enter into a powerful symbiosis. The nude body of the model, doubled in part by its reflected image, occupies three-quarters of the composition. It inhabits the space with a broad and peaceful respiration, and Matisse gently introduces himself into it, touched by grace. In his writings, which are full of the humility of everyday concerns, the question of the model comes up again and again like a refrain, associated with the oceanic aspect of the pictorial act. "I become one with the painting, like an animal with what it likes," writes the wise Matisse.[7]

Through the woman's body, he wants to "condense" the essential, the "religious feeling" of life. "I want to reach the state of condensation which makes the painting." "I have a woman's body to paint; first of all, I give it grace and charm, but there is something more I have to give to it. I will condense the meaning of this body by looking for its essential lines." "What interests me the most is neither still life nor landscape, but the figure. That is what permits me to express the religious feeling I have for life." "The living model, the naked body of a woman is the privileged seat of feeling, but also of questioning: at all costs, one should not try to make the model coincide with a theory or a preconceived effect. The model must mark you, awaken in you an emotion which you seek in turn to express."[8] "But how to paint the nude without it becoming artificial?" asks Matisse.[9]

"My models, my human figures, are never like extras in an interior. They are the main theme of my work. I depend absolutely on my model, which I observe freely, and it is afterward that I settle on the pose which corresponds the most to its nature. When I take a new model, it is in the abandon of her relaxation that I guess which pose suits her, and I then enslave myself to it. I sometimes keep these young girls for many years, until the interest wears

Henri Matisse:
Nude with Mirror, 1937.

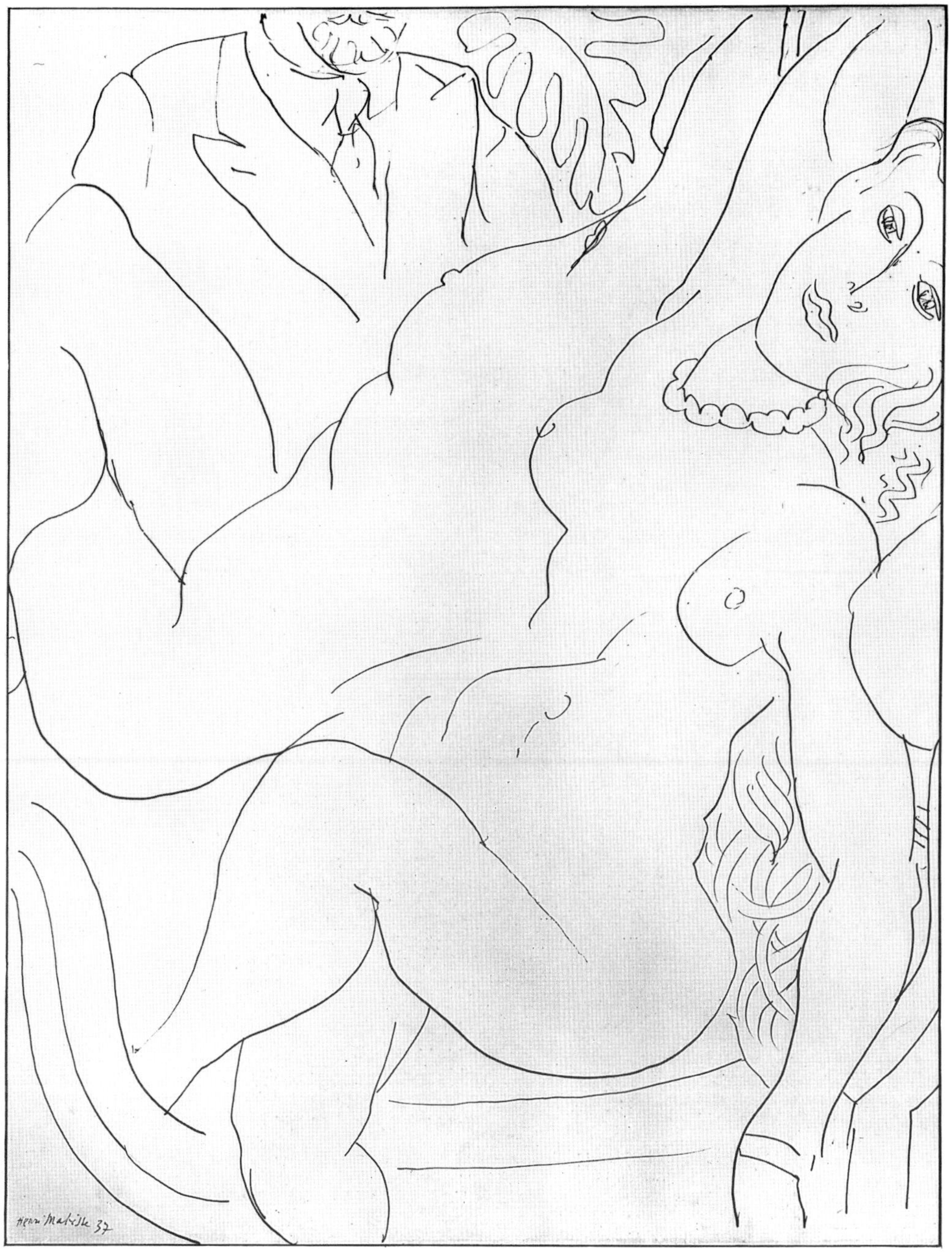

off... Their forms are not always perfect, but they are always expressive. The emotional interest which they inspire in me is not particularly visible in the representation of their bodies, but often in certain lines and special values which are spread throughout the canvas or paper and which form its orchestration, its architecture. Not everyone notices this. It is perhaps a sublimated pleasure."[10]

The model becomes the indispensable focus of the painter's energy. It is the initiator of the painting, and the substance which feeds it. "Most of all, I do not create a woman, I paint a painting... For the other, the model is information. For me, there is something about it that arrests me. It is the focus of my energy... I draw very close to the model—in itself—my eyes less than a meter from the model, our knees at times almost touching. I consider that I have made progress when I observe in my work a more and more evident detachment from the support of the model, from the presence of the model, which counts not as a possibility of information on her constitution, but to keep me in feeling, in a sort of flirtatious state which ends in a rape. The rape of whom? Of myself in a sort of tender feeling before the sympathetic object... The model for me is a touchstone, it is a door which I must break open in order to reach the garden in which I am alone and feel good, even the model exists only for what use I can make of it."[11] "What matters the most to me? To work from my model

Henri Matisse:
Reclining Nude with Mirror, 1937.

until I have it sufficiently inside me to be able to improvise, to let my hand run free while respecting the grandeur and sacred character of all that lives."[12]

The model fertilizes the painting through a closely fusional relationship. Matisse plays footsies, talks about flirtation and rape; he penetrates the model, opens it, plunges into it, but also absorbs it, puts it inside him. There is no longer any opposition between action and contemplation.

The painter then adds this piece of advice: "Fit the parts together, one into the other, and build your figure like a carpenter builds a house. Everything must be constructed, composed of parts that make a whole: a tree like a human body, a human body like a cathedral. Into the work must enter: knowledge, contemplation sustained by the model or by some other subject, and the imagination which enriches what we see. Close your eyes and keep your vision present, then work with your own sensitivity. If you work from a model, take the model's pose yourself; the place where you feel the tension is the key to the movement."[13]

Take the model's pose, appropriate it in order to impregnate oneself with it, to understand it, experience it physically. But by entering into such a symbiosis with the model, Matisse at times fears being engulfed, and so he contrives strategies to detach himself from it. "The ideal thing would be to have a studio with three floors. There would be a first stage of working from the model on the first floor. From the second, one would come "down less often. On the third, one would have learned to do without the model."[14] "It is a matter

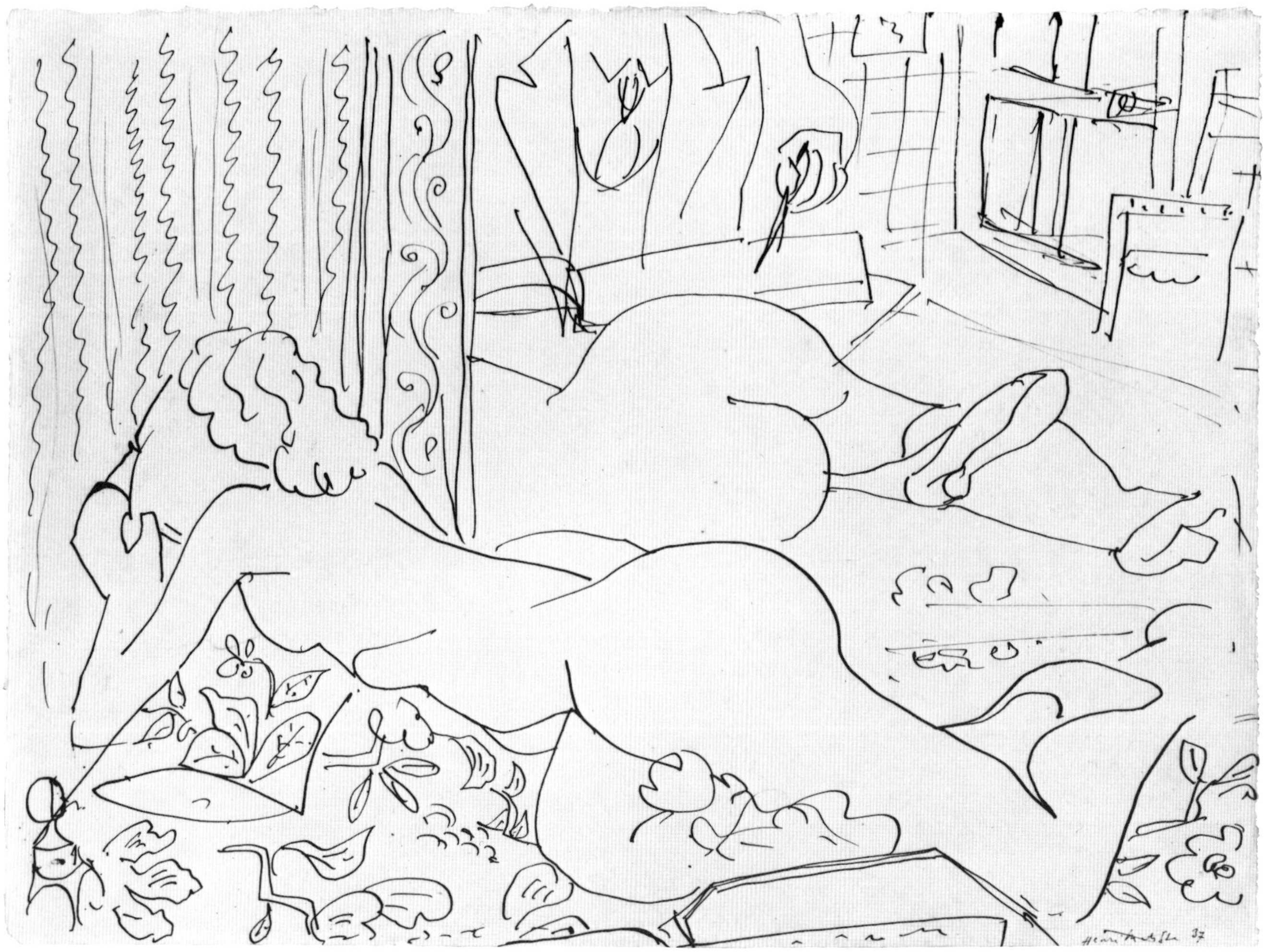

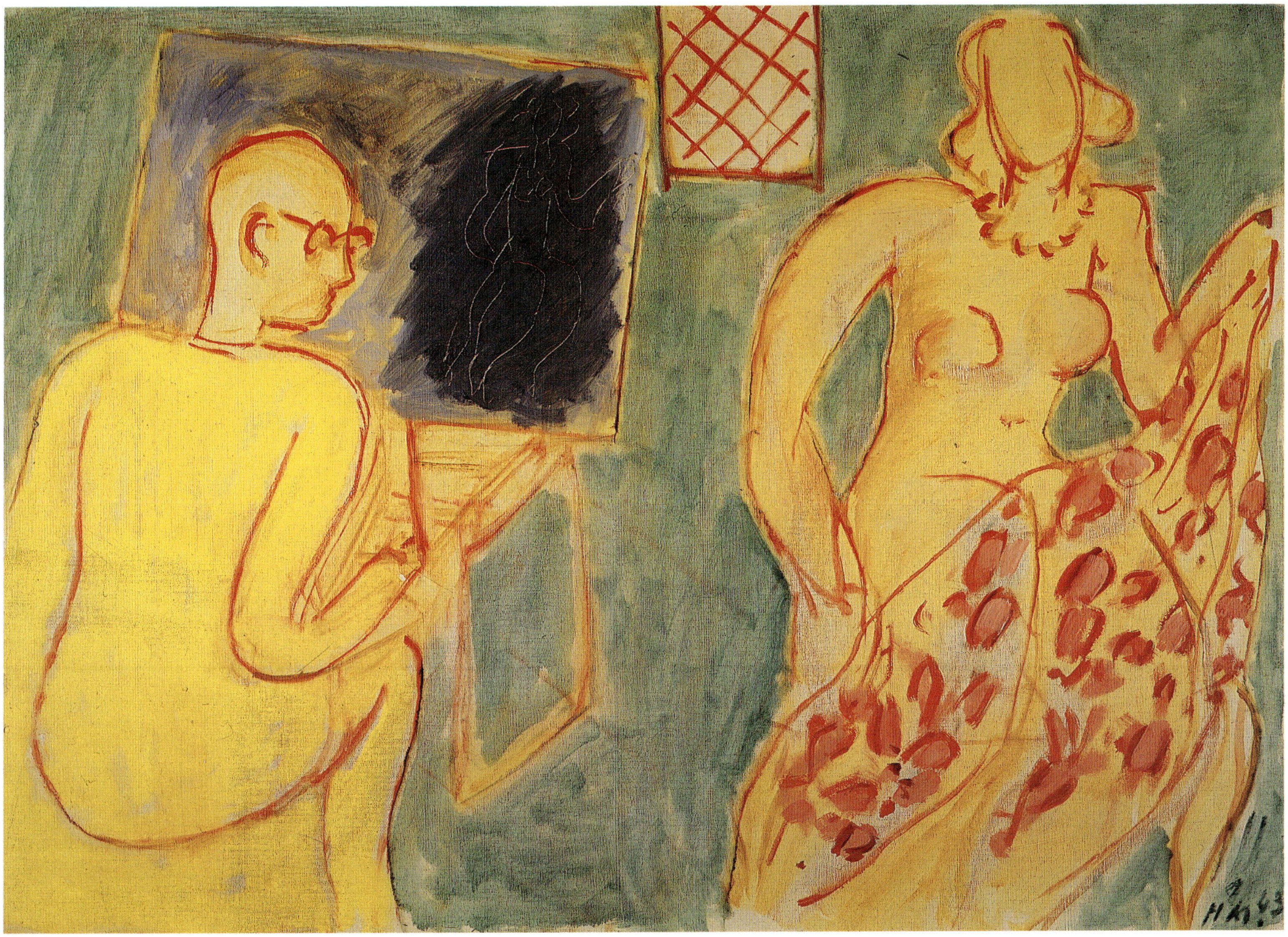

Henri Matisse:
The Painting Session, 1942.

of representing the model, not of copying it, and there can be no color relationship between it and your painting; one should consider only the equivalence of the relationship of the colors in your painting to the relationship of the colors of the model."[15]

To be able to do without the model, one must be completely "impregnated" by it, possessed by it, and it was in order to verify this intimate possession that Matisse drew blindfolded. His knowledge was so internalized that it was situated beyond the eye, it became autonomous and combined with the hand guiding the pencil or the brush.

Throughout his life, Matisse let himself be seduced by his models. To his friend, Rouveyre, he related in plain, almost banal terms, a visionary episode in which he incarnated himself in his model—a beautiful English girl—to the point of altering the color of her eyes! Then, very seriously and literally, Matisse verified the metamorphosis with a witness and even tried to give a medical explanation for it.

"You spoke of an English girl as beautiful as a dream. One hour ago, I had a third drawing session with an English girl perhaps even more beautiful than the one you are telling me about and who, after all, has vanished. Mine is there and will come back the day after tomorrow to look at me in the eyes as people usually do when I work, without defenses, without worries or protection. Her beautiful eyes were hazel yesterday, today, when I could no longer find their color by looking at them, I asked Lydia to come and tell me what was what. She answered that she has eyes of the same color as yours, as my own. I was quite astonished by this. But, I saw the eyes change color during the course of the session, becoming darker, at the same time as a redness colored the face. I swear to you that I did nothing for this, I thought that it was a rush of blood that was making the eyes change. You

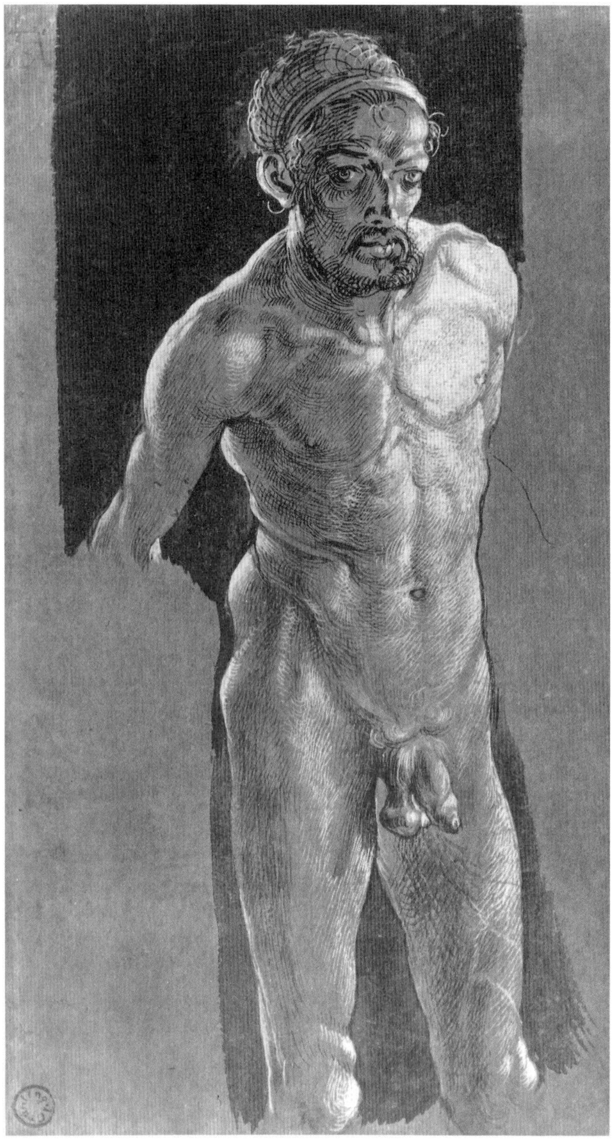

Albrecht Dürer:
Nude Self-Portrait, c. 1503.

cannot imagine the harmony that unites her eyes, her lips and the gentle curve of her chin. I will never be able to render that. So there she is, in front of me like a little pigeon in my hand." Indeed, rarely has a painter gone so far in his identification with the model.

If artists are great consumers and producers of nudes ("What love was to poets and storytellers, the nude was for artists," wrote Paul Valéry), and if they very probably project themselves just beneath the surface in all of the nudes they represent, there seems to be a relative taboo on the direct and official representation of their own nudity in the history of painting.

There were of course a few transgressions. One of the most surprising ones we owe to Dürer.[16] On two occasions, Dürer painted nude self-portraits. In one unfinished drawing done in pen and ink and brush, he represented himself completely naked from the head down to the knees, depicting his own anatomy with as much precision as the features of his face. We see the body of a man in his prime with a relatively athletic musculature. The face, with its bulging eyes, has a hallucinatory quality.

Dürer with a naked torso may also be recognized sitting wearily in the pose of the "Man of Sorrows," with a whip and switches in his hand. He appears more explicitly in a self-portrait in which he showed himself pointing to his spleen with his index finger. An inscription at the top of the page explains this gesture: "The place with the yellow spot indicated by my finger is where it hurts." The spleen, then considered by the theory of humors to be the seat of melancholy, secreted the famous "black bile" which was responsible for dark moods. The "spleen" of the Romantics refers to the same organ as the source of similar pains. In pointing to this area, was Dürer indicating a physiological ailment or a psychological state, or both?

These two self-portraits, unencumbered by religious or mythological costumes, were not intended for the public eye. Dürer's art transfigures them, but they were not the product of idealization, and he depicted himself without any self-indulgence. In the absence of precise historical information, we could even imagine that Dürer executed

Albrecht Dürer:
Self-Portrait When Ill, 1512-1519.

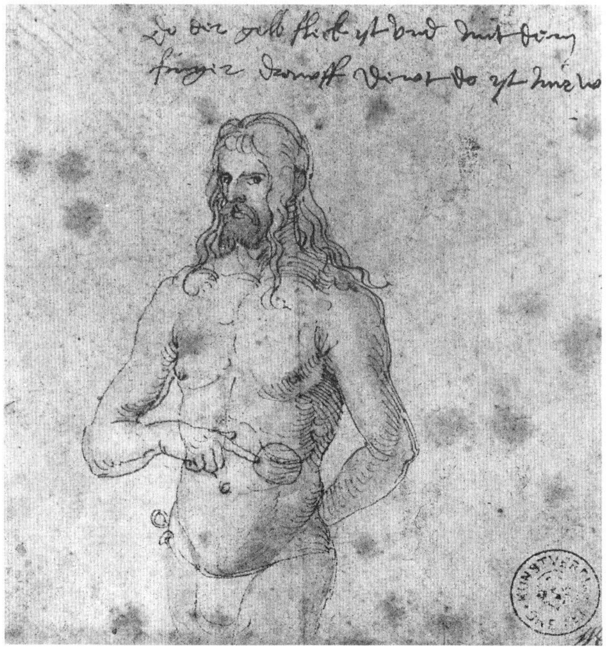

Jacopo Pontormo:
Study of a Nude
(self-portrait), 1525.

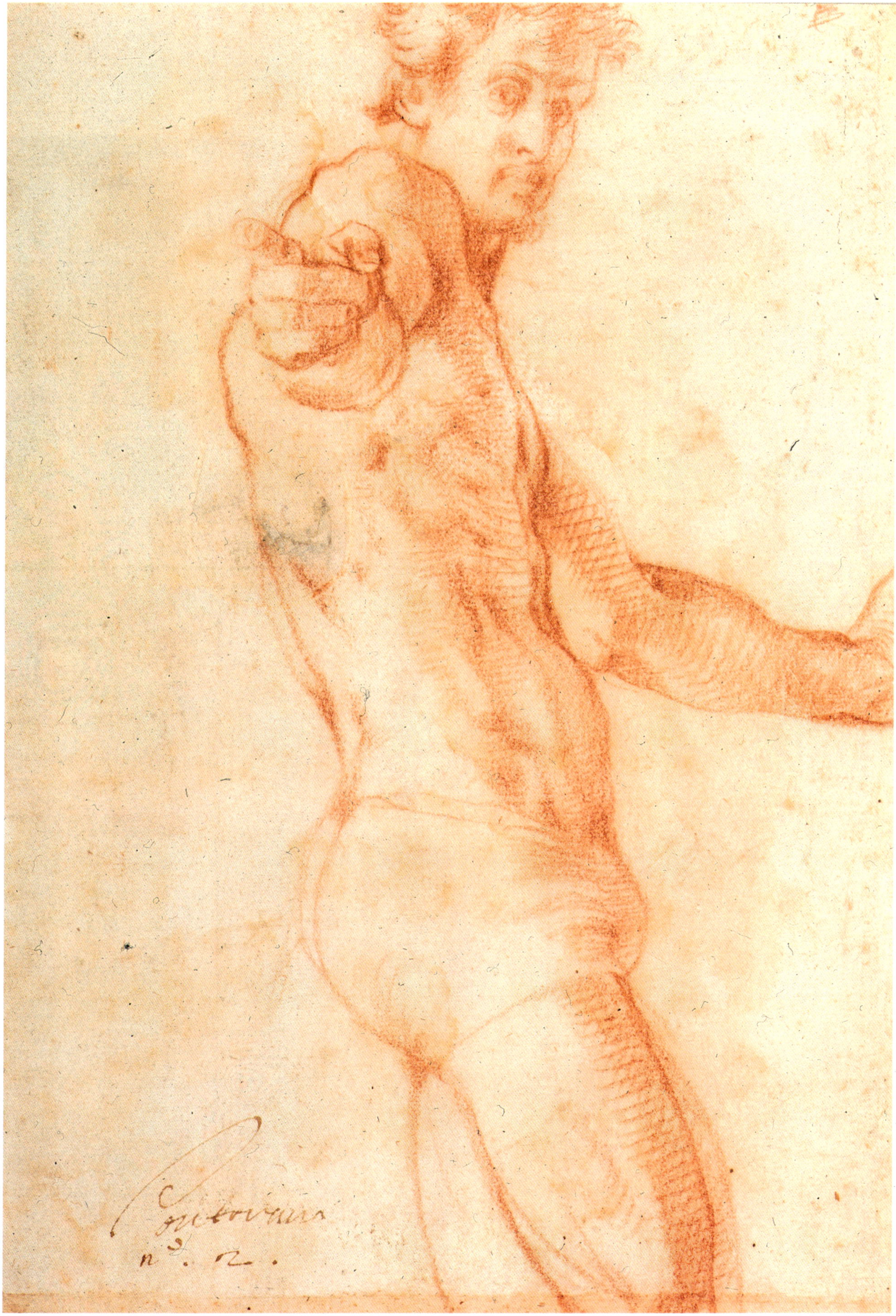

Egon Schiele:
Nude (self-portrait), c. 1910.

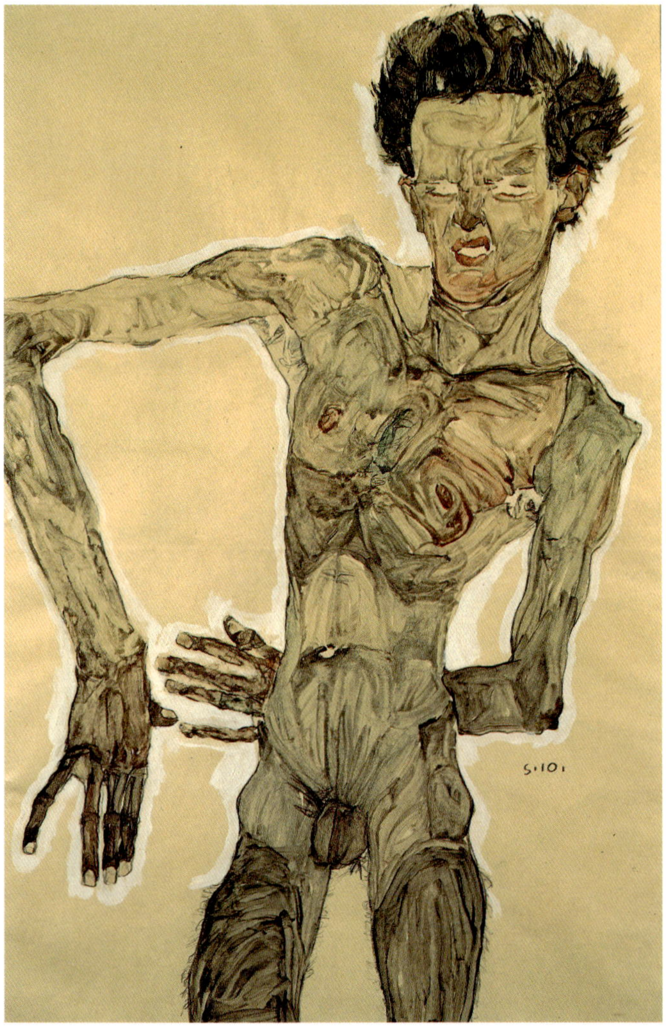

the second nude self-portrait to send to a physician as a sort of illustrated health bulletin.

Pontormo, the Mannerist artist par excellence, who also executed some nude self-portraits, was obsessed with his state of health. His bilious temperament is manifest in every line, every comma of his private journal. He described in detail, to the ounce, the content of what he ingested, and was as obsessed by what went into his body as by what came out of it. His menus and the effects they entailed were combined with dry and summary descriptions of the progress of his work. For example: "The third of April, did the leg starting from the knee with great difficulty because of the darkness, the wind and the coating, and in the evening I ate 14 ounces of bread, two fried eggs, chicory. Friday, I began one hour before daylight the back which is above the other. I ate a half kilo of bread, asparagus and eggs and the weather was fine. Saturday I ate. Palm Sunday, I ate some marvelous fritters at Bronzino's. Monday morning, I had someone in the garden tying the vines and hoeing the garden."[17] And so on for page after page while he was working on the paintings commissioned by Cosimo de' Medici for the church of San Lorenzo in Florence. For years, according to Vasari, Pontormo locked himself up in the chapel without letting anyone enter. Even his patron was not allowed access to the area walled up by the maniacal painter.

Pontormo was also haunted by anatomy. Legend has it that in a fit of melancholy, and to give a natural touch to the figures of bodies drowned in the Flood for the choir of San Lorenzo, he kept cadavers immersed in water-filled troughs in order to make them bloated—and stank up the place in the process. His many sketches and studies prove his constant passion for nudity. In one of them, done around 1525, he used himself as a model, drawing himself like the other figures (unless he drew the others like he drew himself?), that is, with a somewhat bumpy, expressive and animated musculature and set in contorted poses, the eyes like dark holes in the face. Pontormo, according to Vasari again, was exceptionally handsome and had very fine features, "bellissimi tratti." In his account, the biographer remarks that the painter was so afraid of death that he refused even to hear about it. So full of paradoxes is the unconscious.

Among the few known nude self-portraits, there is a head and shoulders of Van Dyck playing the part of the shepherd Paris.[18] It is not by chance that the artist portrayed himself as the judge who had to decide which of the goddesses was the greatest beauty: Athena, Hera or Aphrodite. Beauty naturally belongs to the realm of the artist, it is his "speciality" and he is better trained than others to attempt to approach it.

While "self-nudes," as Michel Tournier called them, are common in photography, they are still fairly exceptional in the painting of the twentieth century. Bonnard, the author of several "self-nudes," did not beautify himself. In his *Self-Portrait in the Bathroom Mirror,*[19] he used that age-old device to depict his naked, somewhat frail torso. The virility of his skinny build is even less convincing in his *Self-Portrait as a Boxer.*[20] Egon Schiele represented himself in scores of nude self-portraits which went even beyond the nude, for he almost looks like a skeleton: the hypersensitive artist who liked skinny little girls is just skin and bones. His gaunt, hollow-eyed face becomes a skull. The collar bone and hips protrude, and his penis seems empty and emptied once and for all. The few traces of hair add a derisive touch to a body that is already almost bereft of life.

Pierre Bonnard:
The Boxer (self-portrait), 1931.

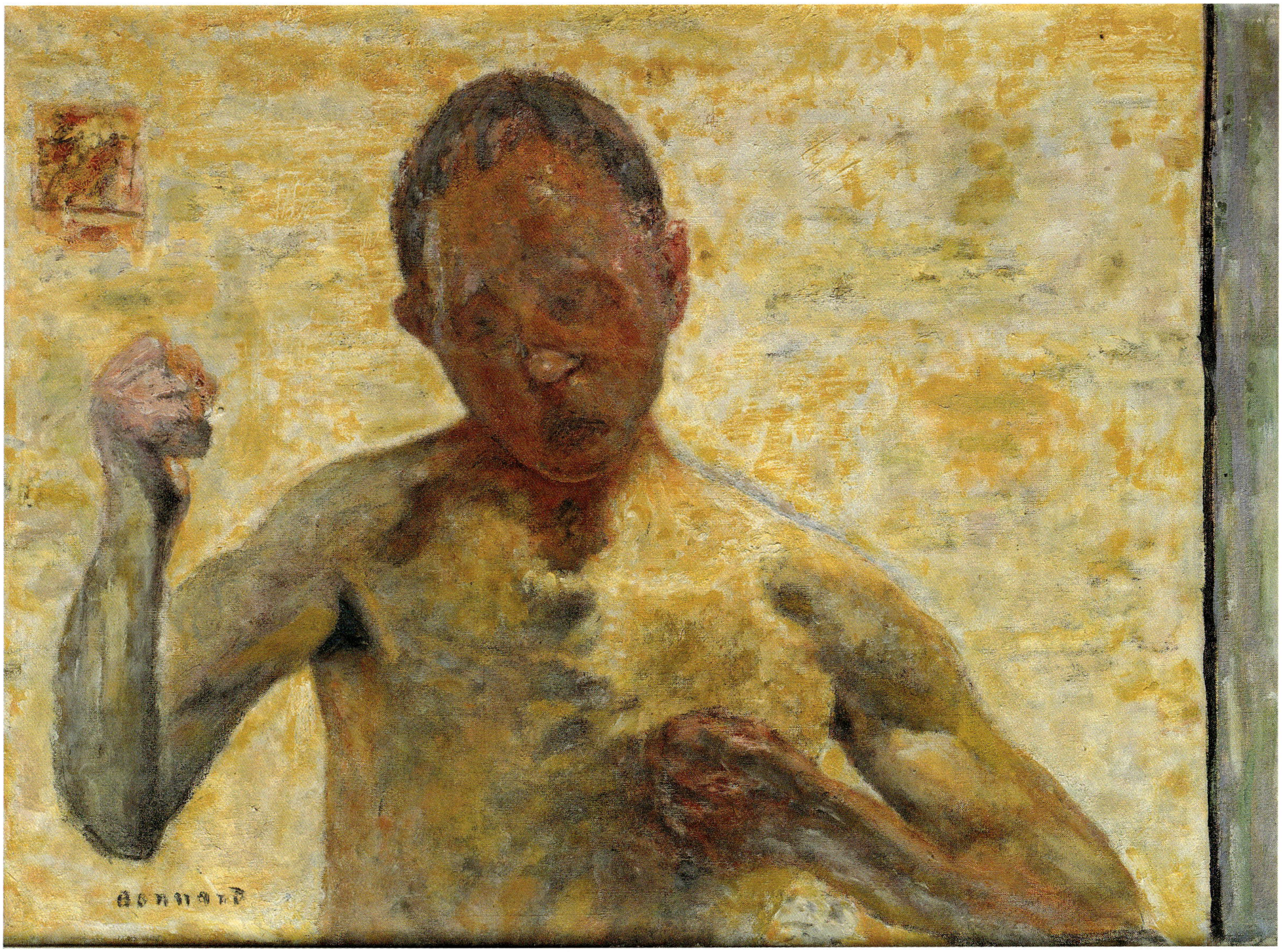

The births of Pygmalion

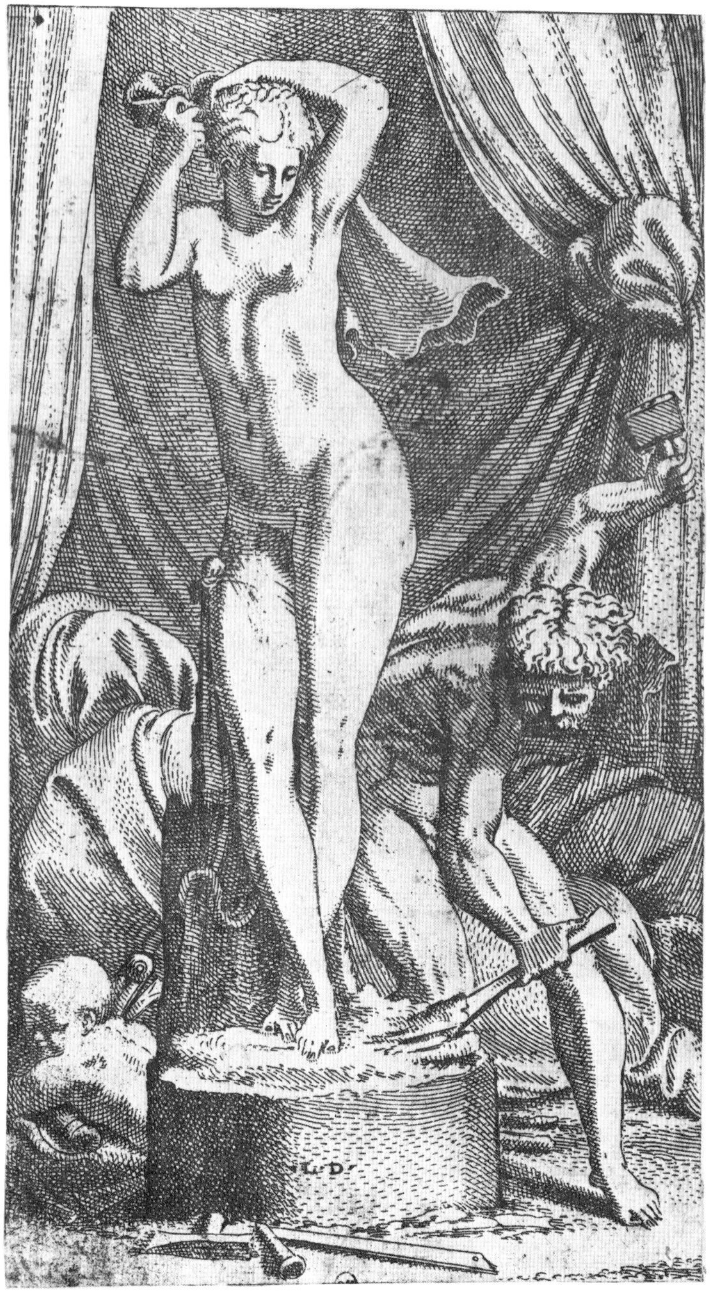

Master L.D. *(after Primaticcio): Pygmalion Sculpting Galatea, c. 1545.*

As he works, the artist creates his doubles of flesh. Through his body and through his desire, he breathes life onto the canvas or into the marble. The story of Pygmalion[21] is worth retelling in this regard. Having seen the faults with which nature afflicted the bodies of women, Pygmalion decides to remain a virgin and a bachelor. However, he carves in ivory the figure of a woman of superlative beauty, and falls in love with this pure being who has so much reality for him that she seems to be alive. "Art hides itself by so much art." The artist pines for this image of his own creation. He regularly touches the statue to ascertain if it is not made of flesh, and cannot believe that it is made only of ivory. He speaks to the statue, holds it in his arms, kisses it and believes that it responds, that the flesh yields to his touch. He is even concerned that his fingers will leave bruises on the limbs they have pressed. He brings it gifts that are usually offered to young women: seashells, smooth pebbles, small birds, flowers of all colors, drops of amber. He dresses it in fine clothing and puts rings with precious stones on its fingers; adorns it with necklaces, gold chains, and pearl earrings. The statue is as beautiful nude as when it is decorated. Everything suits it perfectly. He lays her down on a dyed Sidonian carpet, calls her his love and puts soft feather cushions under her neck,"as if she could feel them."

On the day when Cyprus celebrates the feast of Venus, when gold-adorned ewes with curling horns are sacrificed, Pygmalion makes an offering and asks the gods in a timid voice to give him for wife a woman like the ivory beauty (not daring to say the statue itself).

Venus, also decorated in gold, understands the artists wish, and, when he returns to his workshop to embrace the statue, he feels her body start to become warm. He touches his mouth to hers, feels her breasts, and with each touch, the ivory softens, loses its hardness, yields to his fingers like wax from Hymettus in the heat of the sun. The sculptor still hesitates to rejoice, he fears that he is deluding himself. Again and again, his hands touch the object of his desire, and what he feels is a real body, its veins pulsing with life. The ivory, a material whose smoothness and pallor is so much like flesh, and which lacks only the red glow of living flesh, begins to move, blood courses beneath the skin. His lips finally press the lips of a real mouth, and a live young woman responds to the kisses he gives. She even blushes, an irrefutable proof of her flesh and blood existence. As she opens her eyes, she discovers simultaneously her lover and the heavens. Through desire, the work of art has become flesh.

The wish to see life and its most subtle vibrations imbue the work of art is the obsession of every

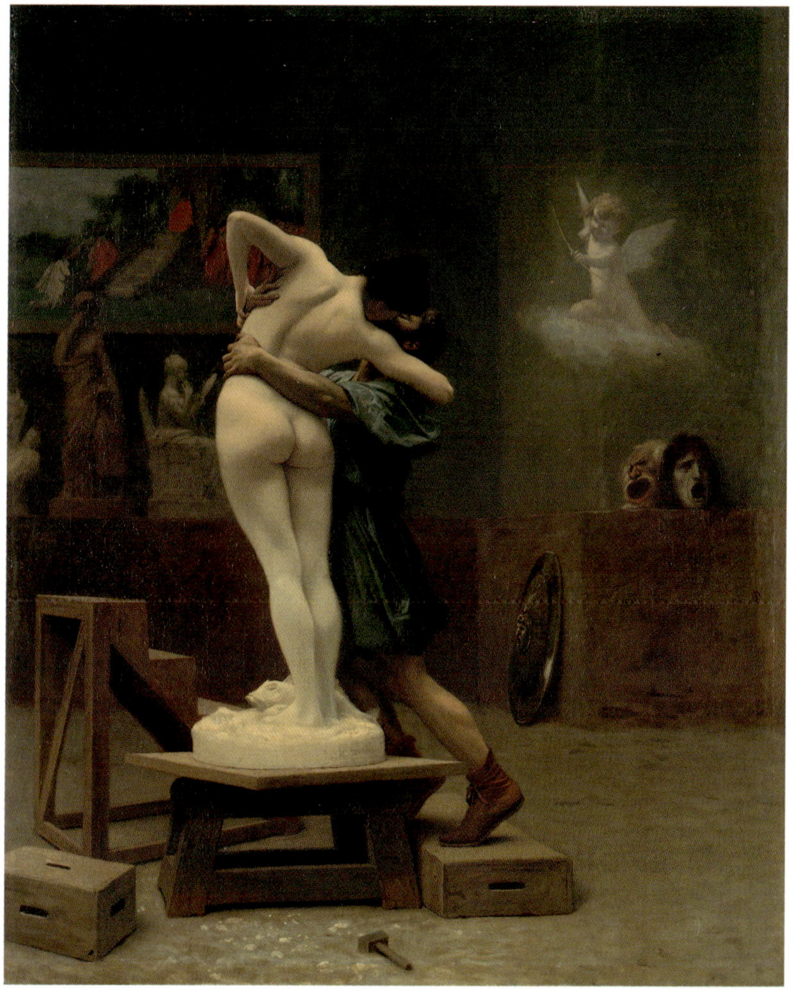

Jean-Léon Gérôme:
Pygmalion and Galatea, 1890.

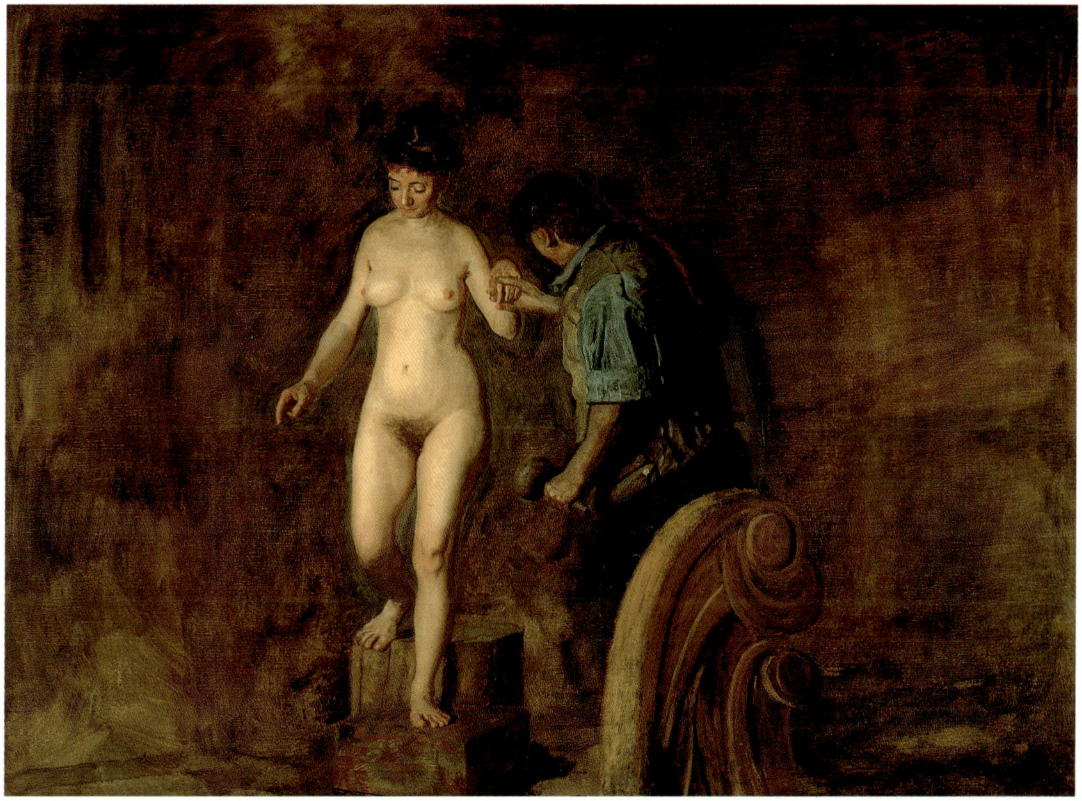

Thomas Eakins:
William Rush and His Model,
1907-1908.

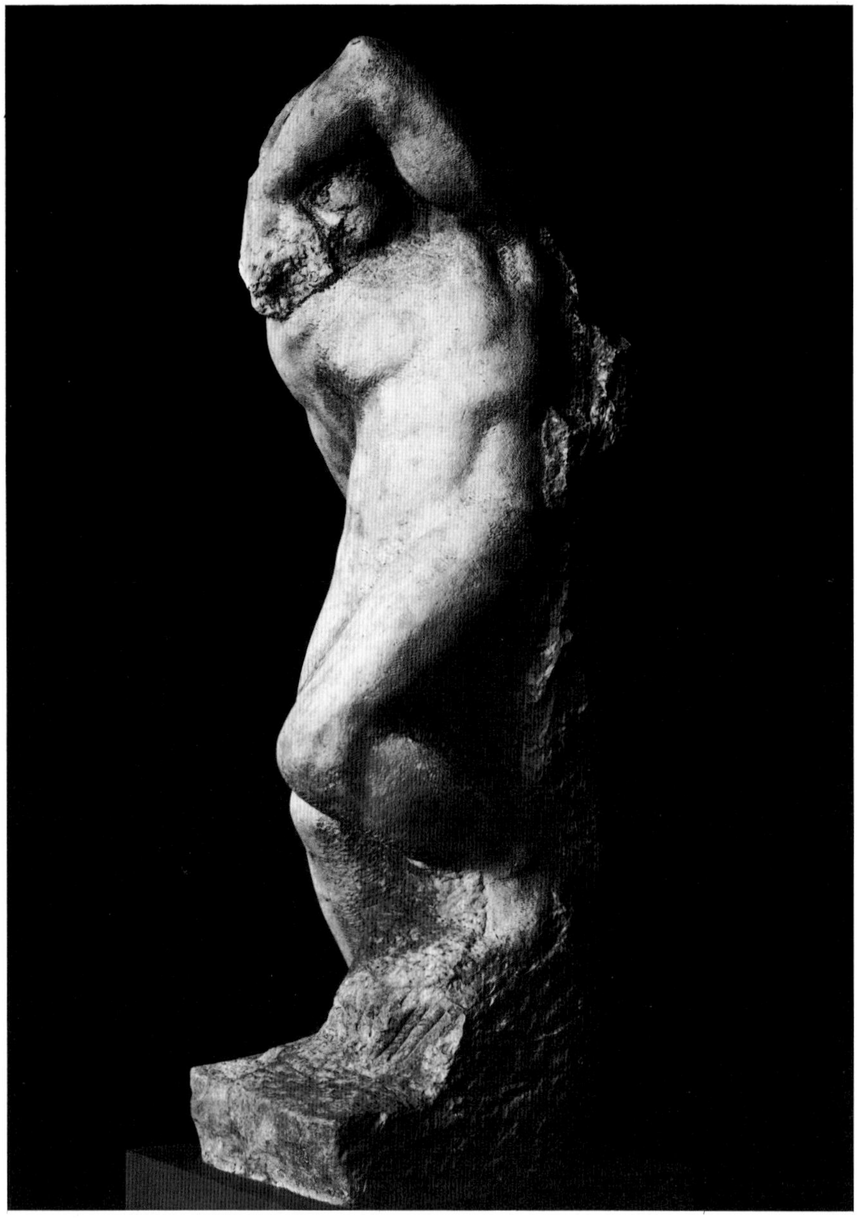

Michelangelo:
Slave, c. 1532-1534.

creator. It is expressed to the point of becoming an *idée fixe* in the poems of Michelangelo dedicated to the beautiful Vittoria Colonna, whom he loved with an unrequited love all through his life. The sculptor treats the sculpture like a woman, a mistress, a lover. "The sublime sculpture is so like a female companion,"[22] and he speaks of the marble as if it were a woman's body: "A great artist can conceive of no subject which marble does not contain in its breast."[23]

In a madrigal, he explains to Vittoria Colonna that "in taking away the pieces of a block with the chisel, one brings into being, from out of the heart of the dense and rough stone, a living figure which grows all the more as the stone diminishes."[24]

In his writings, Michelangelo constantly associated heat and cold, flame and stone: "If the inner fire is friend to the cold stone and if, extracted from it, it surrounds it afterwards, burns it, dissolves it, and yet lives still, so to speak, then joins the other stones together and makes itself indestructible; and if it rises with them to the heavens and defies winter and summer, we ascribe to it an even higher value than before; it appears to elude the winds and storms and even mocks the thunderbolts of Jupiter. In the same way, if, when brought into being by me, the flame which inside me is an occult activity, dissolves me; after having been burned, then extinguished, I hope to have more life."[25]

Through the stone, life grants itself the power to become immortal, and the magician of this transmutation is of course the sculptor beyond his own life. "How can it be, noble lady," he marvels to the glacial Vittoria Colonna, "that a living image carved in rocky stone can live longer than its maker, who is so soon struck down by death?"[26] Knowing that he has this power of immortality, he wants to have the distant Vittoria benefit from it by sculpting her image in stone, like Titian immortalized the mistress of the Duke of Rubino as a Venus with a little dog. He offers the inaccessible lady to execute their double portrait:

> "Perhaps I may give the two of us a long life, either in colors, or in marble, by reproducing our love and our faces; so that a thousand years after our disappearance, people will see how beautiful you were, how I loved you, and why I was not mad in loving you."[27]

But the indifferent beauty refuses, thus depriving herself of the only immortality possible. Michelangelo believed that beauty was what came nearest to eternity. He deified and worshipped a woman who served as his guide and also as his mirror.

Michelangelo knew that beauty was difficult to capture. This precursor of the young Werther suffered and dreamt of a joyful beauty. Like Leonardo, he realized in a very clear way that the artist served as his own model.

> "If it sometimes happens that an artist, making another image, represents himself in stone, livid and cadaverous, I often do so myself who am such by it;
>
> "And it seems to me that I always take my own image when I think that I am doing hers.
>
> "I could indeed say that the stone for which she is the model resembles her; but I will never be able to sculpt anything but my stricken members.
>
> "But if art preserves the living memory of a great beauty, it should then make me joyful so that I can make her beautiful!"[28]

If the sculptor, like the painter, emphasizes the principle of projection, Michelangelo is not in the least shocked by this; he is hardly surprised, considers it natural and would wish only to draw more joy from it.

On the rivalry between art and reality

Jean-Dominique Ingres: Angélique, 1819.

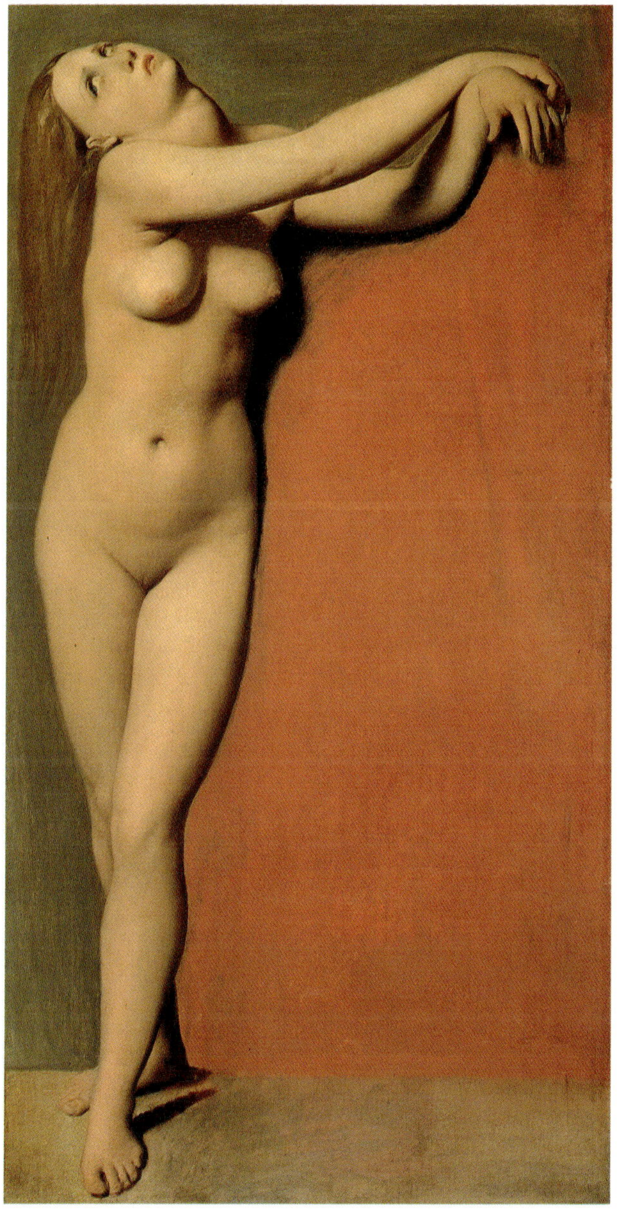

Through his ability to transfigure, the artist blurs the illusory borderline between art and reality. There are many stories that deal with this particular confusion. The libretto of *Tosca*, written by Illica and Giacosa, is full of dramatic situations. Tosca is jealous of a painting and of the gaze of her lover on another woman chosen as model. Interferences between reality and illusion abound.

In the church of Sant'Andrea della Valle, the artist Cavaradossi paints a Mary Magdalen with blue eyes and streams of blond hair.

And you, mysterious beauty,
Crowned with blond tresses,
Your eyes azure blue,
Those of Tosca are black...
The mystery of art which plays
With diversity,
But in painting her,
I think only of you, Tosca.

The sacristan is shocked by the painter's choice of models, whether it be Tosca or the beautiful blue-eyed Attavanti, who often goes to pray there. When Tosca, whose "blood boils with a mad love," discovers the painting, she becomes jealous of the blond beauty. "She is too beautiful... I hid myself to capture her features," the painter explains in his defense: "How she looks at me! She mocks me! She teases me!" Tosca exclaims, so jealous that she finally asks her lover: "Then make her eyes black! Then make her eyes black!" Here, painting asserts its power of ambiguity over reality. Tosca's rival is a painting which, through its trompe-l'oeil quality, evokes the model, and even more her lover's gaze upon her.

Literature is full of anecdotes about the rivalry between art and illusion. In *The Work*, Zola brings these ambiguities into sharp relief. It is said that when Cézanne, the writer's childhood friend, read the book, he took it as a distorted reflection of his own personality, and this caused a fairly definitive break in their long-standing friendship.

The painter in the story is a certain Claude Lantin, who lives alone. One day, he encounters a young

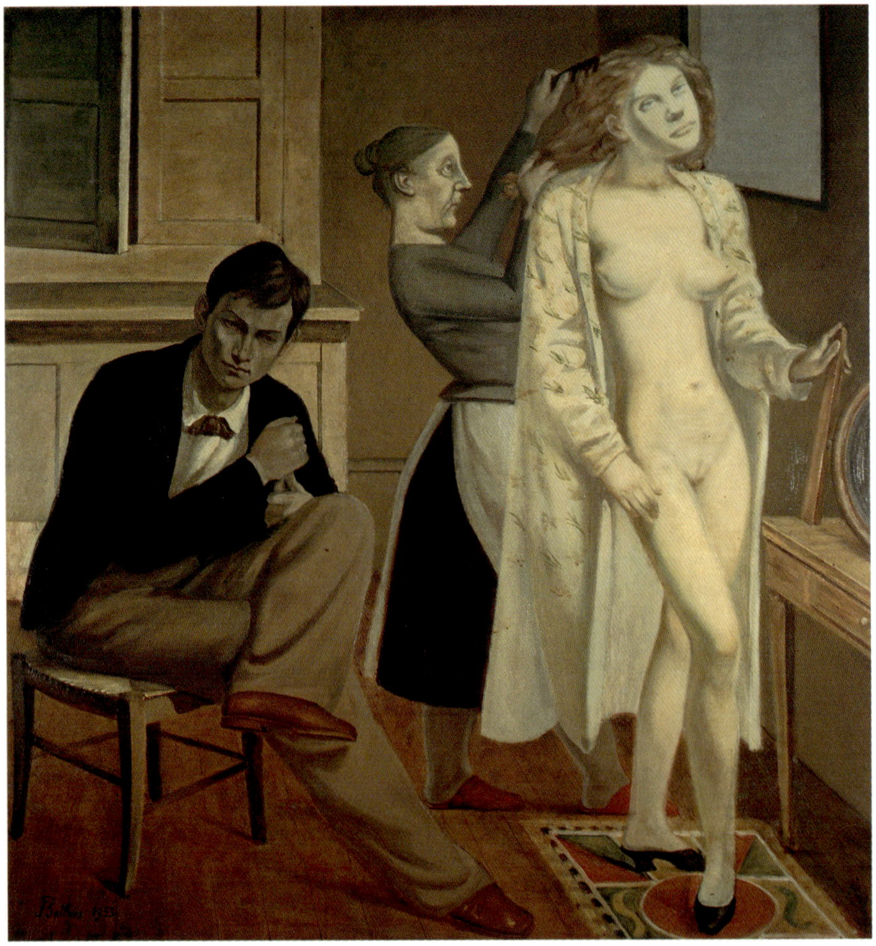

Balthus:
Cathy Dressing, 1933.

girl who lives a hard life, and he takes her home. Exhausted, she ends up falling asleep, and only then does the painter dare to look at her and admire her. Seeing her beauty, he begins to draw her, full of enthusiasm for the skin tones and well-structured muscles. "He had already forgotten the young girl, he was in ecstatic contemplation of her snowy white breasts, which lightened the delicate amber of her shoulders. An anxious modesty made him shrink from the sight of nature, he held his elbows close to his body, he became a quiet, attentive and respectful little boy again."[29]

He sketches her more and more often. She becomes his lover, his official model, and yet remains very modest. However, Claude despairs: he cannot capture this model and introduce it into his painting, as he would like. He makes errors and spoils the motif. At times, "he flees from his work, suffering abominably from leaving it so, marred by a gaping wound."[30] Christine exhausts herself posing for months on end, but, stoically, she lets herself be directed and manipulated, while he strives to "penetrate himself with the quality of this flesh," this flesh which absorbs light and whose blood he wanted to see flow in his painting.

"The nude is a wonderful thing indeed... And it vibrates and it takes on life, as if we could see the blood coursing in the muscles... Ah! a well-drawn muscle, a solidly painted limb, in full light, there is nothing finer, nothing better, it is God himself... I have no other religion, I would go down on my knees and stay there for my whole life... Look, there, under the left breast, well, how lovely it is, there are some bluish veins that give the skin an exquisitely delicate tone... And there, the curve of the hip, that dimple with its golden shadow, what a delight!... And there, under the fleshy modeling of the belly, that pure line of the groin, there is an ever so slight carmine tint in pale gold."[31]

But Christine sees herself like an object, no different than a jug or a cauldron in a still life. The painter's passion for flesh is merely pictorial. His lovers are now only painted lovers. Sublimation, sublimation, Dr. Freud would no doubt suggest. Christine rebels against this illusory quest. She is hurt by this "ménage à trois" in which she feels herself surpassed by the mistress-muse of painting, the only one who makes her lover's heart beat and who separates her from him by an insurmontable wall.

In Christine's eyes, her rival, this cumbersome concubine who is "so terrible in her immobility as an image," is the victor. But Claude struggles without end. He sweats "blood and tears" to create flesh, to breathe life into his painting. He is never completely satisfied, his model does not fulfill his expectations. He searches on and on without ever reaching his ideal. One day, in a blind fit of rage, he makes a hole in the canvas. Christine secretly rejoices at seeing her rival "killed," while the painter gauges the extent of his "crime": "Claude stared at the open gap in the chest. He felt a tremendous grief coming from the wound, from which the blood of his work seemed to be flowing. Was it possible? Had he really murdered what he loved the most in the world? His anger turned into stupefaction, he began to run his fingers over the canvas, pulling the edges of the tear together as if he were trying to close the edges of a wound."[32]

The theme of the obsession of bringing flesh into being haunts Zola's novel. The author himself, a lover of literature, the Pygmalion of his own characters, must have had a close acquaintance with this problem.

In Rudyard Kipling's novel, *The Light That Failed*, there are fairly similar ingredients: a blend of love, sublimation, the solitude of the artist and the ambiguous presence of the live model. The main character, Dick, a sort of globetrotter reporter making drawings of the fighting in Sudan for an English newspaper, is strangely haunted by a childhood love.

Back in London, he runs into this former love by chance; she has become a frigid woman, a failed painter who works out of compulsion. She categorically refuses to give herself to him. The model idealized in his memory falls apart upon contact with the actual reality. Chance, however, provides him with a model: a young woman found unconscious by the friend with whom he shares his apartment. At first, the artist is wary of this unfortunate woman, but he fairly quickly gets the idea of

Edvard Munch:
The Artist and His Model, 1919-1921.

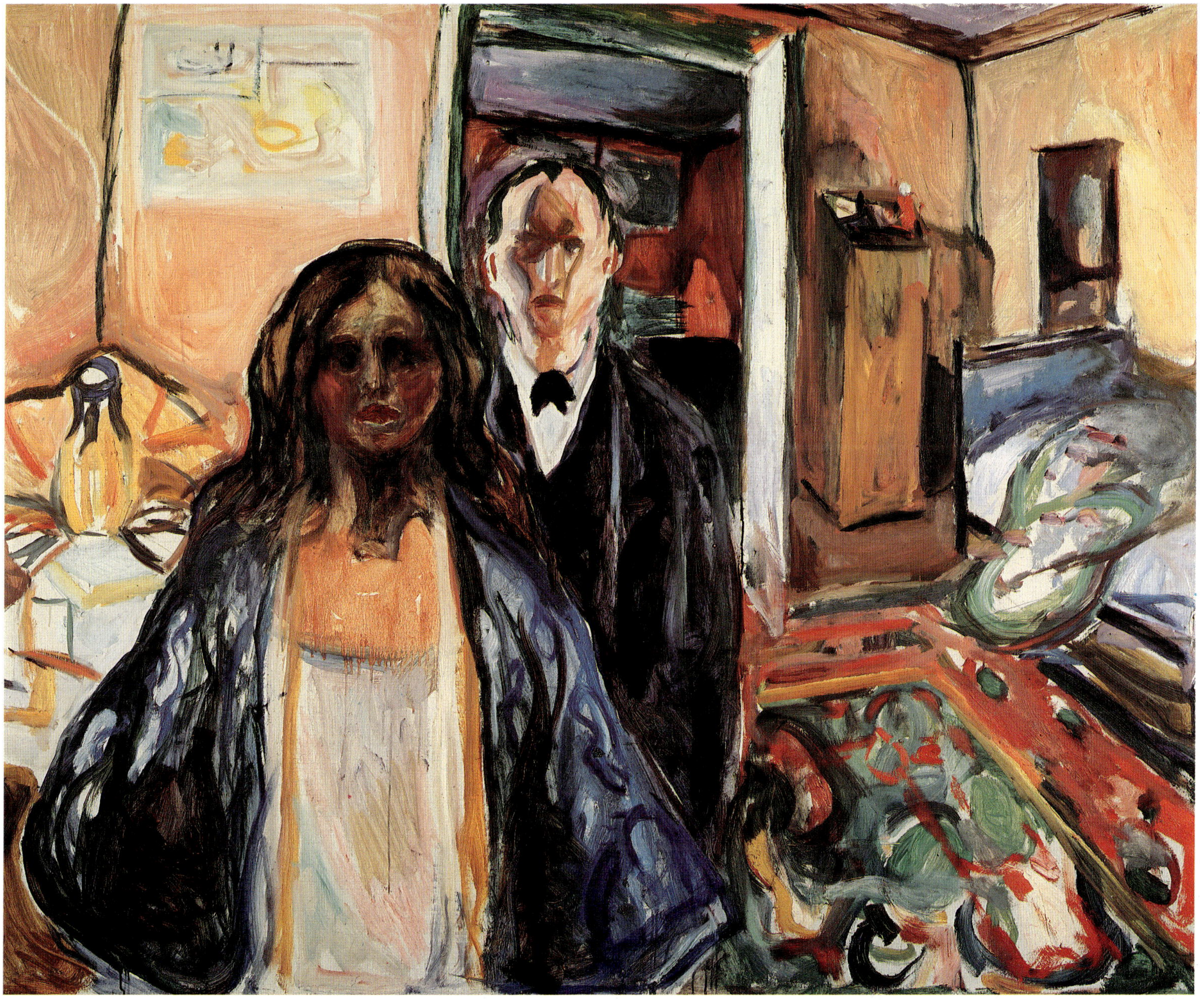

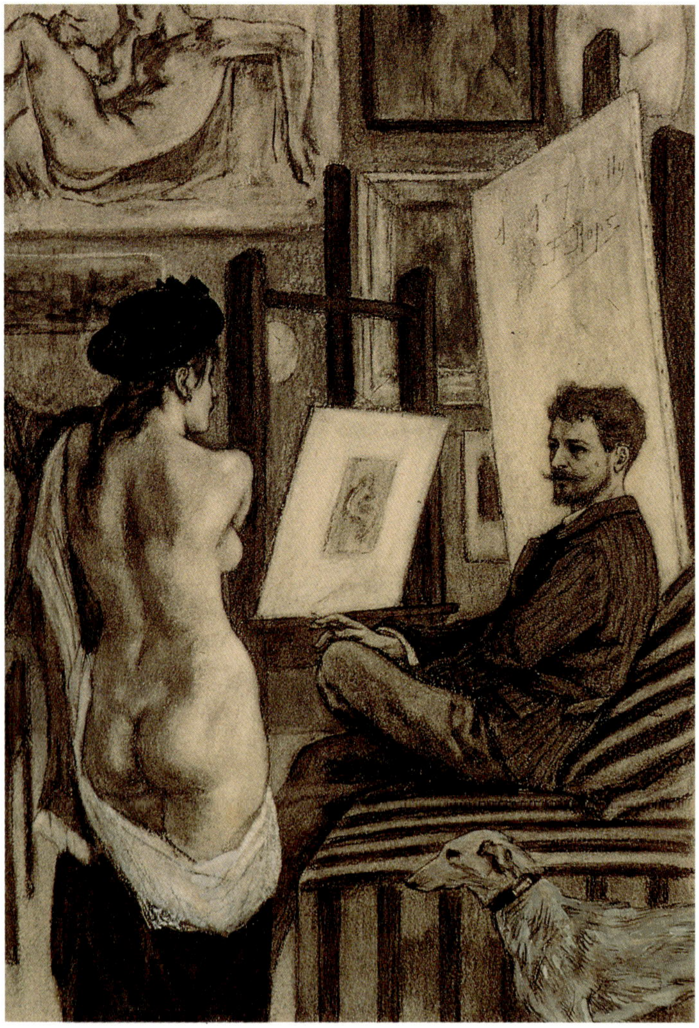

Félicien Rops:
Self-Portrait with Model in the Studio, 1875.

using her as a model. He looks her over as one would evaluate a horse before a race; she revolts, feeling herself outrageously undressed by the painter's scrutiny. However, obliged by her material need, she becomes his model. The painter appropriates her, and warns his friend, Totenhow, to "remember that she is not a woman but my model."[33] He uses her to work on a "Melancholy" which he has not been able to finish. Another strange coincidence, a "Melancholy"!

Dick keeps working, but then, slowly but surely his vision begins to fail; he will eventually go blind. Knowing this, he works frantically, trying to finish the work in which he wants to put a little bit of Bessie, his model, and a little bit of Maisie, his childhood love. Once his "Melancholy" is finished, drunk with exaltation and whisky, he shows it to his faithful friend and neighbor, confessing to him that he went "to Hell" to get it. Bessie, furious at having been forced to pose and even more furious at having been denied a potential husband—Totenhow—by the possessive painter, takes her revenge on his most precious belonging. In her rage, she wipes out the painting.

This crime is not immediately noticed by the painter who, after having put the finishing touches, became completely blind (as if painting had stolen his eyes). When he finally learns, through a long chain of events, that the fruit of his passionate labor has been destroyed, he succumbs indirectly to suicide.

Joyce Cary, another English novelist, in *The Horse's Mouth*, which relates the bohemian life of a sixty-seven-year-old artist and ex-convict, Gulley Jimson, also deals with the problem of the artist's physical implication in his work and his complex relationship with the model.

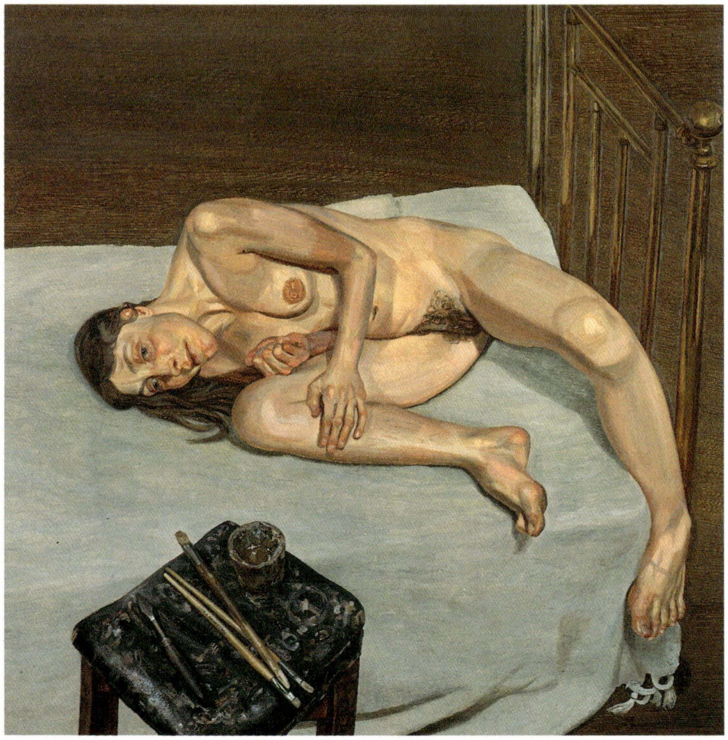

Lucian Freud:
Nude with Painter's Palette, 1972-1973.

Oskar Kokoschka:
Self-Portrait with Doll, 1920-1921.

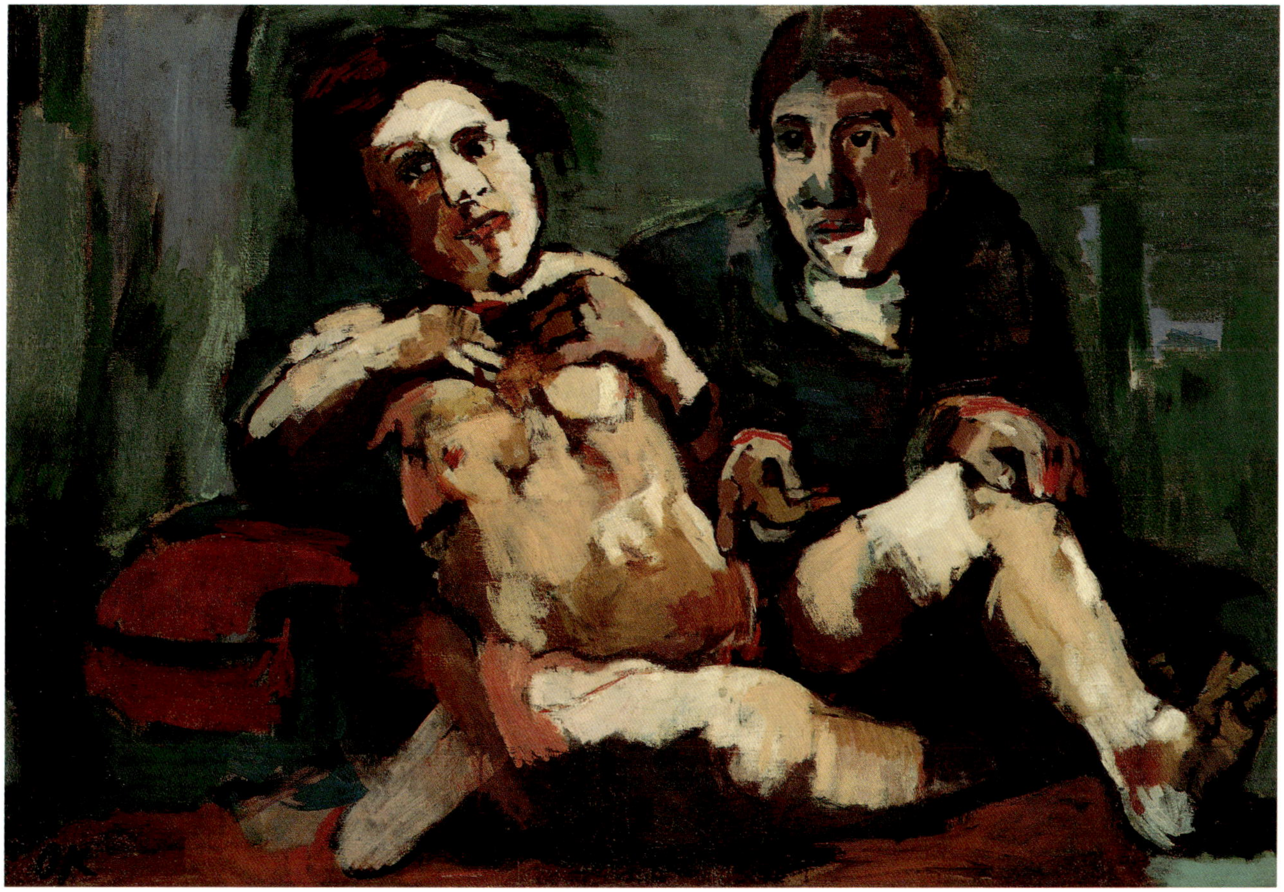

He says of his model (who is also his mistress, if not his mistress and also his model): "I didn't know whether to draw her or bite her." "There was always something about Sara that made me want to hit her or love her or get her down on canvas."[34] When he looks at her he sees the painting he could "get" from her. The interferences between art and illusion accumulate to the point of confusion and Sara, a highly narcissistic character, admires herself through her image in her lover's paintings. In a lengthy confrontation, the woman compares herself to her painted image. She alternately accuses the painter of having betrayed reality ("I didn't think I was so pink as that") or praises the skill that improved her charms (the white highlight that brings out the roundness of her breasts). The artist and the model argue over the origin of the beauty. The artist boasts of having done the breasts well. "You'll admit they were wonderful firm... and wonderful white too," the model retorts. To which the artist replies with: "Look at that vein there, just a drag of the brush across the grain."

Then, like Tosca or Zola's Christine in *The Work*, Sara becomes fiercely jealous and contrives to distract the painter from his objective. The victim ironically complains of her tactics: "And when I was mad to paint, she was for pushing me to bed and getting in after me. Stirring all that fire only to cook her own pot. Growing wings on my fancy only to stuff a feather bed."[35] What bothersome rivalries! And yet, it is precisely the image of this unbearable woman that he wants to immortalize on canvas, even at the cost of his own destruction. He becomes a "bloody adolescent," and she a "radiant virgin." A "radiant virgin" who in the eyes of others is nothing but a vulgar harlot. And yet, the favorite models of Degas and Toulouse-Lautrec were precisely the tenants of brothels.

Pablo Picasso:
The Sculptor, 1931.

In Search of the Model

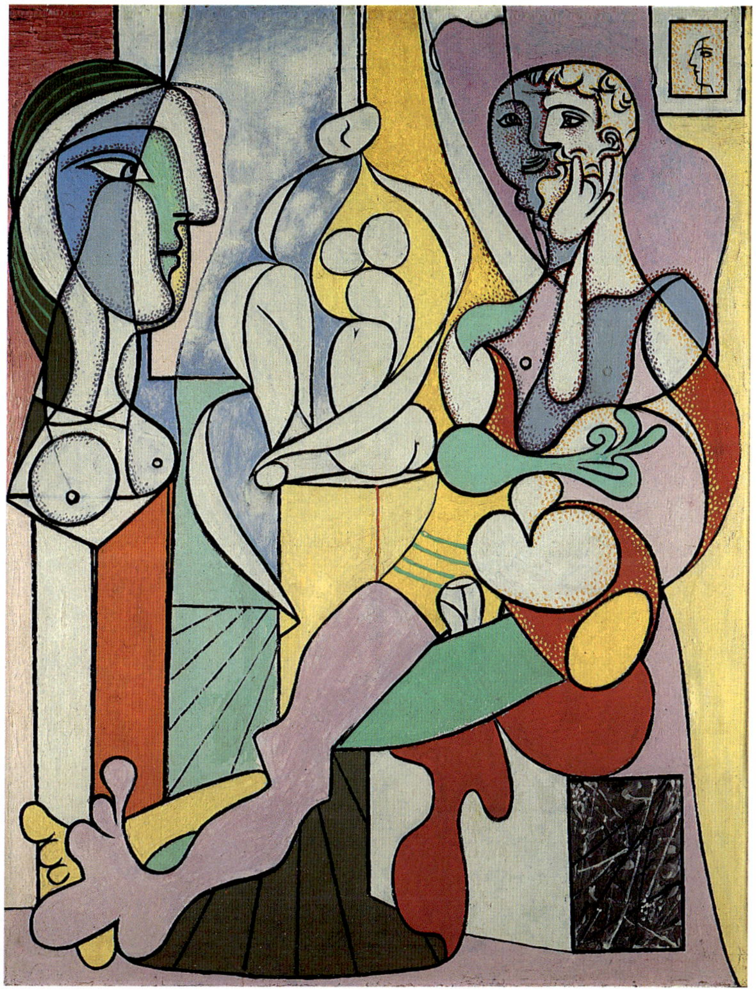

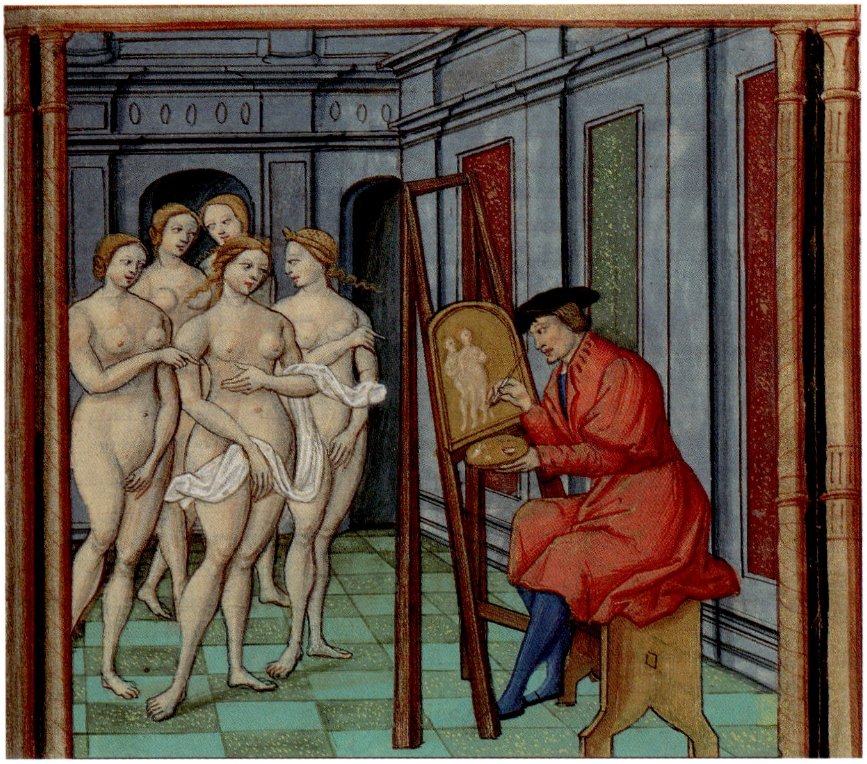

Anonymous:
Zeuxis Painting the Maidens of Croton, c. 1530-1540.

The impossible model

Ever since art has concerned itself with illusion and beauty, the search for the model has been a constant preoccupation. Pliny and Cicero both tell the story of the painter Zeuxis, who was invited to Crotona to decorate a temple of Juno. Wanting to create a perfect image of feminine beauty, he made an announcement calling for all the beautiful women of the city to appear before him. Finding none who was perfect, "for the reason that nature has not assembled all of the graces in one single creature," he selected five among the most beautiful to sit for him and composed his figure from the best parts of each.

Art strives to create something that is "more beautiful than nature" and also "more real than nature." Zeuxis, who was obsessed with illusion, painted grapes with such care that birds would come to peck at them. No wonder that he felt cruelly surpassed by his rival Parrhasios when he himself tried to draw back the curtain which the latter had painted on his canvas. Zeuxis recognized that he could fool only animals, while Parrhasios could deceive human beings. The story continues. Zeuxis paints a boy holding grapes. Again, birds attracted by the fruits come to eat them, and this too angers the painter, for he thinks that his figure should have been painted convincingly enough to frighten the birds away. He had not achieved the illusion of life.

Legends about Zeuxis were often evoked and reinterpreted in the course of the history of art. In the thirteenth century, they were incorporated into illuminated manuscripts. In one, we see Zeuxis perched on a ladder with the five models at his feet.[1] Sometimes he is represented as a sculptor, a maker of statues and images.[2] Later, Zeuxis returned once again to his brushes, and we see him at his easel in the presence of five fairly undraped beauties (as the classical texts stipulated), one hand modestly covering, or accentuating, the pubis. In certain cases, the representation includes a gymnasium, in accordance with Cicero's account. This text mentions the reticence of the Crotonans at surrendering their daughters, sisters and spouses to the gaze of Zeuxis, a foreigner. In an attempt to divert his plans, they take him to the gymnasium and entreat him to imagine the beauty of the women from that of the men! Need we add that the painter did not let himself be taken in by this stratagem?

This recalls, in reverse, an anecdote about Renoir told by his son and by the art dealer Ambroise Vollard.[3] Renoir did not like painting men and did not know how to go about representing a male model. One day, however, he wanted to paint the scene of Paris presenting the apple to Venus, and, on the pretext that he could find no suitable male model, he disguised Gabrielle—his faithful, famil-

François-André Vincent:
Zeuxis Choosing His Models, 1789.

iar and almost familial model—to play the part. Danielle Canneel, who was Paul Delvaux's favorite model for eighteen years because of the ivory-like pallor of her skin and her youthful figure, often posed for figures of young boys.

The endless search for a model is an expression of the search for perfection and also for a correspondence with a mental image and a fantasy, compared to which reality is always out of place, in one way or another. The artist wants to breathe life into his creation, but by bending life to his will.

The power of the ideal was shown with a brisk perspicacity by Théophile Gautier in his novel *Mademoiselle de Maupin*. For Albert, a perpetually unsatisfied esthete, reality always fell short of his expectations. He preferred the women of Rubens and Raphael to real women. When he analyzed the qualities of his mistress, Rosette, he did so with the eyes of an art lover scrutinzing a work in detail: "It is a statue, several parts of which have been brought to a peak of perfection. The others are not so neatly extracted from the block; some parts were rendered with delicacy and charm, but others were done in a slacker and more negligent way. To the vulgar eye, the statue appears to be entirely finished and complete in its beauty; but a more attentive observer soon discovers places where the work is not so coherent. There are contours which, in order to attain their specific purity, need to be rubbed with the finger of the artisan more than once."[4] Like Zeuxis, Albert would surely have liked to compose an ideal mistress out of perfect fragments.

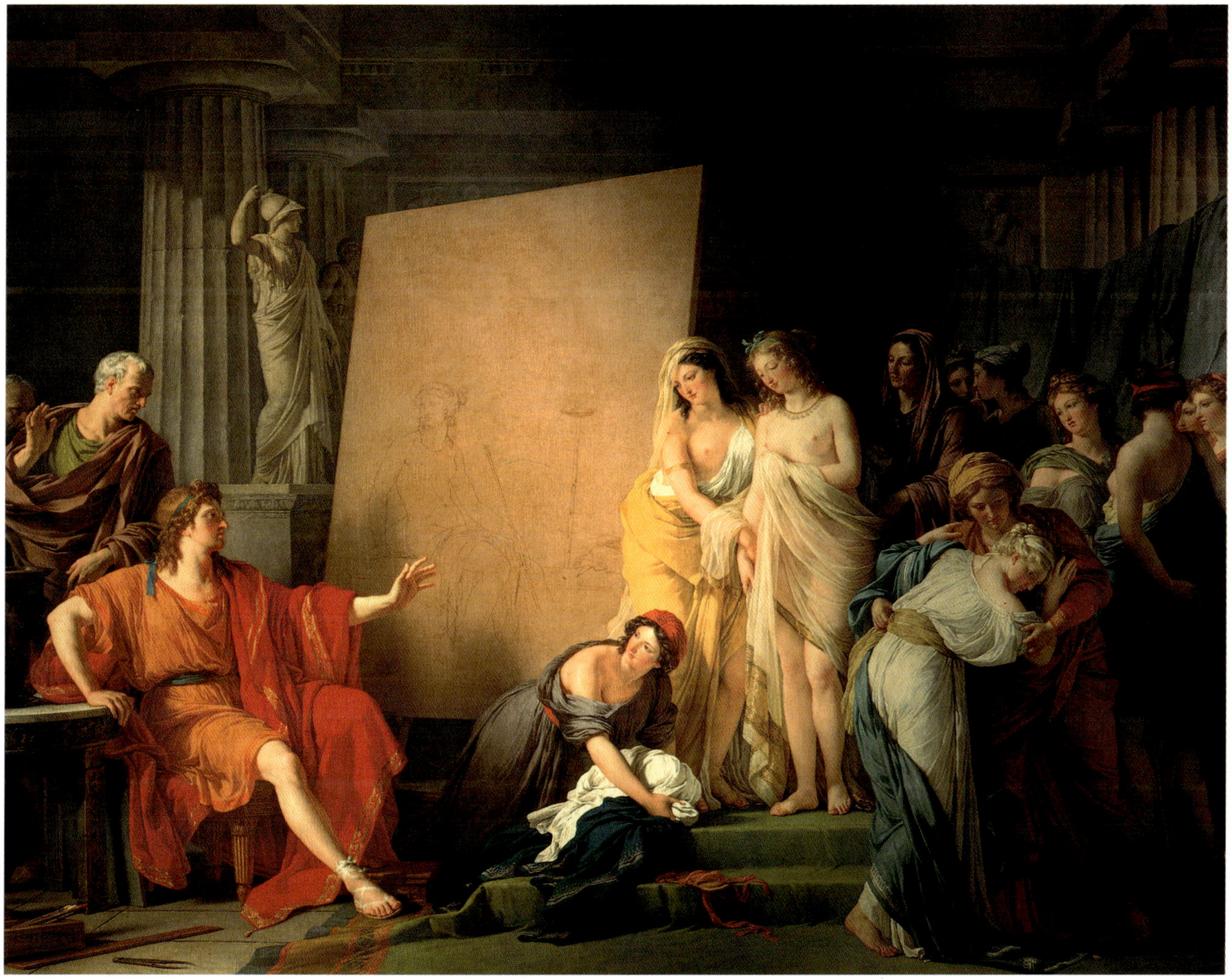

It was probably Balzac, in *The Unknown Masterpiece*, who succeeded with the most penetration in rendering the impossible nature of the model, and also the way in which the painter takes for his mistress a painting, the labor of his flesh and blood. In this story, everything takes place on the level of passion—and we should recall that the idea of passion includes that of suffering.

Frenhofer, an aging painter at the peak of his glory, receives in his studio the visit of his old pupil and friend, Porbus, accompanied by a young painter named Poussin. When Porbus shows the old man one of his pictures of a female figure to get his advice, the latter analyzes the work and finds it not very satisfactory, for the figure is not sufficiently "alive." The dialogue, or rather the monologue, is very enlightening:

"Your good woman is not badly got up, but there's no life in her. You all think you've done what needs to be done when you've drawn a face correctly and put everything in the proper place according to the laws of anatomy! You color this or that feature with a flesh tone mixed in advance on your palette, taking care to make one side darker than the other; and because from time to time you look at a naked woman standing on a table you think you've succeeded in copying nature, you imagine yourselves to be painters and you fancy you have stolen God's secret from him!... I find it impossible to believe that the warm breath of life animates this beautiful body. It seems to me that if I were to place my hand on the firmly rounded throat, I would find it as cold as marble! No, my friend, blood does not flow beneath this ivory skin, the crimson dew of life does not swell the network of veins and capillaries intertwining beneath the amber transparency of her temples and breast. Here is life, movement—there only stillness; in every piece life and death struggle with each other: here is a woman, there is a statue, there again a corpse. Your creation is unfinished... The mission of art is not to copy nature but to express it."[5]

Beauty does not let itself be captured easily; it must be loved, and loved some more, and observed, "press her and grasp her tightly to force her to surrender." There is no end of struggling to seize its vitality. "You give your women beautiful robes of flesh, beautiful draperies of hair, but where is the blood which engenders serenity or passion, and which causes particular effects?"[6]

There are no recipes, no instructions for capturing the likeness of life. How to render the subtle palpitations, "the soul... which wanders like a cloud," "the flower of life"? There are of course ways and means that can help the artist, but they are limited. Frenhofer uses them. Following the advice of Leonardo da Vinci, he examines his painting in a mirror, alternately condemning and defending the drawing: "Drawing gives you the skeleton, color brings it to life, but life without a skeleton is even more incomplete than a skeleton without life."[7]

However, Frenhofer has a secret, a great secret. For a long time, he has been working on the painting of a female figure which he stubbornly refuses to show in spite of Porbus' insistent requests to see "his mistress." The old painter indeed talks about it as if it were a woman with whom he was madly in love, and he evokes it with great emotion.

"Yesterday, as night approached, I thought I had finished. Her eyes seemed moist, her flesh was restless. You could see movement in the tresses of her hair. She was breathing!"[8]

The artist wrestles with nature in the hope of taking possession of it, or even surpassing it. However, being unable to finish the painting of the woman, he invokes the need of a faultless model. " 'So far I have failed to make the acquaintance of a faultless woman, a body whose contours are of the utmost beauty and perfection, and whose coloring. ... 'but where can she be found in this life', he said interrupting himself, 'that beautiful lost Venus of the ancients, sought so often, and of whom we only and rarely come upon some scattered fragments? Oh to see her at last, just once, for one brief moment, this nature divine and complete, the Ideal, I would give my entire fortune, yes I would seek you in your limbo, celestial beauty! Like Orpheus I shall go down into the hell of art, to bring life back from there.' "[9]

The young Poussin thinks immediately of his young mistress, the charming Gillette, a modest girl endowed with a remarkable beauty. It is then that Porbus contrives the clever plan of proposing Poussin's mistress "in exchange" for a look at the painting. "A woman for a woman!" The master rebels painfully against being forced to show his canvas.

"What! Show you my creature, my bride? Tear aside the veil beneath which I have chastely covered my pride and joy? That would be prostitution, horrible! I have lived with this woman for ten years, she is mine, mine alone, she loves me. Has she not smiled at me with every stroke of the brush I have given her? She has a soul, the soul I endowed her with. She would blush if eyes other than mine were to come to rest on her. Allow her to be seen? But where is the husband, the lover, so base as to lead his loved one to dishonor? When you paint a picture for the court, you don't put your entire soul into it, you sell the courtiers nothing but highly colored marionettes! My painting is no painting. It

Pablo Picasso:
The Painter and His Model, 1925-1926.

is a sentiment, a passion! Born in my studio, she must remain there virgin, and only emerge fully clothed. Poetry and women reveal themselves naked only to their lovers."[10] What can be added to such a passage, in which physical identification reaches its climax?

But Gillette goes into the studio. Porbus and Poussin wait behind the door, pressing their ears against it, listening. In a breathtaking denouement, Frenhofer opens the door to his studio after only a few instants and invites the two conspirators to enter. The pair marvel at the wealth of masterpieces on the walls of this secret studio, while the old man, with an excitement worthy of "a love-intoxicated youth," leads them towards the canvas, which he begins to praise in vibrant phrases.

This latter-day Pygmalion cannot contain his excitement before his canvas, he waxes expansive, his speech becomes erectile. The two painters leave the old man to his ecstatic monologue and look at the painting, only to discover that it is nothing but a confused and formless mass. The only recognizable thing is a bare foot, but an exquisite, living foot which emerges as if from the ruins of a demolished city.

"There is a woman underneath," Porbus exclaims, noticing the successive layers of painting which spoiled the figure by dint of his wanting to perfect it. "What enjoyments there are upon that piece of canvas!" he cries out. That evening, after this terrible unveiling, the old painter burns all of his works and commits suicide.

This story by Balzac, which is no more than twenty pages long, condenses with rare power a host of questions on the painter's love relationship with his model and his painting.

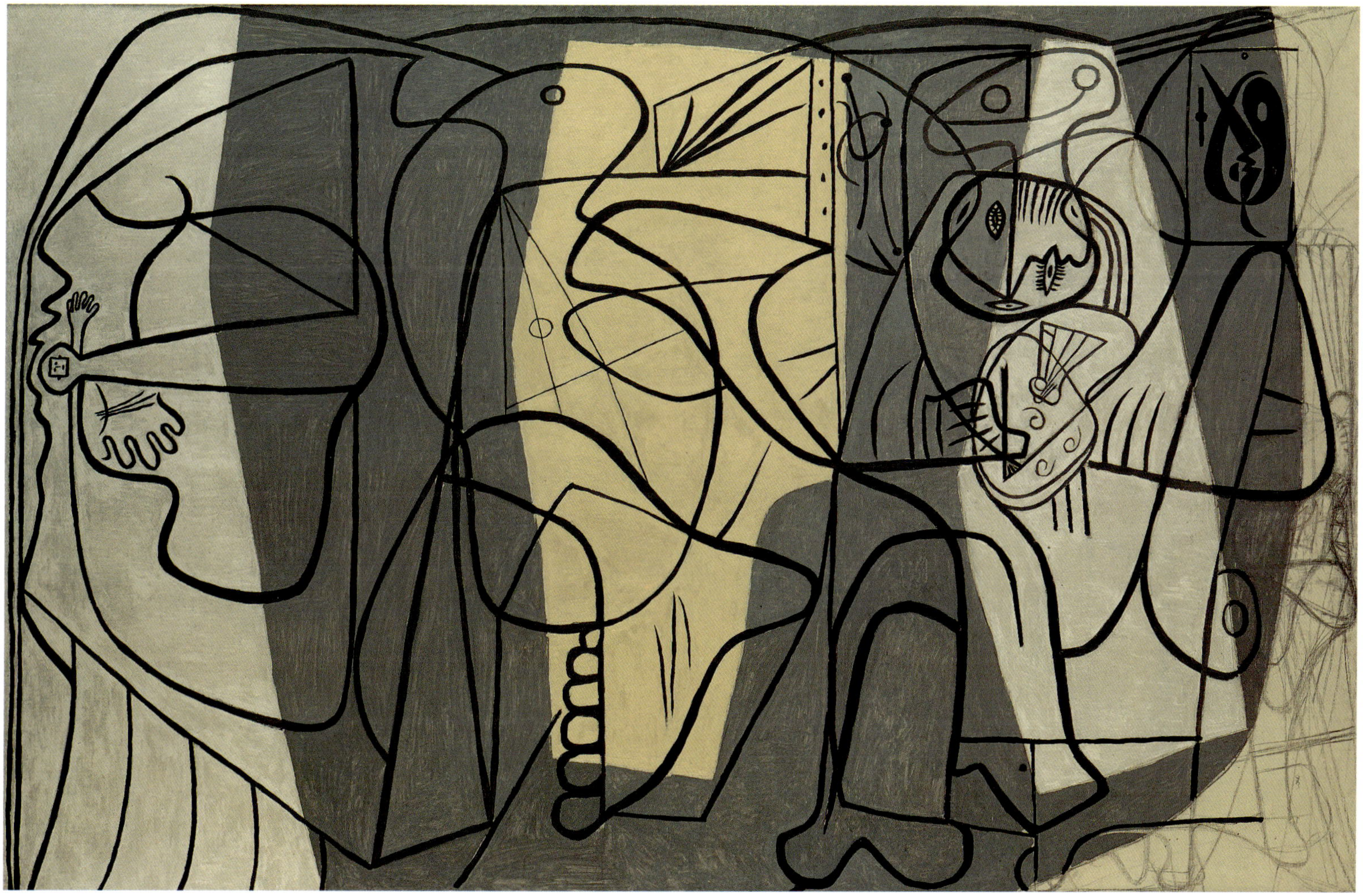

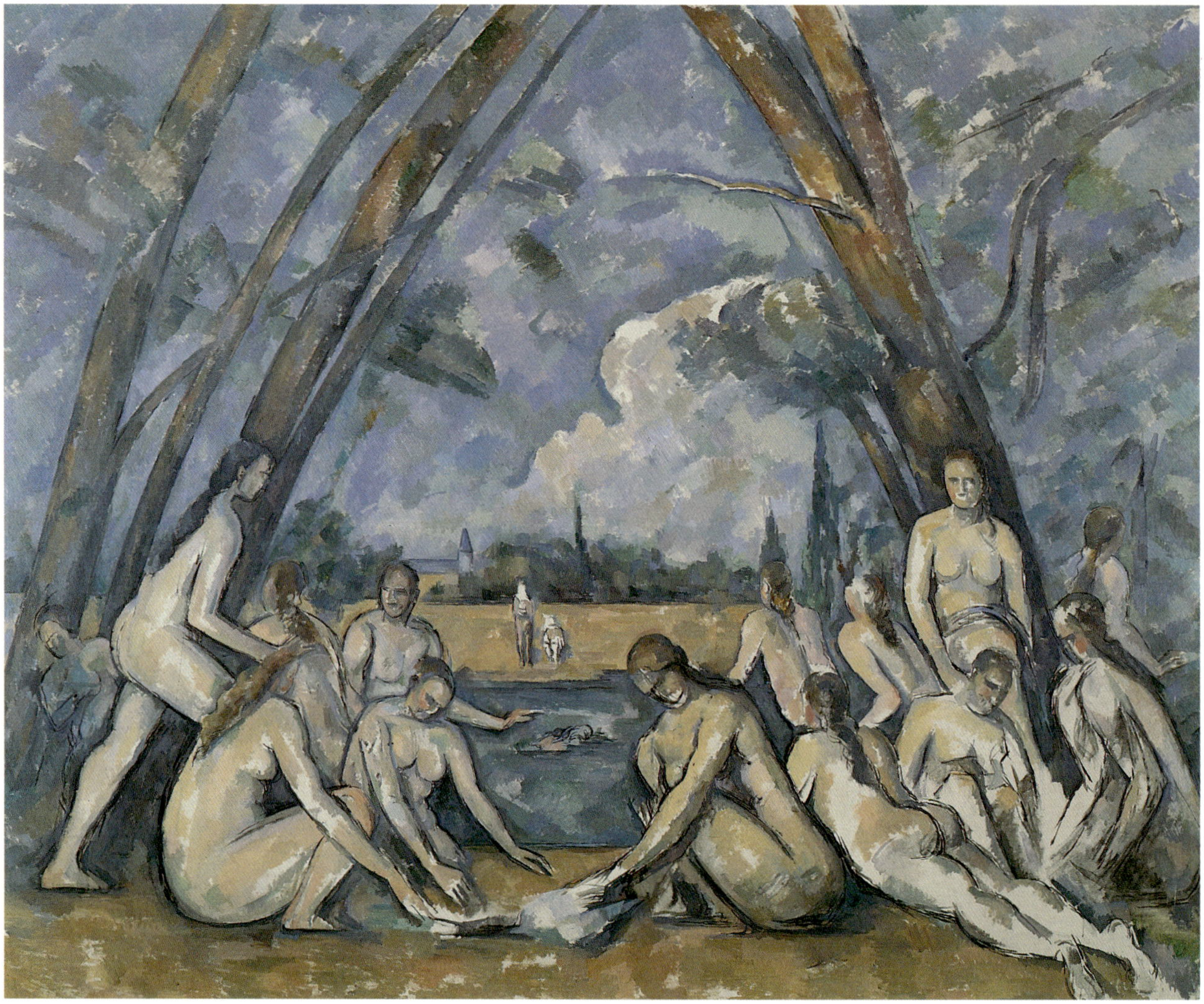

Cézanne, like Balzac's Frenhofer, was probably among the painters for whom the model seemed particularly "untouchable." Throughout his career, he endeavored to represent the male and female bathers which seemed so impossible for him to paint. After reading Balzac's *Unknown Masterpiece*, Cézanne declared: "Frenhofer is me!" He was driven by the obsession of not being able to "realize." "I have a little sensation," he told his dealer, Ambroise Vollard, "but I cannot express myself."[11] He kept searching for a model even though he was very fearful when he was confronted with it. And yet, in his days as an art student at the Académie Suisse in Paris, on the Ile de la Cité, everything had been done to make him and his fellow students familiar with the live model. This academy, founded by the "Père Suisse," a former model himself, based its instruction on the study of the live model: male for the first three weeks of the month, and female for the last week—a form of reward? Zola knew of the Académie Suisse even before Cézanne studied there, and he described it in a letter to his friend Baille: "Chaillan claims that the models are tolerable there, although without being prime material. They draw them during day, and caress them at night (the word caress is a bit weak). So much for the day sitting, so much for the night sitting; it is said that they are quite accommodating, especially for the nighttime hours. As for the fig leaf, it is unknown in the studios; they undress with great familiarity, and the love of art hides all that might be exciting in this nudity."[12]

Cézanne was uncomfortable with physical contact, and also with women, whose importance he tried to diminish: "Women are not for me, that would disturb me too much. I do not even know what they are good for; I have always been afraid of trying."[13] And yet models were a part of Cézanne's life and everyday work in the studio. One sculptor, Jules Gilbert, who went to Paris to see Cézanne, tells the story of their first meeting: "Upon arriving in Paris, I went to see Cézanne. I rang the bell, and the door was opened by a completely naked woman who led me into Cézanne's studio, where he was painting sitting on his cornet case. While we conversed, the model was frying something in a pan on the stove, and the odors of the one were no more pleasant than those of the other."[14]

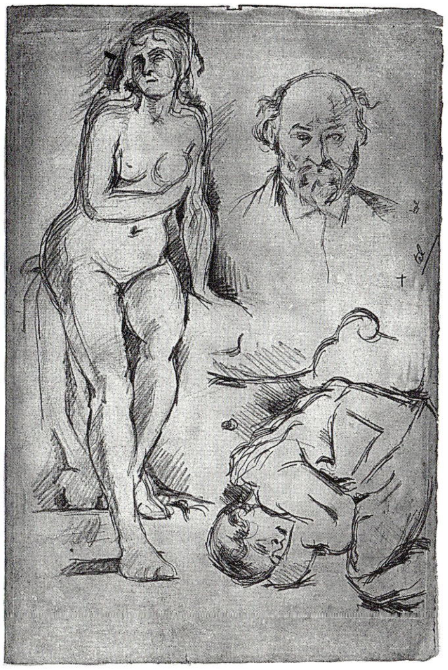

◁◁ *Paul Cézanne: Large Bathers, 1889-1905.*

◁ *Paul Cézanne: Sheet of Studies, c. 1882.*

A considerable number of works by Cézanne give an ardent and exalted expression of the female presence. The painter's fear was probably in proportion to his attraction. That he fled women can only mean that he feared some fatal enchantment. Cézanne regularly rewoked his female bathers and, invoking the narrowmindedness of the French provinces, he confided to the collector Osthaus that he had given up female models and settled for the services of "an old invalid who poses for all these women."[15] The nude became the nude in itself, beyond the identification of its sex. The male bathers were no longer distinct from the female bathers. Cézanne used sketches of female nudes for his representations of male *Bathers* and, conversely, sketches of bathing soldiers for his *Grandes Baigneuses*!

In being hypersensualized, could the kind of painting which Cézanne called "*couillarde*" ("ballsy") be beyond sexuality, or, more exactly, was it the dream of a total sex, the dream of the androgyne? The painter transformed and transfigured human bodies. Here and there we see a bather without a head (which recalls Rodin's answer when asked why the *Walking Man* was headless: "As if we walked with the head!"); others have no feet, or a collapsed torso. The human form is stretched out or shortened according to the demands of the composition.

Cézanne's project was "to marry the curves of the female body to the slopes of the hills."[16] Landscape as a metaphor of the body. The body as a metaphor of the landscape. There was a fusion, or an attempt at a fusion, for Cézanne was never totally satisfied, he never found fulfillment, either with the nude or the portrait. His dealer, Ambroise Vollard, sat for him and found himself constantly being scolded. One day, he fell asleep and collapsed to the floor, knocking down the makeshift pedestal which Cézanne had set up with his usual maniacal care. The artist severely reprimanded him: "You wretch! you are disturbing the pose! I tell you, in truth, you should hold yourself like an apple. Do apples move? do they?"[17] It is a well-known fact that Cézanne used artificial flowers for his still lifes so that his "models" would not change color over time!

Vollard, for his part, was terrorized by the painter's gaze whenever he began to show signs of fatigue. The sittings often lasted three and a half hours, and Cézanne's moods depended on a number of external factors. The most decisive one was the light; only a "light grey" day was favorable. On top of that, silence was required, not only in the studio, but also in its vicinity. The mere barking of a dog could sabotage the session. The painter also could not stand being observed by a third person while working, nor did he tolerate the slightest modification in the familiar surroundings of his atelier. Even the displacing of a carpet could endanger the day's work. And at no time did Cézanne ever give the impression of finishing. At the end of one hundred and fifteen sittings, to his bewilderment, Vollard heard the artist say that his portrait was still unfinished but that he was not too unhappy about the shirt front!

Paul Cézanne: Seven Bathers, c. 1900.

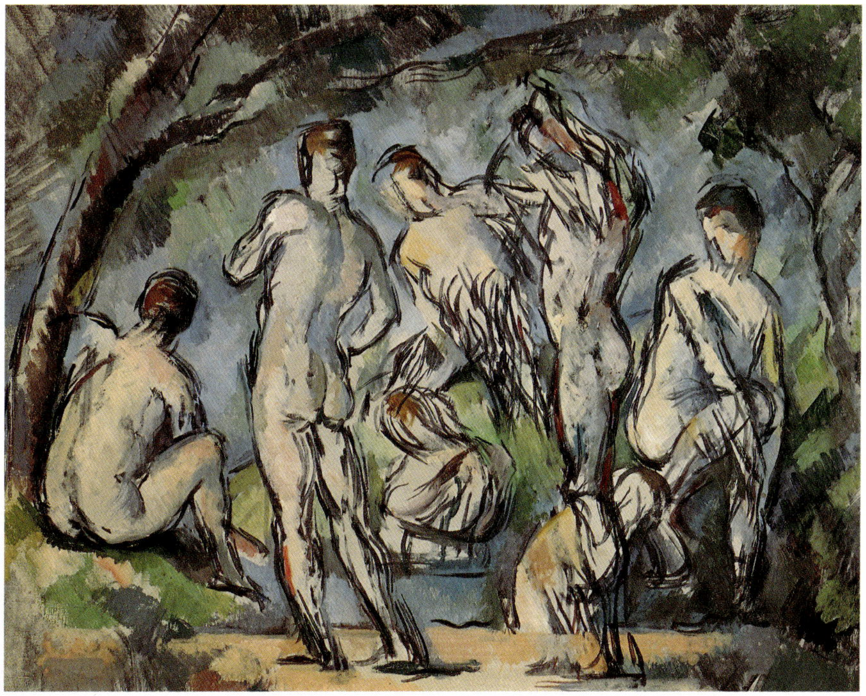

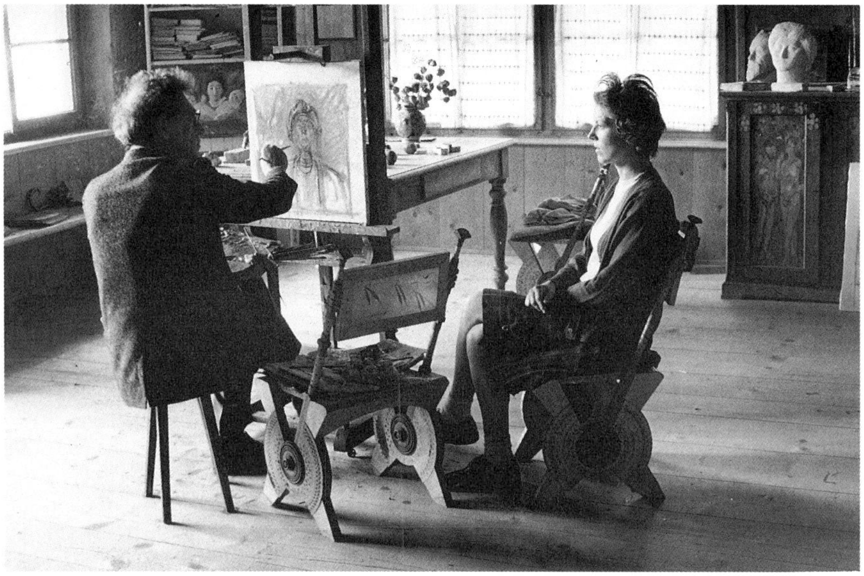

Giacometti Painting Annette in Stampa, undated.

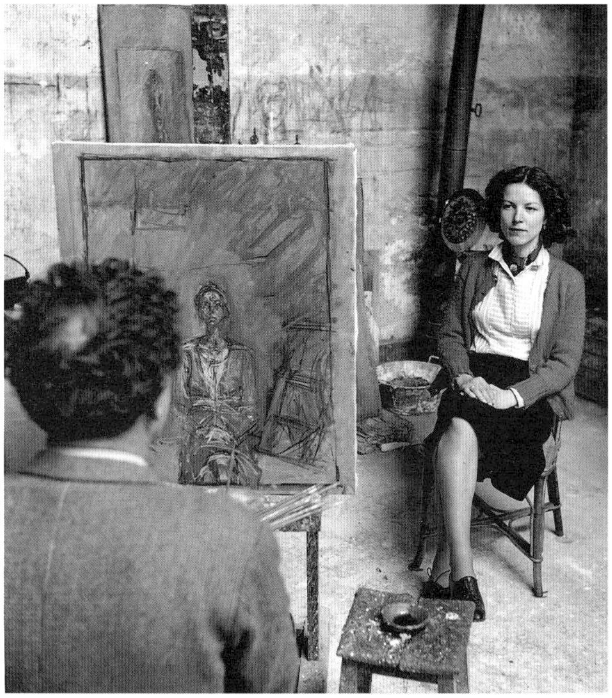

Giacometti with Annette in His Studio, undated.

Giacometti was another artist who seems to have been afflicted with chronic dissatisfaction. This condition is evident in each line of the "journal" which James Lord kept during the eighteen sittings for his portrait. At first, it was just a matter of making a rapid sketch in a few hours. But then, as Giacometti said himself: "The more you work on a painting, the more impossible it is to finish it."[18] The artist had an established ritual: he put the sitter on his chair, whose position was carefully marked on the floor, required him to be motionless and to adopt a gaze straight into the eyes, forbade laughter and insisted on making the session last long into twilight. The sittings were always tinged with despair: "It is going so badly that it is not even going poorly enough for there to be hope!"[19] Art was a matter of life and death.

Moreover, Giacometti identified with the model, and his rage was aroused precisely by the fact the image he would make did not seem to correspond sufficiently to what he had in his mind's eye. The Japanese professor Isaku Yanaihara sat many times for him. "We were together so much that one day I had a strange experience. Yanaihara was sitting for me, and all of a sudden Genet walked into the studio. I thought he looked odd with his roundish face, his pink complexion, and his lips seemed to be swollen. I could not understand why. Then I suddenly realized that I was seeing Diego and Genet as they must have appeared to Yanaihara."[20]

This strange fusion is reminiscent of Matisse's identification with the beautiful redhead with chameleon eyes. Not only does the artist fuse with his model to the point that he even sees through his or her eyes, but he closely identifies illusion with reality. One day, having inadvertently made the canvas fall from the easel, Giacometti apologized as if he had been addressing himself to a living person!

With each stroke of the brush, Giacometti put his body on the line, anxiety was omnipresent. The portrait would sometimes even disappear: "The head is going away," he told his sitter, "it is going completely away... The canvas will perhaps empty itself completely, what will become of me then? It will kill me!"[21] He strove constantly to draw what he saw from out of the void. The painting was constructed and deconstructed. The portrait became a "hell." Giacometti badgered his sitter as if he wanted to possess him, and, his constant recriminations aside, he was supremely conscious of the sitter's role.

Alberto Giacometti:
Large Nude Seated, 1957.

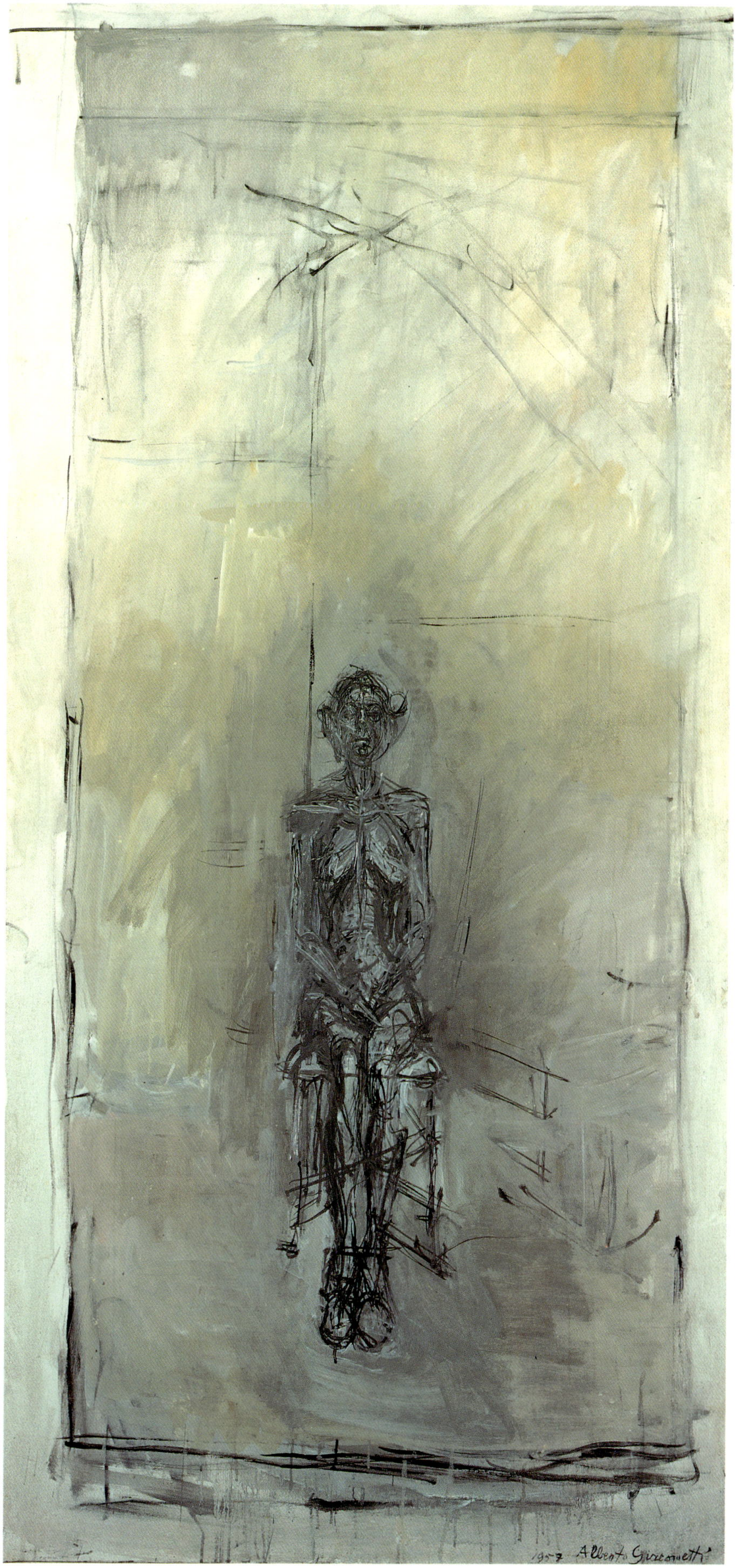

For him, "everything holds by a thread, we are always in danger."[22] As for the sitter, he had the impression at times that he would remain forever paralyzed in the pose and he anxiously apprehended the final result as he saw, day after day, his likeness coming into form and dissolving again. The narcissistic feeling finds its satisfaction, however. While, for the model, it was the "final" image that counted, he understood that for Giacometti, this represented only one step in the progress of his work. On reading the journal of the eighteen sessions, which James Lord wrote in a plain, unadorned style, almost like a police report, one easily imagines that it could have gone on indefinitely. In fact, the completion of the portrait was interrupted only by Lord's departure and by Giacometti's promise to send the picture to an exhibition. But at no time did Giacometti express the feeling of having finished. As with Cézanne, dissatisfaction seems to have been the very motor of his work. Both painters were famous for destroying their own works out of rage.

Throughout his life, Giacometti wondered if he could show woman as he saw her, without knowing if for him she was a goddess or a whore. Giacometti was an assiduous frequenter of bordellos, a worshipper who saw the prostitute as an implacable divinity. As Jean Genet recalled: "He is sorry that the brothels are gone. I think that in his life they took—and their memory still takes—too much room for us not to mention them. It seems he entered them like a worshipper. He went there to see himself kneel in front of an implacable and distant divinity. Between each naked whore and himself, there was perhaps this distance which his statues constantly establish between us and them. Each statue seems to withdraw into—or emerge from— a night which is so thick and remote that it merges with death: thus each whore must have seemed to be part of a mysterious night in which she reigned supreme. Within himself, abandoned on a shore from which he would see her become smaller and grow larger at the same time. I would also venture this: is it not in the brothel that woman could pride herself in having a wound that will never again deliver her from solitude, and is it not the brothel that will divest her of all utilitarian function, thus making her achieve a certain purity?"[23]

For Genet, the wound was the origin of beauty itself. "Beauty has no other origin than the wound, which is singular and different for each, and which each man keeps within himself, visible or hidden; he preserves it and retreats to it when he wants to leave the world for a temporary, but profound solitude."[24] Beauty, the wound and the strange inaccessibility of the model are all links in the same chain.

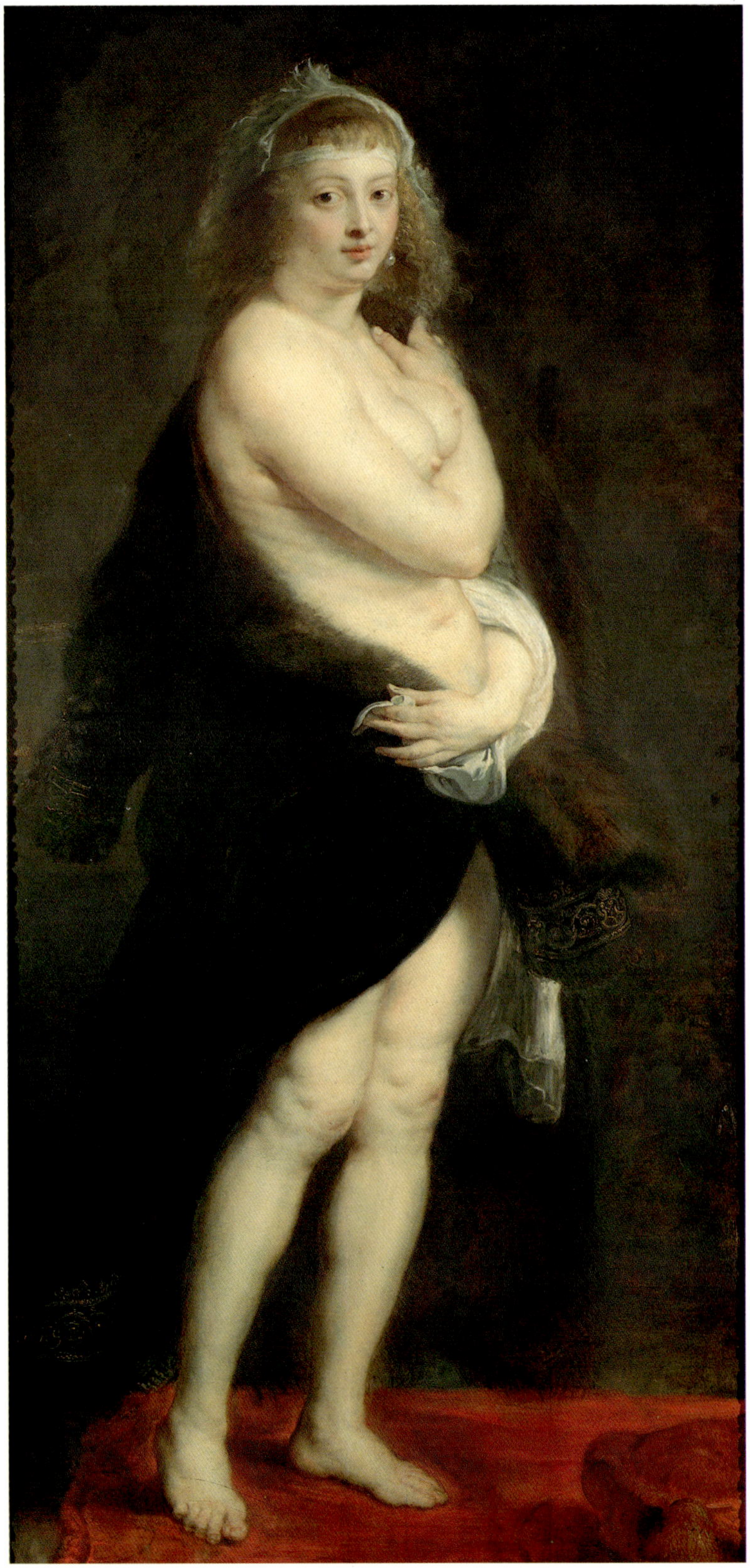

Peter Paul Rubens:
The Pelisse, c. 1638.

The question of flesh

The artist's *idée fixe* is to give life to his subject by extracting it from an ideal model. But he also transmits it through his blood and his bile. Painting and sculpture are eminently physical acts. Cézanne himself was surprised when he realized that he could remain in a sort of ecstatic trance for more than twenty minutes between two brushstrokes. "My eyes bulge, they are bloodshot... I cannot take them away... they are so glued to the spot I am looking at that it seems they are going to start to bleed. A drunkenness, a sort of ecstasy makes me falter as if I were in a fog when I rise from my canvas... Tell me, am I not a bit mad?... The *idée fixe* of painting... Frenhofer..."[25]

It is by the injection of the artist's blood that art exists. The artist offers his flesh and that of his model to the work of art. The question of carnation has always haunted painters. How to paint the flesh? But, above all, how to make the flesh pulse with life? The color in itself does not give the solution. There is a special "something" that is not so easy to define. Color is not only a garment, or even a form of make-up. It is not something that is put "on top of," it must actually be "inside" in order to become "natural."

Titian fascinated his contemporaries with his ability to render lifelike flesh. He was suspected of mixing blood with his pigments, like Apollo flaying Marsyas to nourish his palette and make his painting "alive." The very word pigment, from the Latin "pigmentum," refers both to the colors for painting and to the epidermis.

Painters experimented constantly in order to obtain recipes to reproduce the color of flesh. During the Renaissance, Cennino Cennini recommended the use of green earth, some white well mixed with glue, and, specifically for the skin color of youthful figures, the yokes of eggs laid in town; they were better, because lighter than those of eggs laid in the country. The latter, however, were better for rendering the complexion of old people or dark-skinned men. He also recommended adding some cinnabar, a red color which, like blood, turned brown upon drying. This mythical color was said to have been extracted from dragons killed in combat, or drawn from an antediluvian animal with a strange and lethal odor from which one had to protect oneself.

In fact, the production of cinnabar required a strange alchemical process whereby a mixture of melted sulphur and mercury was put into a piece of skin. The result was a substance of a very red color streaked with long brownish veins which was said to have medicinal properties that were especially effective in the treatment of venereal diseases. Cinnabar was considered the best pigment to imitate the color of blood. Cennini recommended it both for the surface of the skin and for wounds; in other words, for open, living flesh. However, it had to be used with caution. Flesh does not let itself be approached without danger. At every moment, the painter runs the risk of "killing" his picture.

Diderot remarked that the thing that finally drives great colorists mad is the alterability of flesh, the constant changes of the skin as it registers the emotions, blushing or paling, radiant or dull, full of life or as livid as a cadaver. The emotions run skin deep. The body's envelope vibrates and resonates with the movements of the soul. And so, depending upon our sensations, we change skins. The painter strives to keep up with these changes, to seize the slightest pulsation. In the act of painting, he tries to fix an ineffable and indescribable movement.

The carnation of flesh is the most "impossible" of colors. "It is a coloring through which painting could dream itself as body and as subject: the coloring of vicissitude, and so of the awakening of desire. If a painting sleeps, awakens, suffers, reacts, resists, transforms itself or changes color like the face of the beloved when she feels her lover's gaze, this is the most one could dream of in terms of the efficacity of the image."[26] Carnation is the painter's ultimate fulfillment, it is his ideal, the element par excellence of his art, and the very essence of painting. In order to approximate it, some tried to imitate the structure of the body, playing on its transparency: the red of the arteries, the blue of the veins, the yellow of the skin, rendering the surface by what is underneath, in the depths, by what is known from the science of anatomy and the dissection of corpses.

All means are good, but none is ever completely satisfactory. The integrity of flesh thwarts the brush. In the eyes of the artist, there is inevitably a discrepancy, however slight, which stimulates him to further effort, bringing him sometimes to the brink of despair. Flesh and color are surrounded by ambiguities and contradictions. Although they are surfaces, they both imply depth; like the visible tip of an iceberg, they exist by the hidden, mysterious part which determines their appearance. Their diaphanous quality is asked to say much more: to express water, air, fire, humidity, blood, the visible and the invisible, the palpable and the impalpable. Color should be as changeable as the humors, as vacillating as air and water, unpredictable, alterable, fragile.

In discussing the question of "coloring," in his *Analysis of Beauty, written with a view to fixing the unstable ideas of taste*,[27] Hogarth showed the importance he attached to carnation. For him, the most beautiful coloring is that of flesh. Art consists in varying the tints of the flesh. When faced with a subject which captivated and eluded him, he felt the need to elaborate "fundamental principles," principles which rested on a fascination with flesh.

"It is well known, the fair young girl, the brown old man, and the negro; nay, all mankind, have the same appearance, and are all alike disagreable to the eye, when the upper skin is taken away: how to conceal so disagreeable an object, and to produce that variety of complexions seen in the world, nature bath contrived a transparent skin, called the cuticula, with a lining to it of an extraordinary kind, called the cutis... The cutis is composed of tender threads like network, fill'd with different colour'd juices. The white juice serves to make the very fair complexion;—yellow, makes the brunnet;—brownish yellow, the ruddy brown;—green yellow, the olive;—dark brown, the mulatto;—black, the negro;—These different colour'd juices, together with the different masses of the network, and the size of its threads in this or this part, causes the variety of complexions."[28]

The beauty of the complexion becomes a concentrate of beauty, it must be captured by the blue or the blood vessels, the redness of the flesh and the yellow of the fat. The painter as a carnivore or vampire! But his venture was not a simple one, for the fine colors associated with fine complexions are extremely variable. They are affected by heat, fever, and cold. Confronted by this diversity, "the brush is powerless," Hogarth lamented; only by nuances and complicated techniques can one hope to get close to beauty. "If this intricate disposition of the tints is wanting in the general hue of fair flesh the whole is a doughy white or like drowned flesh, the unnatural even colour of a waxwork hand or arm would be a frightfull sight alive. Nay the finest pale red silk as near the colour of flesh as it could be made, would still be more offencive with its eveness: and a black moor even colour'd as a cloath [sic] whole or velvet mask perhaps would shock the moors as much as one milkywhite. So a statue painted all over with even red and white would be less agreeable than the marble milky white one & where animated they would be the same."[29]

Thus, uniformity was the enemy. The tonality of snow, ivory, marble, or wax uniformly applied to living flesh would be "hideous." Through the problem of coloring and carnation, we come back to the unfathomable and strongly sexualized mystery of beauty itself. Thus, in the eyes of Hogarth, there were colors that were "chaste" and others that were not. The study of anatomy could, of course, further this understanding by giving "a true idea of the elegant use that is made of the skin and fat beneath it, to conceal from the eye all that is hard and disagreeable, and at the same time to preserve to it whatever is necessary in the shapes of the parts beneath, to give grace and beauty to the whole limb...The skin, therefore, thus tenderly embracing and gently conforming itself to the varied shapes of every one of the outward muscles of the body, soften'd underneath by fat, where, otherwise, the same hard lines and furrows would appear, as we find come on with age in the face, and with labour, in the limbs, is evidently a shell-like surface (to keep up the idea I set out with) form'd with the utmost delicacy in nature."[30]

What passion in this approach to flesh! What sensuality in these spontaneous affirmations! What delight in the precise observation of the epidermis! We can readily imagine the painter touching and caressing his models, the better to practice his craft. The caress as an apprenticeship of the fine arts!

Flesh, the artist's inevitable standard, is the delicate frontier between the inside and the outside. This limit, however, is not as distinct as it might seem. It is full of orifices, places of passage and transformation. It is a sort of crossroads of the sensible elements, a halfway house in which the senses are condensed in a labyrinthine network; it is a "thick surface," so to speak, and also an interstice into which a chaos of fantasies project themselves, a tissue of entrails that turns itself inside out like a glove and exhibits itself. Flesh is where touch takes place, it indicates distance and proximity, openings and closings. The visible coils itself around the flesh, charged with sexuality and love.

Frenhofer looked at the imaginary woman in his painting and felt that she was looking at him. "She loves me," he would even say! The flesh of the model, of the dream image and its reflection in the painting, is both near and far. Approach it and it flies away. It oscillates in an unpredictable manner between the optical and the tactile, absorbs and reflects light, attracts caresses. It is blood, illusion, fiction and passion. All the while belonging to the realm of the eye, it is the flesh that possesses the eye. It blurs the limits between vision and touch, verges on hallucination. The eye embraces

Paolo Veronese:
Allegories of Love: Infidelity, 1565.

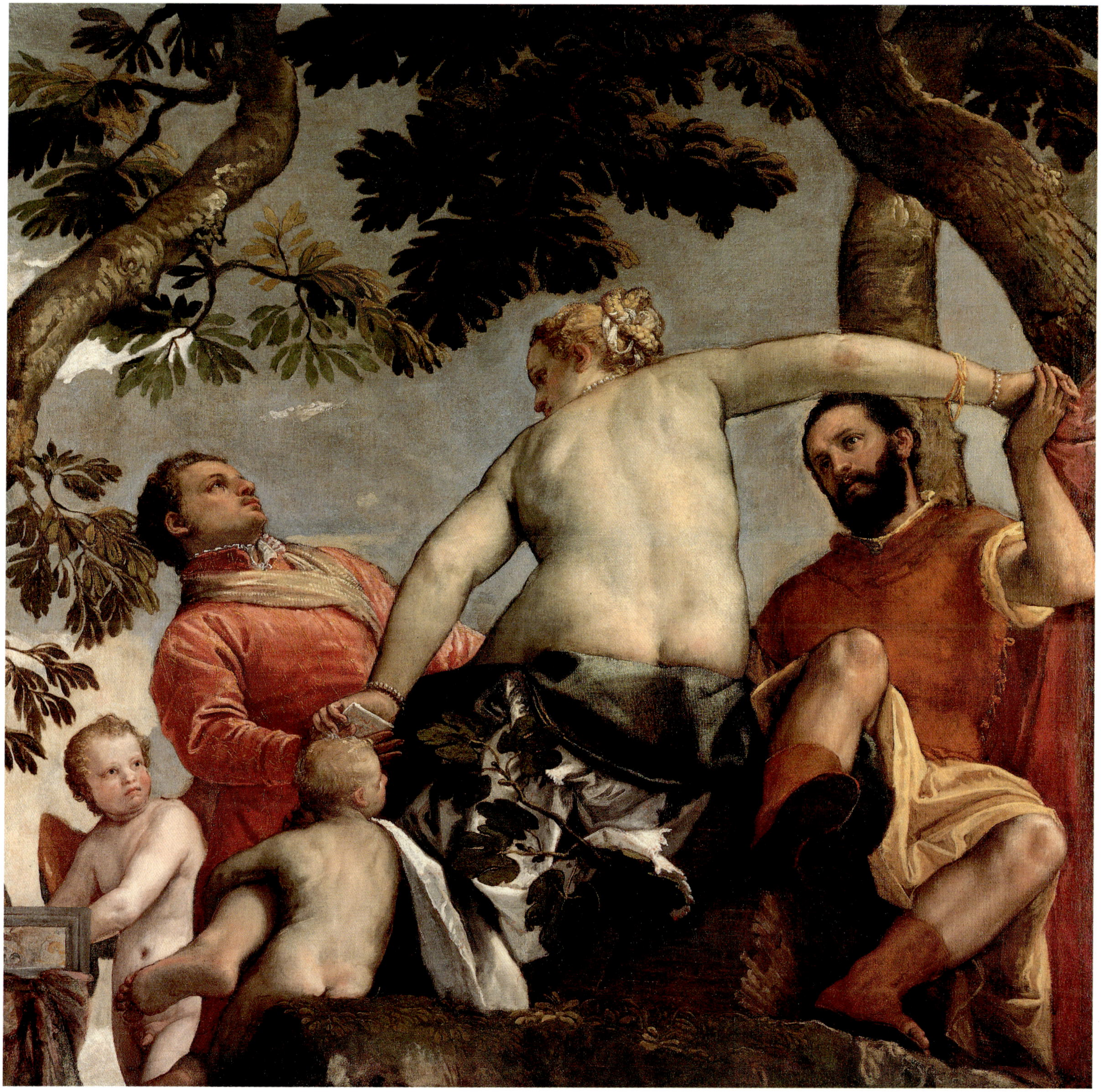

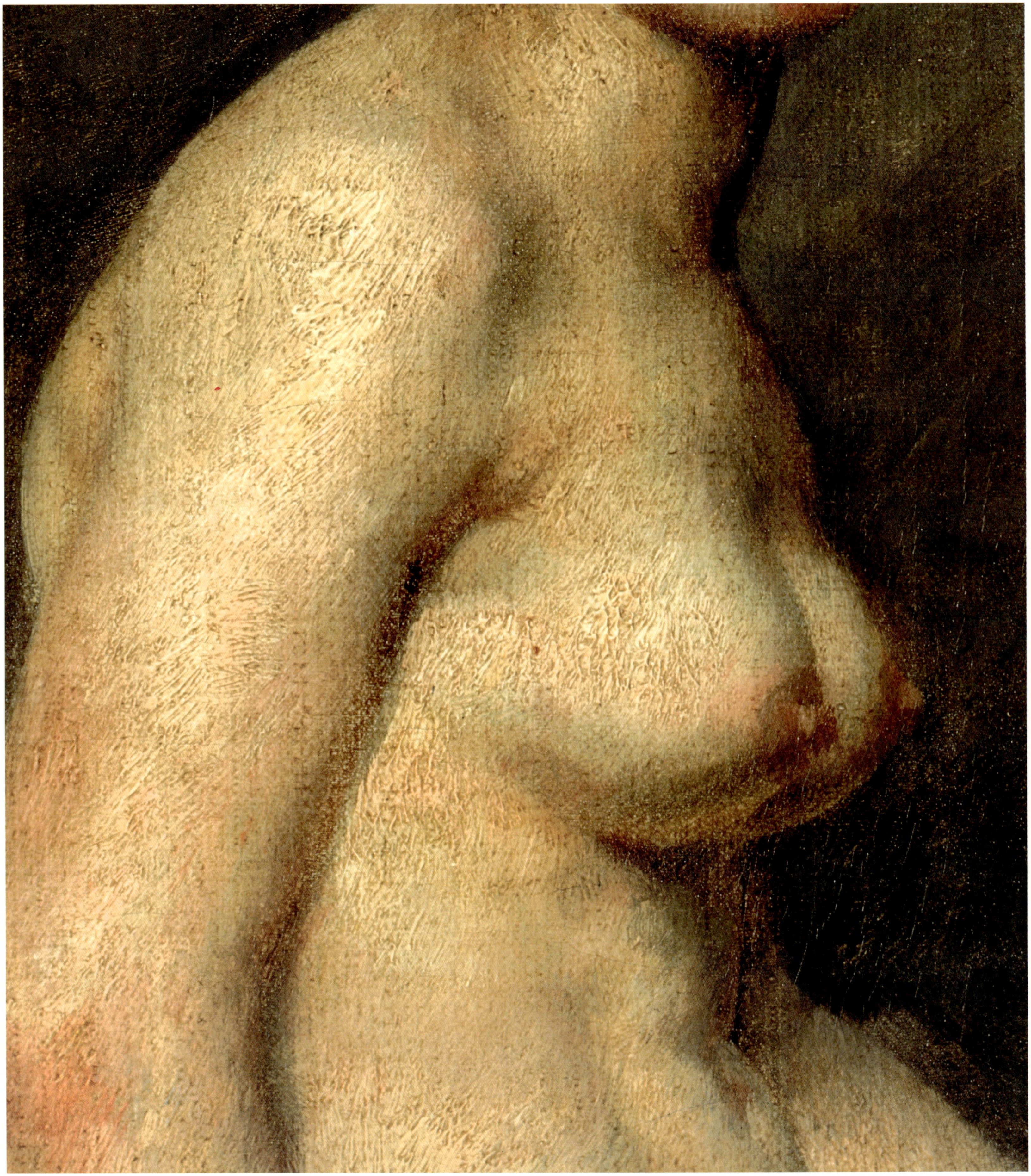

Eugène Delacroix:
Nude Seated (Miss Rose), detail.

images. Color is a capricious mistress, as coquettish and infernal, as bloodthirsty and diabolical. It feeds on the life of the painter; possessive, it demands an exclusive cult, eliminates rivals, compels the artist to celibacy and solitude; in other words, to sublimation.

Carnation, once called the "voice of the flesh" *(voce della carne)* signifies the desire for love, the pleasures of love. In it, painting finds its source and its bottomless, never-ending abyss. In it, more than anywhere else, the painter unites with his painting in a sort of hierogamy in which blood, with its feminine and fecundating qualities, is one of the main actors, like an "ultra-nudity" which courses through all bodies in a universal, even cosmic way. Thanks to his passionate love, Pygmalion makes blood run through veins of ivory; the virgin figure comes to life. But even before its transmutation, the sculptor was afraid of damaging it with his embraces, of spoiling it with bruises, with black and blue marks, or "*livor*" (a term which also refers to jealousy).

Throughout the ages, the "mania" of painters was to find recipes for the rendering of flesh. Delacroix's *Journal* is full of remarks on flesh tones. He minutely set down the ingredients each time he made a discovery: "Fine brown skin tone, very sanguine; dark chrome yellow and purple tint of brown and white lacquer."[31] "For the pink green tint of the cheek of a fresh brunette, cadmium and white, light zinc yellow and emerald green, white and lacquer..."[32] And so on.

Delacroix's admiration for Rubens and Titian was also determined by the quality of their flesh tones: "It is difficult to say which colors were used by Titian and Rubens and others to make those brilliant skin tones which have not altered, and in particular the half-tones in which the transparency of the blood under the skin was perceptible in spite of the grey which is included in all half-tones. I am convinced for my part that, in order to produce them, they mixed very bright colors together."[33] Rubens indeed intermingled reds and greens to render the coloring of flesh. Delacroix was also subjugated by his models, whose addresses he inscribed in the flyleaves of his notebooks, and he even recorded his emotions before sittings: "Whenever I wait for a model, every time, even when I am the most pressed for time, I am overjoyed when the hour passes and I tremble when I hear the key turn in the door."[34] Even more, he "suffered for the model," by identifying with it and also by giving himself, body and soul, to his painting. "I go to work as others rush to see their mistresses, and when I leave, I take back with me to my solitude, or in the midst of the distractions that I pursue, a charming memory that does not in the least resemble the troubled pleasure of lovers."[35]

If, according to his writings, he occasionally succumbed physically, he deplored it immediately afterwards as a loss of precious energy for his painting. Regretfully, he writes of Hélène, a pretty model, that "she has taken away part of my energy for today." The muse is a demanding and very exclusive mistress. "In truth, painting harasses and torments me in a thousand ways, like the most demanding mistress; for four months, I have been leaving at daybreak and flying to this captivating work, as if to the feet of the most cherished mistress."[36] The muse, however, is grateful when this

Eugène Delacroix:
Nude Seated (Miss Rose), c. 1821.

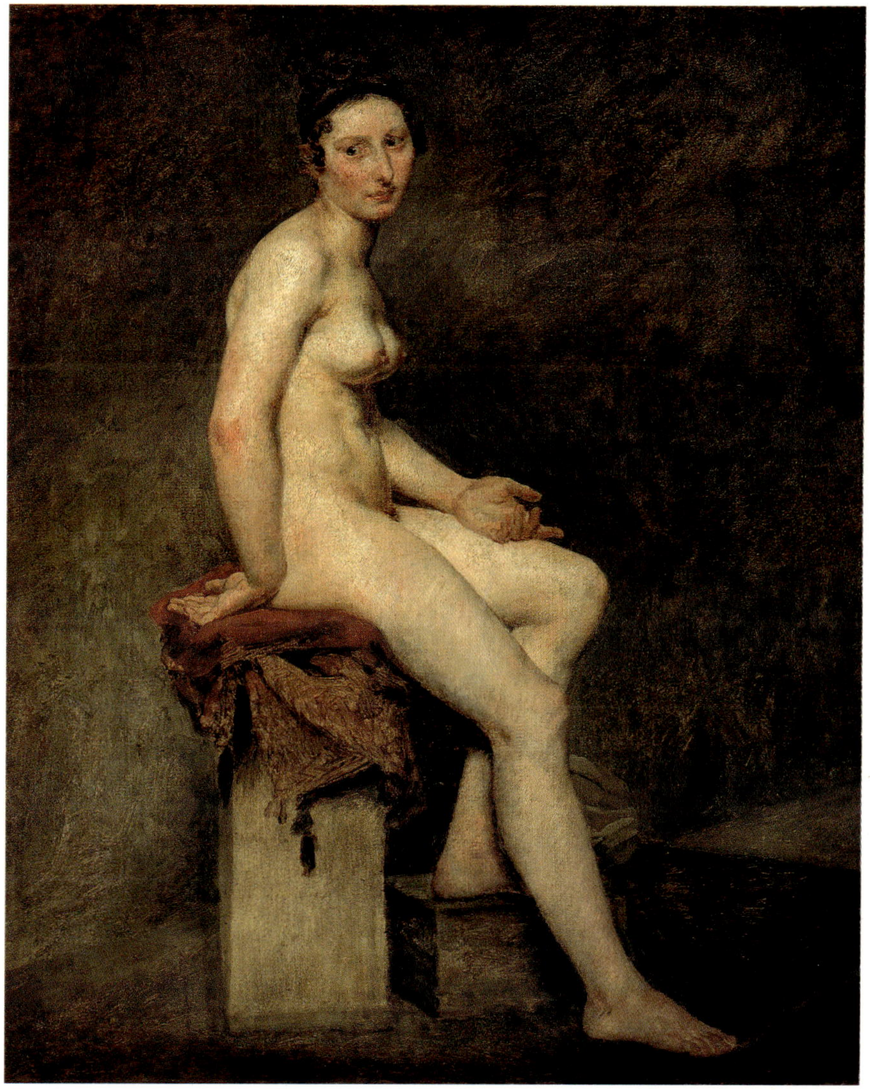

Paul Gauguin:
Annah the Javanese, 1893.

cult is exclusive. "Nothing charms me so much as painting, and now, on top of all else, it gives me the health of a man of thirty. It is my sole thought, and I scheme only to give myself entirely to her, that is, I plunge into my work like Newton (who died a virgin) into his famous research on gravity (I believe)."[37]

Was it in order not to succumb to temptation that Delacroix liked to use daguerreotypes, and especially daguerreotypes of men? "I looked untiringly and with a passion at these photographs of naked men, at the admirable poem which is the human body, on which I learn how to read, and the sight of which has told me more than the inventions of the wordmongers."[38] Did he need to put the nude at a distance in order to be able to analyze it better?

Flesh and color remain the primary purposes of painting, as well as its sensual reasons. The colorists "must massage with color as the sculptor does with clay, marble or stone."[39] They must also exercise their attention closely in order to find the right tones and the most essential ones, the most determinant ones being very likely those of carnation.

In his letters to his brother Theo, Vincent van Gogh also made some very specific remarks on the difficulty of rendering flesh, and when he saw his portrait painted by Gauguin, he rejected it in part because of his treatment of carnation: "This is not flesh in the least, but boldly we may attribute this to his [Gauguin's] will to make a melancholy thing, the flesh in the shadows is lugubriously bluish... Once more, one must not do flesh with Prussian. Because then it ceases to be flesh; it becomes wood."[40]

Often, the quality of the rendering of flesh constitutes the prime criterion for the painter. That is where he is judged, for that is perhaps where one can best measure his degree of implication, as well as his technical ability in approximating something that is impossible to achieve totally: a glorious and corruptible substance in which life, by manifesting itself, betrays the shadow of death. At the least mistake, flesh becomes morbid. When Baudelaire wrote to Manet with a warm tenderness to say that he was "not alone in the decrepitude of his art," it was because one of the signs of the birth of modern art in *Olympia* and the *Déjeuner sur l'herbe* was the handling of the color (which in the meantime had become "chemical"). With Manet, the painter, whose trade is to deal with visible things in general, and the human figure in particular, exhibited a body free of mythological or religious pretexts.

The canvas and the paper are skins: onto them the body and soul of the artist project themselves, and sometimes even become bogged down in it. To suggest the representation of flesh, painters invented imaginary structures that corresponded to them like so many indices of style. To show it, they used spots and lines, the epidermis is represented streaked, dotted, patched, shimmering, constellated. The cutaneous robe is woven in every possible manner; it is speckled with color. The inaccessible nudity is covered with layers of paint like so many chaotic veils of a more or less complex structure. The flesh identifies itself with the canvas and the canvas with the flesh, like a woman who makes herself up, tracing, as Michel Serres put it, "the tender map of tact,"[41] from which beauty springs, and renders visible her sensible world by covering it feature by feature, an eye for an eye. "The artist or the artisan, with a brush, hammer or pen, at the decisive instant, fights a flesh-to-flesh combat. No one who has refused contact has ever struggled, shaped, loved or known anything."[42]

If the canvas is a skin, it is also a shroud, the receptacle of the painter's sweat and blood, a flexible veil in which the traces of the suffering body are impressed. Veronica, the patron saint of painters, caressed and wiped the face of Christ with her veil on the road to Calvary, and immortalized this mask of pain on the cloth. This analogy can be extended, for the painting is also a relic, the memory of a moment of passion (in all senses of the word), a memory of the body, a memory of sensations, which then becomes a cult object, a ritual object. It summarizes the totality of sensations. A fragment of cloth condenses the entire world. The part refers to the whole. Fetishism and more fetishism! In the veil of St. Veronica, the entire martyred body of Christ is suggested. In the canvas, the entire body of the painter is represented in filigree, a discreet structuring shadow.

Like the tunic of the *écorché*, a cutaneous robe, the painting contains the sensations and the memory of an individual and collective existence; its scars, its pigmentation, record a past that is always present. Sense and sensation streak its surface. The grain of skin, the grain of the canvas, the grain of paper, and the beauty mark (called "*grain de beauté*" in French). Painting and flesh are the prime surfaces of seduction and simulacrum, with their receptive and vulnerable places, they are truthful and deceitful, overcharged and exposed, transparent and opaque, the territory of paradoxes, films of dreams in which inside and outside meet.

Through carnation, painting renders fantasy tangible. The story of Renoir is particularly savory in this regard. He was systematically attracted to rotund female forms, and this conditioned his judgement of painting, whether his own or others'. The first painting that ever "grabbed" him, he said, was a *Bathing Diana* by Boucher. For him, a painter

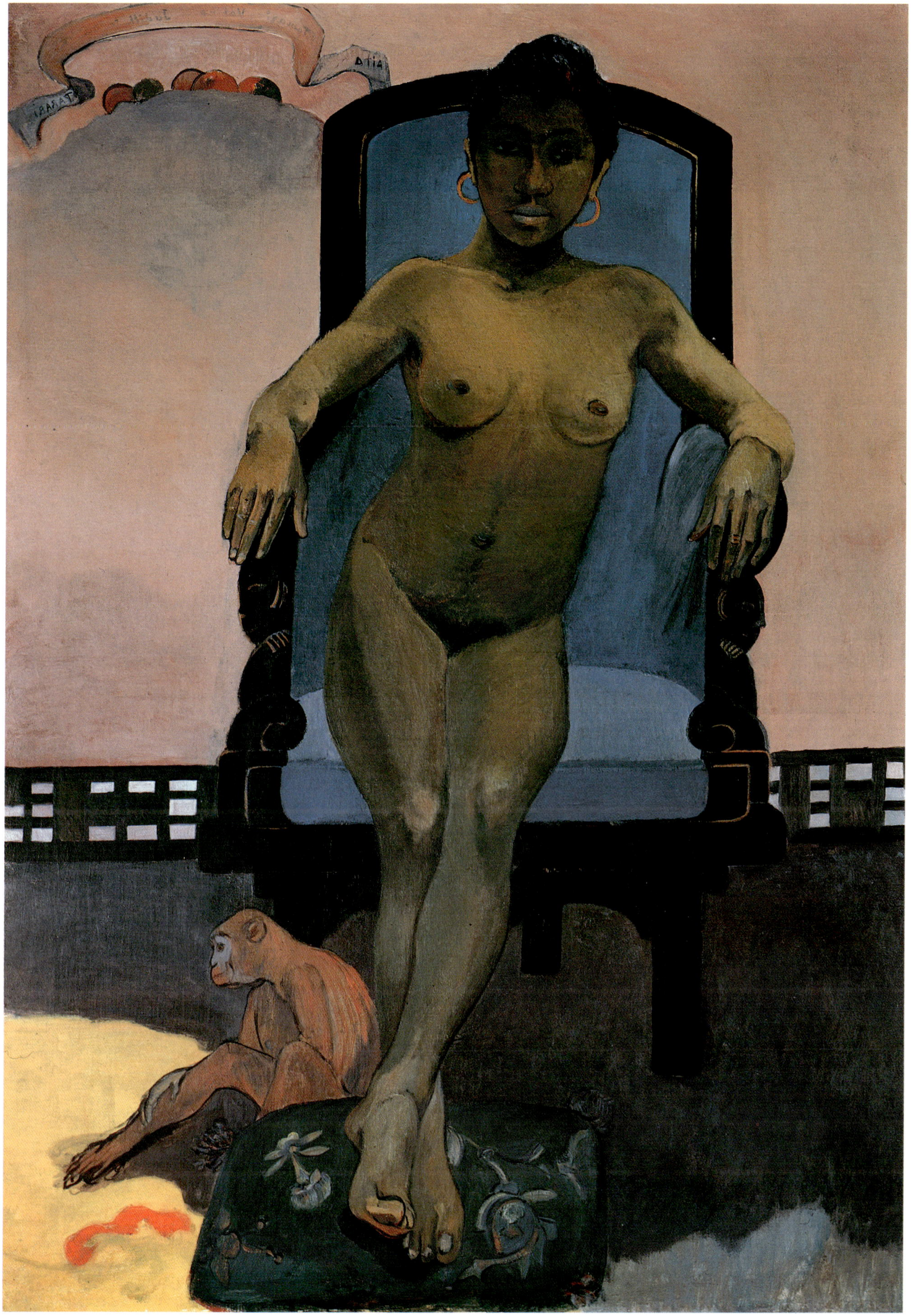

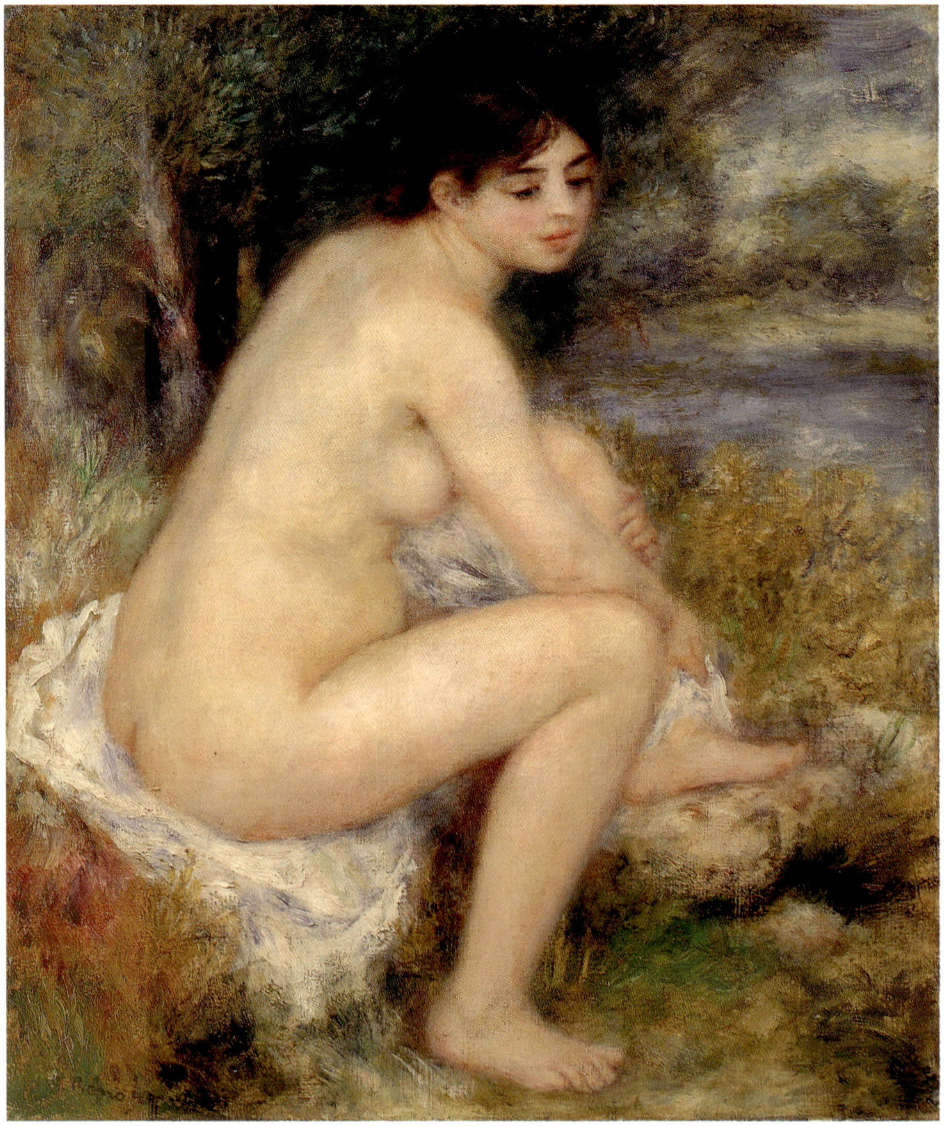

Pierre Auguste Renoir: Nude in a Landscape, 1883.

who had "a feeling for boobs and bottoms was a saved man," and Boucher precisely "painted youthful behinds with little dimples, just right." Rubens appealed to him because, among other things, "he was never short of buttocks."[43]

Throughout his career as a painter, he looked for well fleshed-out models; he feared having to do the portraits of skinny women who did not have a pink flush to their cheeks. When he had to paint the portrait of Madame de Bonnières, he would rage against this woman who ate too little and who, moreover, immersed her hands in water before the sittings to make them appear whiter. For Renoir, a model had to have a certain thickness, her hands should be marked by work and, when she posed, she should think of nothing. Renoir liked only well-rounded figures softened by opulent flesh. Not surprisingly, he criticized Michelangelo for having studied too much anatomy and, "for fear of forgetting the least muscle, he included some which must surely have hindered his figures at times."[44]

As fundamental in his choice of a model as the forms, was the way in which the skin reflected light. He boasted of the quality of the skin of Mademoiselle Savary when she sat for him: "What a charming young lady! And what skin! She positively illuminates everything around her!"[45]

During a trip in "dismal Holland," he rejoiced when he discovered a particularly fine model: "A real madonna! With the skin of a virgin! You cannot imagine the breasts of this young girl, heavy and firm. And the lovely fold underneath, with its golden shadow... Unfortunately she had no time to sit because of her work, which she did not want to leave; but I was so happy about her docility and this skin which took the light so well that I wanted to take her to Paris with me. I was already telling myself, may she not be deflowered too soon, so that she will keep this peach-like complexion! And so I asked her mother to entrust her to me and promised that I would see to it that no man would touch her. 'But what will she do in Paris, if she does not work?' the mother asked me in stupefaction. It was then that I understood what kind of work my virgin was doing."[46] But the "morals" of the model mattered little. Degas, whom Renoir especially

Pierre Auguste Renoir:
Reclining Nude (Gabrielle), 1903.

admired, endowed girls from bordellos with a chaste and almost religious appearance.

Vollard, after having "naively" recommended a "morally very good" model to Renoir, was told by the painter: "when she undressed, I would not have minded her being morally very bad, but I would have preferred her to have firmer breasts at least!"[47] All through his life, Renoir's perennial subject was the female figure: "The nude woman may rise out from the sea or from her bed, she may be called Venus or Nini, no one will ever invent anything better."[48] For his servants, which were his most faithful models, the only thing he required was that they had "a skin which takes the light well." He hated professional models and their predictable poses.

He was constantly trying out flesh tones. One day, going into his studio, the art dealer noticed an oil sketch of roses; surprised by this unusual subject, he was told by Renoir that it was an experiment in flesh tones for a nude! The painter would say that nothing delighted him more than painting a bottom. For him, painting was evidently a question of enjoyment, and he rebelled against the "need to look for thoughts in painting. When I see a masterpiece, I am happy just to enjoy it... When I see in a painter the passion he felt in painting, he makes me enjoy my own enjoyment. The enjoyment that I have had when I see masterpieces has really given me a second life."

Art must be taken on wholeheartedly, and the body—incarnated in its generosity—is its absolute criterion. "When I have painted a bottom and I feel like giving it a pat, that is when it is finished!"[49] Could there be a more explicit way to appreciate a successful carnation? This success was often too apparent in the eyes of his contemporaries, and Renoir tells how, for one of his nudes judged as being indecorous, he had to add an animal hide, a doe, and bow and arrow, to transform it into a "Hunting Nymph."[50] Such were the demands of the time. The painter's own vocabulary, however, did without such euphemisms. He expressed in almost violent terms his enthusiasm for Titian's *Venus with an Organ Player* in Madrid: "The limpidity of this meat, how one would like to caress it! How one can feel all the joy that Titian had in painting this picture."

To be sure, when flirting in such a vigorous way with life, painting simultaneously transfigures it. Renoir was not fooled, as we can see from the following anecdote: "One day in the Louvre, I was waxing ecstatic over a Fragonard, a shepherdess with a delightful petticoat which all by itself made the painting. Then what do I hear but someone saying that the shepherdesses of those days must have been as dirty as those of today. So I said, first of all, I don't give a damn, and then, if that was the case, then we should have all the more admiration for the painter who made such jewels out of such filthy models."[51] As for Renoir, when his models were not curvaceous enough, his eye and his brush took over and elaborated. Madeleine Bruno, a model of very slight build who posed for a picture of bathers, had difficulty in recognizing herself in the generous forms on the canvas.

To the very end of his life, when he could paint only with brushes tied to his arthritic fingers, Renoir continued creating full-bodied, blossoming female forms brimming with the rosy glow of life.

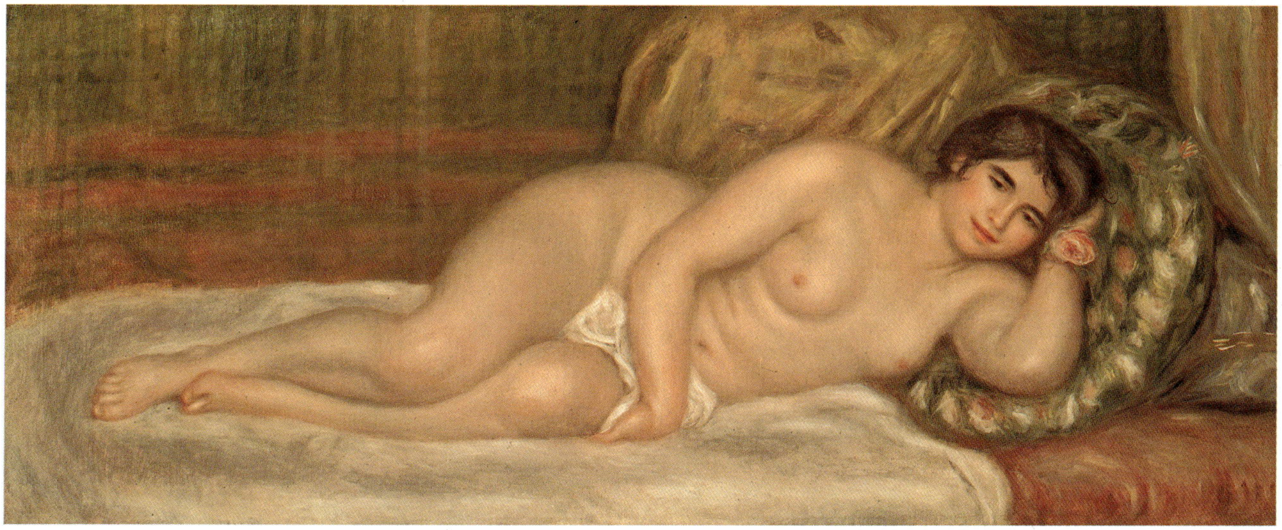

Johann Heinrich Füssli:
The Desperation of the Artist before the
Grandeur of Ancient Ruins, 1778-1780.

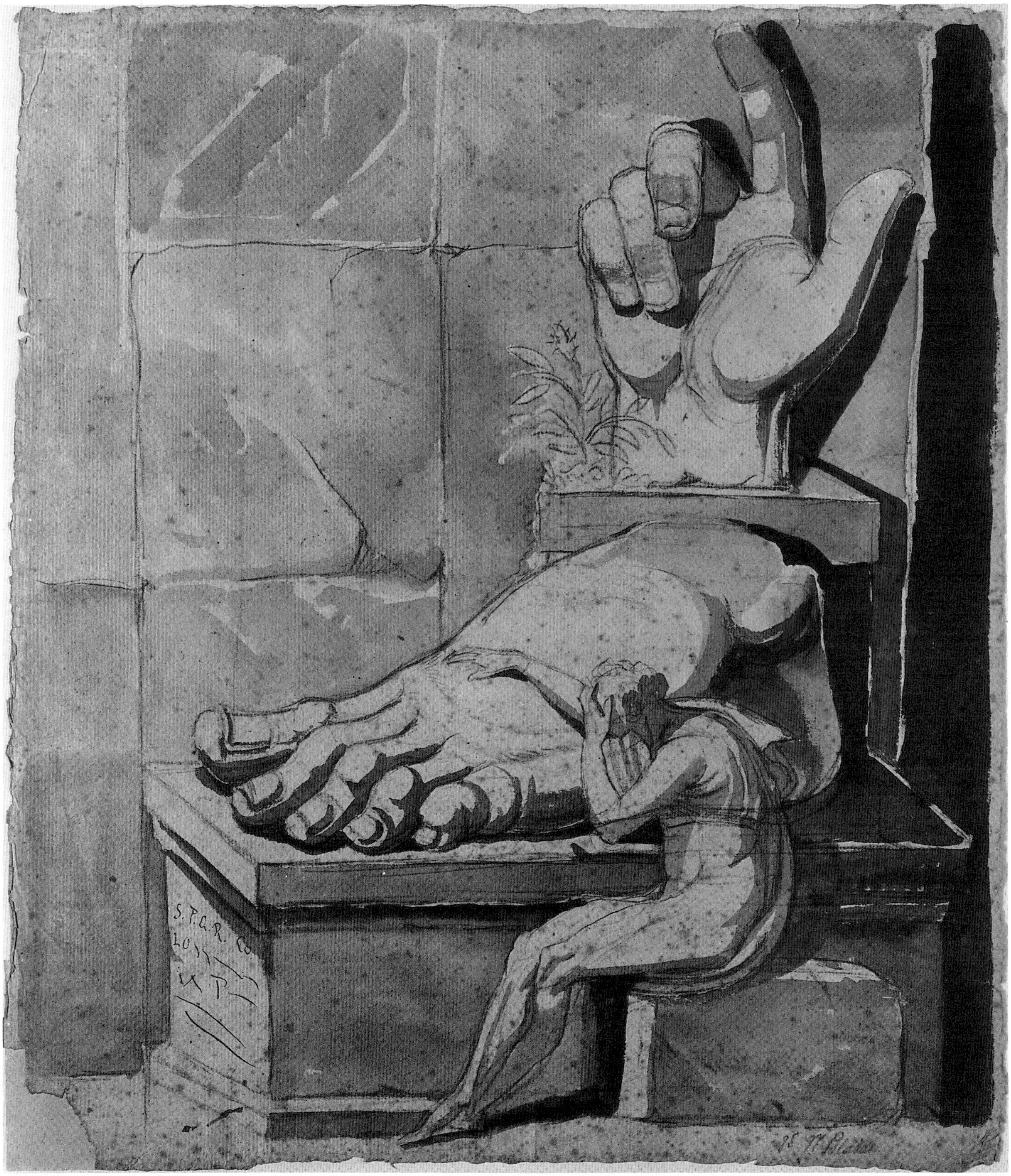

How to domesticate the body: canons of beauty

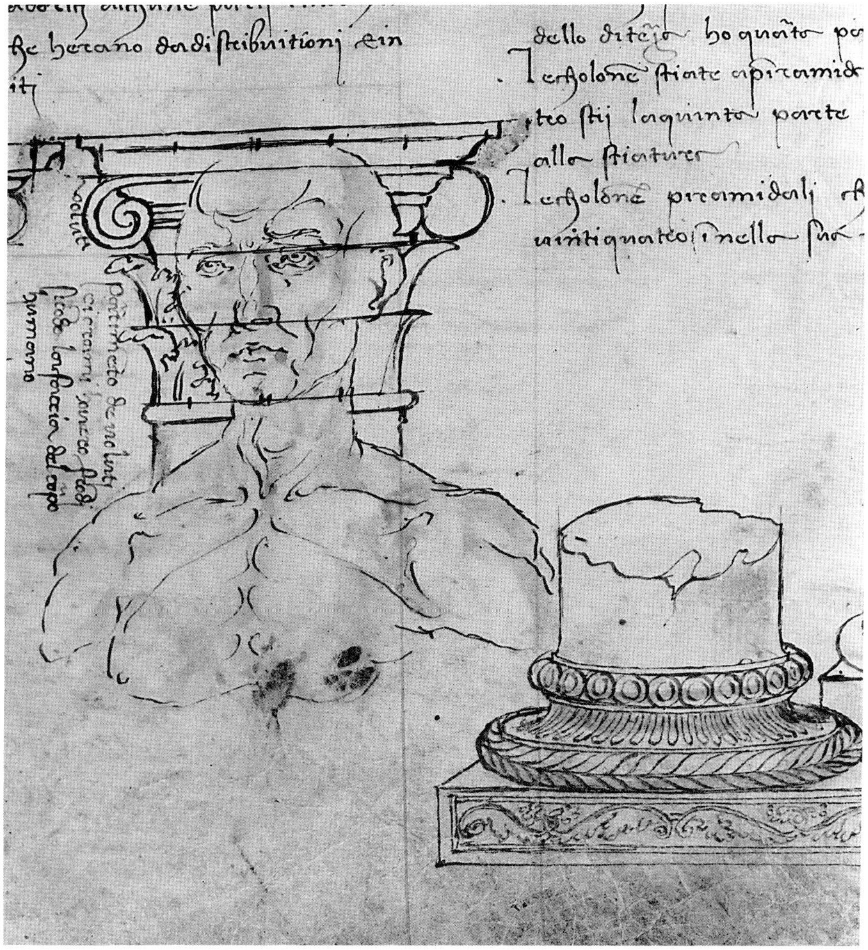

Francesco di Giorgio Martini: Study of Proportions, c. 1470-1480.

In order to approach the human figure, that strange and elusive form, artists have resorted to canons of beauty and theories of proportions of all kinds. Since antiquity, that is, as soon as there was an organized attempt to elaborate illusionism, men like Polycletus and Vitruvius endeavored to extract from numbers the secrets of beauty, harmony and balance. It was as if artists were striving to tame the impenetrable human figure, to come into possession of it by instituting rules, to prevent it from escaping their grasp by applying formulas which, unfortunately, never excluded a touch of the arbitrary.

The desire for beauty and the need to establish conventions went hand in hand. The mathematical relationships between the various parts of the body of living beings could be expressed either by a division of the whole, or by the multiplication of a unity.[52] According to Galen, it was Polycletus, the author of the famous sentence, "Beauty comes little by little through many a number," who set down the correct proportion of each finger in relationship to each other, of the fingers in relationship to the hand, of the hand to the forearm, and so on for each part in relationship to every other part of the entire body.

The Italian Renaissance had a boundless respect for the theories of proportions handed down by antiquity. They were considered not only technical devices, but also metaphysical postulates. At that time, when artists were assimilating the whole of scientific culture, the theory of proportions was held to be the rational basis of beauty; it was the prerequisite for artistic endeavor and for an expression of the pre-established harmony between microcosm and macrocosm.

The proportions of the human body were seen as the visible incarnation of harmony. Vitruvius had identified the proportions of man with those of buildings. This point was seized on and developed. Two artist-theorists, Leon Battista Alberti and Leonardo da Vinci, worked methodically on this question. Both had the same determination to make an empirical science of the theory of proportions. They boldly confronted nature and set about measuring the human body with compasses and protractors. They also carefully chose their models. Their goal was to discover the ideal, the better to define the norm. Proportions not only provided artists with a simple planimetric armature for drawing, they also defined the organic articulation of the figure and its three-dimensionality.

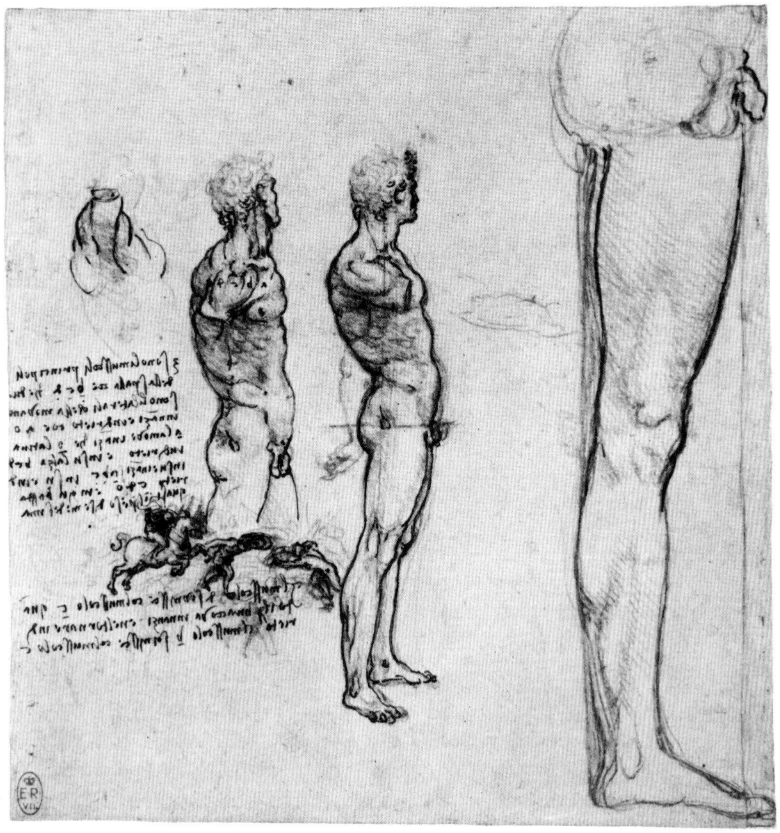

◁ *Leonardo da Vinci: Nude Study for* The Battle of Anghiari*, c. 1503-1504.*

▽ *Leonardo da Vinci: Proportions of the Human Face, c. 1505.*

Alberti established a table of measurements which he claimed to have tested by scrutinizing a large number of people. Leonardo da Vinci based organic unity on the correspondences between the various parts of the body, and undertook a systematic study of the mechanical and anatomical processes that altered the objective dimensions of the body. The anatomist-painter observed that joints thickened when there was a flexion, and that muscles dilated and contracted.

Leonardo da Vinci persisted in trying to quantify the ideal proportions:

> "From the chin to the hairline, there is 1/10th of the figure.
> From the junction of the palm to the tip of the middle finger, 1/10th.
> From the chin to the crown: 1/8th.
> From the pit of the stomach to the crown: 1/4th.
> And from the fork of the ribs to the crown: 1/4th.
> And from the chin to the nostrils, a third of the face.
> And as much from the nostrils to the eyebrows and from the eyebrows to the hairline.
> And the foot represents 1/6th; the distance from the forearm to the arm, 1/4, the width of the shoulders, 1/4."[53]

A grid of this kind can be quite useful when it is a matter of tackling the formidable subject of the human figure, to say nothing of the nude. In his notes, the painter lavished advice on imaginary pupils: "When you draw a nude, be sure always to represent the entire body; then complete the limb which seems the best done and study its relationship with the other limbs, otherwise you will adopt the habit of never assembling them well."[54] It is of course necessary for the constituent elements of the human body to combine in such a way as to give the effect of a well-knit unity. In order to achieve this, Leonardo wrote, a knowledge of anatomy was helpful.[55] Leonardo corrected Vitruvius, fixed the proportions, squared the profile of a mature man with a dense grid of lines and numbers.

As for Dürer, following his trip to Venice and his meeting with Jacopo de' Barbari, he assiduously

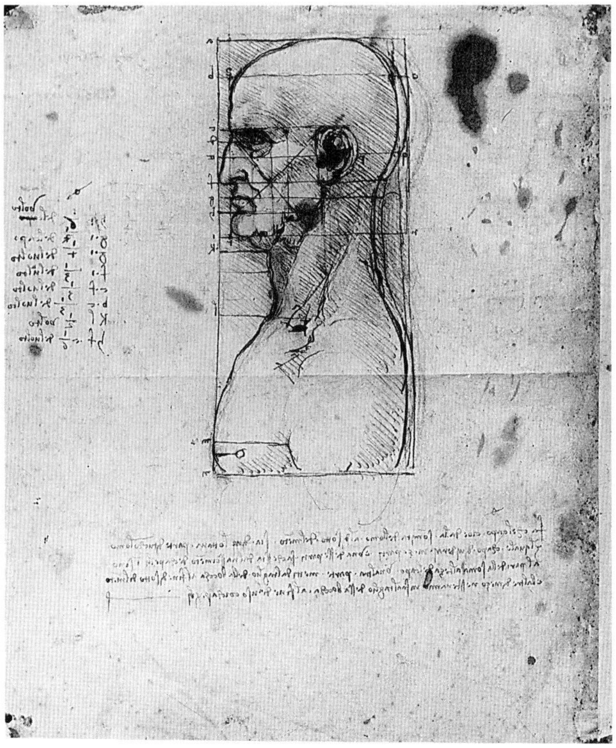

Albrecht Dürer:
Study (The Measured Man), c. 1505-1510.

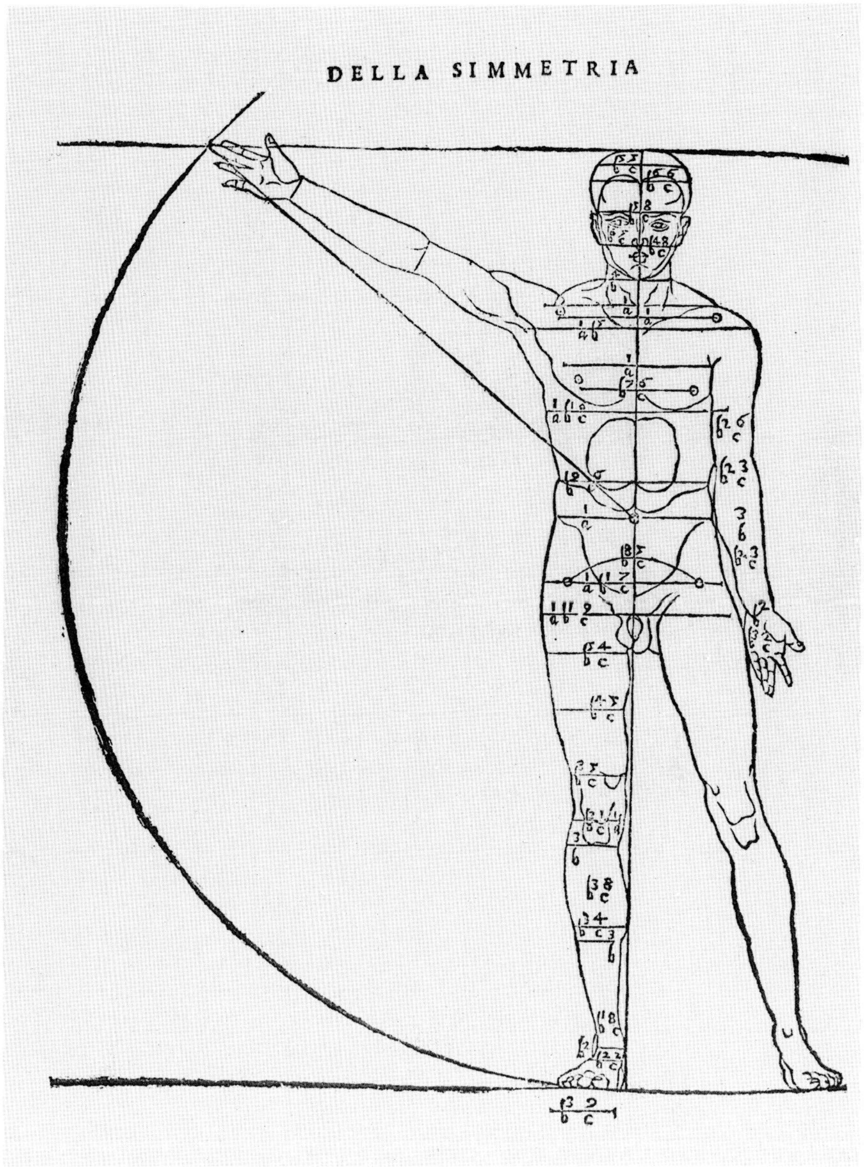

studied the problem of proportions and of working from the live model. Anxious to discover the intrinsic rules of beauty, he discouraged him: "It often happens that one can study two or three hundred human beings and find only two or three things fine enough to be useful."[56]

The artist established classifications, eliminated anomalies and created a typology. Beauty, however, does not let itself be imprisoned in norms so easily. Faced with its enigmas, Dürer confessed humbly: "Beauty is the thing that I know not." He nevertheless wrote a *Treatise on Proportions*, a book which he thought would serve the future painter. At times, his advice to users turns in a vicious circle: "It is a fact that he who would be helped by this book without knowing about the subject it discusses will experience great difficulty at first. But let him set before him a man with the necessary proportions, and then let him trace the external contours according to his talent and his knowledge of drawing. For he earns consideration if he follows life so closely in the reproduction he makes of it that the latter resembles it and becomes like unto nature, and in particular when that which is reproduced has beauty, the reproduction then is held to be a work of art and it is praised as it deserves."[57]

One may legitimately ask at this point what were the desired proportions, the famous universal proportions for which Dürer tried to find the key. He resolved to instruct himself, and consulted all the available documents; he studied the notes of Leonardo da Vinci, analyzed the reflections of Luca Pacioli in his *Summa Arithmetica*, learned Vasari's system of measurement, and borrowed techniques from Alberti's *De statua*.

Sometimes, however, the painter became disillusioned and wary of the mathematico-philosophical speculations of the Italians. Regretfully—or with relief?—he came to the conclusion that neither universal proportions, nor ideal beauty existed. Beauty was relative: "In a man's judgement, a form may be considered beautiful at a given moment, and be passed over in favor of another form at another moment." The artist radically denied an abstract concept of beauty and finally declared: "Only God is able to conceive supreme beauty." Could this have been a relative abdication?

Unlike Leonardo da Vinci, Dürer took little interest in anatomy. He did not practice dissection, but attached himself to the external image of the body. The study of the live model, however, was indispensable. To the presence of live models, which he stipulated had to be nude, he added the use of geometry and provided "instructions on the way of measuring with a ruler and a compass lines and entire bodies." The Northern painter recommended intensive work from the nude in order to obtain good results in the practice of representing the draped body. He considered the drawing of the nude as the best way to capture the balance between the four limbs: "One achieves the clearest vision of the world when one often reproduces living people, for we see them then in the same way that each thing presents itself."[58]

Hendrick Goltzius:
Apollo Belvedere, 1617.

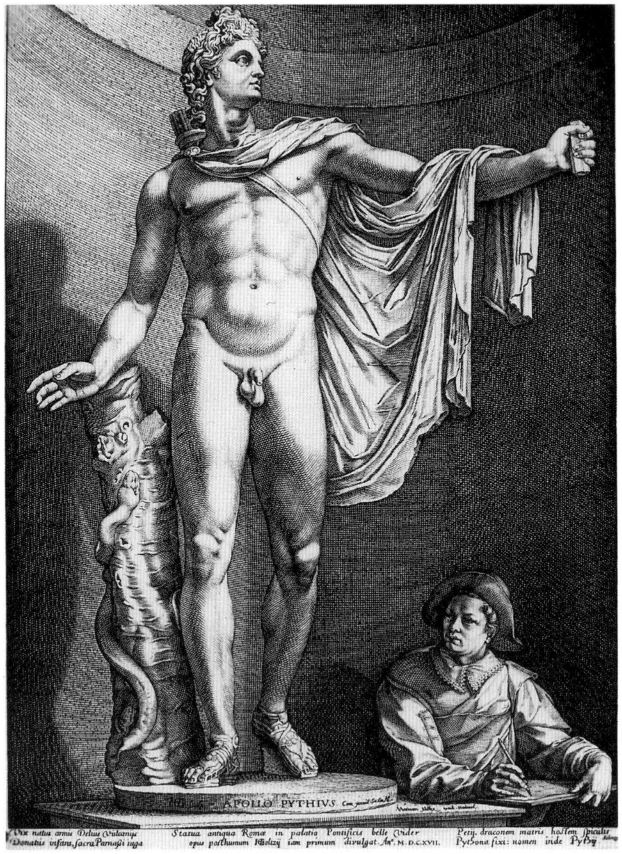

Juste de Juste:
Human Pyramid, undated.

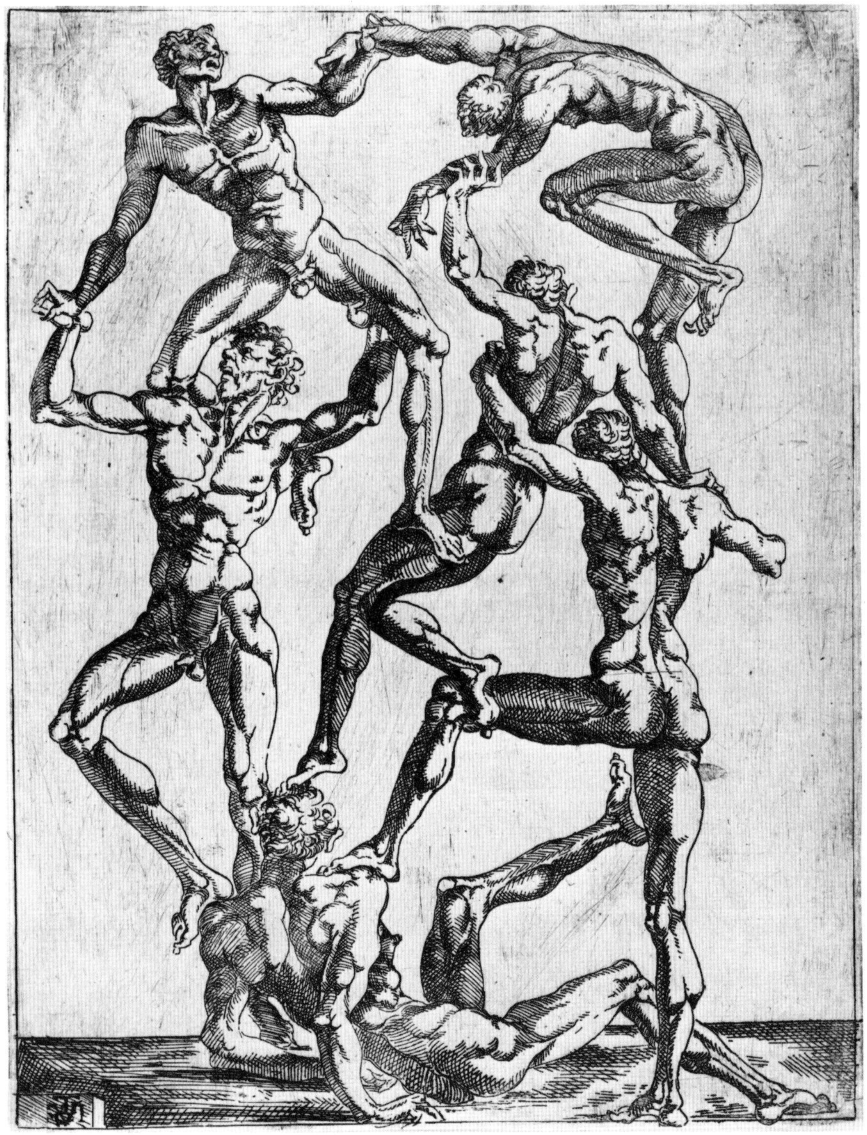

Michelangelo:
Nude Study for
The Battle of Cascina, *1505-1506.* ▷

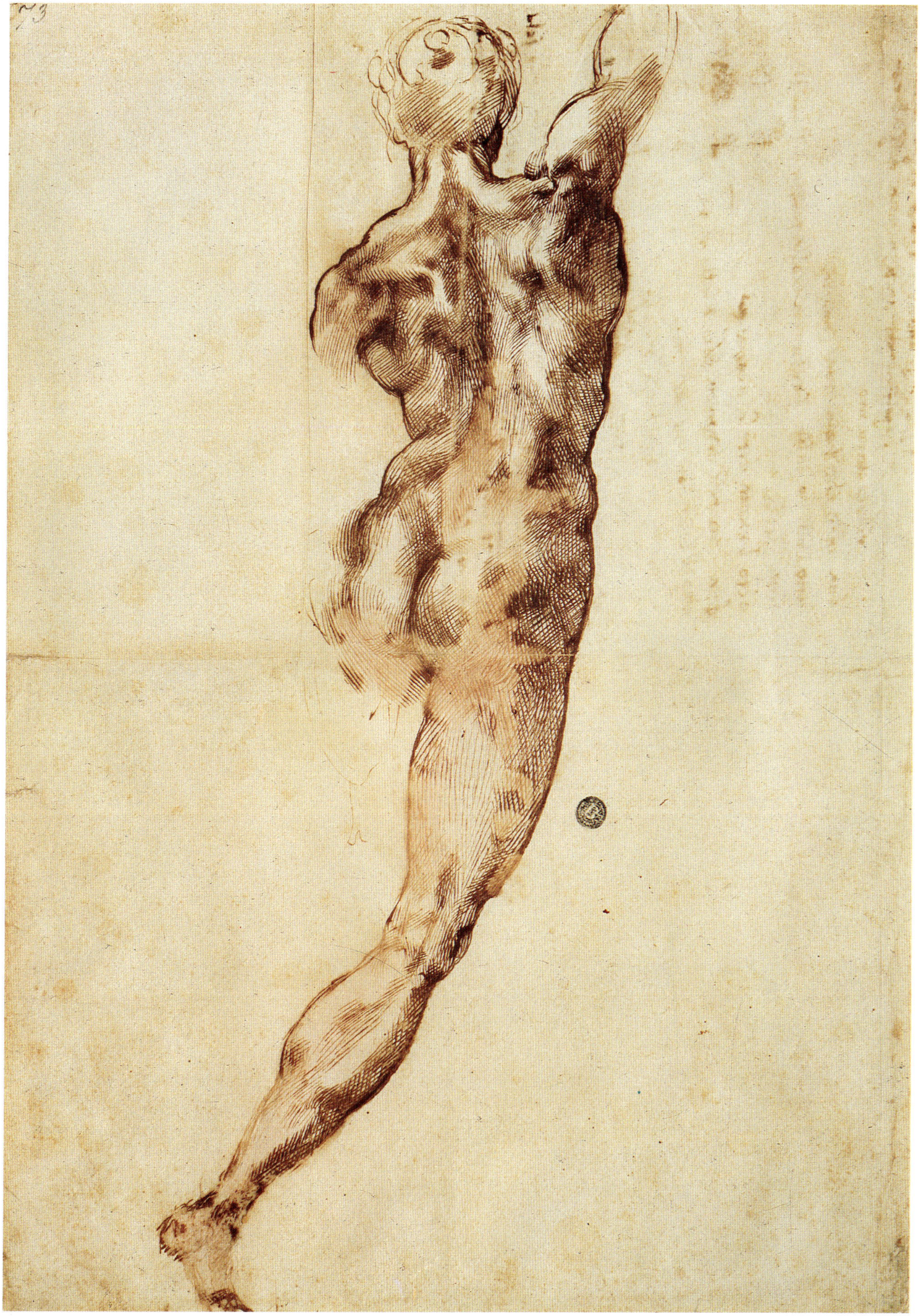

William Hogarth:
The Analysis of Beauty, plate 1 - 1753.

Jacopo Barozzi, called Vignola
Squaring the Canvas, 1583

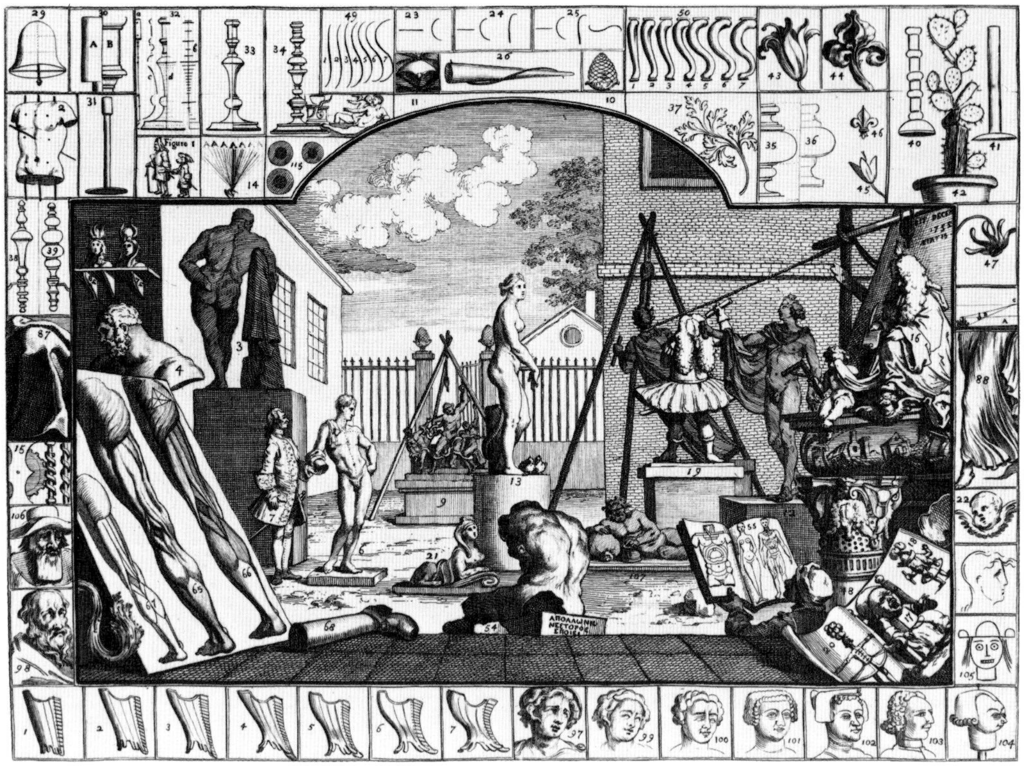

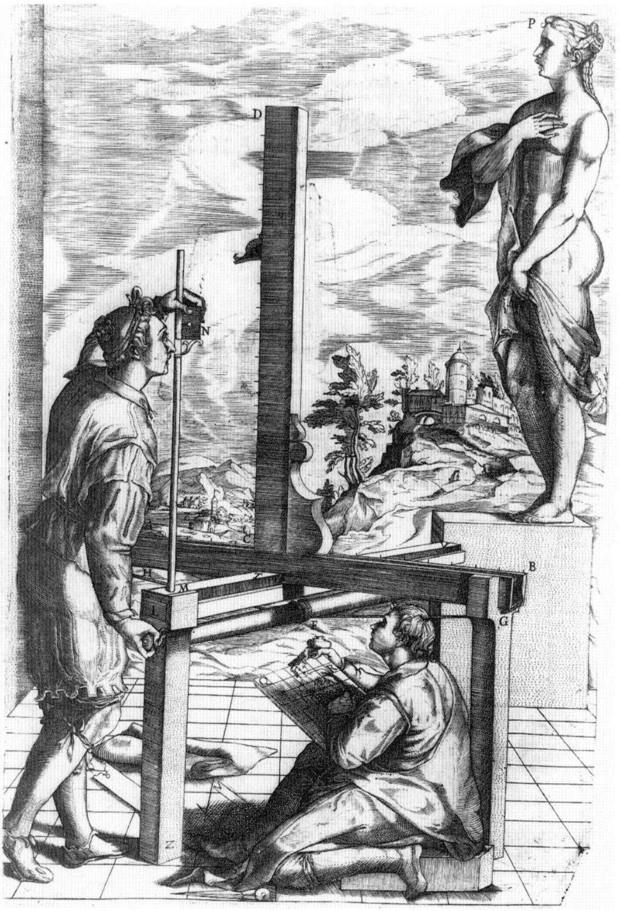

Accordingly, his 1493 study of a *Woman Coming out of Her Bath* is the first drawing of a nude executed by a German painter from a nude model. Dürer, however, was not short of paradoxes. While he fervently recommended the observation of the human body, his fourth piece of advice for the education of the future painter was that he "be preserved from the female sex, and that no woman live near him; that he does not look at or touch any nude woman, and that he guard himself against impurity. Nothing weakens reason so much as impurity!"[59]

In his outline for the ambitious *Book of the Painter*, measurement appears to have been a major concern. He planned to give instructions on the measurement of a child, an adult man, a woman, a horse, etc. The master pointed out that this science of measurement borrowed from Vitruvius and Pliny should be applied with complete flexibility. It was in no way a matter of fixing forms once and for all.

If beauty does not let itself be tracked down easily, the artist can nevertheless turn around it and associate it with "homogeneity," "harmony," "coherence." The search for beautiful living models is part of this process. It is necessary, Dürer pointed out, to copy with application, "people who are considered beautiful." Confronted with the difficulty of finding perfect beings in real life, the master—unwittingly perhaps—adopted the same method as Zeuxis for the temple of Juno, and

Albrecht Dürer:
Eve, 1507.

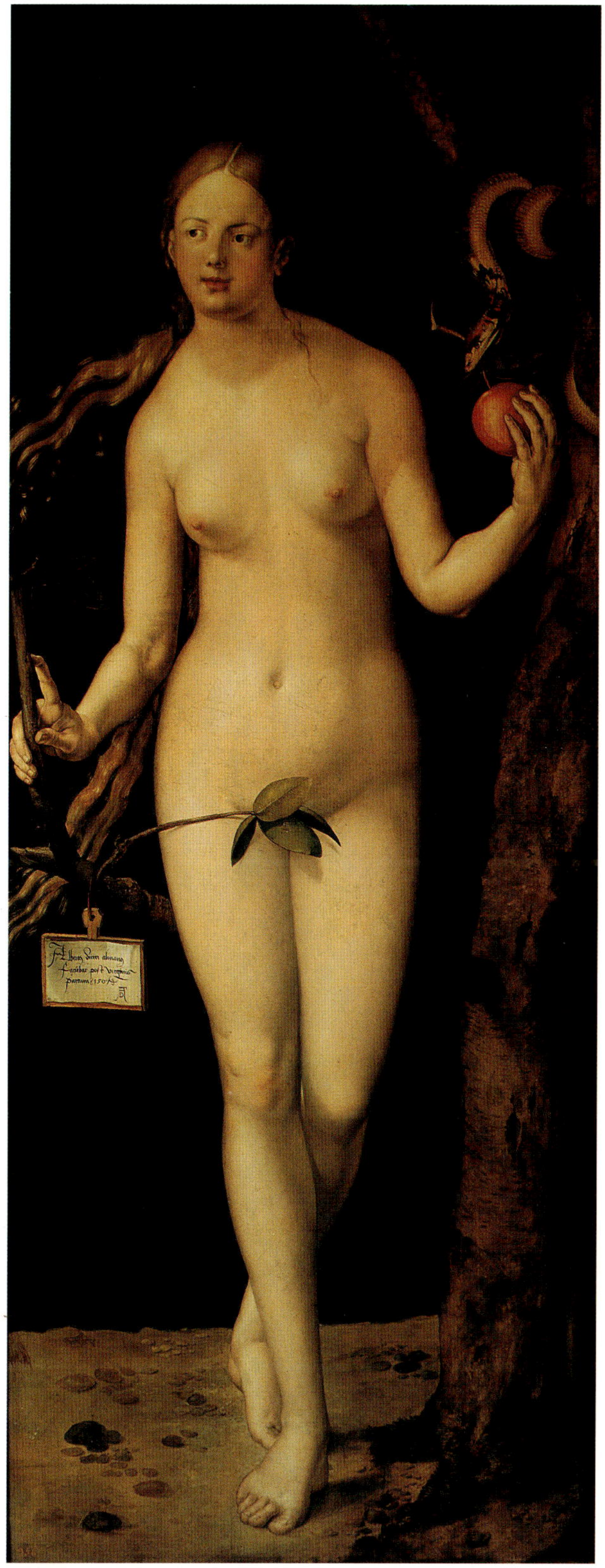

recommended an assemblage of parts: "For, starting from several different men, an intelligent artist can achieve a good result by combining different parts of their members."

Theoretically, when the apprentice is ripe, he should have integrated the model to such a degree that he is able to do without it. This is the dream of autonomy and of the integration of the ideal subject. But the obsession with beauty always ends in paradox. "Beauty is so composed in the human body and our judgement in this matter is so full of doubt that we can meet two human beings, both very comely and likeable, but which do not resemble each other in any part of their bodies, either in the proportions, or in their character, and we do not even know which is the most beautiful, so blind is our faculty for knowledge. This is why, when we make a judgement on an object of this sort, it is uncertain. Even if one actually does surpass the other in some respect, this will remain unknown to us."[60]

In thus endeavoring to circumscribe beauty by different means, Dürer was an innovator, and it was he who executed the first nude figures of Adam and Eve in Germany, which he represented lifesize, as if their scale would make them more compatible with reality. Dürer untiringly searched for the most appropriate models, using himself as his own models for his many self-portraits, and even his wife (for a St. Anne), whom he measured, observed and drew from memory.

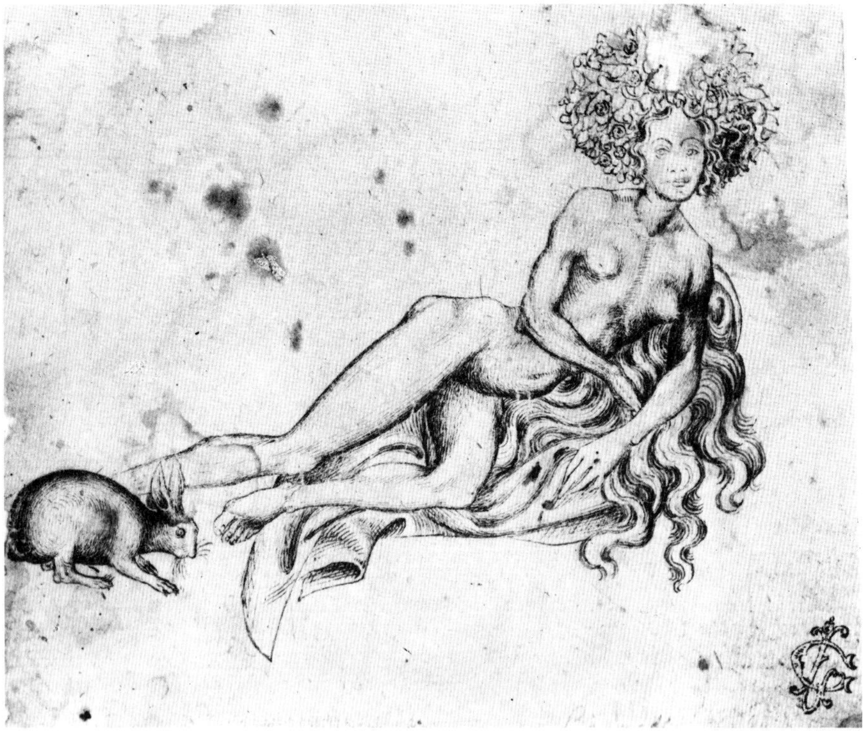

Antonio Pisanello:
Allegory of Lust, c. 1430.

The beauty of the devil

Elusive beauty flirts constantly with the devil, to the despair of the creator, yet it is also what motivates him. Baudelaire dedicated a hymn to this fatal goddess in his *Flowers of Evil*:

> What does it matter if you come from Heaven or Hell,
> O Beauty! awesome, frightful, artless monster!
> If your eye, your smile, your foot, should open the way
> To an infinity which I love and have never known?

The she-devil toys with her neighbor and rival: ugliness. Beauty—of which Balzac said: "We ask her only to exist"—knows more than one trick to disorient, surprise, or escape. "She is what drives to despair," exclaimed Paul Valéry, and Rainer Maria Rilke declared that she was "the first degree of the terrible." Definitions roll off her many shells, over her successive skins superimposed like the layers of an onion of which the center (and the meaning) can never be reached without entailing its destruction. She is the ineffable par excellence; "words fail" on her account, she leads to powerlessness. "Beauty is negative," Paul Valéry anxiously asserted, while Georges Bataille underscored its disquieting relationship with bestiality, animality and filth.

Leopold Sacher-Masoch, author of the famous *Venus in Furs*, wrote a short story which is about the adventure of a particularly loathsome hunchback painter who went to live with a family full of charming children, and especially a young girl of rare beauty, Valeska. This story, called *The Esthetics of Ugliness*, shifts constantly between the beautiful and the ugly. The hunchback painter succeeds in winning over the entire family, including the dour Aunt Rose. The playful painter, who loves costumes, disguises himself as a witch. Attracted by Valeska's beauty, he wants to paint her portrait, but this superb model runs away. The artist then devises a scheme in order to attract the young beauty: he tells a fairy tale and assigns roles to the children so that they will put on disguises. The author of *Venus in Furs* has the ravishing Valeska garbed in a sumptuous fur wrap which further accentuates her natural charms. "She becomes so completely captivating," the painter remarks, "that all we can do is fall at her feet and put ourselves at her mercy."[61]

Beauty, for Sacher-Masoch, was answered by submission. The painter in the story, however, becomes master of the situation; he organizes the sitting like a sort of ritual. Although the artist's appearance is repulsive, he is secretly in love with his sitter. He works feverishly on the painting. He realizes that he is in love and knows also that involvement in art has a diabolical side. "Let the dark one stir a bit. He helps me in my craft. We never paint better than when the brush is led by desire."[62]

After various episodes in which death almost intervenes, the painter marries the beautiful Valeska. The hunchback stands in front of his easel, and the beauty, an admirable model, is enthroned in her princely furs. The relationship between beauty

▷ *Frédéric Léon: The Studio, 1882.*

▽ *Pablo Picasso: Woman and Old Man, 1954.*

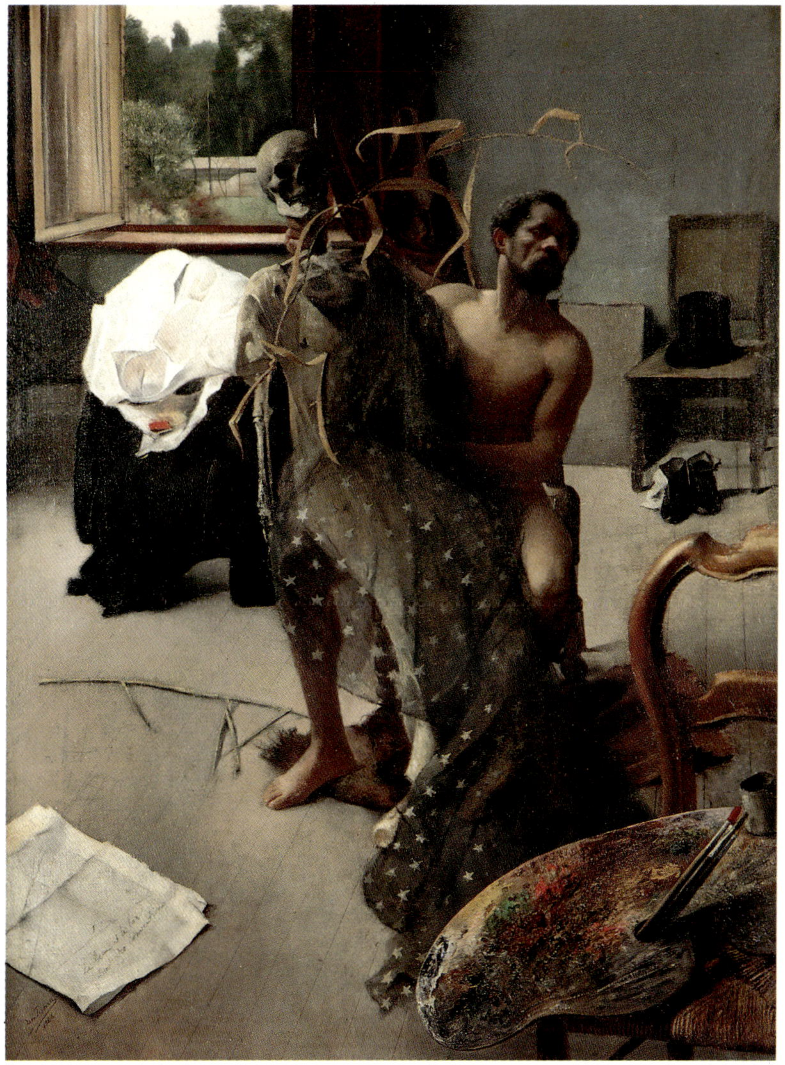

and the beast is charged with meaning; by playing on contrasts, it accentuates the character's power of evocation; the painter's satanic side, and the woman's beauty, which is so extreme that it takes on an abstract, unreal aspect.

The artist is always working on an unknown and unfathomable terrain. Through stone or pigments, he worships that unnameable goddess: Beauty. "Study beauty only on your knees,"[63] was Jean-Dominique Ingres's peremptory advice. And Baudelaire, once again, turned towards beauty only to stress its petrifying nature, its statue-like immobility and its sovereign impenetrability, its dazzling and mirror-like attributes.

I am beautiful, O mortals! like a dream of stone,
And my breast, on which each has expired in turn,
Is made to inspire in the poet a love
As eternal and speechless as matter.[64]

Archly, beauty takes over the energy of the artist, leaving him unsatisfied, on the verge of powerlessness, armed with his norms, conventions, and recipes, which lose their power to move and become sterile as soon as they repeat themselves or become too obvious. Beauty imposes her fluctuating and unpredictable laws. Capriciously, she dictates her models to desire. And Rimbaud writes:

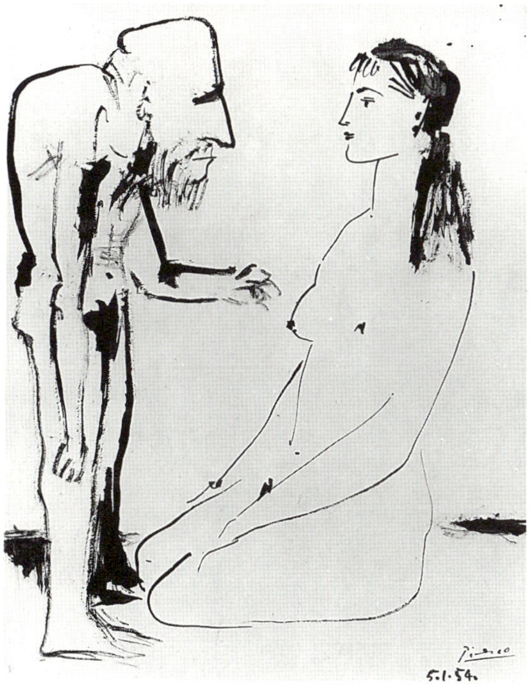

One night, I sat Beauty on my knees
And I found her bitter
And I insulted her.

Beauty is tyrannical. But this did not stop the Surrealists from composing her apology. André Breton defended a violent beauty: "Beauty will be convulsive, or will not be at all; veiled-erotic, exploding-fixed, magic, circumstantial, or it will not be."[65] It must emerge from the poignant feeling of the thing revealed and have the characteristics of a crystal: "It is a find, a marvelous precipitate of desire,"[66] which contains the magic power of expanding the universe. Beauty, woman and love (fusional love) are all associated. Each of these elements arises like an apparition. And beauty, like woman herself, is a thing of scandal. Love is both something adored and a poison, the fascination it exerts is as fatal as the woman of the same description. Which recalls Delacroix's statement that, "without daring, and an extreme daring, there is no beauty."[67] In beauty lurks cruelty, and desire is the only thing that makes the world and creation turn round.

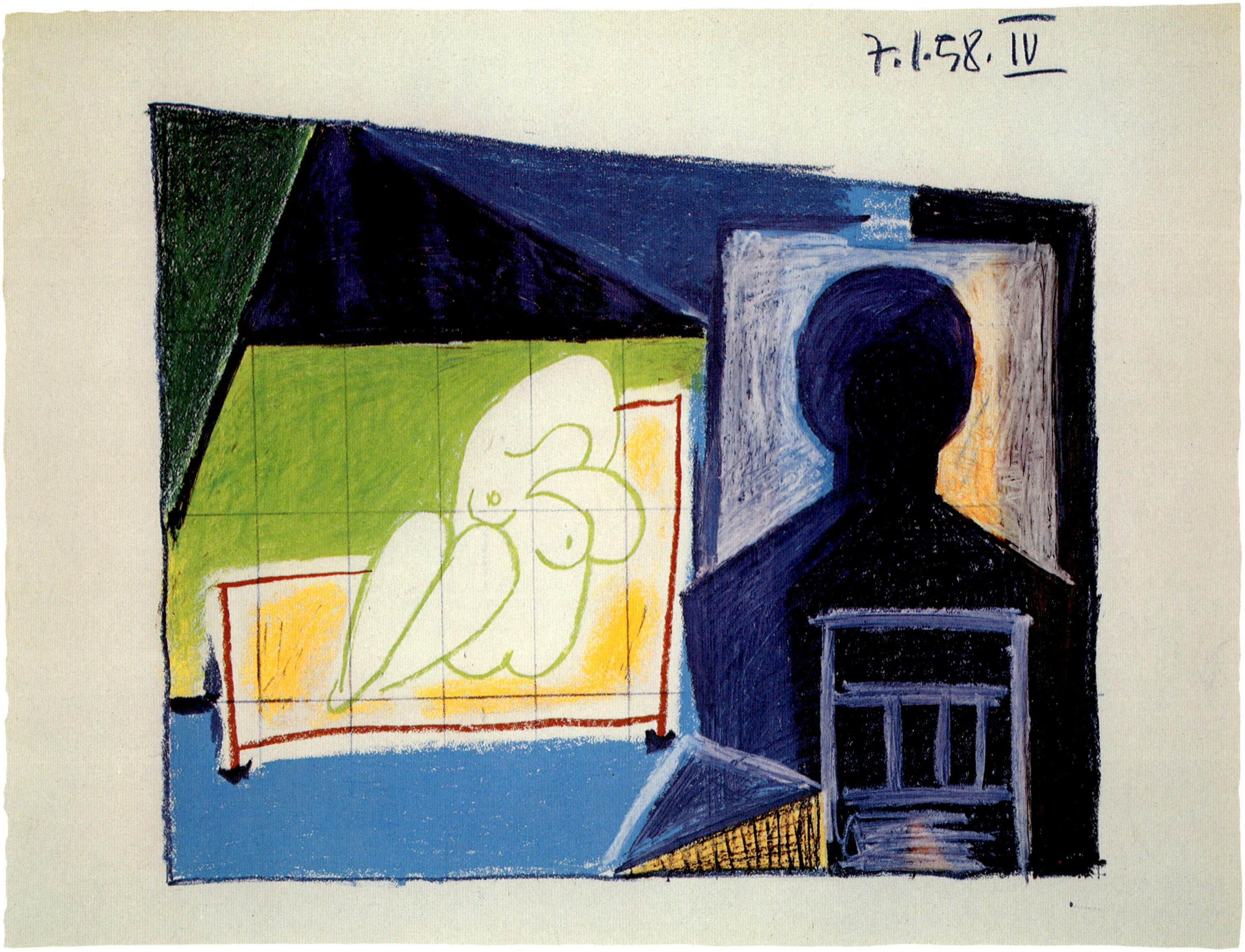

Pablo Picasso:
The Painter and His Model, 1958.

The two-way seduction or the seduction of the gaze

The relationship between the artist and the model is the stage of a seduction the prime mover of which is the gaze. On one side, the artist armed with the tools of his trade; on the other, the model, immobilized in a pose. Between the two, the eye-beams of the creator strike his subject, enveloping, penetrating, caressing and assaulting it. It is this avid gaze that welds their strange relationship together. The eye is involved everywhere, directs the performance, establishes the modalities of the ritual. It is the third actor, rapid, mobile, eminently active. Undoubtedly, the artist is in love, thirsting avidly for lines and forms, colors and textures. He takes hold of the model, appropriates it with the tip of his brush or the point of his chisel. He delves into secret reaches, scrutinizes the skin. He is both rapist and robber. Faced with this languid, available flesh, he acts, transforms.

The artist seduces the model and is seduced by her; it is a two-way seduction. Seduction is founded on a diabolical strategy. As an event the pose, which is anything but "natural," takes shape as a ritual. It relies on various artifices which, through a sort of black magic, permit the artist to channel the vital energy concentrated in the nudity of the model—who is usually a woman. "It should be said that the feminine is seductive because it is never there where it is being thought."[68] Constantly slipping out—of her clothes, of the artist's sight—the model becomes that much more attractive in a game of hide and seek. Hers is the power of superlative concentrated seduction; here more than anywhere else, seduction comes into sharp focus. Because of the presence of her naked body and its artificial attitudes, the model commands a special power. Desire condenses in her contours, runs skin deep, floats like an aura about the observed female body, a body constructed by the artifice of the pose, transformed beyond its anatomical destiny, its naked truth, by the eye of the artist. It is a deified body (as in Baudelaire's poetry), both malefic and fertile.

This insidious faculty is both symbolic and physical. Through the body, the model establishes a realm of appearances, the realm of a "deep surface," into which the eye of the artist strives at all costs to introduce itself and to penetrate. On the indefinite surface of the model charged with a diffuse and diffracted eroticism, the painter endeavors to encounter painting, the sculptor to encounter sculpture. The muse displays her masks; she is ever veiled yet ever present. Uncertainty is the name of the game; she gives herself to the eye, but without offering any guarantees. The artist tries to reassure himself through her, but she keeps him off balance, she fuels the ambiguities and the paradoxes. She disguises herself with her various nudities, hides herself behind the varied poses, presents a vertiginous display to the beholder. She is endlessly travestied for the artist's eye dresses her with his style, his brush or his chisel. She is sublime.

The sitter is a "star" become intemporal. At the same time as the artist brings her into being, he is born through her. "This is my body," he could very well say of her. A transubstantiation takes place. The movie star, that celestial divinity, singularizes herself and finds her immortality in the creation of an ephemeral image made up of make-up and fixed in time by the film. The model, however, less made up than the goddesses and vamps of the silver screen, is herself painted, reworked, reconstituted by the intervention of a creator.

Starting from the naked body of the live, very much alive model, the artist elaborates his own artifices, his own particular style. He appropriates the model's energy to such a degree that he attaches his name to it. We commonly speak of paintings and sculptures as being nudes by Matisse, Modigliani or Rodin. To what extent do they still involve a well-known English redhead, a Jeanne Hébuterne, a Camille Claudel? The model seems to be dispossessed, the better to be reborn elsewhere, in another form, in the immortality of the work of art. Reincarnation, strange avatar. It is a game in which the loser wins. Moved by his passion for cold Vittoria Colonna, Michelangelo meant no more than that by his desire to immortalize in marble not only her beauty, but also the attraction he fostered for her, an attraction which made her that much more beautiful.

The model is a woman doubled by the artifice of the pose, doubled by the gaze of the artist. She exhibits herself like a sacred prostitute, displays the facets of her opacity, while the artist creates images, engenders forms and colors. Seduced by a body, he is impelled to produce. The woman lounges and lingers, the artist conquers, lays down his marks. The ritual of the pose is a codified strategy, an impossible strip-tease afloat in illusion and illusionism, and dizzying passion. The artist selects his model, dictates the poses while "keeping his eye on her," holding her under his rule. Though occasionally a dictator, he is nonetheless dominated by his subject and the mental images to which he tries to give form, a human form, via the implicit or explicit obsession of figuration.

Given form, the model sacrifices herself in the present in order to live eternally in the work of art. It is at once barter, blackmail and defiance of death.

Man Ray:
Kiki of Montparnasse, 1922.

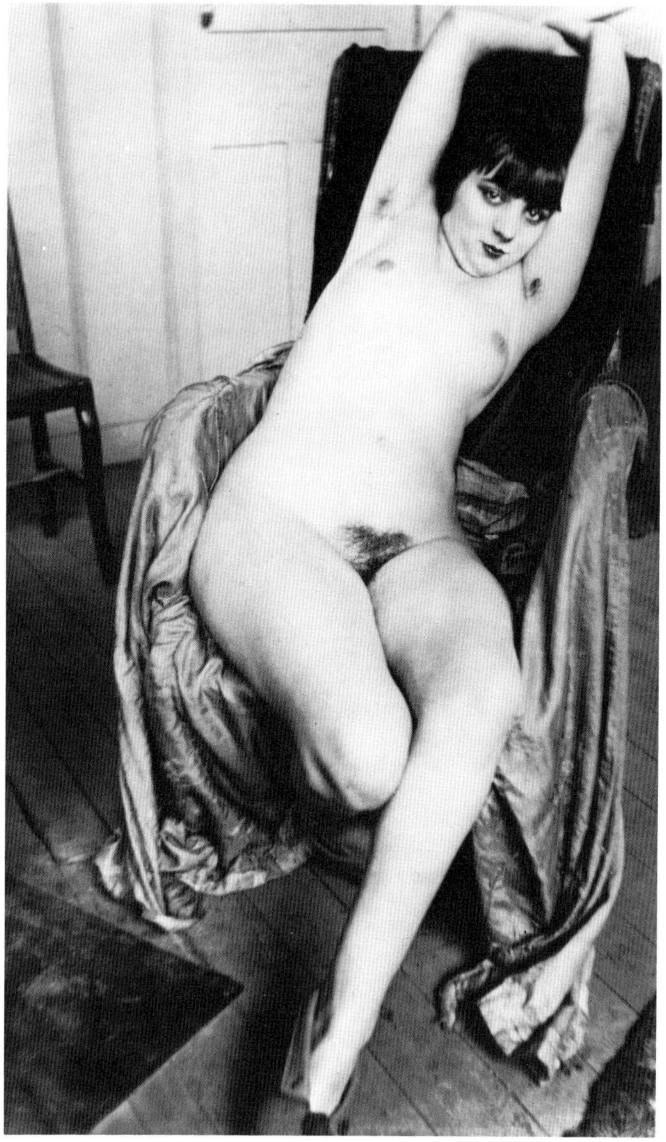

The woman exposes herself, renders herself visible (without gaining in transparency for all that—on the contrary!); the artist does the rest, probes into her, emblematizes her. It is upon the model's body that the artist struggles against death. As in all strategies of seduction, shifting, dodging, diversion come to light (the etymology of seduction, "se-ducere," suggests diversion, divergence, separation).

In her novella *Les relations d'incertitude* ("The Uncertainty Relation"), Anne Walter weaves a quite unusual web of relations between the painter and his model. What is rare, if not all together exceptional, the alchemy of this relationship is described by the sitter herself, a young woman who has the uncanny feeling that she has taken the place of the previous model, a certain Olga, who died under mysterious circumstances. The narrator-model meets the painter Volodia seemingly by chance, although their meeting was in fact cleverly planned in advance. The narrator is progressively and ineluctably bewitched; trapped, she consents to remain so in a manifestly dangerous relationship, a commerce which can only be called diabolical. The sittings exhaust her, but she has fallen under the artist's spell and lets herself be absorbed by him, a certain pleasure of existing in paint captivates her. "I like the studio more and more. The charm of metamorphoses. I become completely different in these paintings; seen from inside, meditated, loved. I don't know who I am, it is Volodia who discovers me little by little. Or does he force me to become that?... Something of me insinuates itself into these canvases, impregnates them, and escapes from me."[69]

Sittings are tiresome and painful as she suffers from cramps and the cold. But their spell makes her put up with everything, and as the painter works away, the sitter identifies with the canvas. "The canvas and I, it's the same thing, we belong to him... Pleased with the effect of a well-placed glaze, he lightly touches my hair, slips down my neck, slides along my waist." But the painter remains unsatisfied, and suddenly, as brutally as a rapist, he pushes the "smooth and rounded end" of a brush into the model's vagina: "pleasant pain," she sighs, swooning, sweating, her eyes closed, wondering if she is victim or accomplice, and certain that she will return to the studio the next day with her cheeks ablaze. This simulacrum of a rape, carried out with the help of an object, makes the painting blossom, "a work so subtle, so pure, and nourished by the most secret recesses of my flesh." The model is now at the painter's complete disposal, subject to his every whim, as docile as clay, "shameless and annihilated," "frightened by the pleasure she glimpsed."

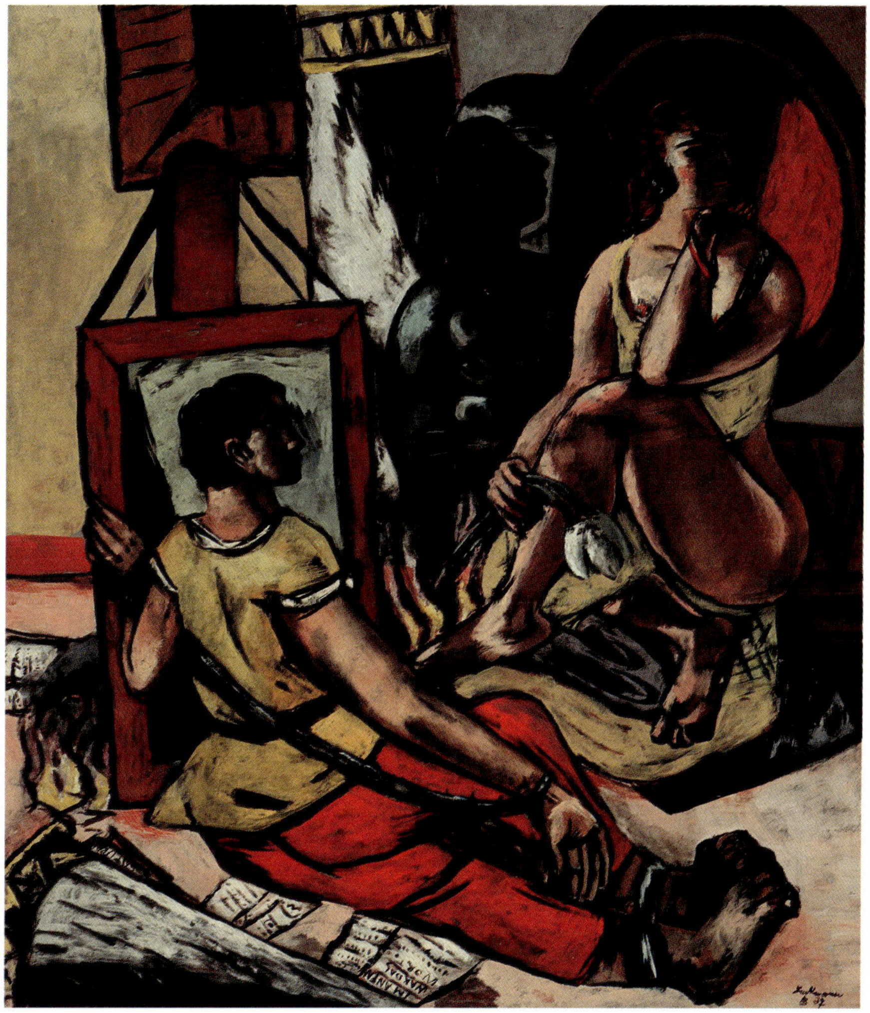

Max Beckmann:
Central panel of The Temptation of St Anthony, *1936-1937.*

Volodia gives his model to various men, observes their lovemaking; he "sells" her (in the most commercial sense of the term), the better to possess her, yet without ever touching her; only the eye is active. No matter what happens to her, the woman does not interrupt the diabolical process, despite its violent and glacial torments. "I will persist, go to the limits of this deviation. Accept everything, and no longer leave the closed, but troubled confines of the work of art... I fall asleep not knowing if I am wanton or forsaken... For Volodia, I am merely the means to a work which is embellished by my suffering." In a ritual celebration, which is perhaps only an ordinary business deal, the model is violated by the painter at the hands of unknown men. This ceremony is repeated without change until the painter dies.

In this brilliant tale, the woman has a sharpened awareness of her role, or of what one might be tempted to call her duty; it is a consequence of the progress of the painter's work. Drained and ravaged by the brutality of the ceremonies, the model nonetheless blooms; she becomes more relaxed. Her wounded look suits her; she plunges into her inner being as the gaze of the painter reveals her to herself. The "insatiable and lusting" eye of the painter, as Gauguin called it, kills her and brings her back to life.

In this continuous ritual exchange between the painter and his model, the roles of the protagonists are probably less clearly defined than it might seem at first. There stands the model in the stark factuality of her physical presence, but how clear is this presence? The painter looks at her very closely, sometimes at very close quarters (Matisse's account of being knee-to-knee with his model). He "zooms in," like a voyeur, an "erectile seer," a voracious ogre, a cannibal. By his gaze he "vampirizes" the vamp, tries to capture the nudity of the woman.

But the woman posing is also an ogress; she attracts the artist, magnetizes his gaze, directs it to the edge of her own self. She is beyond the sex object. She stimulates an energy which does not go

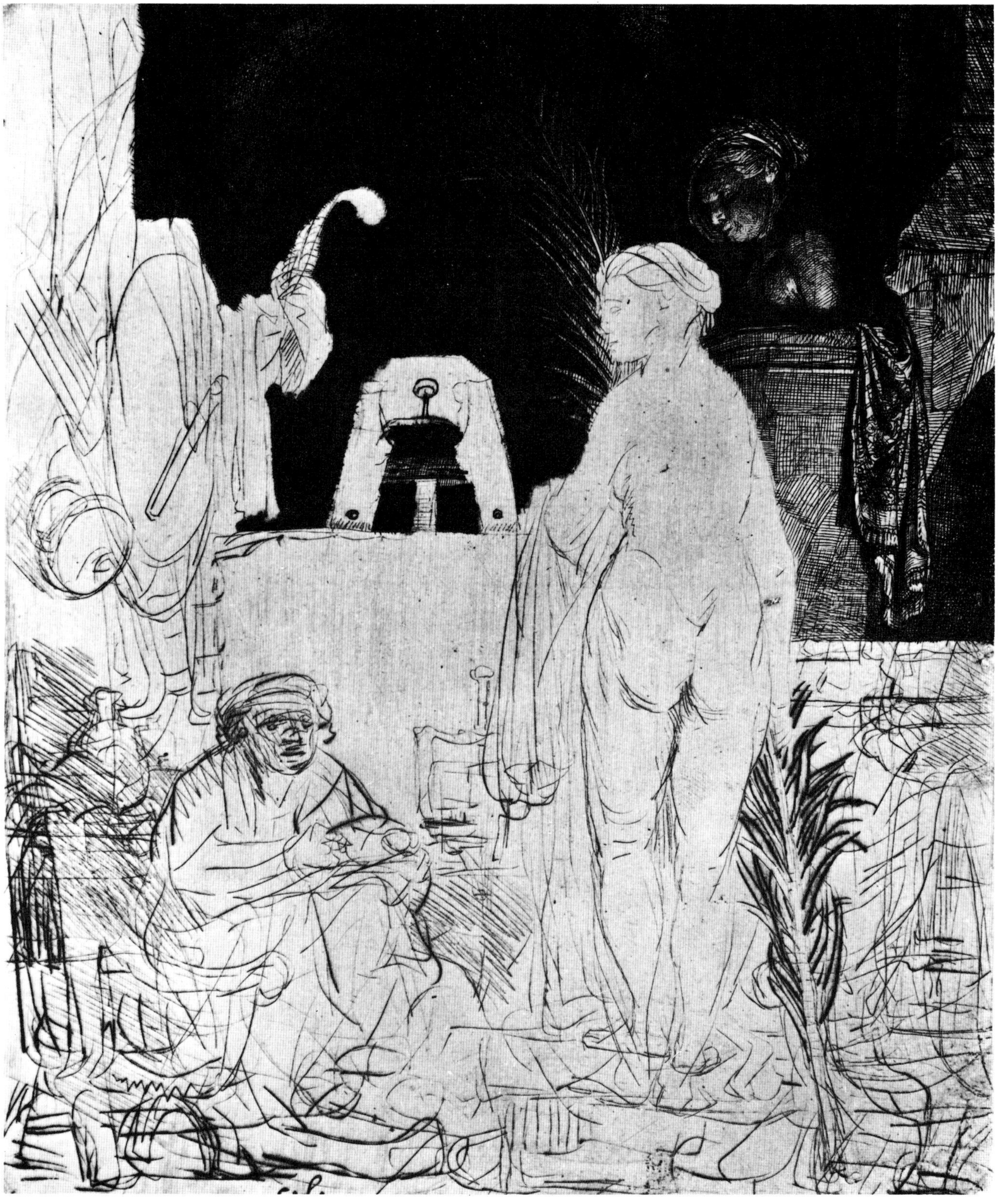

"into" her, but "onto" her, at the surface of her appearance, and which will nourish the canvas or the stone. Gifts and counter-gifts. The relationship exceeds that of mere usefulness. It is a privileged means of access to something that is inaccessible. It is the special realm of essential affinities, of hallucinations. Seduction is inevitable and yet undefinable. To attempt to define it would be to kill it, kill the fascination. It would result in a complete disenchantment; a plain, flat, reality would take over, as in certain failed paintings. Seduction works its troubling wonders only if it preserves its enigmas. As Nietzsche once wrote: "We do not think that truth remains truth when its veil is removed," and, "Art is a lie which makes us understand the truth."

Art and seduction elude the grasp of words, and by this very fact, the rapture is renewed—the rapture, but also the abyss. Circling the model, the artist circles an absent presence. The model, beyond her tangible, physical, earthbound reality, is also composed of emptiness and illusion. The model abolishes reality. What is hidden behind the "trompe l'œil" if not a certain absence? The model seems a simulacrum; she blurs the distinction between reality and illusion. Moreover, her fetish-attribute is often a mirror. The woman who poses for an artist is a sister of Narcissus, but it is through the eye of the painter that she sees herself; it is this very gaze which sends back to her her own image while simultaneously nourishing the creative act.

The artist absorbs the model. The scene between the painter and his mistress-model Sara in Joyce Cary's book[70] highlights this dual relationship. In Magritte's Surrealistic world several works represent an eye that has become detached from the rest of the body and acts as a mirror. It is the strategy of the lure; the artist turns to the model, like the falcon towards a decoy, thinking he will finally find there the reality that has slipped away. He encounters the model as if he were meeting his fate, an abyss into which he falls, sinks, loses himself and is reborn. If the forces of attraction and the power of desire are particularly intense, it is because the artist does not "circumscribe" the model; rather, he is bewitched by her. "The spell is worked by what is hidden," Baudrillard writes.[71]

The artist's and model's eyes cross and clash in a voluptuous duel. They intermingle in the "discreet charm of a silent orgasm."[72] The tactile gaze of the artist desires to form, to bring to light the obscurity and opacity of both the model and world. Between the artist and his model there is, strictly speaking, no exchange of services, but if there were, the only currency possible would be death. The artist strives to capture life in his "live model," the better to immortalize his model. The model

Rembrandt:
An Artist Drawing One of the Virtues, c. 1639.

Henri Matisse:
Study for The Nude in the Studio, *1904.*

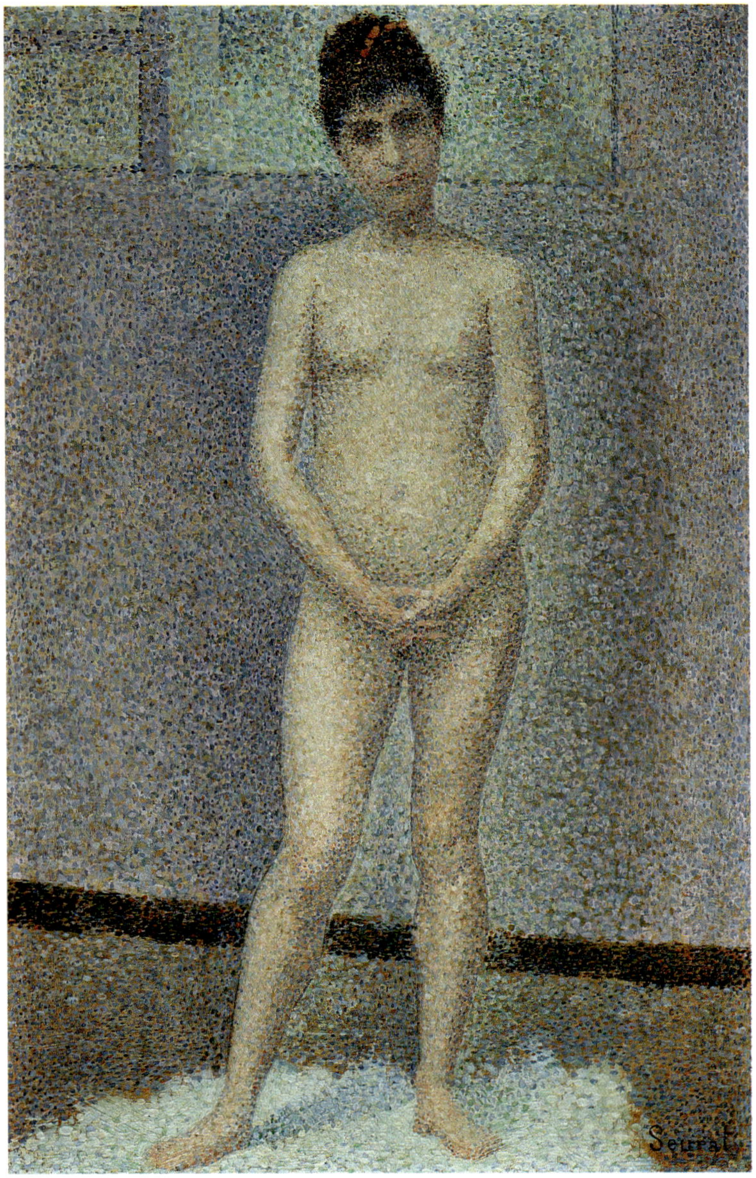

Georges Seurat:
Model Standing, 1887.

sacrifices herself in the present and is reborn in the realm of the intemporal. Jeanne Hébuterne, Amedeo Modigliani's model and mistress, commits suicide on the day after the painter's death.

Beauty, so ardently sought by the artist, partakes of this challenge; she absorbs energy, accumulates it around her, but does not allow the artist to capture her, for none can possess either the infinite or the void. The attraction to this strange void is part of a dizzying experience verging on sensual delight.

Through seduction, the model initiates the artist into his art. The courses in drawing "from the live model" of the academic tradition clearly display the features of some initiation. The artist had to take this necessary step: it was the very essence of his apprenticeship. By studying the live model, he was supposed to learn how to see—perchance to love. Through this semi-public display of nudity, students endeavored to penetrate the enigma. In the silence of the studio, they obstinately tried the key. Violence and passion. Grace and defiance.

Through the impossible schooling in the study of the body, the artist and the model sign a pact, a tacit agreement. The stakes are enormous, unlimited; destinies are played out here. The scope is so great that it cannot be uttered. Death prowls about furtively. The artist and model are invested with considerable power, yet they remain infinitely fragile and vulnerable. There is always the risk, in seducing each other, that they will falter.

"We seduce with our mortality, our vulnerability, the void which haunts us," writes Baudrillard.[73] The woman who poses, the seductress, is never exactly where the artist wants her to be. Her presence short-circuits itself, blinks on and off, vanishes and emerges elsewhere. She is discontinuous, lives her life by slipping in and out. Appearance adorns and dissimulates her. The beautiful model is cruel, hypothetical. On the surface of her various appearances, the desire of the artist endlessly immolates and immortalizes itself.

Seduction oscillates between two poles: between a strategy, the artist's willful, determined obstinate application to his work, the untiring repetition of the sittings, a patient conjuration; and an animality, the nude model's brutal, physical suggestivity, flung into the face of the dissecting gaze, the visual embrace.

The model posing is an absent star enacting the simulacrum of nudity, entrenched behind the infinitely superimposed masks of seduction. She is the object of an almost religious sacrifice, a sort of sacred prostitute surrendering herself to the cold drama of the pose. The artist, the esthetic seducer par excellence, wants to dispossess her, to appropriate a supreme power that is impossible to locate or situate. In sketching the model, or as the French say, "croquant le modèle" (making a "croquis" of, but also, literally, "crunching" the model), the artist seeks to ravish her energy, her beauty, her life... Art is rape, murder, sacrifice, rebirth, and its means are hypnosis, seduction, the orgy of the eye.

The demurely codified ritual of the pose masks a confusion, chaotic fusions, a delirium, desire, bloodthirsty crimes (the question of carnation), magical reincarnations. All of this is worked through the gaze, an oblique gaze which doggedly seeks to elucidate the mystery. The model, who is both powerful and disarmed, awaits the verdict of her image. The artist acts like a god, but a god stricken with doubt; he suspects the model—the crux of the enigma—of possessing its resolution and withholding it for her own benefit.

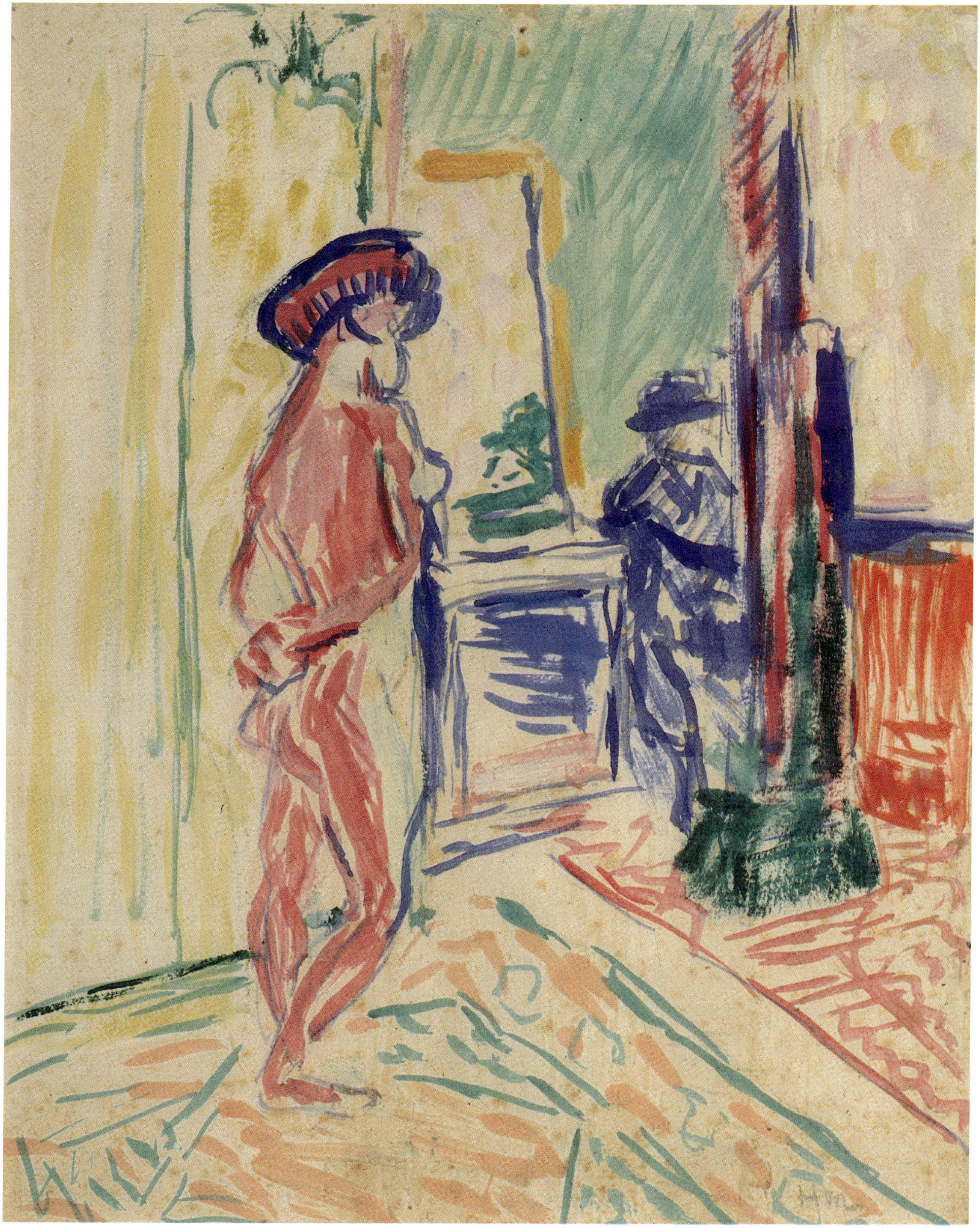

Henri Matisse:
The Studio in Quai Saint-Michel, 1916.

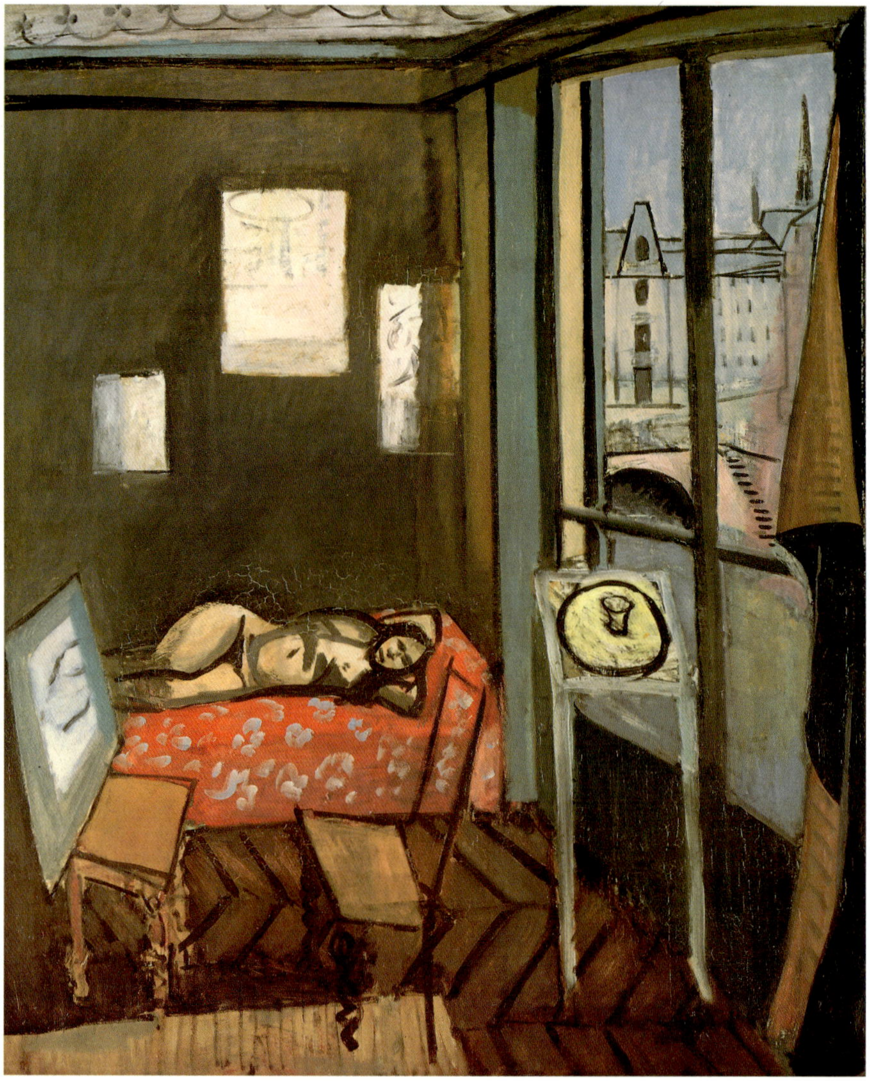

Henri Cartier-Bresson:
Matisse and His Model, 1944.

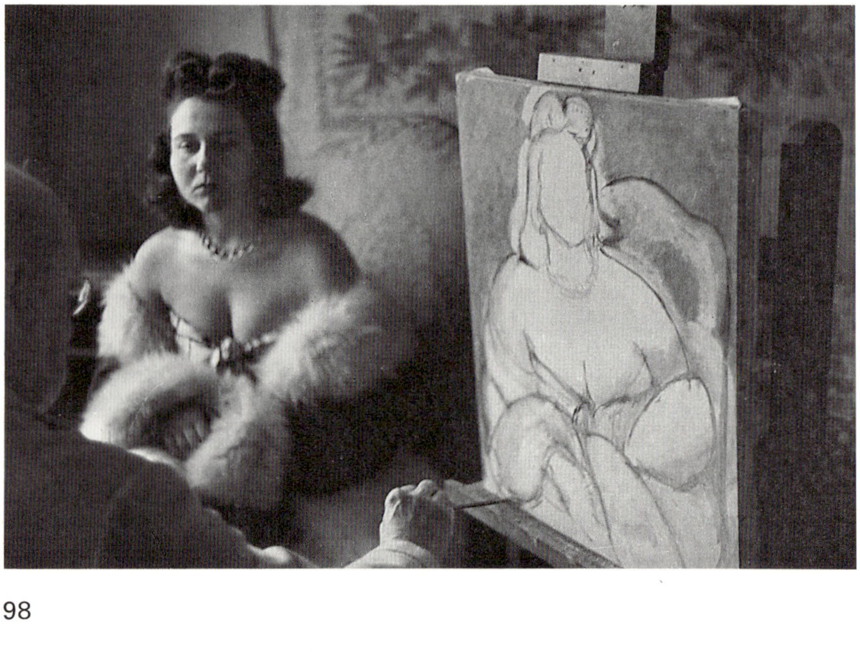

There is a subtle perversion at work. It defies natural order by putting a nude woman at the artist's disposal, a woman which he "uses," which he looks at but cannot touch; a sort of idol placed on a pedestal, shared on occasion as in an academic setting with other voyeurs. The only physical act that is permitted (theoretically speaking, of course), is of a plastic or pictorial nature. It is strongly advised not to cheat. One story, anecdote really, which is the most symptomatic of such stories tells us that Rembrandt was angered by the conduct of a student who, after having shut himself up in his room with his model to paint, undressed himself because of the heat saying to his sitter, "here we are then, like Adam and Eve." The story goes that the master, having observed the scene through a keyhole, furiously chased the naked couple out of the studio with his stick, exclaiming, "Well, now that you know that you are naked, you must leave paradise."[74]

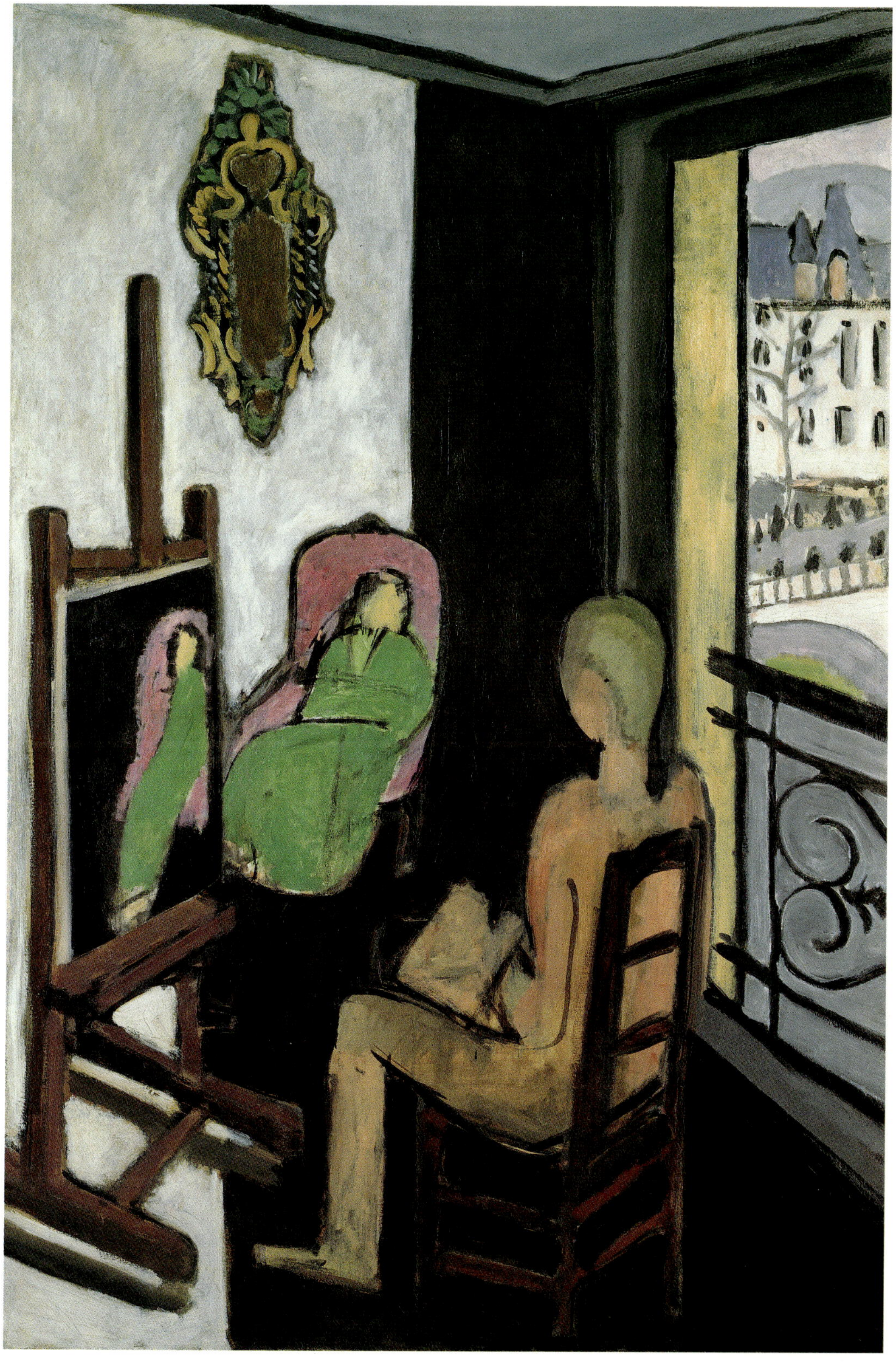

Henri Matisse:
The Painter and His Model, 1917.

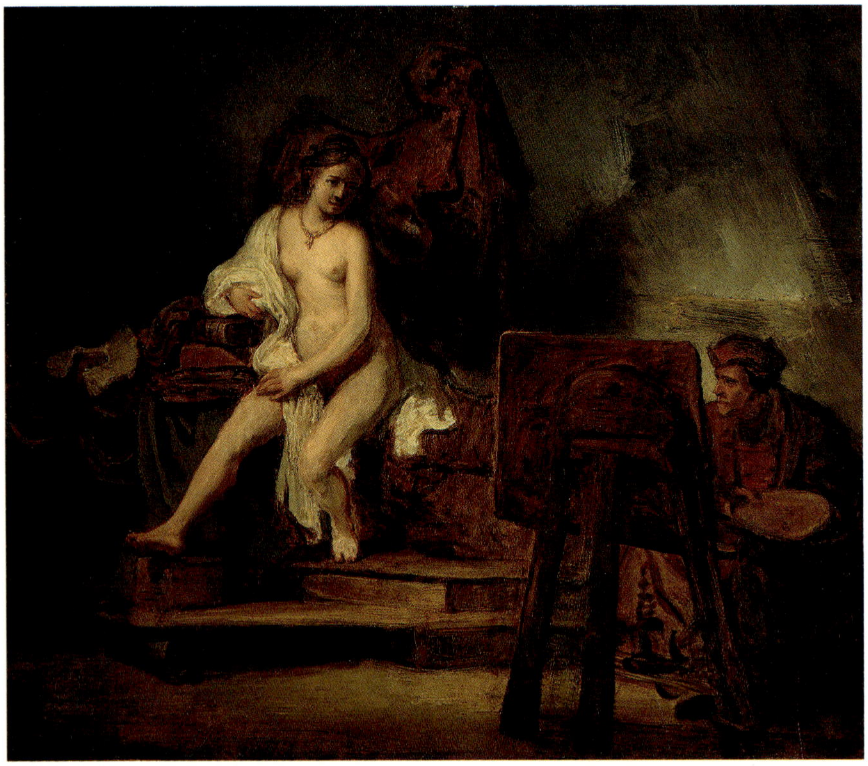

Anonymous (follower of Rembrandt)
A Painter and His Model
(Rembrandt Painting Hendrickje), undated.

The chastity associated with the model (relative and always theoretical) is probably intended to recharge desire through a solemn taboo, to lead it to the brink of the sexual act and to divert it to fertilize the creative work. The energy of love is accumulated, contained, channeled. As in all perversions, there is codification; rules are laid down, a ritual is repeated, relatively immutable in a relatively identical decor. Transgressions are forbidden because they would jeopardize the theatricality necessary to the ceremony which attempts to draw immortality into its web and neutralize the natural effects of death. The staging of the pose is a ritual drama in which several fates are at stake: that of the artist, the model (or more exactly, her image) and, most importantly, the act of painting. No one is completely master of the situation. With almost maniacal care, the academic system fixed to the point of stereotype and conformity the conventions of the pose in order to contain the delirium of fantasy and reassure the protagonists as to the definition of their roles.

Partners in the artist-model relationship may be associated in aggressivity (as in Bacon, for example), in plenitude (Matisse), in unsatisfied tension (Cézanne), or in fulfillment, in enchantment or disenchantment. They are contiguous in their separation or in fusion (Picasso). Ritual exchanges without end. This codification, in light of the "dangers" of the situation, involves a sort of exorcism. The conventions channel the energy, generated by the encounter giving form to what is untamed, transforming bestiality into something sacred, putting a semblance of order into the immensity of the challenge, namely, the will to capture life, and, at the same time, to make it immortal.

Artists and the models cast spells on each other, intimidating one another by the gaze or the pose. As in amorous seduction, they hypnotize each other. The model parades in a statuesque immobility which masks her. She is kin to coquettes, avatar of the witch; her charms frighten, terrorize and magnetize, and thus she initiates the young artist.

The sitter, sacred prostitute, high-priestess transfixed in her incarnated beauty, isolated on her dais, is religiously offered, yet gives herself sexually to none (theoretically of course). The model is also artist. It is no coincidence that throughout the Renaissance and the four succeed-

Albert Marquet:
Fawn-Colored Nude, 1898.

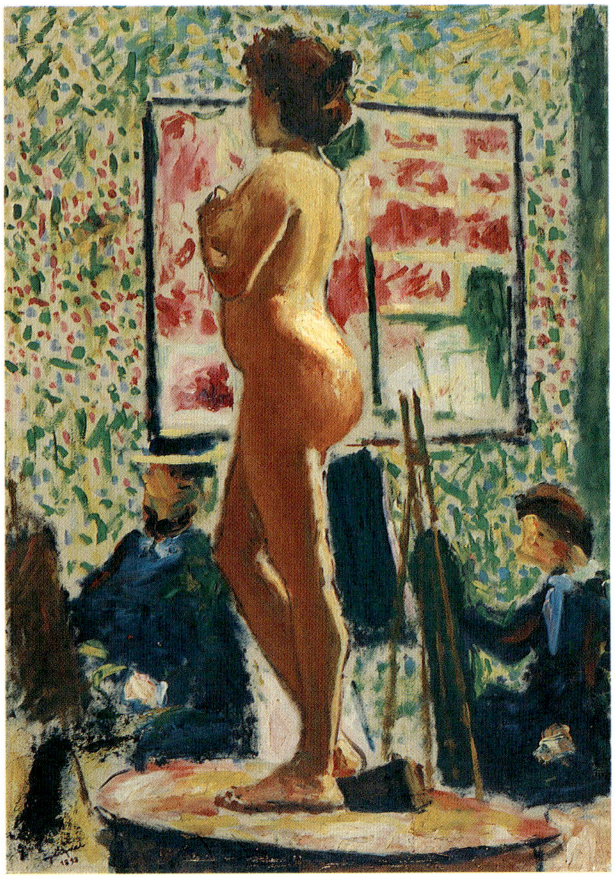

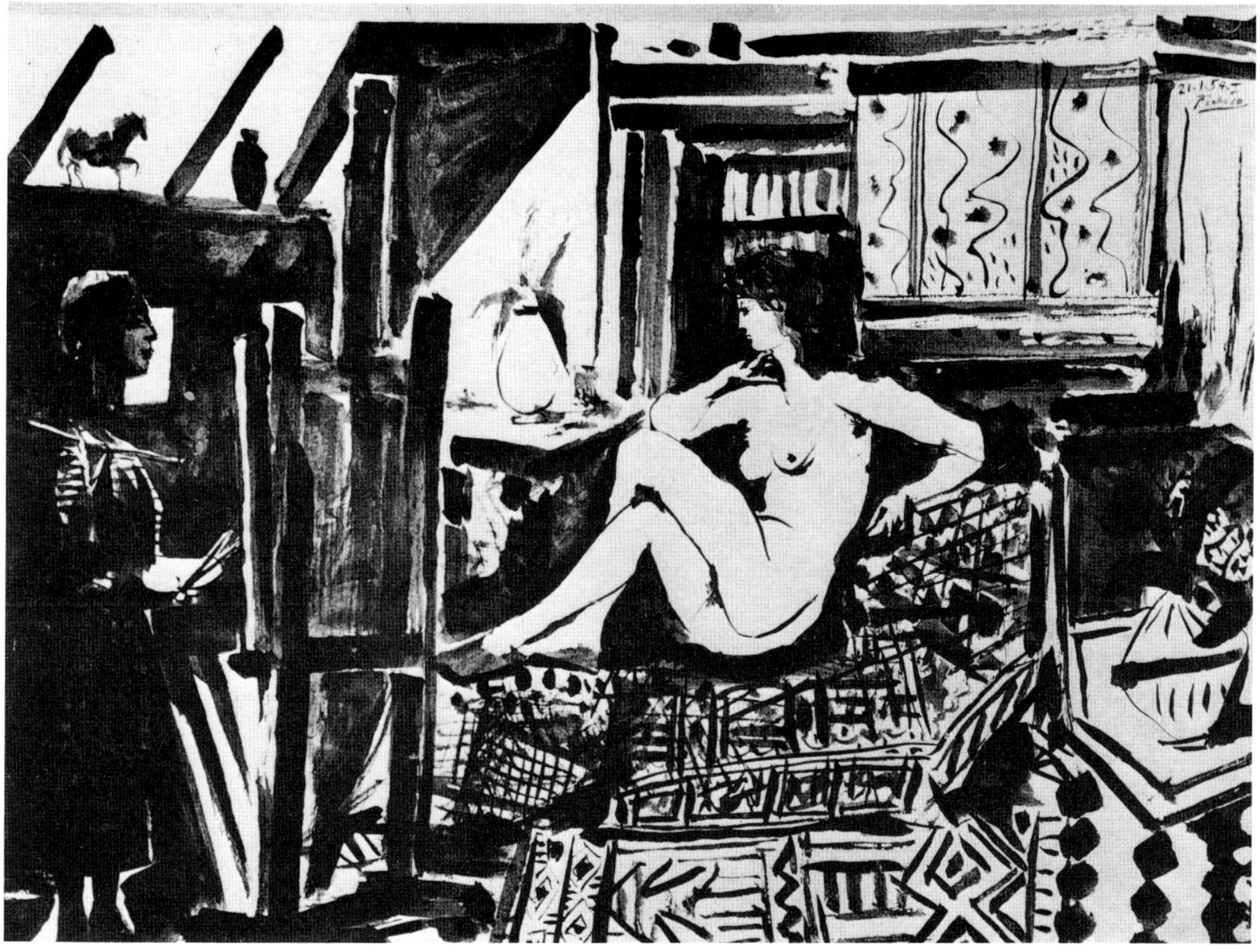

Pablo Picasso:
Interior (Woman Painting and Nude in the Studio), 1954.

ing centuries the allegory of painting, the personification of painting, was represented as a female figure usually draped in the classical style, like the Muses, holding palette and brush. Nor is it by chance that a painter like Picasso who was obsessed with the dangerous and close relationships that arise between artist and model, should represent female painters, thus endowing the model with his own identity as an artist. Could these so very particular relationships also involve a rivalry?

As the model's body can never be reached in its entirety, it may be that the artist sees in this opaque corporeality an envelope hiding unsuspected talents. Conscious of being dependent on the model, the artist guesses that he is himself brought into being by her, and so he may easily suspect her of containing a superior force. He fetishizes her in this way too, attributing to her the ruses of a goddess. Apart from a few, all-too-deceptive appearances, the relationship of the artist to the model is not that of a master to a slave. It is truly a two-way relationship.

By catching the artist's eye, the woman exists; she is the enchantress who, behind the deceptively innocent appearance of sleep, is capable of unleashing madness. She is the seductress, the one who would provoke a parting, create a scandal (from "skandalon," that which brings evil), were her living force not domesticated by the academic ritual. The proof, if proof is necessary, would be the effect of paintings like Manet's *Olympia* or *Déjeuner sur l'herbe*, in which the models are represented as such, and not as "academic" nudes clad in convenient mythological references.

All the while being absorbed in herself, the model is a mediator (her danger being proportional to her effectiveness) between art and the artist. The latter suspects at times that she is only feigning sleep and innocence, and that, behind her slightly weary appearance induced by the lengthy session, are concealed unlimited powers. And so the seduction is never innocent; it upsets and overturns situations and the order of things. In his dizzying experience with the model, the artist is afraid of being engulfed, dispossessed, by this disquieting mediator; he works at executing her icon, but senses that this image is not due solely to the human hand.

The model is surrounded by the aura of a sacred light which fascinates and petrifies the artist. Her sacrifice brings power. Although obscure, the model can give birth to light, and the artist, realizing his debt to her, risks not being tolerated by this protean substitute. Fear is the sister of seduction. The sitter, the seductress, occupies the empty space of an imaginary divinity dreamt up by the creator, but she immediately becomes a tentacular divinity which overflows all bounds and proliferates in an unpredictable fashion.

In the stratagems of the coquette (like Marivaux's Marianne) or the seducer (as in Kierkegaard's *Diary*), each gesture, each move refers, by its theatricality, to a protocol of courtship, to a representation. In the relationship between the artist and his model, the pose elaborated on the dais in a deliberately orchestrated liturgy is also a representation, which the artist evokes in turn by a sort of "mise en abyme," or image within an image.

In being exposed, the body of the model is vitrified, and so demonstrates the impossibility of nudity. It places itself beyond the ken of classification and yet encompasses all classifications. It displays a sort of second skin which—who knows?—may be the artist's second skin. Clothed in artifice, it lends itself better to fetishization. Strictly speaking, there is nothing "natural" in the existence of the model, but she enables the artist to pursue an inaccessible naked truth, which, being unattainable, compels him to produce.

The model, like the strip-teaser invented by the Western world, exhibits a deceptive nudity,

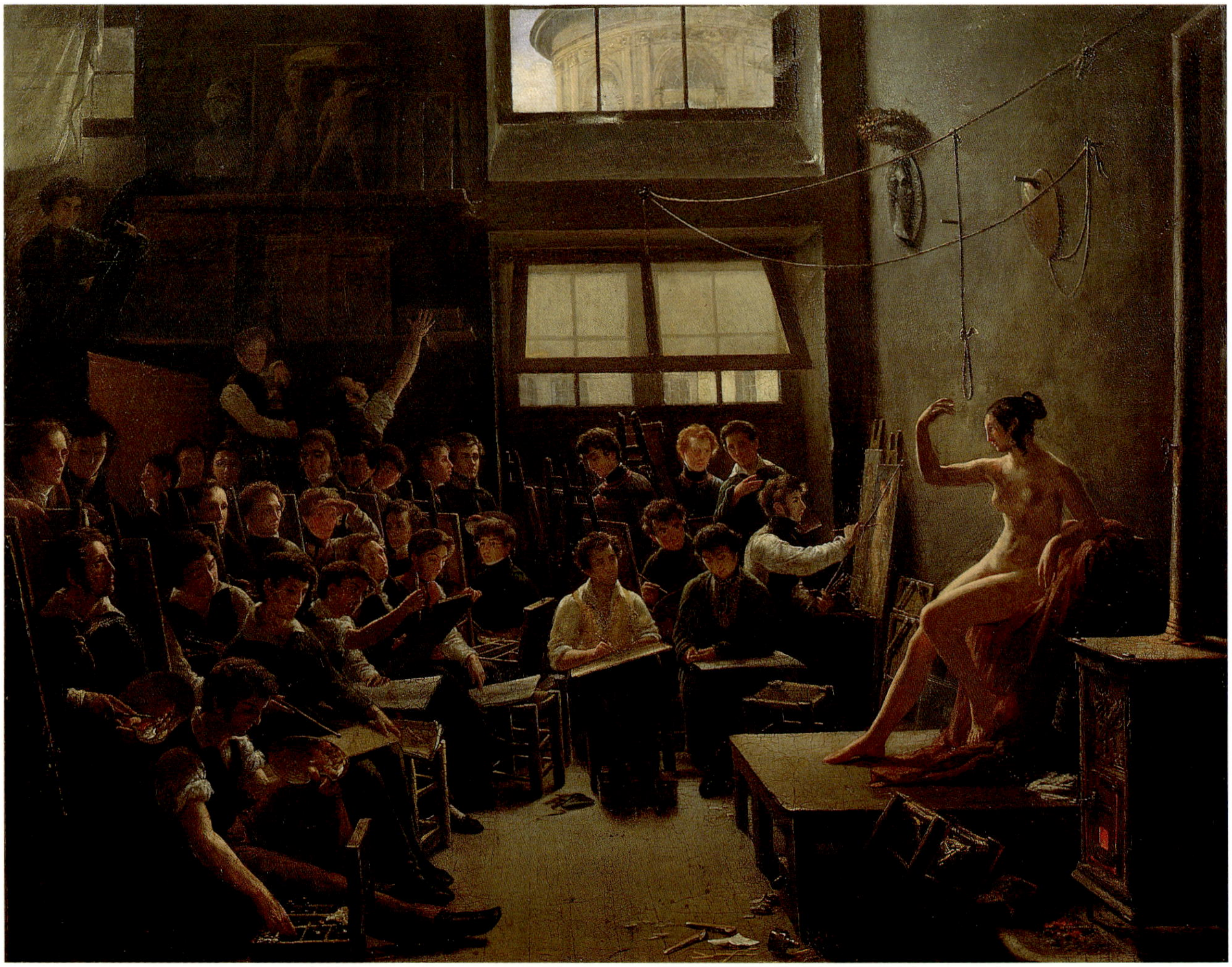

Paul Duthoit:
Young Ladies' Studio, 1896.

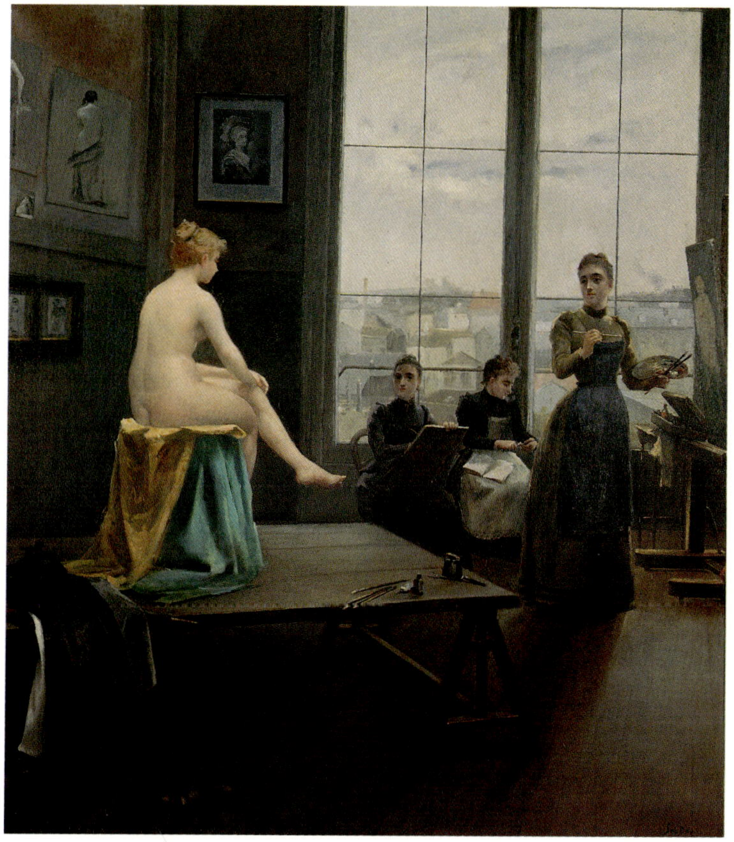

abounds in artifices (fetishes or fetishizable attitudes) without letting herself (and this is logical in the logic of fantasy) be either approached or "taken." The model's disrobing never ends. In both instances, the body stands for an illusion, a simulacrum of nudity in the presence of spectator-voyeurs in need of a mediator. In the immobility of the pose, the model intercedes between art and the artist. In the deliberateness of her show, the stripteaser intercedes between man and sex.

Artists' models, fashion models, and stripteasers learn to maintain a blank, expressionless face in order not to "distract" those who watch them. It is known that Renoir would not tolerate his models seeming to think of something. This is why he especially appreciated the "ideally relaxed" Gabrielle Renard, his maid and the nurse of his children, who regularly posed nude for him between 1900 and 1912. For more than twenty years, Paul Delvaux kept the same model, whom he appreciated not only because of her blond pallor, but also because of her ability to relax, or, in a sense, her ability to be absent. There are countless examples. Through his own style, the artist dresses the model, kills her, "has her hide," and makes her live again in a skin extracted from his own flesh.

Art, like theater and fashion on another scale, is governed by artifice. In the esthetic imagination, the artist makes use of an illusory natural nudity of the model as a spark, a detonator. "Nature" is only a pretext. "The more we study Art," Oscar Wilde wrote in his *Intentions*, "the less we care for

Auguste Massé:
The Studio of Gros's Pupils, 1830.

Attributed to Antonio Palamedes:
The Painter's Studio, undated.

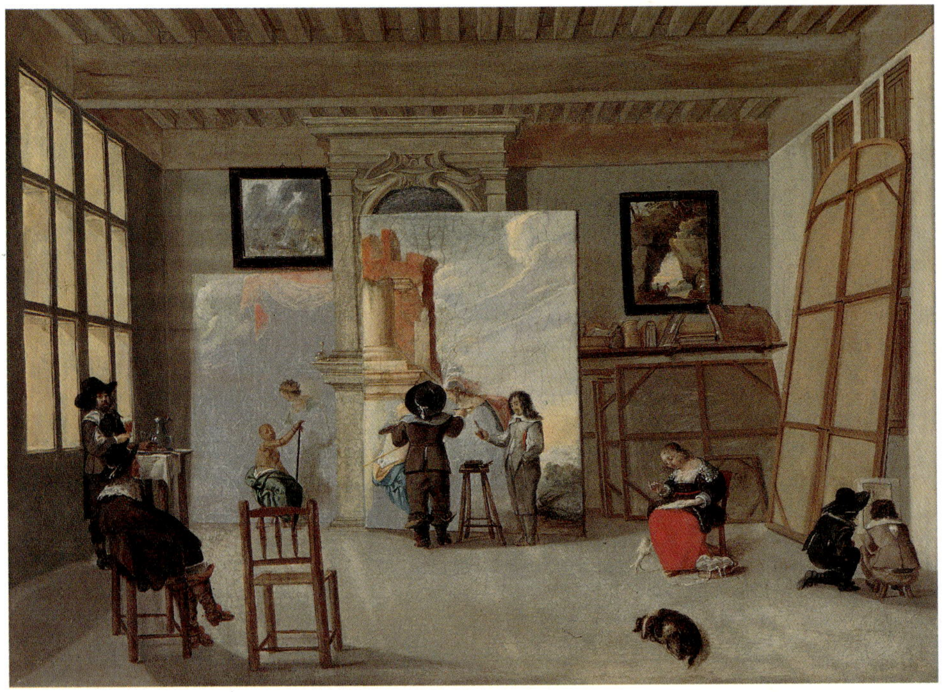

Henri Matisse:
Nude (Male Model), 1900.

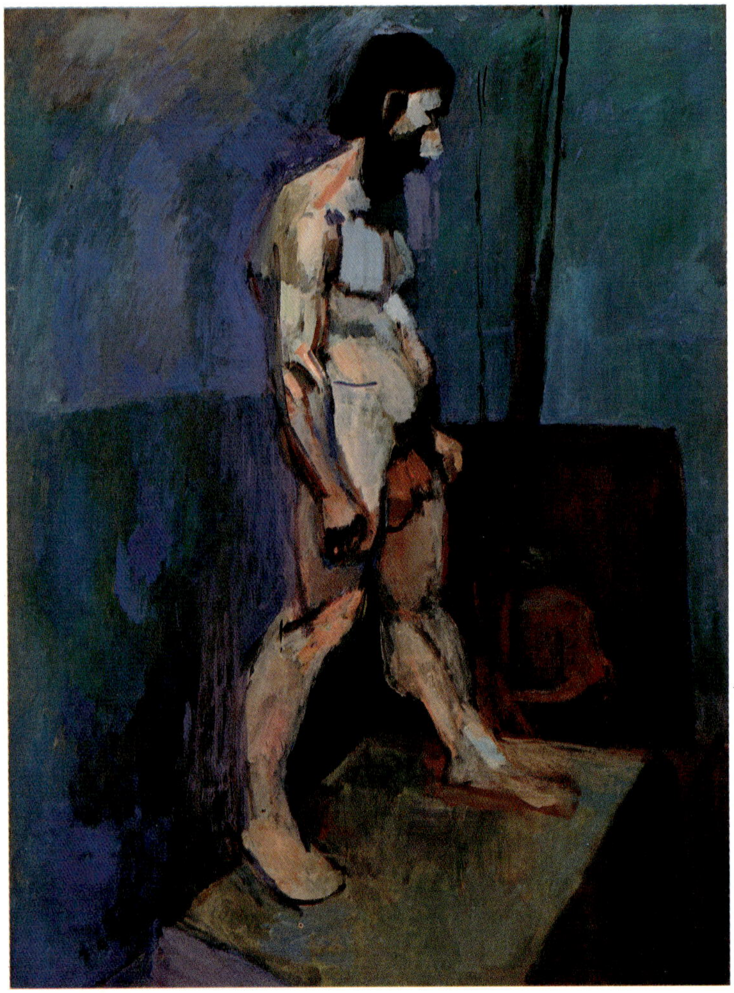

Nature."[75] We may follow the author of *The Picture of Dorian Gray* on this particularly familiar terrain. "Art is our spirited protest, our gallant attempt to teach Nature her proper place."[76] Art is always superior in the complexity of its beauty. It finds its perfection in itself and nowhere else. "Life imitates Art far more than Art imitates Life."[77]

The model, somewhat put at a distance by the studio situation, is never completely an external object; by drawing her body, the artist takes hold of it, interiorizes it, makes it his own, an extension and rebirth of his own body. Then Greeks, who were greatly concerned with illusion, made art a radiant presence in their everyday lives. In the bedroom of newlyweds, they would place statues of Hermes and Apollo so that the future mother could conceive children equal in beauty to the works of art seen during the amorous embrace. A strange twist in the Pygmalion tale!

"The only portraits in which one believes are portraits where there is very little of the sitter and a very great deal of the artist,"[78] declared Oscar Wilde, speaking as a connoisseur. The creator forces life to accept his conditions. Thus Degas, in his attempt to transpose the instantaneous into a durable form, invented complicated postures imitating natural ones and obliged his models to adopt them, poses so difficult to hold, moreover, that

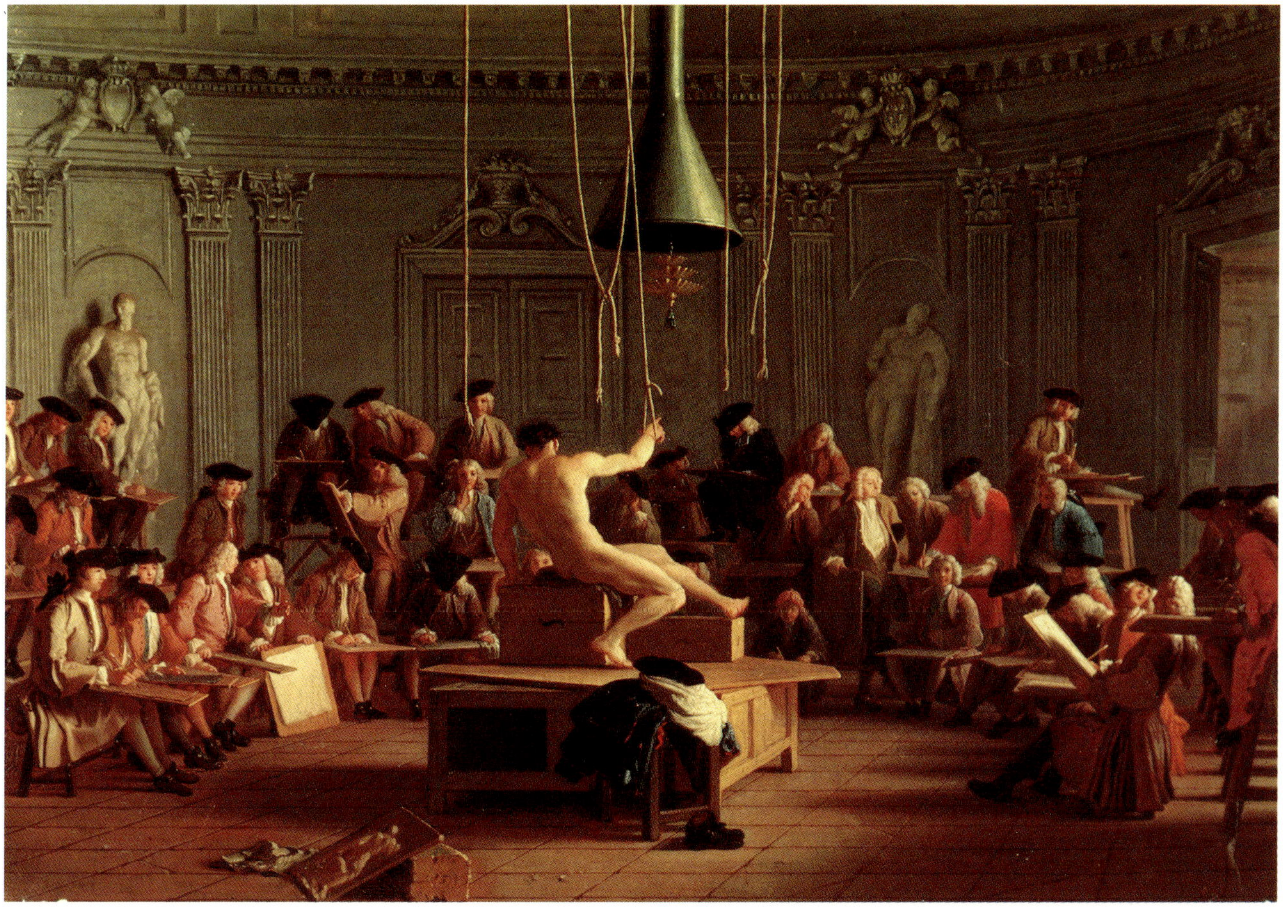

Michel-Ange Houasse:
The Drawing Academy, c. 1715.

Henri Godet:
Model Posing as "Ivy," c. 1898.

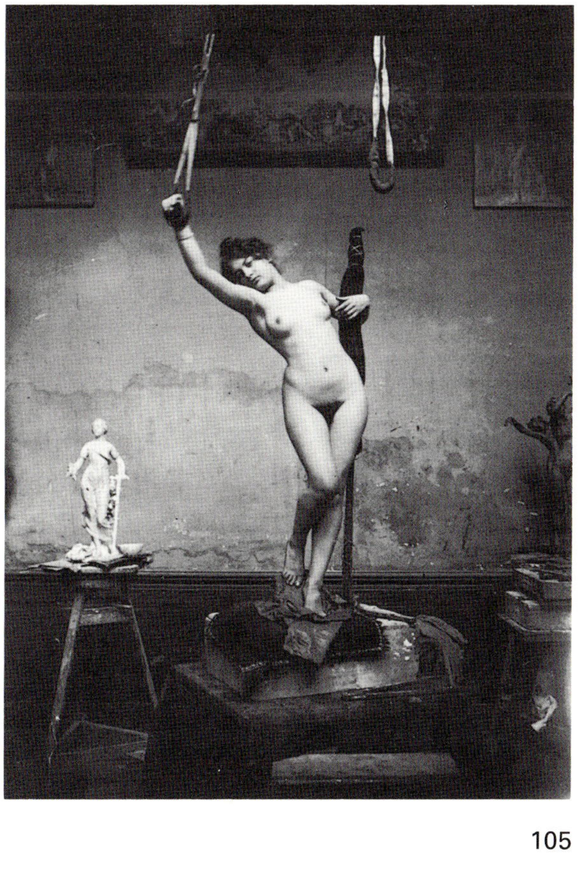

Degas called on the services of photography to take over from his live models; his pictures of contorted attitudes seem nevertheless to have been taken from life.

The pursuit of the model always takes on the appearance of a seduction, of an artificial quest. The artist sets out in search of a model who corresponds as closely as possible to the image he has in mind. This gives rise to a relative dissatisfaction with reality, which always seems to fall short of the imaginary. And so artists take all sorts of material and contingent steps in order to get their hands on a "good" model. Delacroix, writing plainly at the beginning of his *Journal* that he risked the pox with one nineteen-year-old model, did not forget to set down the addresses of those who posed for him. On the backs of his drawings of nudes, Ingres scrupulously noted the names and addresses of the models, so afraid was he of losing them. In his notebooks, Degas indicated the qualities of his models, evaluating them like racehorses. He would rejoice when he had made a "find," which he exhibited to his friends like a filly before a race. As for Renoir, he was always on the lookout for a "bottom that reflected the light well." Manet, who liked the milky-white skin of the redheaded Victorine Meurent, kept her as his favorite model for ten years.

Paul Cézanne:
A Modern Olympia, 1872-1873.

Particular and dangerous relations

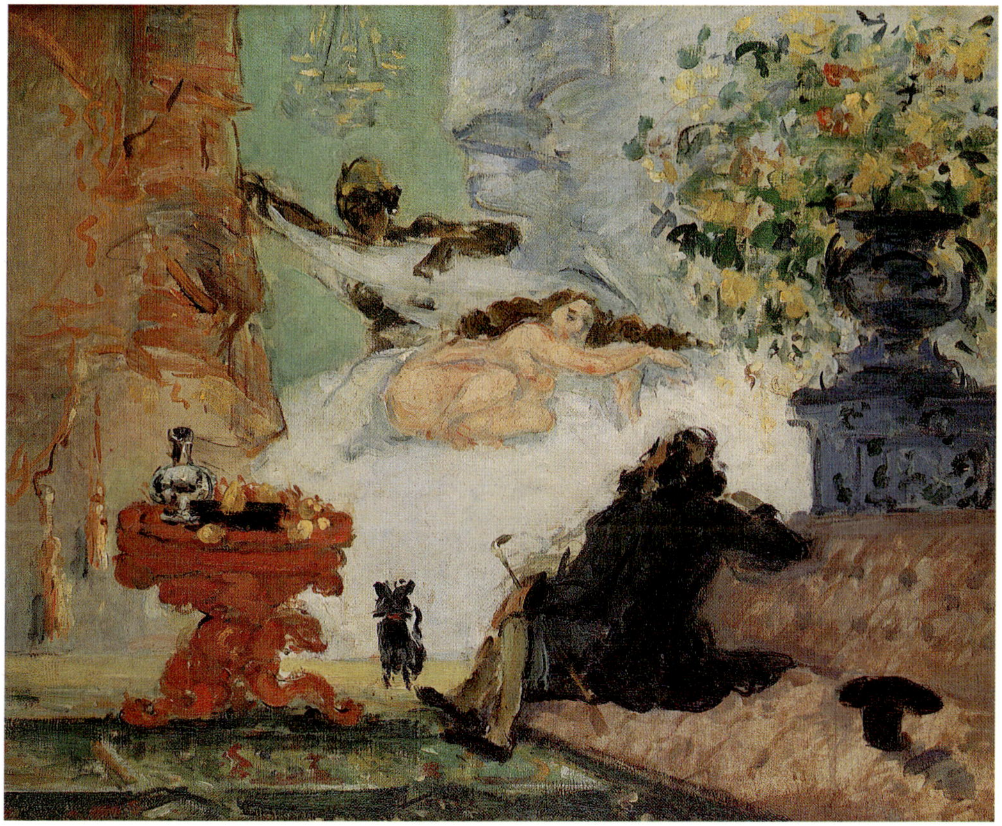

The scandalous model

With Manet, historically, a change arises in the relationship between artist and model. The latter was no longer dressed in a mythological pretext, but in pictorial artifice alone. Small wonder, then, that when it was presented at the Salon des Refusés in 1863, *Le Déjeuner sur l'herbe* raised an unprecedented outcry. After having savored the delights of Cabanel's *Venus*, visitors burst out laughing when they came to Manet's canvas. Contemporary critics lashed out with corresponding verve. "Manet will have talent the day he has mastered drawing and perspective; he will have taste the day he renounces subjects chosen deliberately to create a scandal... We do not consider it a very chaste undertaking to have sat a woman down in the woods, clad in nothing but the shade thrown by overhanging leaves, and in the company of students wearing berets and frock-coats. That is a quite secondary matter and I regret, much more than the composition itself, the intention which inspired it... M. Manet wants to achieve celebrity by shocking the bourgeois... His taste is corrupted by a love of the bizarre." The picture inspired scores of outraged descriptions: "A common *bréda*,[1] as naked as can be, lounging shamelessly between two guardians as well dressed as can be in coat and tie... These two characters look like high-schoolers on holiday, perpetrating some enormity to play at being men; I search in vain for what this unseemly logogriph could mean."[2]

Antonin Proust alone gives a somewhat sympathetic account of the genesis of *Olympia* and *Le Déjeuner sur l'herbe*. "One Sunday in Argenteuil, on the eve of the day he painted *Le Déjeuner sur l'herbe* and *Olympia*, we were lying down on the river bank, watching the white skiffs passing by on the Seine... Some women were bathing nearby. Manet's eyes were glued to the flesh of the women as they came out of the water. 'So it seems I have to paint a nude. Well, I'll paint them a nude, then! When we were in the studio, I copied those women of Giorgione, the women with the musicians. It is a very dark painting. The background has receded. I am going to do that over again, and do it with all the transparency of the atmosphere, with figures like the ones we see over there. I'll be torn to pieces. They'll say that I have got my inspiration from the Italians after having got it from the Spaniards.' "[3]

So Manet is supposed to have exclaimed "I'll paint them a nude!" What a program! There is something vigorously new in his tone (no pun intended), and yet the history of painting throughout the centuries had been full of nudes. Manet relegated these nudes of the past to the props room, only the better to use them as models. His picture is full of borrowings from the *Country Concert*, *Moses Saved from the Nile*, the *Surprised Nymph*, the *Judgment of Paris*, and various river allegories. And yet, the *Déjeuner* is simply a rural outing, a picnic around the figure of Victorine undraped not like a goddess, but like a model taking a rest between two poses. What the painter had unveiled was the behind-the-scenes of the open-air academy.

Odilon Redon's reaction to the *Déjeuner* is singularly eloquent. "The painter is no intellectual if, after having painted a nude woman, we are left with the feeling that she will immediately dress again... There is one, in Manet's *Déjeuner sur l'herbe*, who will hasten to put her clothes back on after the discomforts of the cold grass, next to the young men devoid of ideals who accompany her."[4] Contrary to traditional painting, with the *Déjeuner* the nude has become a model and not vice versa. This work, which Manet himself called *"la partie carrée"* ("the four-way party"), presents the illusion of the prosaic. It refers as well to a fashion of the period, that of taking students and models to "a picturesque site, a sort of great natural park where a vast clearing was well exposed to light from the sky, and near the wood a pond, reflecting the upside-down images of the great trees. A few models were hired for the expedition; they were asked to walk, sit and run, either nude or clothed in drapery; mythology was right there, alive in front of us."[5] The models, too, were very much alive.

In Manet's painting, on the contrary, there is no drapery, no mythology, just the rather plump forms of Victorine and her coarse feet betraying her lowly origins. Where artifice was concerned, painting triumphantly took over from accessories. For the Emperor, however, decency has been outraged; the painting offends virtue! In spite of all common sense, art and morality were confused.

In a striking contrast, the model, with her portly forms and earthy flesh bared to the eye, is seated in the company of two men wearing the dark three-piece suits which had recently become popular in nineteenth-century fashion. Remarkable contrast! The model no longer strikes a pose but takes a

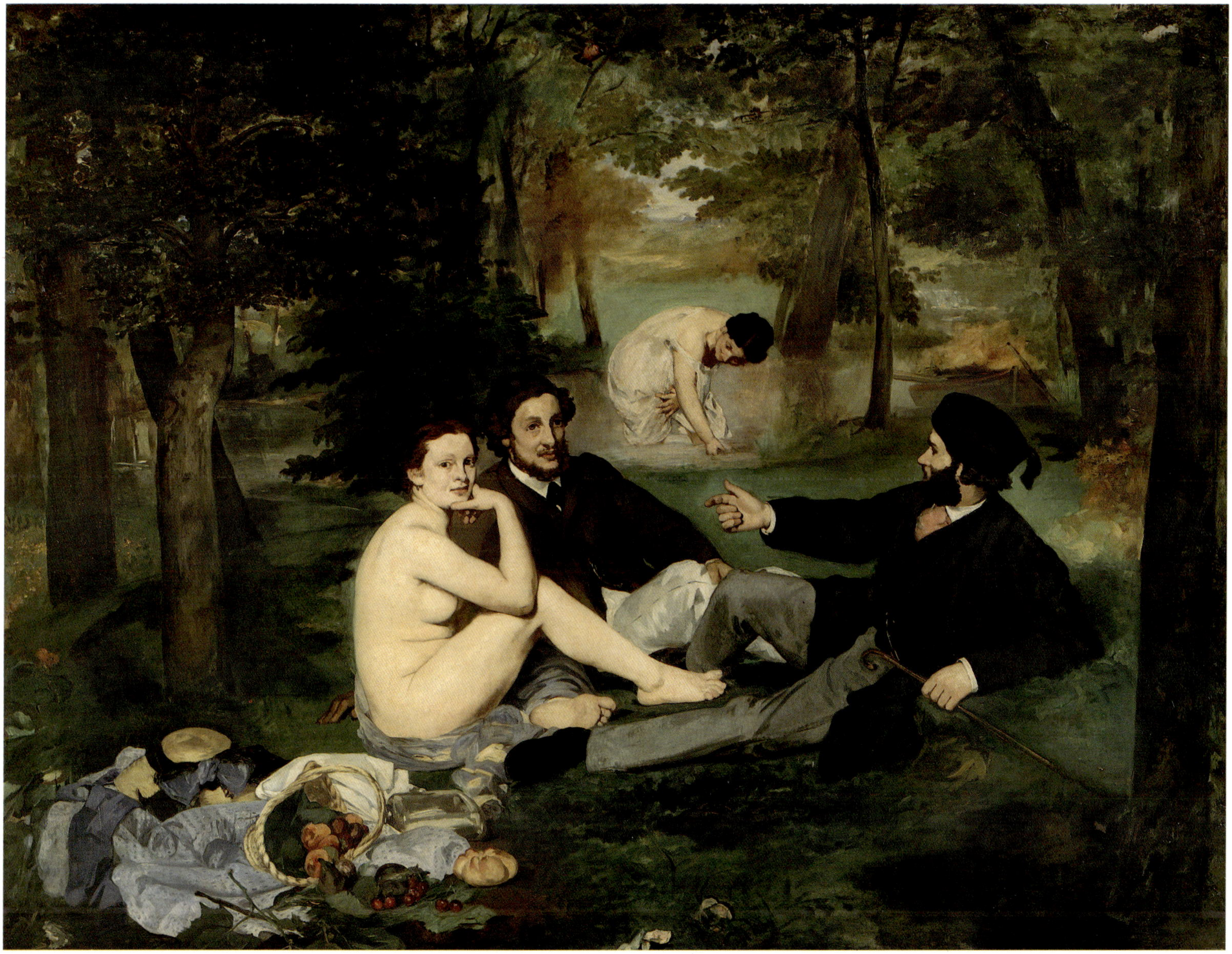

Edouard Manet:
Le Déjeuner sur l'herbe, 1863.

pause. Jumbled still life cleverly composed by the artist's brush, the food spread before the model attests to the sensuality of an "off-season" repast complete with cherries and figs. Make no mistake about it; there is nothing "natural" here. There is something grating about the ease with which the formally dressed men chat about who knows what next to the arrogant nudity of this woman, who has turned her head to face the spectator, himself suddenly turned into a voyeur caught in the act. The woman may not be very "seductive," but the picture works its spell; it has a grating charm. Manet's contemporaries, not daring to let themselves be seduced, resorted to uproarious laughter to hide their uneasiness—not to say fear.

What, indeed, is going on here? An overturned basket displaying its contents, clothing lying discarded on the grass in a pleasantly picturesque confusion, a conversation caught just as one man is listening to another argue a point, and then... and then, there is this woman with her incongruous nudity, who looks as if she were "somewhere else"—but where? Absolutely no complicity with the decor, no exaggerated lassitude either; just an absence. She is "offsides," her presence is connected to nothing, justified by no narrative. And, finally, to know that it was the practice to plop models down in the outdoors from time to time explains very little. The painting continues to intrigue us, and that is why the scandal was repeated (which is fairly rare for a scandal, and would be absurd for a scandal which only touched upon morality); but once again, let there be no mistake, it was above all a question of painting.

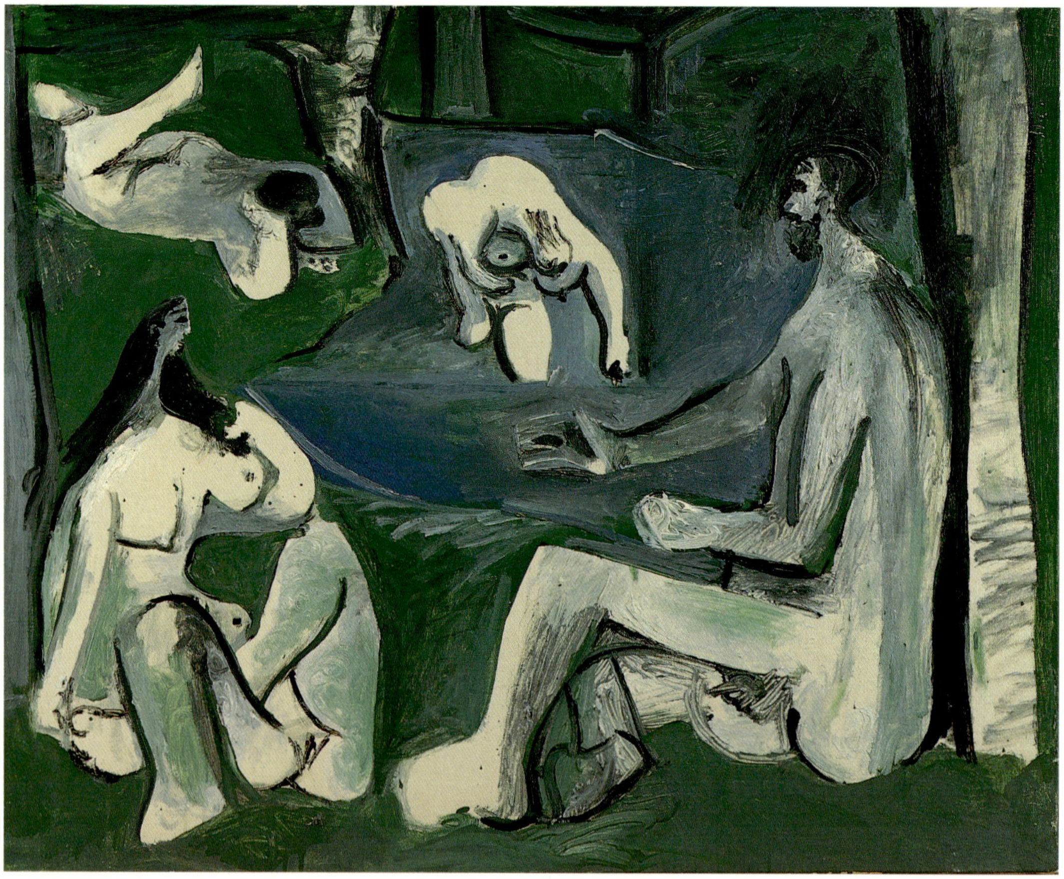

Pablo Picasso:
Le Déjeuner sur l'herbe after Manet, 1961.

The presence of Victorine, the model resting in between poses, is indecent not because she is nude—her attitude is much more modest than that of many a Venus from previous centuries—but because she is nude next to men who are dressed to the hilt and act as if this were nothing out of the ordinary. In no way do they seem concerned with her. Paradoxically, the place she occupies is empty, like a protruding hole, an evident and silent gap whose silence echoes—in a suspended time—the conversation of the men. The woman coils about herself, enclosed in her body, but her gaze, which is intentionally expressionless, without any identifiable content, remains unfathomable. Where does it lead? Towards the eye of the painter, or towards that of the spectator; towards some abyss, or nowhere at all?

Picasso, in his craving for historical references in his later years, also took painting as a model and enthusiastically tackled his fetish masterpieces, namely the *Meninas* of Velázquez, Delacroix's *Women of Algiers*, and *Le Déjeuner sur l'herbe*. Already in 1929 we find him scribbling on the back of an envelope this prophetic phrase: "When I see Manet's *Déjeuner sur l'herbe*, I tell myself: some suffering for later."[6] Between 1954 and 1961, he recomposed the *Déjeuner* in a series of works that undress the protagonists, move them around, remove one of the figures, render even more indisputable the relationship between the painter and his model; a confrontation without being one. The combined atmosphere of an outing and an open-air studio, with boaters resting, straw hats and food, a great Cézannian bather testing the temperature of the water, artists on a spree and models available for a pause. Intermission.

Manet's *Olympia* created a resounding scandal too. As Zola remarked, this canvas is "truly the painter's flesh and blood. It contains him entirely and contains only him."[7] Moreover, Manet would keep *Olympia* with him throughout his career, taking it along to his successive homes and studios. Zola was one of the few contemporaries who realized the intentions of *Olympia*'s incestuous father. "For you, a painting is simply the pretext for an analysis. You needed a nude woman, and you chose Olympia, the first one who happened along; you needed some light and luminous touches, and you added a bouquet; you needed a few dark touches and you placed a negro woman and a cat in one corner. What does all of this mean? You scarcely know yourself, nor do I. But what I do know is that you have admirably succeeded in doing the work of a painter, the work of a great painter; that is, by energetically translating into a particular language the truths of light and shade, the reality of objects and creatures."[8]

Edouard Manet:
Olympia , 1863.

And as Paul Valéry points out in a very dense text: "Olympia shocks, exudes a sacred horror, asserts herself and triumphs. She is scandal, idol, power, and the public presence of a miserable mistery of Society. Her head is empty: a black velvet ribbon separates it from the greater part of her being. The purity of a perfect line encloses the Impure par excellence; she whose function requires the blissful and candid ignorance of all modesty. A bestial Vestal devoted to absolute nudity, she makes one ponder over what is hidden and preserved of primitive barbarity, or of ritual animalism in the customs and deeds of prostitution in the great cities."[9] Marcel Proust, in *The Remembrance of Things Past*, has Oriane de Guermantes speak of *Olympia* in terms nuanced with reticence: "Her place is perhaps not quite in the Louvre." The duchess may well have seen there an image of Odette, the *demimondaine* who, contrary to the duchess's wishes, became the wife of the refined Swann.

And yet Manet cannot be accused of outright savagery. At *Olympia*'s feet, references abound: the *Venus Pudica* of Antiquity revised by Titian's *Venus of Urbino* (whose little dog has become a cat), Velázquez's *Venus with a Mirror*, Goya's *Maja Desnuda*. These pictorial allusions are further artifices that attempt to dress the model in another way. The scandal of *Olympia* was of a very peculiar kind. It was not the worldly scandal of the *Woman Bitten by a Snake* by the contemporary sculptor Clesinger, who used Madame Sabatier for a model; nor that provoked by Chassériau's nude paintings

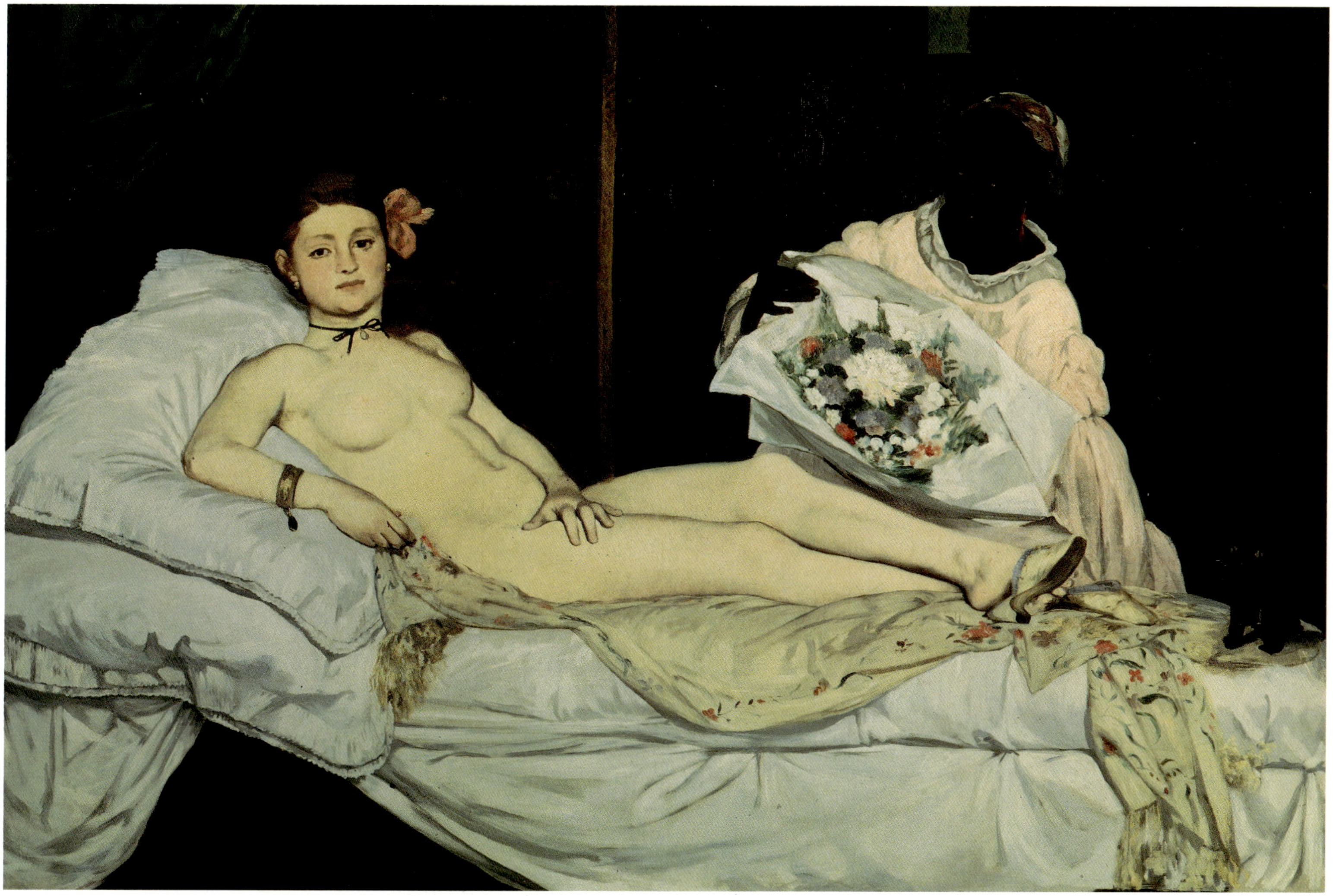

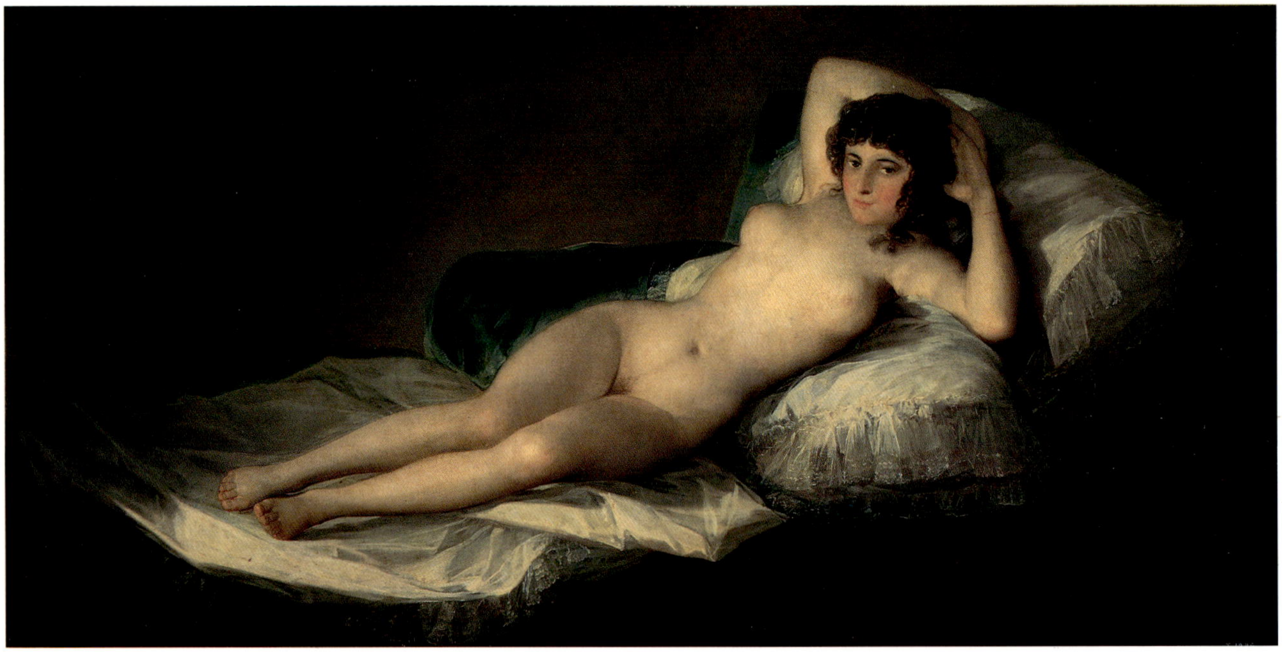

Francisco Goya:
The Maja Nude, 1800-1803.

of his mistress, the courtesan Alice Ozy, which drew the fire of ribald, but finally quite flattering verses.

There is a further "fault" in the fact that Manet granted as much importance to a slipper as to a bouquet, a black cat, a rumpled bedsheet. The scandal was repeated several times: when the painting was first shown in public at the Salon of 1865, the same year at the Exposition Universelle, and in 1890, when it was given to the Nation by a group of friends and collectors. The work then remained for a rather long time in the purgatory of the Musée du Luxembourg. The Louvre welcomed Manet, yes, but not his *Olympia*. The attitude of this institution makes one think of those lukewarm friends who are slow to accept the new mistress of one of their number. There was yet another commotion in 1907 when *Olympia* finally crossed the sacrosanct threshold of the Louvre and was hung next to the *Grande Odalisque* of Jean-Dominique Ingres. There was a last storm in 1932 on the occasion of a major Parisian retrospective.

That Olympia was nude, nothing out of the ordinary there; that she was in contemporary undress, that was completely unacceptable! She was transfigured not by the artifices of idealization or mythology, but by those specific to painting itself. The rather short legs of Victorine Meurent, her high-set breasts, her square face and pointed chin, her unaristocratic hands, and her cold eyes were set down in broad brushstrokes with the "stark brutality of fact." The subject of the picture is explicit. Without resorting to any symbolic ruses, Manet bluntly painted the picture of a prostitute lounging on her bed, waiting for her next client.

In Manet's time, there were many photographs of naked prostitutes boldly displaying their charms, a kind of business card to inform clientele. *Olympia*, steeped in the spicy fragrance of the harem and the Second Empire bordello, indifferently receives from the hands of a negro servant—nanny and go-between—an offering of flowers, which emerges from the dark background like fireworks. A further derisive twist is the fact that the nickname of Olympia (and of Olympe) was very common among the successful *cocottes* of the day; the rival of the *Dame aux Camélias* and the fatal doll of Hoffmann's *Tales* bear some traces of this. There is nothing in this painting, either in its subject or title, which is not directly intelligible. At the Salon, Manet's mother blushing, explained to her friends that Edouard could paint very well when he wanted, but that he was letting himself be led astray by the unwholesome company he kept! No one was fooled.

For having so brutally overturned the taboos, Manet was showered with scorn. Once again, virulent critics loosed their caustic epithets: "What is this yellow-bellied odalisque, this ignoble model picked up who knows where?" The crowds press together as if at the morgue to see Manet's gamy *Olympia*. An almost infantile ignorance of the basic elements of drawing, an inconceivably vulgar point of view. This brownish redhead is perfectly unsightly. The white, red and black together make an awful racket in this picture.[10] "The exhibition now has its buffoon... Among all the other artists, there is a man who has decided to turn somersaults and stick out his tongue... Never have eyes beheld such a spectacle before, nor once so cynical in its effect: this 'Olympia,' this female gorilla," guffawed in the *Grand Journal* a certain Amédée Cantaloube, whose name has so very justly fallen into oblivion.

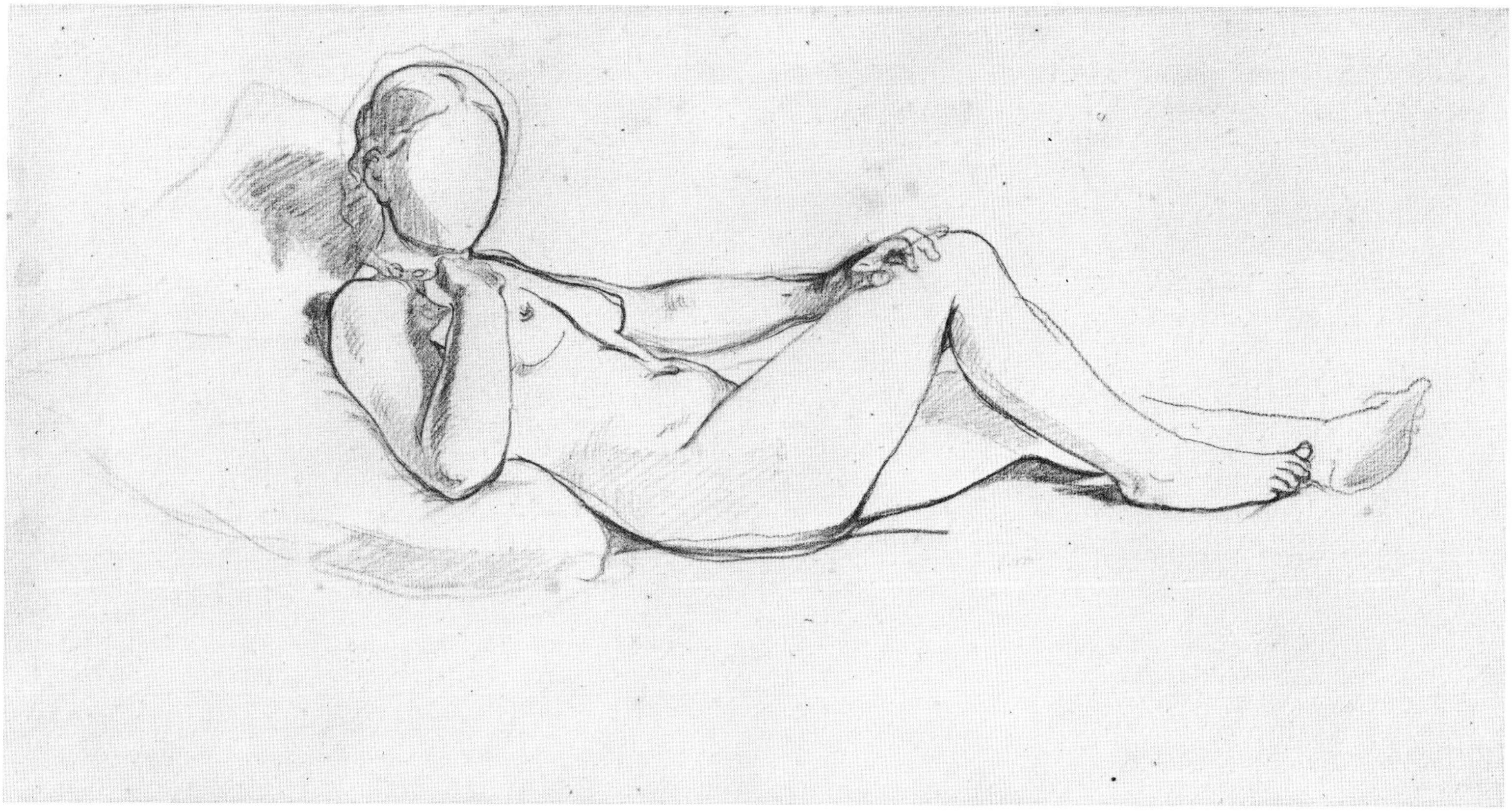

Edouard Manet:
Study for Olympia, *1863.*

Théophile Gautier, who had loudly applauded Manet's first efforts, joined the ranks of his detractors, but with a nuance: "In the eyes of many, it would suffice just to laugh and pass by; but this would be a mistake. M. Manet is not just anyone; he has his school, his admirers, and even fanatics; his influence extends farther than we think. M. Manet has the honor of being dangerous. The danger has passed now. Olympia is not to be explained in any way whatsoever, even in taking her for what she is, a sickly model lying on a sheet. The tonality of the flesh is dirty, the modeling non-existent. The shadows are indicated by more or less wide bands of shoe polish. What can one say of the negro woman bringing a bouquet wrapped in paper and the black cat leaving the soiled tracks of its paws on the bed? We might excuse ugliness; an authentic, a studied ugliness relieved by some splendid color effect. But here, there is nothing more, we are sorry to say, than the wish to attract attention at all cost."[11]

But what is it that worries and shocks the most, the subject or its pictorial treatment? In the obvious reference to Titian, the public and press saw an insult, a blasphemy, while for certain painters and writers, *Olympia* became a sort of prototype. Gauguin studiously copied it. Cézanne interpreted it, adding a client with a top hat. Picasso parodied it and included two clients, one of whom was a self-portrait in the altogether, a surprising "self-nude."

Michel Leiris waxed ecstatic over the little ribbon tied around Olympia's neck. In this "night-trimmed ribbon," the writer sensed "a cruel wound... the unutterable, the ineffable. The last obstacle to complete nudity, the ribbon—almost a string—around the neck, with its natty bow like a ribbon that seals a package containing a gift, forms above the sumptuous offering of the two breasts a double loop which apparently could be easily untied merely by pulling on it."[12] Paul Valéry celebrated the "Triumph of Manet in the bestiality of the cold and nude Olympia, a monster of banal love flattered by a negress," while Bataille sang the praises of the "revolution" effected by the painter, the "acerbic overthrow" of the history of painting and one's relation to the model. Manet inaugurated a "rogue's gallery." "*Olympia*," Bataille explains, "is the first masterpiece over which crowds of viewers laughed an immense laugh." Bataille saw in this symptom the beginning of the destruction of the subject, as well as the transformation of the model. Manet, he writes, "introduced disorder into the pose."[13]

It is true that very early on, Manet could barely put up with the tyranny of Thomas Couture's teaching, and, among other things, the way in which he directed his models (which was in keeping with the academic practices of the times). "On Mondays, the day on which the pose for the entire week was given, Manet invariably had problems with the professor's models... When they climbed onto the table, they traditionally struck outlandish poses. 'Can't you be natural,' Manet would cry out. 'Is that how you stand when you go to the greengrocer's to

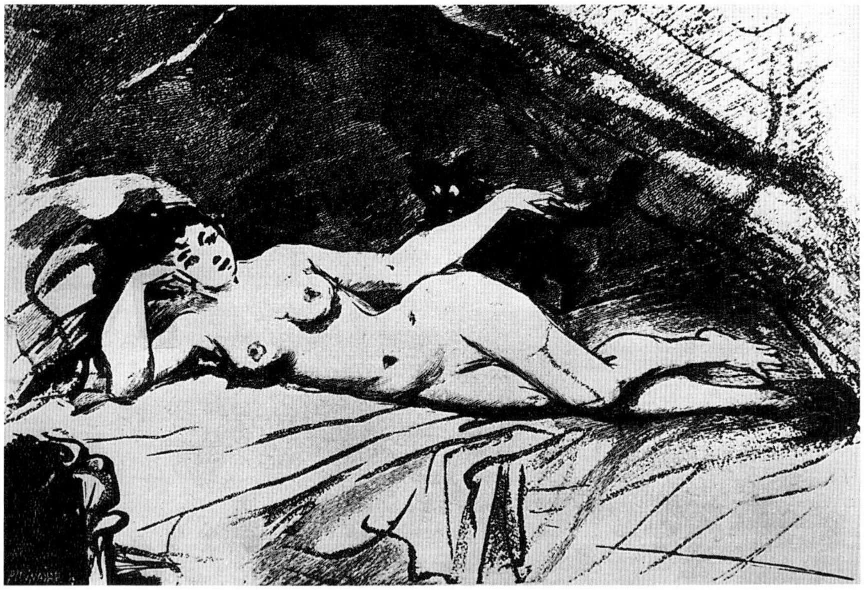

Edouard Manet: Woman with Cat, 1865.

buy radishes?' He had discovered a model named Donato... In the beginning everything went well. But after having frequented other models, Donato would puff up his chest, make his muscles stand out, and strike heroic poses. Manet was dismayed... One day, he had managed to get the model Gilbert to take a simple pose, even letting him keep some of his clothes on. Couture walked into the studio. Seeing the dressed model, he flew into a rage. 'Are you paying Gilbert not to be nude? Whose silly idea was this?' 'Mine,' said Manet. 'Well, my poor lad, you will never be anything more than the Daumier of your time.'"[14]

If Manet rejected these models set like actors in artificial poses, it was not because he refused artifice as such, but rather because, for him, the principal artifice was painting itself. Contrary to what some asserted at the time, Manet's nudes are in no way "realistic"; moreover, realism does not exist in a painting worthy of the name. The "mute simplicity," the "gaping simplicity," of *Olympia* hides a fundamental break. In this new type of painting, the model becomes incongruous, violently incongruous; a certain grace which should characterize it has been brutally eliminated. With this work, the painter's relationship to his model is changing. Manet is jostling in a way models who posture when posing. If his Olympia, an aggressive negation of Olympus, appears as a naked woman, a model "in the buff," and not as a goddess, she is not any more "realistic" for all that. Let us make no mistake about it. She was a spearhead assault on convention, with "bitter colors" that "enter the eye like a steel saw" (caustic remarks attributed by rumor to Delacroix).

Bataille, coming to us through the hubbub that history has recorded, rendered a sensitive and sensually literary homage to Manet, an intimate accomplice in his eyes: "In the secrecy and silence of the bedchamber, *Olympia* attains the stiffness, the flatness of violence: nothing eases that bright figure composing with the white sheet a sharp brilliance. The negro servant entering in the background shadow is reduced to the light, pink sharpness of her dress, the black cat is the depth of that shadow... The blaring notes of the large flower hanging from the ear, the bouquet, the shawl and pink dress, alone stand out from the figure, emphasizing its 'still-life' quality. The brightness and dissonance of the color is so powerful that the rest falls silent: nothing then plunges into the silence of poetry. In Manet's own eyes, the process itself of fashioning a work of art was fading away. *Olympia* as a whole is hard to distinguish from a crime or the spectacle of death... Everything in her shifts towards the indifference of beauty. The effort begun with *Le Déjeuner sur l'herbe* has been brought to completion: the slow preparation is accomplished. Sacred play of technique and light, modern painting is born."[15]

While the scandals created by the *Déjeuner* and *Olympia* have become official and officialized, one of their sources is more hidden than may appear. Manet overturned the conventions of artists' relationship to their models and took painting itself as hostage. There is a shift and a break. The traditional model has been sacrificed, modified. The victim has been killed, assassinated; the subject has been nullified for the sake of a form of painting that aims to be more than naked, flayed alive and without the least concession to prettiness. The sensuality of Olympia is "heavy" and "irritated," the nudity of the girl has the simplicity of obsession.[16] Her gaze is the gaze of insignificance. Presence is in her absence, and it is in a "noli me tangere" of indecency that the void reveals itself. The little ribbon around Olympia's neck is an allusion to the fault, her hand on her pubis tries to hide the crack. With violence, and in a peremptory and wounding way, Manet displays and demonstrates the extent to which woman—the model—is irrepresentable. At the cost of scandal, he paints painting.

The sacred prostitute and the respectable w...

Historically, the academic models were often women of easy virtue. Many were the prostitutes in the nineteenth century who exposed their bodies the better for painters to try their hand at depicting the human anatomy. Whore and goddess. How many of them were dressed up and disguised in the precious and elegant attire of a Madame de...? It is known that Jean-Dominique Ingres liked to draw his figures in the nude in order to dress them afterwards. For the portrait of Madame de Moitessier, for example, it would have been perfectly inconceivable at the time to make this noble lady pose nude; another model, some modest sitter, lent the noble woman her own nude form and flesh like an intermediary wet-nurse of sorts.

Degas and Toulouse-Lautrec openly turned to the world of the brothel and found their favorite models there. Degas lived in the rue de Douai, a few steps away from those special houses which Paul Valéry called *maisons entr'ouvertes* (lit, half-open houses, a pun on the expression *maisons closes*). There he assiduously tracked down his models going through the most mundane motions of everyday life. From the very beginnings of his apprenticeship with Gustave Moreau at the Villa Médicis, Degas worked a great deal from the live model. By a strange twist which surprised no one at the time, the models (mostly male) would strike poses inspired by antique statuary. For example, Degas drew a model in the pose of the *Athlete* of Lysippus. The marble, inspired by life, inspired the living in turn!

Very soon, however, Degas broke away from the traditions of the nude. In his painting *The Young Spartans* he dropped the convention of giving male figures a dark skin-coloring to distinguish them from the fair-complexioned women. However, what seems to have interested him even more than the nude itself, was the undressed, the semi-nude, the transitional, the intermediary state,

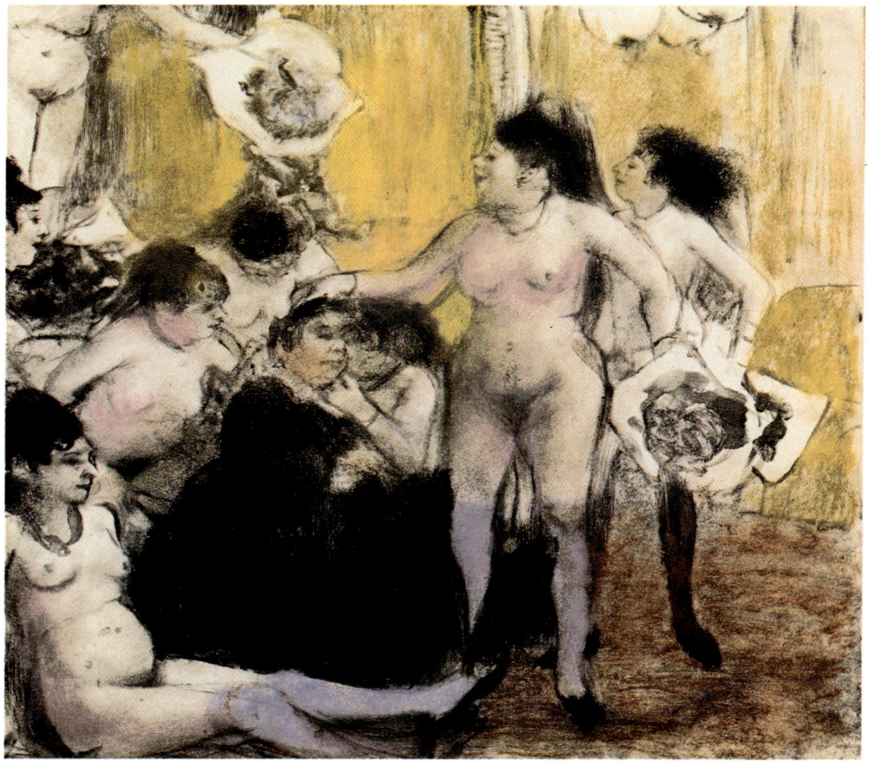

Edgar Degas:
The Madam's Birthday Party 1876-1877.

Edgar Degas:
After the Bath (Woman Dressing), 1885.

a passage very strongly evoked by the act of bathing. "Undercover" drama inspired by a shift from one situation to another. Degas observed intimate events which art had not yet touched upon. We no longer see Susannah surprised at her bath by the elders, but prostitutes performing their ablutions. Degas himself remarked: "See what a difference time makes; two centuries ago I would have depicted *Susannah and the Elders*, but I paint only women in their tubs."[17] "Until now, nudes have always been represented in poses which imply a spectator. But my women are simple and honest folk; they are concerned only with their physical occupations. Look at this one here, washing her feet... it is as if you were watching through a keyhole."[18]

If, in the process, the subject seemed to be rushing toward the prosaic, art was there to transfigure it. The little milliners, laundresses, streetwalkers became so many sacred divinities brought into being by the caress of the charcoal pencil. The voyeur Degas watched them through the keyhole and said of his own bathers that they were "human creatures taking care of themselves." This voyeur had a sharp eye and "took matters directly in hand" (in the strict sense of the expression). He worked directly with his fingers on one series of monotypes, for example, and ran his hands over the body of the little Pauline in order to transpose his sensations directly into wax.

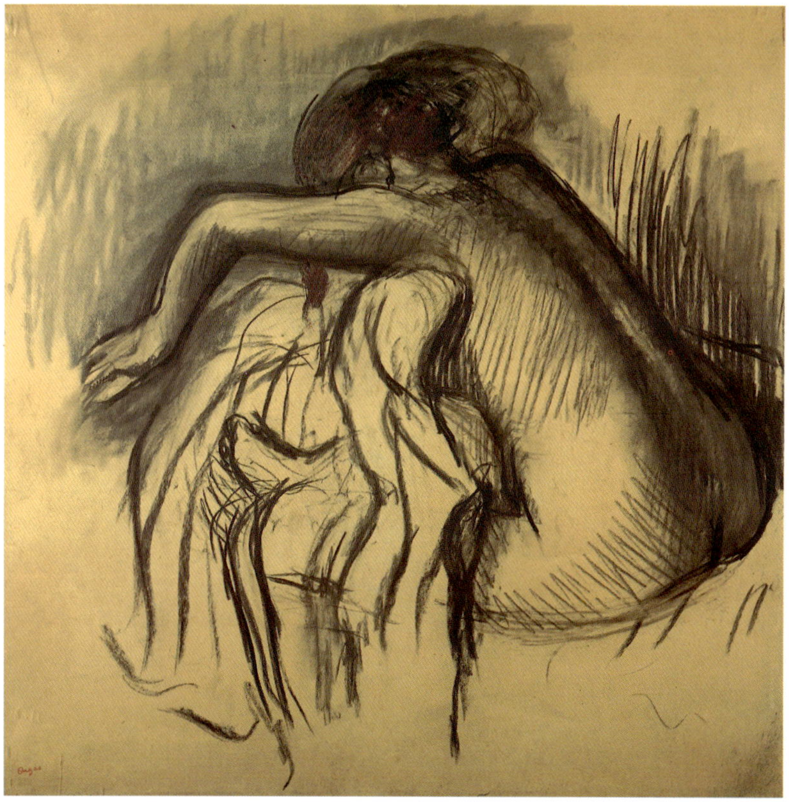

Such sensual work on such forbidden subjects could only be greeted by his contemporaries with anxiety. Some compared Degas' women to *batrachians*. True, they were quite fond of water, the fusional element par excellence. The critics voiced their disapproval: "M. Degas displays for our benefit, with the fine and powerful immodesty of the artist, the modern, pasty and puffy flesh of the public female. In the sordid boudoirs of registered houses, in which ladies fulfill the socially useful role of great repositories of love, we see rolly-polly tarts washing, brushing, rinsing, and wiping themselves in tubs the size of troughs."[19] On one of these women in a tub, a critic wrote: "Degas has done nothing to hide her batrachian aspect, the sagging of her breasts, the ponderousness of her lower parts, the ungainly twists of her legs, the length of her arms, the astounding appearance of her belly, of her knees and feet in unexpected foreshortenings."[20]

The writer Joris-Karl Huysmans, a subtle observer of his times, leveled virulent criticism at Degas' choice of subject matter and yet, discovering the nudes of 1886, although his commentary is again violent, he glimpses something more in these works—true painting. Moreover, it is Huysmans who would later speak of "civilized flesh tones" in the pastels of Degas. "Here, there is a plumb and stuffed redhead who bends forward, making the bone of the sacrum protrude from the taut globes of her bottom; she painfully contorts herself to bring her arm behind her shoulders in order to press the dripping sponge... There is, in these pastels, something of the maimed stump, the goitered throat, the waddling of legless cripples, a whole series of attitudes inherent even in young and beautiful women, adorable enough when reclining or standing, but froglike and simian when they have to lower themselves, as here, in order to mask the decay of their bodies with bandages. But over and above this particular note of loathing and scorn, what must be seen in these works is the unforgettable veracity of these types, drawn with a broad, flowing, easy line, a lucid and masterful fervor and a cold passion; what must be seen is the ardent and muted color, the mysterious and opulent tonalities of these scenes; the supreme beauty of the flesh tinted blue and pink by the water, lit by closed windows, veiled in muslin; in dark rooms where we can make out in the filtered daylight of courtyards walls hung with Jouy cretonnes, washstands, basins, flasks and combs, brushes with

Edgar Degas:
Woman Drying Herself, c. 1890.

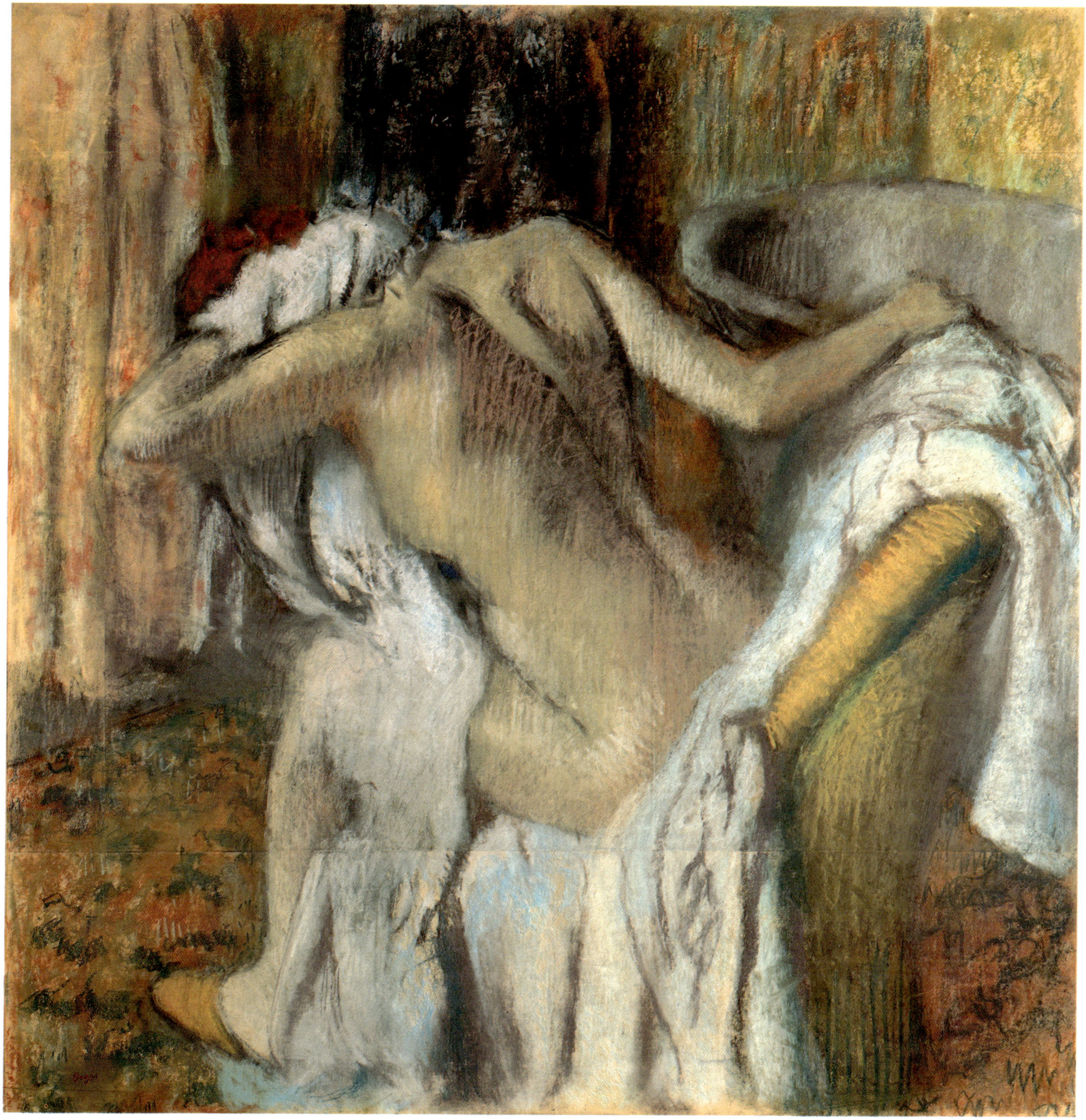

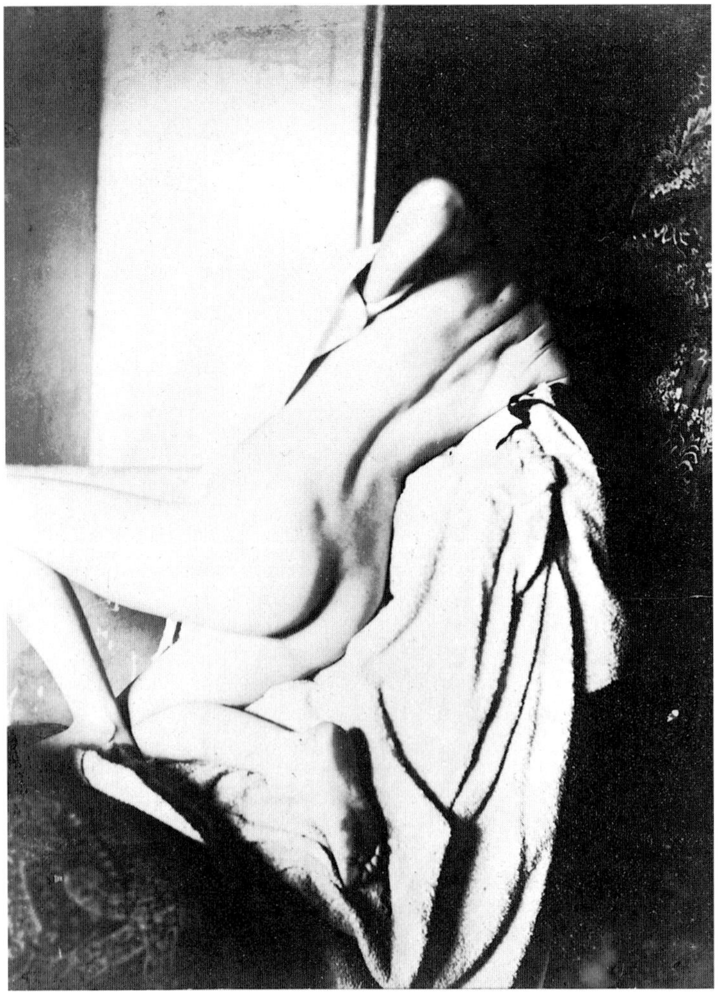

Edgar Degas:
After the Bath (bromide print), 1896.

briarwood handles, kettles of rose-colored copper!... A powerful and isolated artist, who is without any known predecessors, and without a lineage to speak of , M. Degas creates in each of his paintings the feeling of a strange exactness, of the unseen, something so precise that we are surprised at our being surprised, and are almost angry with ourselves for it."[21]

Beyond the inherent repulsiveness of the subject matter, critics realized the extent of the break effected by Degas. "The masterpiece is the plump, short-legged woman, her back turned to the viewer, holding her bottom with her two hands. The effect is tremendous. Degas has done what Baudelaire did—he invented a new thrill. The eloquence of these figures is much too fearful. During the Middle Ages, cynicism was one of the preferred vehicles of eloquence; the art of Degas expresses at the same time the pessimism of the saints of old and the skepticism of our century."[22]

Degas indeed had an attachment for these models who posed without any fuss. The heavy forms of the butcher's wife are relieved by an iridescent play of light. To a pretty woman who solicited Degas to honor her with a portrait, the master is said to have replied pointblank: "Yes, I would like to paint your portrait, but I would first have you put on a bonnet and apron like a little housemaid."[23] Degas was fond of women who were unencumbered by modesty and who surrendered themselves without reservation. Perhaps it was that the painter rightly guessed he was dressing them in light, like Rembrandt transmuting the earthy flesh of stout Dutch women into streaks of gold.

These women presented in near-nudity, Degas often came back to this theme. He turned constantly around his models. "One should work the same subject ten times, a hundred times over. Nothing in art should look accidental, not even movement."[24] At the eighth Impressionist exhibition, he showed a "Series of women bathing, washing, drying, combing their hair or having their hair combed." So fascinated was he by the intimate relationship between women and their bath that he even furnished his studio with basins, sponges and a tin washtub. Completely missing the point, his models joked sarcastically: "You know what they are posing at Degas's studio," one asked Gustave Coquiot in a dance hall, "Well, just women in bathtubs washing their arse!"[25]

While at her bath, a fascinating moment for the artist, a woman enjoys a fusional relationship with herself, she is without onlookers and face to face

Edgar Degas:
After the Bath, 1896.

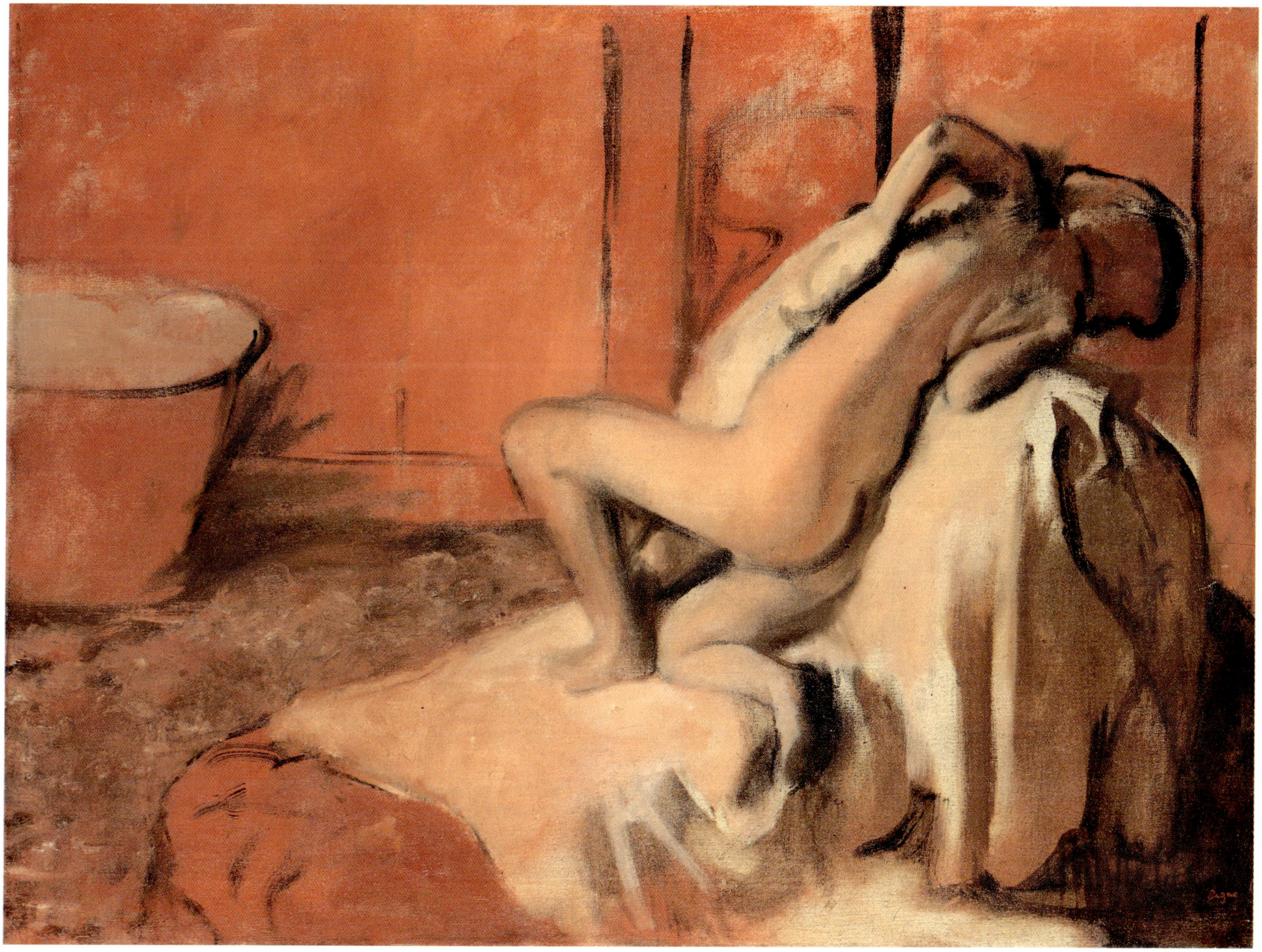

Edgar Degas:
Actresses in Their Dressing Room, c. 1880.

Edgar Degas:
The Great Arabesque, 1882-1891.

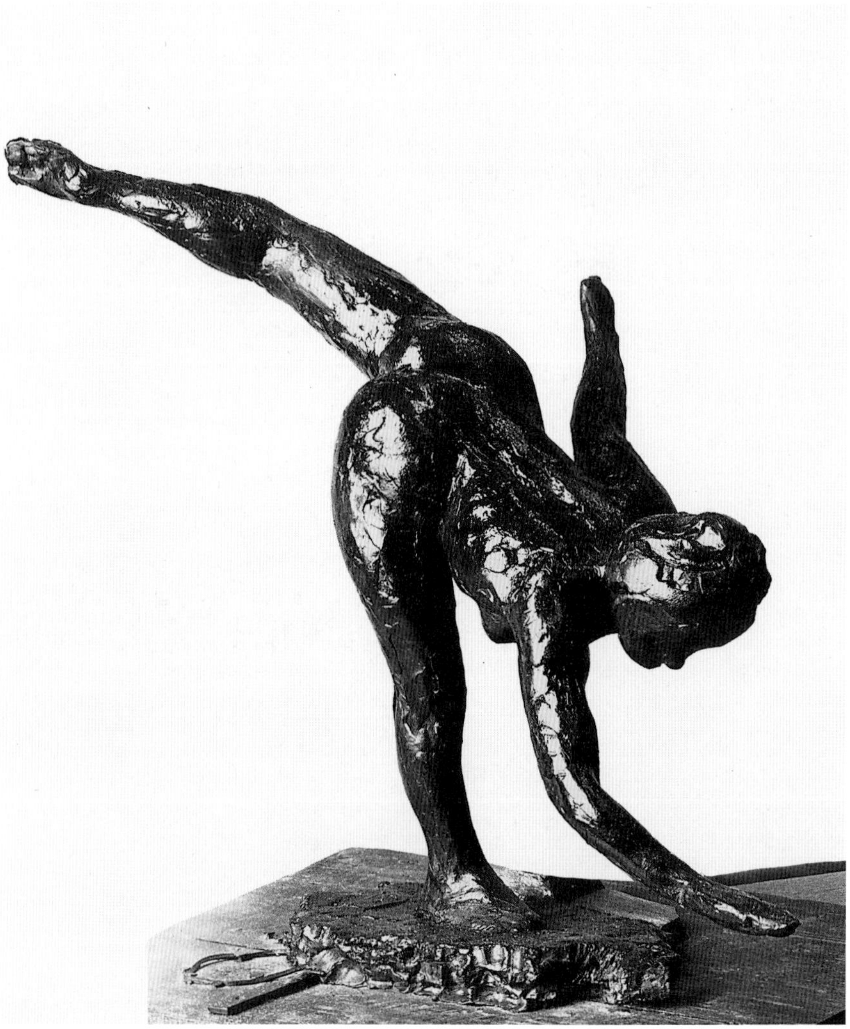

with herself in a highly narcissistic encounter. The mirror sends back to her her own image. Degas purported to show women divested of their coquetry, "like animals cleaning themselves." The artist associated them with "the idea of the cat licking itself." One day, while showing his sketches of nudes bathing, Degas wondered out loud if he had "not considered woman too much like an animal."

In peering through the keyhole, Degas secretly reveres his models. By stubbornly and untiringly repeating the same subjects, he seeks to resolve an enigma, the enigma of a gaze, the closed gaze of woman upon herself, a gaze wrapped up in a sort of self-sufficiency and auto-eroticism. The woman at her bath is taking care only of herself, oblivious to her surroundings, oblivious to the gaze of others, concentrated on herself and within herself. In the water, she returns to foetal positions, the elementary positions of the most intimate fusion. The artist dives into this sensitive flesh. The bath is a crucial experience of sensation. In Degas's work, the sacred prostitute is not enshrined on a pedestal, but in a bathtub; she ignores her admirers, never lowers her gaze upon them, looks only at herself, into her own center, her navel. Such independence renders her supreme. There, more than anywhere else, she escapes. Degas undertook to pursue her, drew the same model in the same pose, the same model in different poses. Like Marcel Proust with Albertine, he wanted to make this elusive figure his captive.

If Degas, like some stealthy photographer, seems to have stolen these images behind the backs of his models, he nonetheless held a rather dictatorial attitude regarding them. He demanded complex poses that were difficult to hold and would quickly

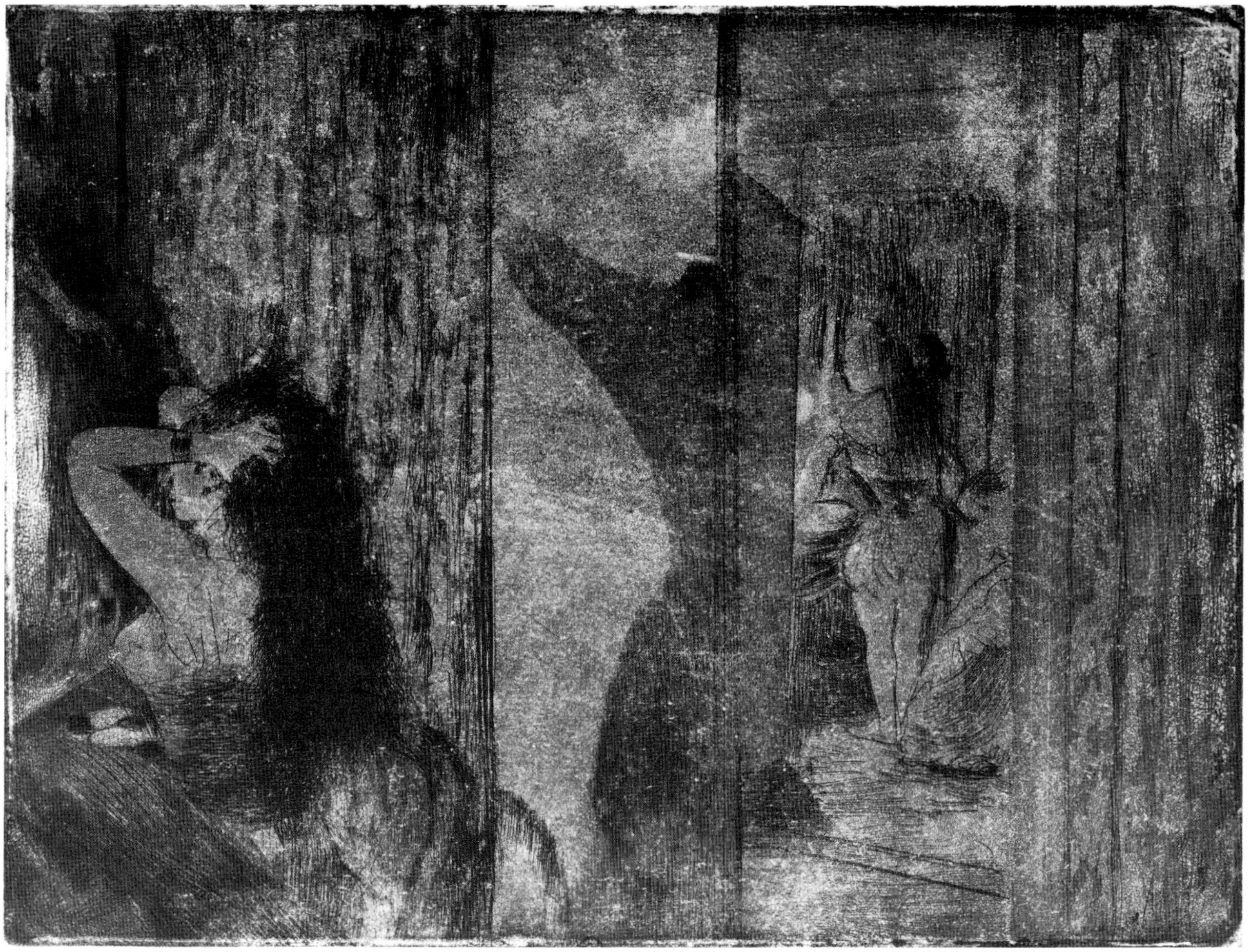

fly into a rage if the poor model expressed the slightest inclination to interfere with his choice. Paul Valéry, however, in an admirable book entitled D*egas - Danse - Dessin*, reports that the painter talked freely with his models and listened to the amusing gossip they brought from one studio to the next. "In the world of painting, the models played a part other than that of just offering their bodies to the analytic eye. Some, like insects in a garden, flew from flower to flower, fertilized them and randomly created various hybrids, transmitting from studio to studio remarks and judgments they overheard, sowing in the ear of one artist the joke heard at another's."[26]

The cynical Degas, who was well known for his vitriolic tongue, was constantly attracted by the private world of women. He delighted in observing the young ballerinas, not just in their official role on the stage, but especially behind the scenes. He represented their hidden side: their yawns, their fatigue, their feet and backs worn out by exercises. He sketched them at rest, off-stage, out of range, their bodies exhausted, abandoned, when they thought that no one was paying attention to them. Only Degas was watching.

Degas's models are seemingly beyond the range of representation. In bordellos, he "caught" the women as soon as they rose in the morning, stretching out like cats, in the sticky warmth of rumpled sheets; a servant smooths their hair, they twist around to wipe their backs, to rinse their underarms with a sponge. The clients have returned to their snug bourgeois existence. Here was the true hidden side of bedroom scenes. With Degas, the sublime finds its roots in the most remote recesses of the commonplace. The poet Valéry followed the transfiguration brought about by the artist's hand like a magic spell: "Not women, but beings of a matchless substance, translucid and sensitive, flesh like glass, madly excitable, domes of floating silk, hyaline diadems, long living vines traversed with rapid vibrations, fringe and flounce which they fold and unfold; while they turn, change shape, float away, as fluent as the massive fluid which encircles, embraces, holds them all around, yielding to their slightest movement, replacing them in their form... No human dancer, no impassioned woman drunk with movement, with the poison of her overwrought forces, in the ardent presence of eyes charged with desire, ever expressed the imperious offering of sex, the mimed call of the need for prostitution, like this great Medusa who, with undulating pulsations of her festooned skirts, which she hitches up over and over with a strange shameless insistence, transforms herself into a dream of Eros: and, all of a sudden, casting aside all of these vibrating frills, her skirts of cut-up lips, she throws herself back and exposes herself, furiously open."[27] Beneath her air of domesticity, Degas's Medusa is a bewitching w...

Like Degas, Henri de Toulouse-Lautrec hated professional models and their conventional poses, and like his elder, he recruited his sitters in brothels. Toulouse-Lautrec was commissioned to decorate a parlor of one famous establishment in the rue d'Amboise, and from then on the bordello haunted his painting. Between 1892 and 1899, he executed over fifty paintings and over a hundred drawings depicting this special world. Day-to-day life is described in these works. Prostitutes wait for their clients, receive them, or resignedly submit to the routine medical examination.

Regularly, the count would desert his studio in the rue de Tourlaque and take up digs in the rue d'Amboise, the rue Joubert or the rue Richelieu. He would move in, leaving, as he said, "the others on the balcony." His disappearances were carefully planned; he would pack his bags, announce a trip, hail a cab and ride the several hundred meters to settle into his temporary place of residence, as if he were going to a spa for a rest cure or to a monastery for a retreat.

The malicious little man liked to give his part-time address to certain people in order to create confusion. The prudish art-dealer Durand-Ruel must have blushed long after one of Toulouse-Lautrec's invitations when the artist welcomed him surrounded by various paintings in progress and... his all-too familiar neighbors. Yvette Guilbert, whose repertoire of stories was reputed for its spicy audacity, was shocked by such dealings. She tells the story of the time she asked the painter if this address was intended to keep his creditors at bay, a question that made the painter burst out laughing: "Ah, his laugh! His laugh! And in bits and pieces, all the while sharpening his pencil, he told me how much he liked living in bordellos, observing the throbbing life of prostitution, listening to the sentimental problems of these poor creatures, the bureaucrats of love... He was their friend, their counselor, their comforter, never their judge... When he spoke of these poor women, the emotion in his voice betrayed the great pity in his heart, and I have often wondered whether, for Lautrec, this fraternal and Christian commiseration was not a mission of beauty."[28] What is certain is that, in such places, he found women who posed to his liking.

During these retreats, Toulouse-Lautrec entered into a symbiotic relationship with his models, immersed himself "body and soul" in their world. "Monsieur Henri" listened to their little secrets, strolled and hummed through the corridors during off-hours and worked a great deal. Sometimes the

Henri de Toulouse-Lautrec:
The Drawing-Room, rue des Moulins, 1894.

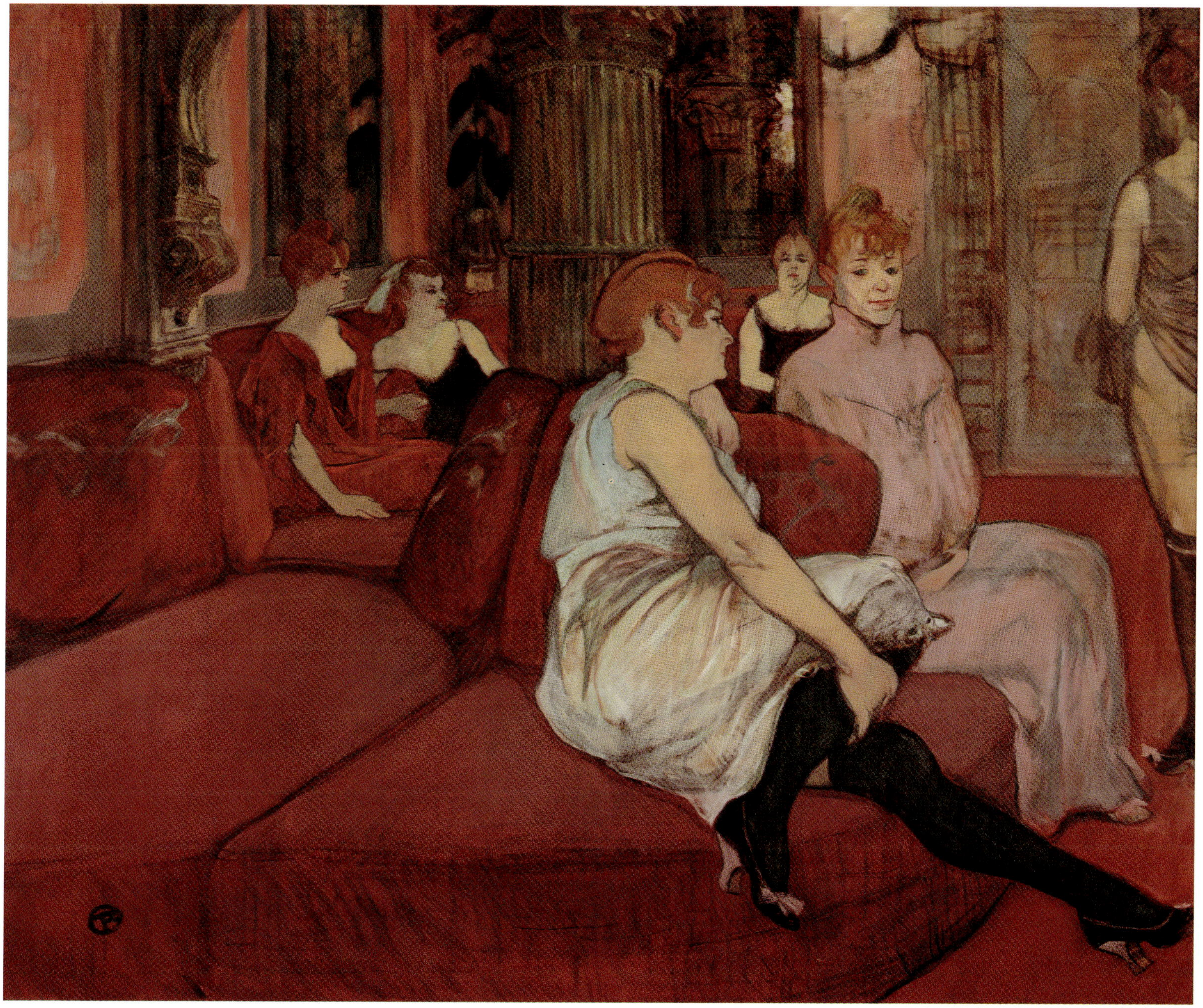

Henri de Toulouse-Lautrec:
The Model's Repose, 1896.

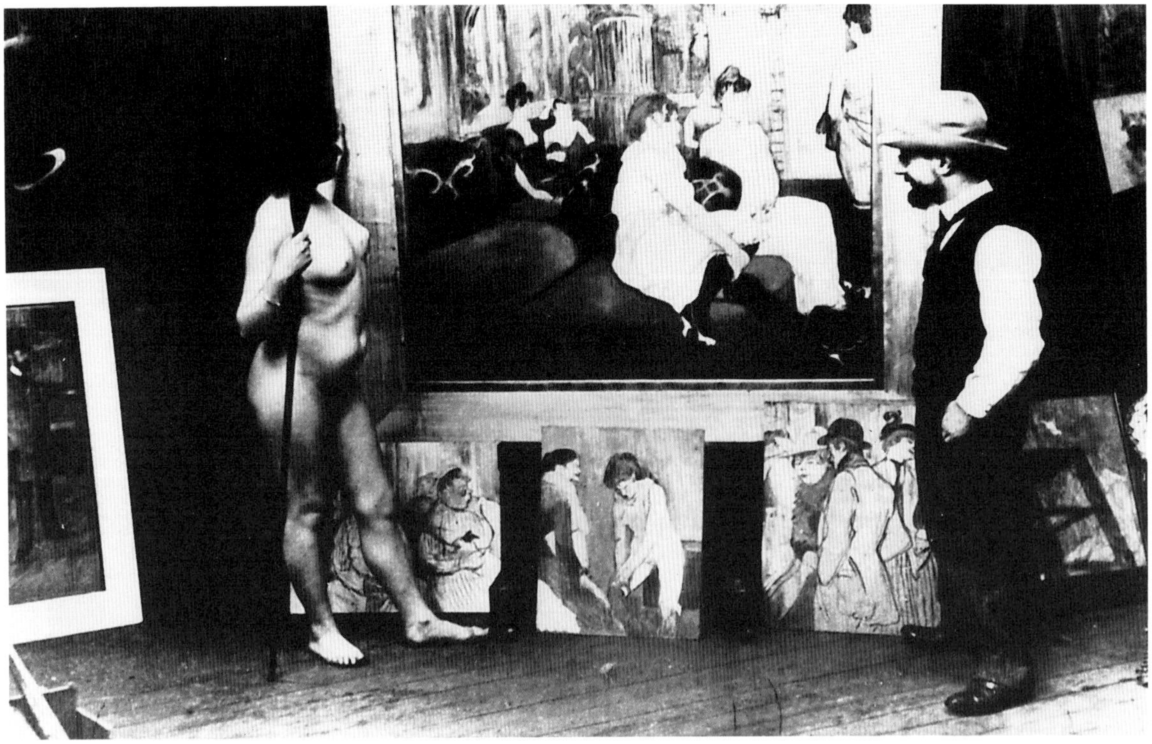

Toulouse-Lautrec and his model, c. 1894.

ladies left the confines of the house and posed for him in his studio. Accustomed to living as they did, scantily clad, they were indispensable to his work. "He asked several women half undressed in colorful shifts and dressing-gowns to dance to a player piano, holding each other by the waist. He had them move forward and back, so that they would face him, and went into raptures over attitudes that reminded him of Botticelli's *Primavera* or the frescoes of Benozzo Gozzoli."[29]

As an adolescent, he had already learned about these women from such scandal-tainted books as the Goncourts' *La fille Elisa*, J.-K. Huysmans's *Marthe, histoire d'une fille,* and Zola's *L'assommoir*. Discovering them as they were in reality, he exclaimed ironically, "I have found women of my own size." Telling his friends about these very special residences, he would point out, no less ironically, that they were the only places in Paris where one could get one's shoes shined properly. In his *Journal*, Jules Renard noted that Lautrec had his own room in an obviously registered whorehouse. From among his "field trips," the artist published an album of twelve lithographs entitled *Elles*, which show his subjects in their everyday lives. One of his contemporaries described the atmosphere with which "Monsieur Henri" nourished his art: "There he plunged into another favorable medium. He liked women; but he also liked the atmosphere of the place, the hushed calm, the lounging around in plush settees. Savoring there the very different times of the day, the gossip of the tarts, he found an intimacy which existed nowhere else for him, so disconcerting was his appearance. In such a reassuring setting, he was very happy, talkative, and could be heard humming popular tunes. Believe me, the girls in these establishments, be it rue d'Amboise, rue des Moulins, or anywhere else, were never nasty with this kind little man who surrounded them with his attentions; on the feast days or birthdays of each of these wanton girls, he would shower them with gifts, pastries and flowers; and when he happened to preside at a gala banquet in one of these infernal houses, you can be sure that he played his part with a distinction and a cordiality which delighted all the ladies. Since he had been drawn there by his desire to paint them, was this not the best place for him to learn about such ladies and produce paintings that went beyond the usual banal hackneyed remarks

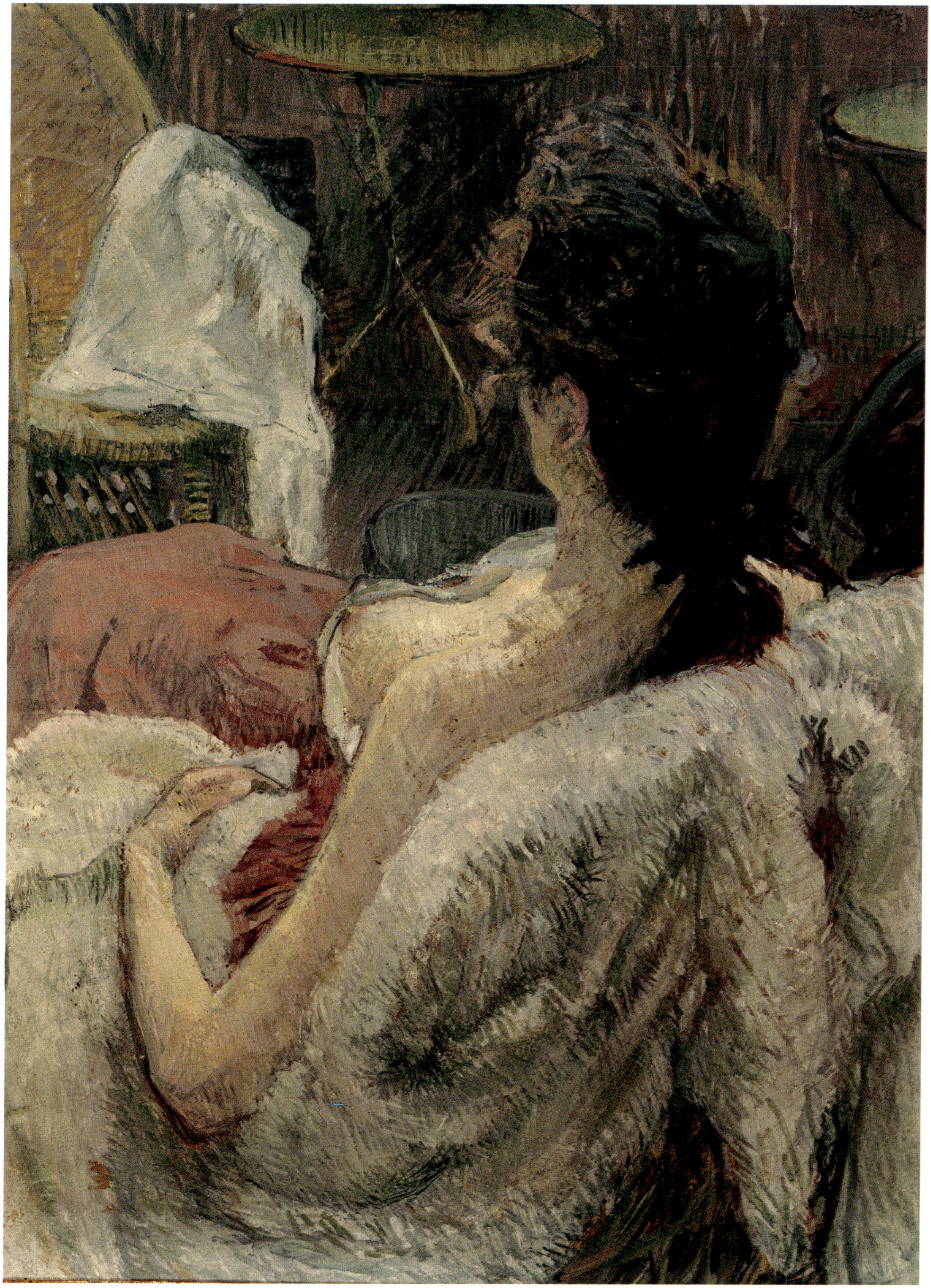

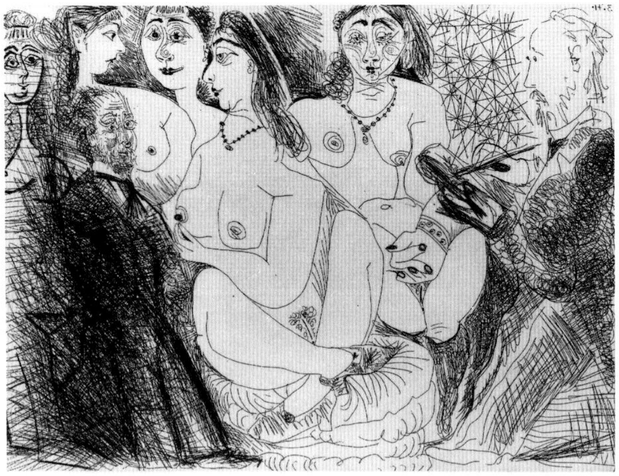

Pablo Picasso:
Etching from the series "Degas in the Brothel," 1971.

Pablo Picasso:
The Models, 1954.

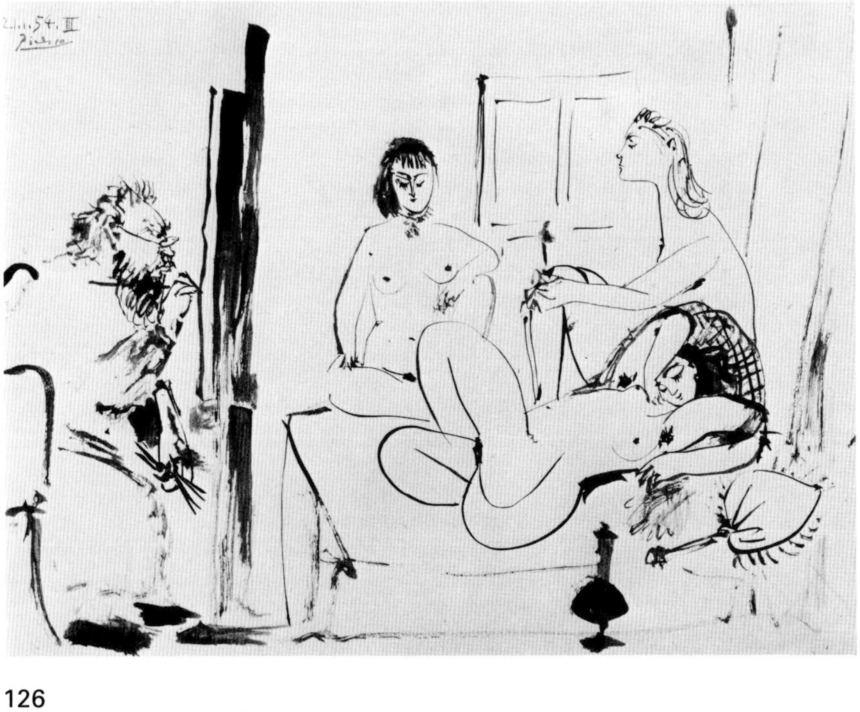

and remonstrances made on this subject? He learned to see women walking, to see them in a state almost as natural as the ones that Gauguin saw in Tahiti." Such was the little man's source of inspiration.

It was—lest we forget—the image of a brothel that gave birth to the *Demoiselles d'Avignon*. So much has been written about this picture that its subject has almost been lost in the process. Generally, Picasso was not very outspoken about his work, however we know this painting's original title was *Le bordel d'Avignon*, or *Le bordel philosophique*. The title, which was supposedly coined by his friends, and probably by Apollinaire, refers to a house of ill repute in Barcelona—with a passing nod to Sade's *Philosophie dans le boudoir*. The showcase of this imaginary house features a typical reception scene. The women stand there, in the act of presenting, or better yet, of "exhibiting" themselves to the clients. The art critic André Salmon, wishing to exhibit the picture, preferred to avoid a scandal by omitting the word "bordel." At the time, out of either indifference or inattention, Picasso accepted this change, which he would later regret however, exclaiming: "What an irritating title!" Whores puritanically disguised as "Demoiselles" hardly correspond with the temperament of a man who once declared, "For us Spaniards, it is church in the morning, the bullfight in the afternoon, and the whorehouse at night. What is it all mixed up with? With sadness, I guess, a funny kind of sadness."[30]

Later, in 1933, he explained the origin of the subject to David-Henri Kahnweiler, his art dealer: "You know of course that it was called *Le bordel d'Avignon* in the beginning. But do you know why? Avignon for me was a name I had always known, a name connected to my life. I used to live a few steps away from the Calle d'Avignon. It was there that I bought my paper, my watercolors. Then, as you also know, Max [Jacob]'s grandmother was from Avignon. We joked a lot about this painting. One of the women was Max's grandmother; another, Fernande, and another, Marie Laurencin, all in a whorehouse in Avignon."[31] Kahnweiler adds that Max Jacob told Picasso about a special bordello in Avignon: "a fabulous place, full of women, tapestries, flowers and fruit." A high sanctuary of carnal pleasures in the heart of which still life and very real life were found side by side.

It should be said that the name of Avignon had become synonymous with debauchery since the days of the papacy. Petrarch mentioned it as being "the sewer in which all of the filth on earth has come to congregate," and medieval chroniclers spoke of it as "the cesspool of every vice and infamy." Is it any wonder that this city happened to

Pablo Picasso:
Les Demoiselles d'Avignon, 1906-1907.

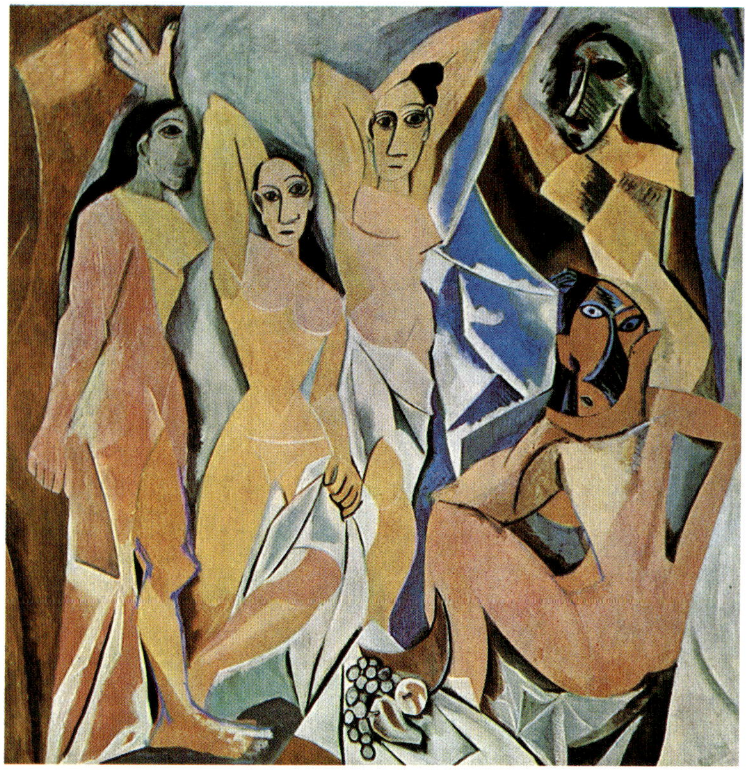

be the birthplace of the family of the Marquis de Sade? This aspect of Avignon's reputation spread abroad, and great cities of Europe like Rome and Barcelona baptized their red-light districts with its name. So widespread was this connotation that, in Italy, the expression "andare agli avignonesi" was a slang expression suggesting a visit to the bordello.

Curiously enough, while the subject matter of the scenes depicted by Degas and Toulouse-Lautrec shocked critics to the point of blinding them to their artistic qualities, beyond the painting's censored title it was the *Demoiselles*'s pictorial handling more than its theme that shocked viewers. With an artist like Picasso, however, it would be absurd to think that the theme was just an innocent pretext. This painting, a veritable "field of maneuvers," is also an evocation of Eros. Leo Steinberg considers it a "sexual metaphor" in which the "figures personify pure sexual energy as a vital force. The space is not a visual continuum, but an interior apprehended by trial and error, a nest explored by feeling one's way through it, or by letting oneself tumble into it, stretch out inside it. While it presents itself symbolically only to the sense of sight, Picasso's space supposes a total initiation, like going into an unmade bed."[32] A very eloquent praise of pictorial fusion.

Brassaï, Picasso's friend and the photographer of his sculpture, saw things with the same eyes and remarked on the role of the artist's "private sketchbook": "In it he consigned the very first stirrings of his inspiration and especially his sexual obsessions... Undoubtedly the fears haunting his masculinity seaped through his work born beneath the sign of Eros. What an amazing anthology could be made of these bodies of women with their underscored vulvas, aggressively tipped breasts, immense, quivering rumps; these masculine fingers kneading flesh, these Minotaures panting with desire. Even the *Demoiselles d'Avignon*, the mother of Cubism, should be included in it. Was it not the product of a lascivious phantasy, and was it not originally called *Le bordel d'Avignon*? And yet, in all of these images of desire, a slight veil of modesty disguises and transposes these obsessions into the realm of the symbolic, the magic, the mythological... It is only in his private sketchbooks that Picasso gives free rein to his eroticism... Like most great masters, next to his official work, he keeps an inferno going. He always has a little sketchbook on hand, ready to receive his most immediate and personal confidences. 'Art is never chaste,' he said to me one day, showing me the erotic prints of Utamaro..."[33]

In the *Harem*, a precursor of the *Demoiselles* dating from 1906, eroticism is but suggested by the slight discrepancy between the time and place of the work's exoticism. Fernande is incarnated there as a series of houris. In the preparatory sketches and studies for the *Demoiselles*, the display of female flesh depicted in the finished work was intended for a sailor, while a medical student carrying either a skull or a book intrudes in the scene. Much ink has been spilt over that skull by observers eager to see in this element a confrontation between Eros and Thanatos, and an allusion to a sort of *memento mori*.

Pablo Picasso:
Drawing for Les Demoiselles d'Avignon, *1906.*

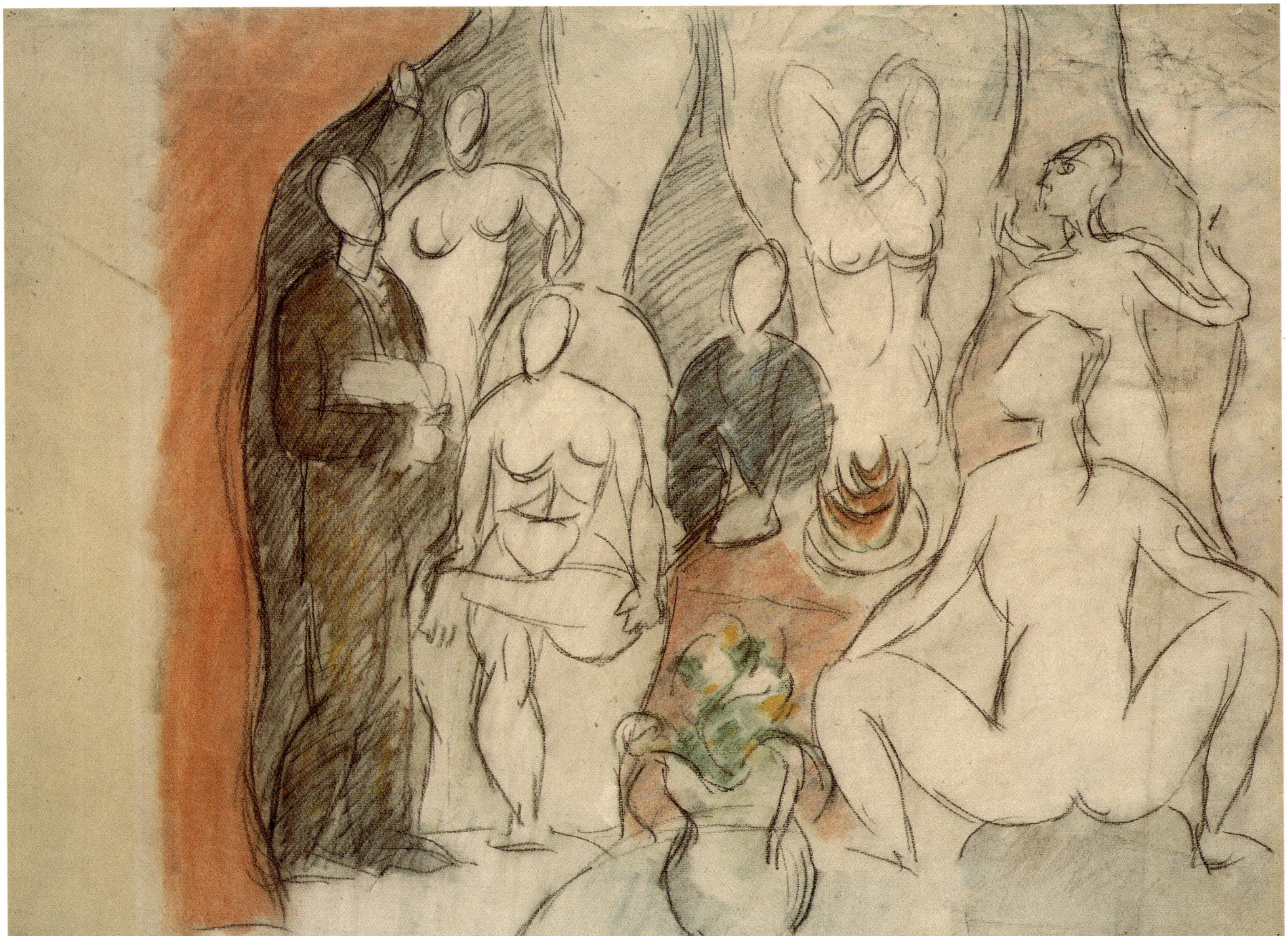

Be that as it may, in the preliminary sketches the med student parts a curtain and reveals a "tableau vivant," a show put on by the tenants of the establishment to whet the customers' appetite. This combined presence of medicine, death and eroticism has been linked by some to the anxiety tinged with fascination that Picasso cultivated with regard to venereal disease. He is known to have visited the morgue in Barcelona and the hospital of the Saint-Lazare prison in Paris, a rare privilege since such visits were—for reasons of propriety—usually limited to a few specialized physicians. The sight of the facial deformations caused by syphilis overwhelmed the artist and clearly left him with indelible memories whose presence has perhaps been too obscured by the debates of art historians concerning the influence of "Negro" and Iberian art. Yet the figure squatting in the lower right corner probably also suggests a face eaten away by the disease. The *Demoiselles* depict a vision of death, an "apocalyptic bordello."

Nevertheless, while we should in no way ally the *Demoiselles* to an all too material reality, we must bear in mind above all that the history of the "Cubist revolution" began with these five great nudes displaying their spatio-temporal distortions and the great variety of their flesh tones. Picasso, in any case, was an unrivaled debunker of interpretations of all stripes. To a critic who asked him in 1910 if he used models, he is supposed to have replied: "Where would I find them?" His eyes sparkled with humor as he made this nod at his "overseas" ogresses, women whom the critic qualified as: "monstrous monoliths," "Alaskan totem poles," "sub-African caricatures."[34] To an equally perspicacious journalist who asked him if "feet should be painted rectangular or square?" Picasso retorted: "I don't know, there are no feet in nature!"[35]

Such questions remind us of the silly and malicious joke making the rounds among the models who wanted to mock one of their number whose forms deviated from the current canons of beauty, suggesting that she go work for the Spaniard. Picasso told Malraux that, at the Bateau-Lavoir, Fernande's friends would tell "unsightly" models to work for him.[36] All humor aside, Picasso himself said that "women are either goddesses or... doormats!" Like Degas, to whom he referred on several occasions throughout his career, he often made his models into "creatures." Picasso also knew the famous "secret" black-ink monotypes of Degas's "filles." Captivated by these prototypes of female animality, he acquired in 1958 eleven of these monotypes from Ambroise Vollard, and in March 1970 began a series of engravings on the theme of brothels featuring his predecessor. The painter is represented as a bearded voyeur watching a procession of bodies displaying sexual parts rendered with great anatomical precision. Degas, however, never quits the dignity of his coat and tie. In one engraving Picasso represents him drawing; in another, he appears in a rectangular frame which could be a window, a mirror, the edge of a painting, or a photograph; in yet another, he merely watches the spectacle.

Legend has it that Picasso took out the monotypes ten years after having bought them, pondering what it was that had motivated Degas. "What was he going over there to look for? Do you think that he was simply taking notes?" he asked Pierre Daix. Picasso worked on a series of variations on the theme of "The Madam's Birthday Party" and Degas's "Salon."[37] A portly matron with hands crossed on her belly, like an old peasant woman, is surrounded by festive women with painted fingernails and curvaceous breasts, wearing pearl necklaces, ribbons around their neck à-la-Olympia, and laced bootees. In most instances Degas's silhouette, like a silent and immobile shadow, hovers over these busy and agitated scenes. He stands there an anonymous client cut by the composition, sometimes squeezed to the very edge of the paper. No one bothers with him; he observes without being observed.

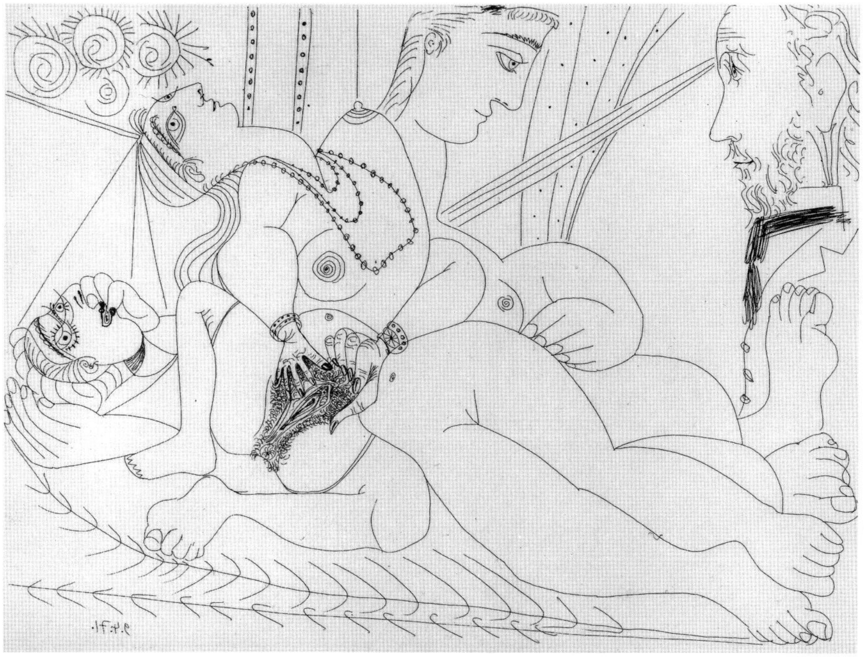

Pablo Picasso:
Etching from the series "Degas in the Brothel."

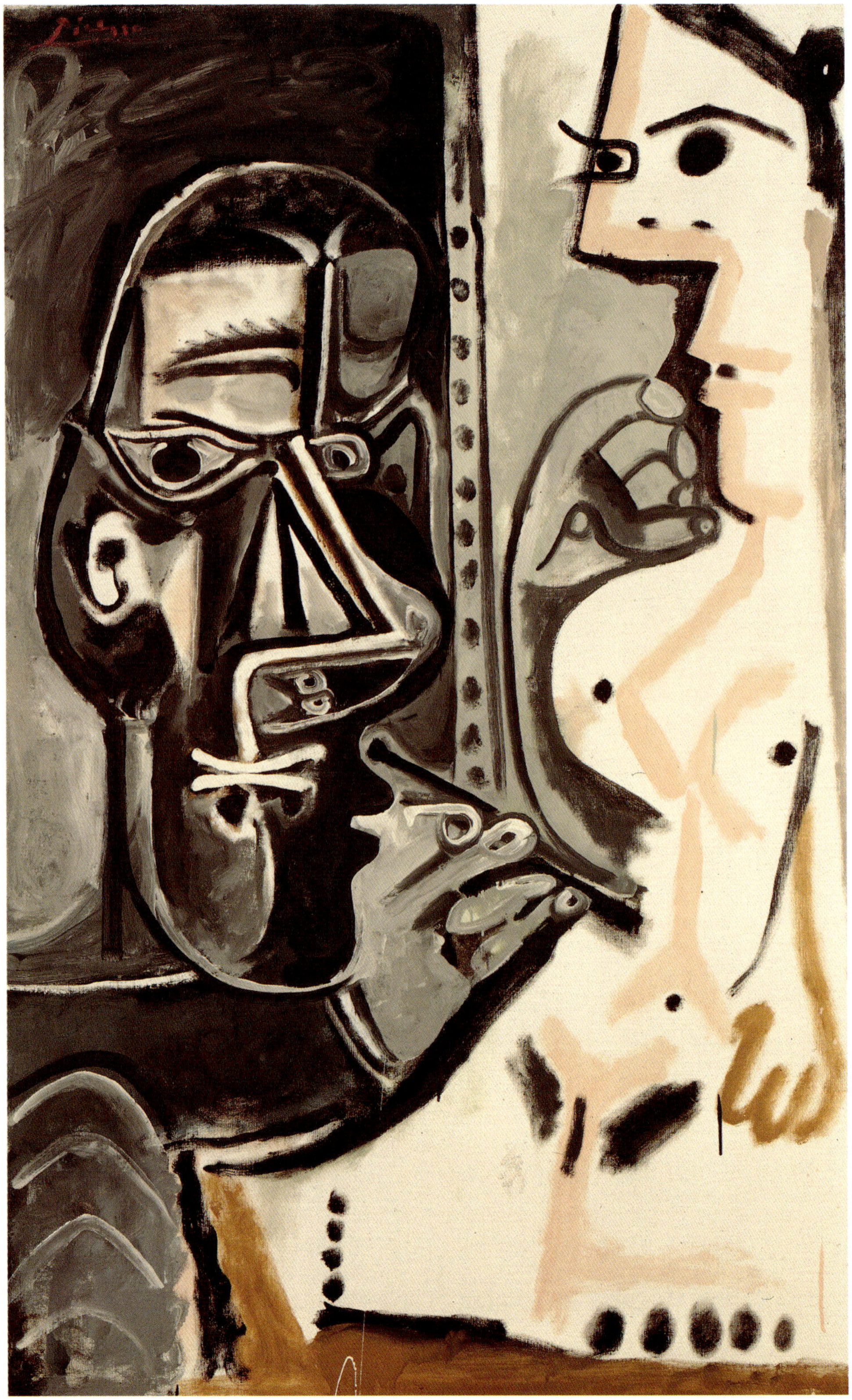

Pablo Picasso: The Painter and His Model, 1964.

The voracity of Eros, the voracity of the model

The themes of the nude and the relationship of the painter to his model are a constant presence throughout Picasso's life and work. Among the more than one hundred prints of the *Vollard Suite* executed between 1930 and 1937, a large number are devoted to the theme of the sculptor's studio. The sculptor is represented with a beard and a lion-like mane, and just as nude as his model. Most of the time a trio of "characters"—sculptor, model, sculpture—existent side by side in a very relaxed atmosphere. The sculptor lies tenderly next to his muse, who cuddles up to his side like a cat, or is shown at times wearing a mask pushed back on her head; a crown of flowers binds her hair. The proximity of the scene's three figures suggests a great gentleness. The sculptor, more contemplative than active, seems to be dreaming in the complete fulfillment of his state; his muse is motionless, and he revels in her. Their symbiosis seems to be without flaw. The only other presences allowed are the sculptures, which appear singly or in groups, sharing the same intimate, maternal space of the studio.

Sometimes Picasso played at blurring the distinction between the model and its representation. "Who is who?" is the question that springs to mind before we find the pedestal which indicates the difference between flesh and stone. The sculptor, crowned with ivy leaves like an antique Dionysos, could revert to animality. For the moment, the beast is resting, but the Minotaur is never far away, and one wonders who brings whom into being, the sculptor or the model? Even if the sculptor is sometimes shown with his tools in hand.

It is the warrior's repose, intermission, the break. Something has happened, and something more will probably happen. Picasso chose to depict that intervening time when the artist and his model settle into inactivity, a suspended time. One mission has been accomplished, others will follow, but before then the primordial couple takes a good breather, as if after a long amorous bout. It is the very instant of fulfillment after pleasure, after the pictorial act which Picasso captures in the web of his undulating lines.

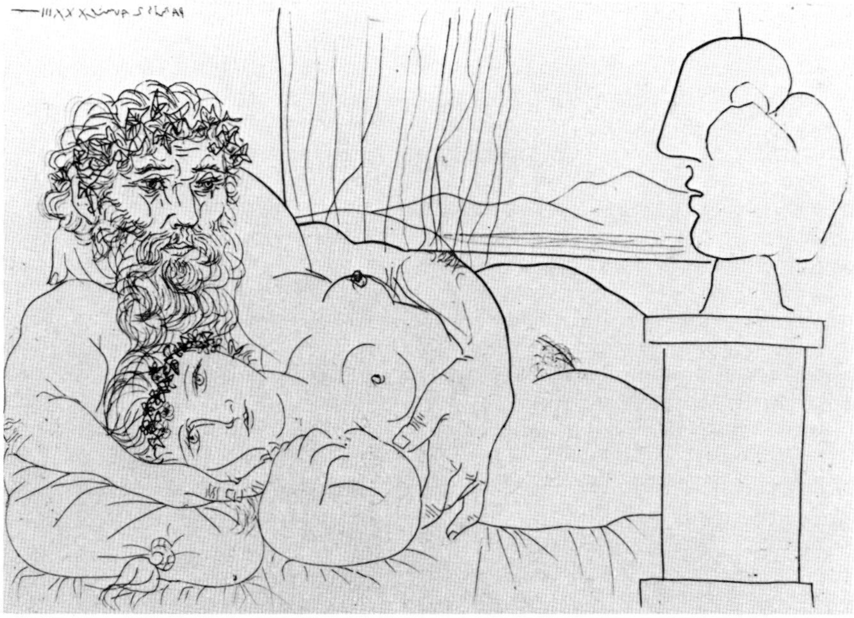

Pablo Picasso:
The Sculptor's Repose, 1933.

Pablo Picasso:
Nude in the Studio, 1953.

Between November 18, 1953 and February 3, 1954, in the wake of the departure of his companion Françoise, Picasso executed a series of one hundred and eighty drawings around the central theme of the painter and his model. He called upon a great variety of techniques to illustrate what he called a "detestable season in Hell." At the same time as these "brio" drawings, he painted a canvas called *The Shadow*, which shows a reclining model (or the painting of a reclining model, try and guess), in front of a dark and ghostly figure (the painter?). Another painting, *Nude in the Studio,* also shows a woman reclining in the closed space of a studio filled with paintings, but without the painter. After that, the painter occupies the pictorial space and the studio in order to observe his model attentively. As Michel Leiris so rightly remarked[38], Picasso depicted the theme of the painter and his model so often that it nearly became a genre in itself, like landscape painting or the still life for others. The situations represented, however, correspond little to Picasso's actual artistic practices; he usually painted without a palette or easel, directly on a canvas laid flat.

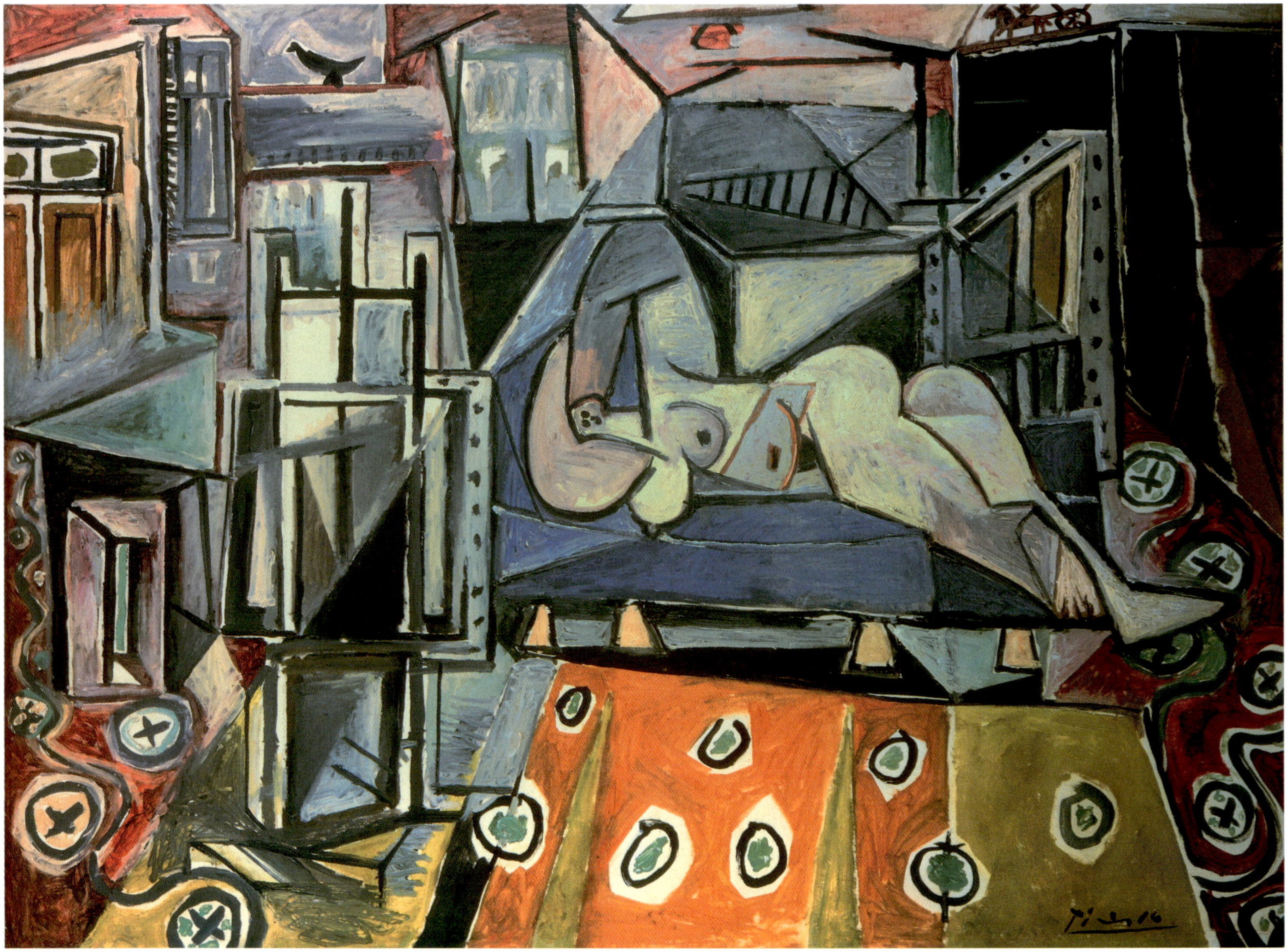

Pablo Picasso: The Painter and His Model, 1963.

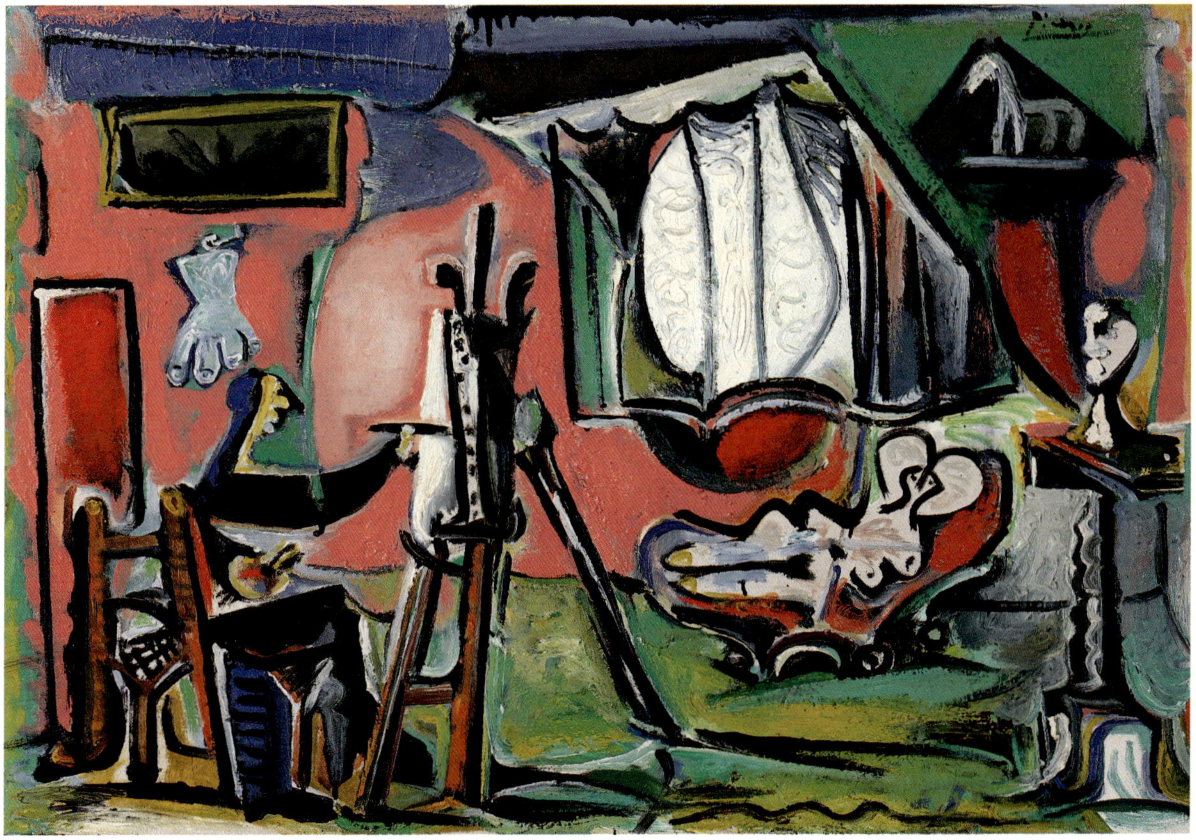

Starting in February 1963, Picasso's passion for the nude precipitated a flurry of paintings all constructed once again around the theme of the model. Picasso described this long series as "the bedroom secrets of a studio," by which he meant, "a raw, immediately transcribed mixture of works, objects, materials, and tools."[39] The canvases were reeled off at a dizzying rate, as if the painter were in the grips of some great urgency. The same setting, with some variations, appears in work after work.

The painter is seated in front of his easel, brushes and palette in hand, caught in the act of painting. Tense, seen in profile concentrating on his work, the painter displays an activity which contrasts with the passivity of the languorously reclining model, whose arms are sometimes thrown behind her head in a posture of peaceful repose. In some instances, the two protagonists are brought closer together and an unexpected spatial ambiguity makes it seem as if the painter's brush were caressing the model's belly in order to take its measure, capture its roundness or snatch up the skin itself. One recalls the incident that took place during the preparations for *Parade*, a ballet for which Picasso designed the costumes. The painter wanted to add a few last-minute touches to the costume of the dancer Lydia Lopokova; she became irritated with the ticklish contact of the painter's indiscreet brush, and finally rebelled, saying that she was neither his canvas nor his mistress!

Picasso wanted to "get his hands" on skin and nudity, all the while wondering if his art would not in the end "skin" him instead. "One can take horrible pains and all of a sudden lose one's skin to these paintings."[40] The stakes are high in this interplay between painting, the body and nudity. "Painting is stronger than I am, it makes me do what it wants,"[41] he once declared, neglecting to add that he always had his way with that mistress of his—painting.

The obsession with the nude recurs like a leitmotiv. Picasso confided his preoccupations to Pignon, another practitioner of the nude: "I do not want to be the one who makes the nude, I want things to be such that the nude cannot be seen other than as it is... There is a point, if you succeed in doing what you want to do, where the breasts fall in place all by themselves, without our needing to draw them."[42] "I want to 'say' the nude. I do not want to make a nude like a nude. I only want to say breast, say foot, hand, belly. To find the means to say it, and that is enough. I do not want to paint the nude from head to foot, but rather get to the point of 'speaking' it. That is what I want. A single word suffices in talking about it. You, a single look and the nude tells you what she is, without words... You know, it is exactly like the fruit vendor: you want two breasts? Well, here you are, two breasts. The necessary thing, for the gentleman looking on, is to have on hand everything he needs to make a nude. If you

Pablo Picasso:
Etching from the series "347"
(Painter and Models), 1968.

really give him everything he needs, the best of it, he will put it all together in place himself with his eyes. Each will do what he wants with the nude that I'll have made for him."[43] All in all, an ambitious program—the open work of art.

When Picasso commented on his paintings (if his statements may be called commentary), filled with presence of the painter and his model, he always spoke of the artist as the "poor artist" and would make fun of his little palette and the care he brought to his painter's goatee. "He thinks he is going to pull through, the poor devil!" One should not forget, however, the pinch of irony with which the Spaniard liked to salt his utterances. Didn't he often say, "How I wish I were a painter!"

These variations notwithstanding, the two main actors, the painter and his model, remain bound, tied, just as Picasso felt chained to painting. "This is how painting is. You take your freedom and you shut yourself up with your idea, that one and no other. And there you are, back with chains on again."[44] The model probably suggested the most generic incarnation of painting, the model "is" painting, or at least the territory on which painting gives the illusion of crystallizing itself. At one point in Picasso's production, a woman (the model?) becomes the painter, as if the artist were fertilized by the woman, or rather, as if painting were fertilized by her. Picasso declared without boasting: "Jacqueline has the gift of becoming painting to an unimaginable degree."[45] Did he mean by this that she was an ideal model, or/and that she made him a painter? Or, again, that his love made him a kind of Pygmalion? Labyrinthine ramifications...

The representations of the painter and his model oscillate between the active and the passive, dualities appear. Movement and sleep, application and relaxation, concentration and abandon, straight and even stiff pose (of the painter) and roundness (of the model). One gaze scrutinizes, perhaps with desire, the other is turned inward in a sort of self-sufficient absorption. And suddenly, abruptly, the model's taboo is transgressed. In *Rembrandt and Saskia*, the painter takes the model on his knees. This passage from model to mistress is depicted in a series of engravings, *Raphael and La Fornarina* after Ingres, as if Picasso had to arm himself with references in order to transgress such an interdiction.

Like Frenhofer in Balzac's *Unknown Masterpiece*, Picasso was in love with his model, in love with nudity. For a time, the painter even lived and

Pablo Picasso:
In the Studio, 1954.

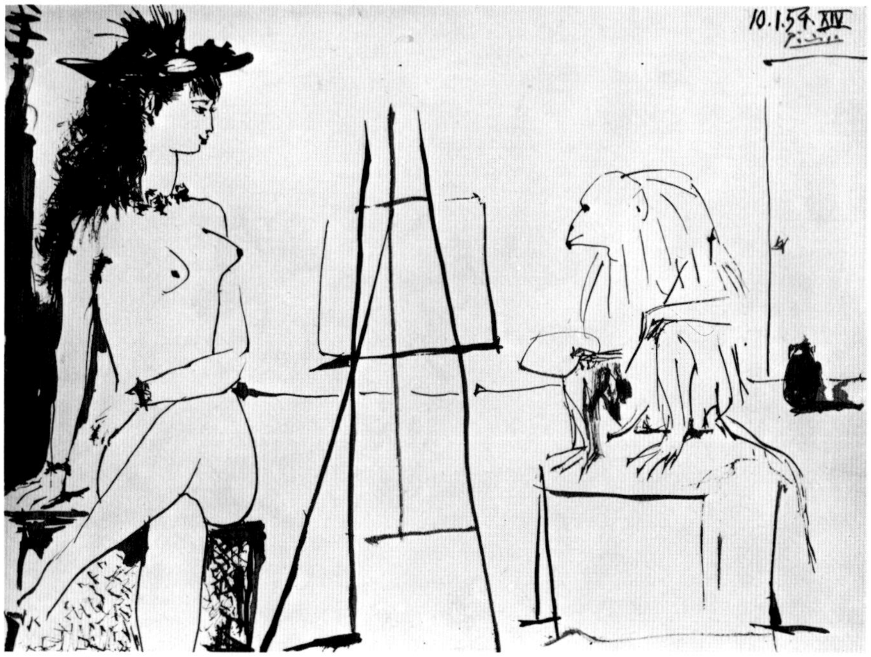

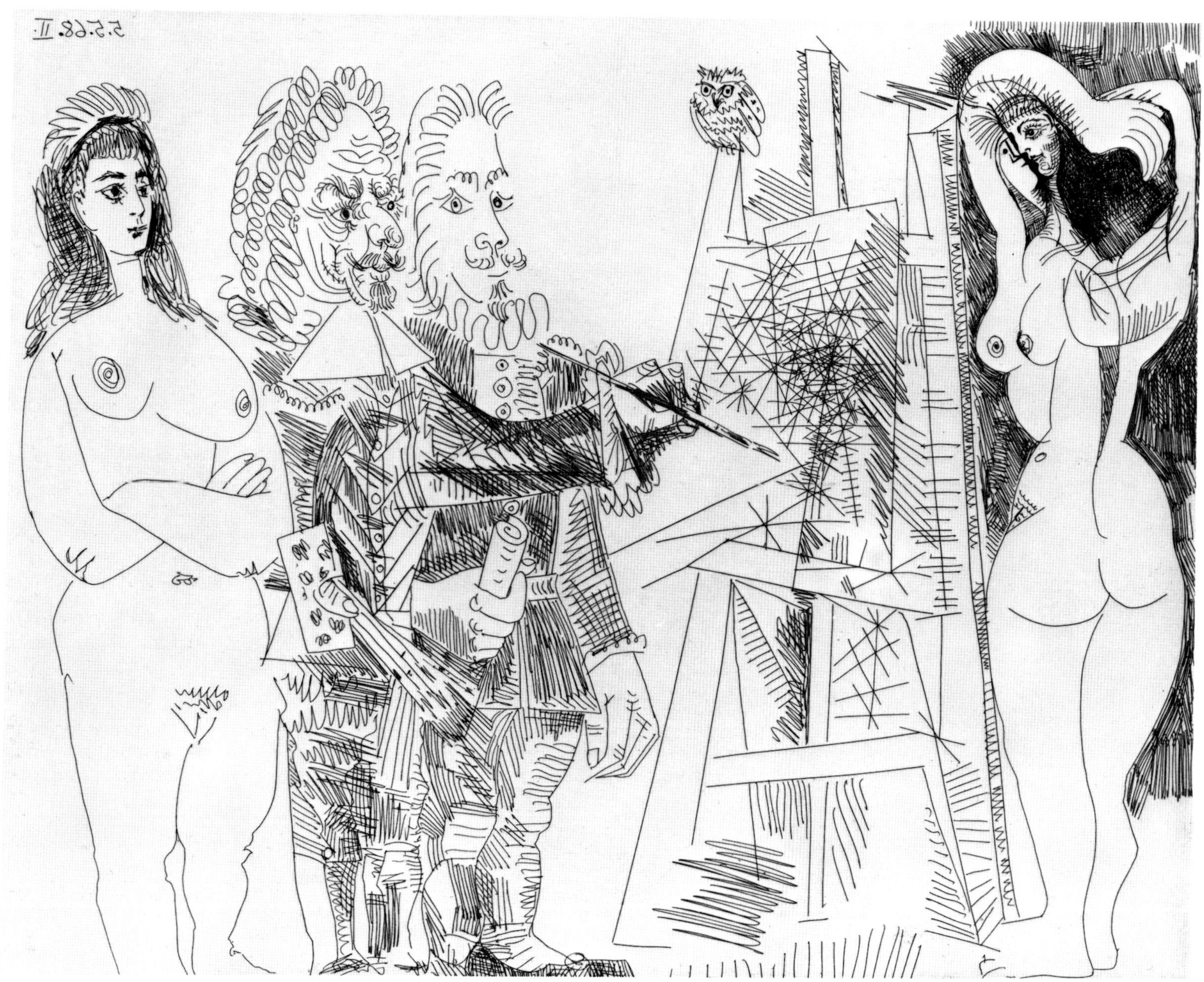

worked at 7, rue des Grands-Augustins, in the same house which Balzac used as the setting for his short story. Picasso often spoke about this story and how he was "moved and stimulated by the idea of taking the place of the illustrious shade of Frenhofer."[46]

During the same period as the series on the painter and his model, Picasso executed a series of "portraits" of figures illustrating the archetype of the painter, the painter decked out with his hat—Rembrandt, Van Gogh, etc.—which he often called "the painter fellow," "eternal crony of the easel," the dauber or demiurge who takes himself for God, the artist who cannot do without a model. "No model, no painter," he would say. The scenario between the painter and his model presented many a variation, but Picasso took the drama to its extremes, a hand-to-hand combat with painting and with the woman who inspired it: a model, not a professional sitter; the woman he lived with, not the model of a woman, but a model woman, a woman who was not painted directly from life, but who was omnipresent. "Jacqueline is said to be Picasso's model," writes Hélène Parmelin, "A model poses, but Jacqueline does not pose, she lives. While Picasso paints her, she may be there watching him, or somewhere else. Her face floats through the workdays at Notre-Dame-de-Vie. The eyes of painting are forever open on her, whether she is in the studio or not. In paintings called 'the painter and his model,' Picasso is not the painter, Jacqueline is not the model, and yet at the same time, in living, they do not stop playing their respective roles."[47]

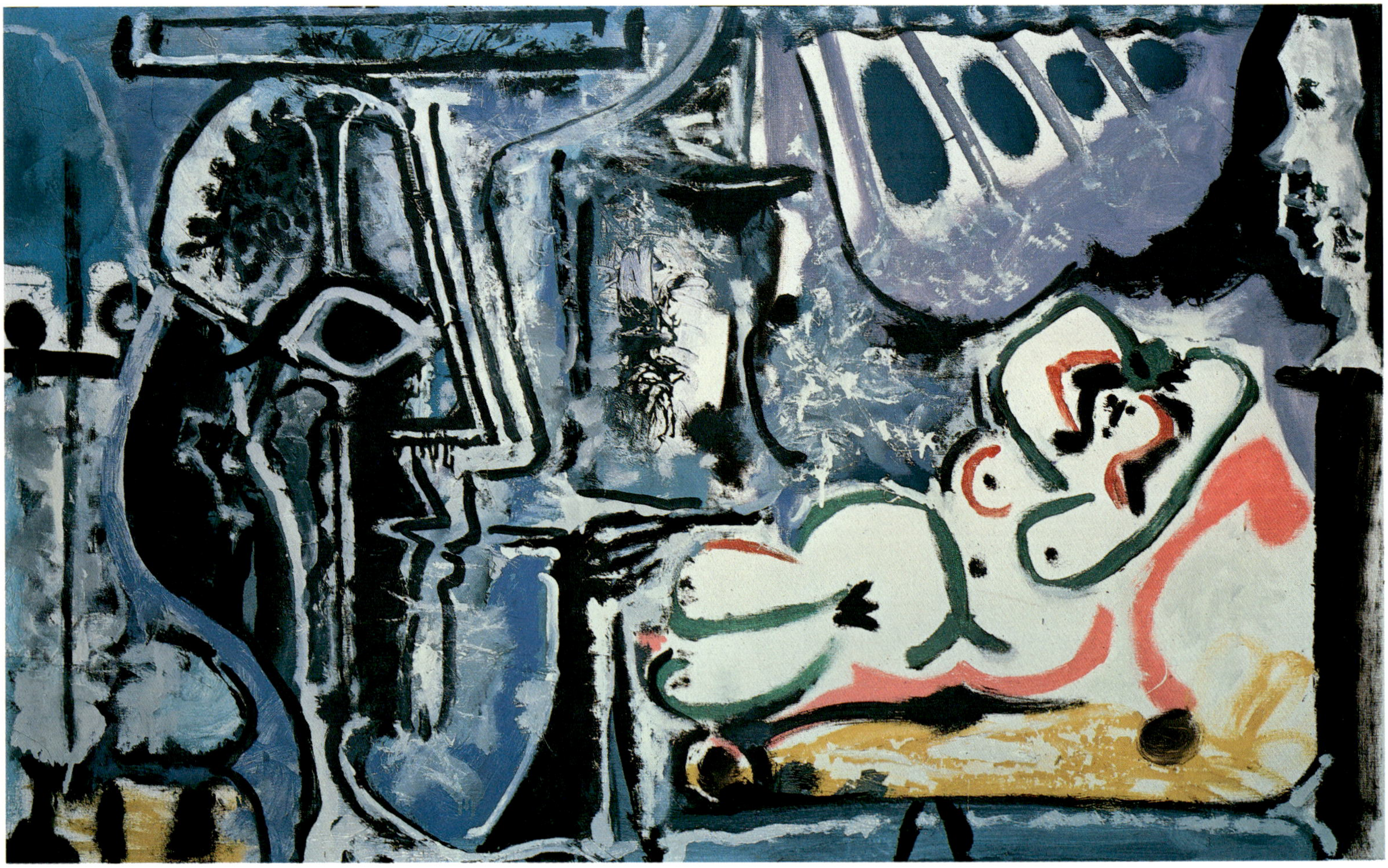

Pablo Picasso:
The Artist and His Model, 1963.

Picasso showed the nude from every possible angle, and applied his ingenuity to representing the sexual parts in infinite variations on the fissure, relentless efforts to depict the cleft. "If I make a nude, people should think that it is a nude, and not a nude of Mrs. So and So."[48] His was an obstinate search to transcribe the carnal reality of a body to the point that one does not know if it is a woman or a painting. Picasso, showing Braque a painting, would anxiously question him: "Is this woman real? Can she go out into the street? Is it a woman or a painting?" Insisting further, he would say: "Do her armpits smell?"[49] And so, for the two painters, underarm odor became the criterion for truth in painting!

Under his brush, woman played all her roles: antique goddess, *alma mater*, devouring mantis, abandoned pebble in sleep, ogress, sacred prostitute... the multifarious aspects of womanhood. In their embrace, one cannot say who engenders whom, who devours whom. The brush is wielded like a phallus, unless it is the phallus which is wielded like a brush. Bodies intermingle. From the beast with two backs, painting bursts forth in joyful spurts, free-flowing streams. We are reminded of a passage in Paul Klee's journal: "In the beginning, the motif, the insertion of energy, sperm. The work as creator of material form: fundamentally feminine. The work as sperm determining form: fundamentally masculine."[50] The aging Picasso worked fast and furiously, without encumbering himself with allusions, and made eroticism explode on the canvas in a loud and howling rhapsody. "You have to know how to be vulgar, how to paint with four-letter words." The artist was painting for his life, committing to canvas his last crimes. "Each painting is a vial of my blood," exclaimed the Andalusian. To a journalist (yet another) who wanted to know what the master would do if he were imprisoned for life and

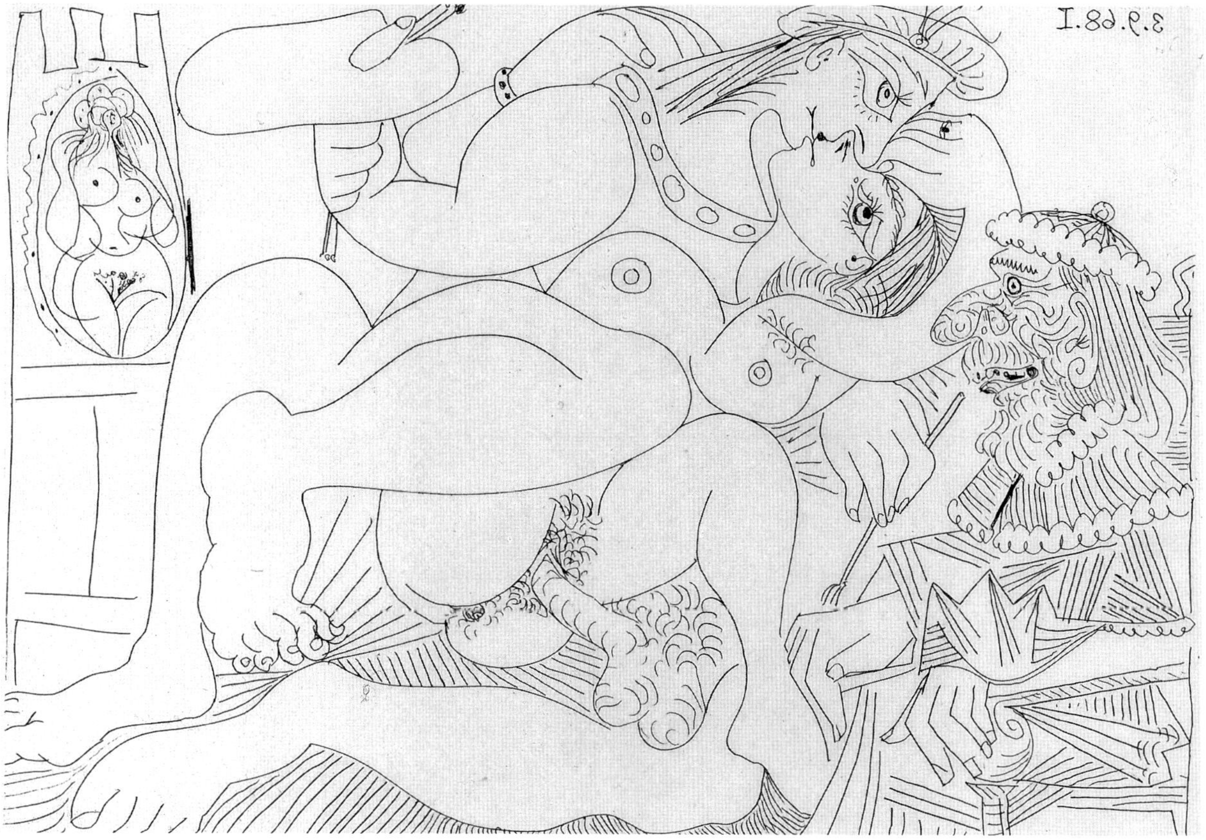

deprived of the tools of his trade, Picasso replied squarely: "I would paint with my shit!" Painting comes into being through the body of the artist, it is the body of the artist itself. This giant of a painter once rightly wondered: "What will painting do when I am no longer around; it will have to pass over my dead body! It won't be able to get around me, no?"[51]

In the series of etchings on the theme of *Raphael and La Fornarina*, Ingres appears as a voyeur. Pictorial references fit together like Russian dolls. Picasso is curious about Ingres, who was curious about Raphael; there is both a curiosity and a desire to kill. References to ward off the fear born of transgressing taboos. The figures spy on each other. The voyeur peers through the curtain. A woman exhibits herself. The painter has an erection with his brushes and palette in hand. On the easel, an image waits. Coitus is explicit, clearly incarnated in superlative and minutely rendered sexual organs. In order to fulfill the destiny of painting, the model is raped. Penetration becomes a magic ritual like that of peasants fornicating in a field to fertilize the earth. Picasso (along with his mediator, Raphael) "dies" in his work, fertilizing art with his climax, which the French aptly call the "petite mort." Picasso reads Bataille.

△▽ *Pablo Picasso:*
Etchings from the series "Raphael and the Fornarina," 1968.

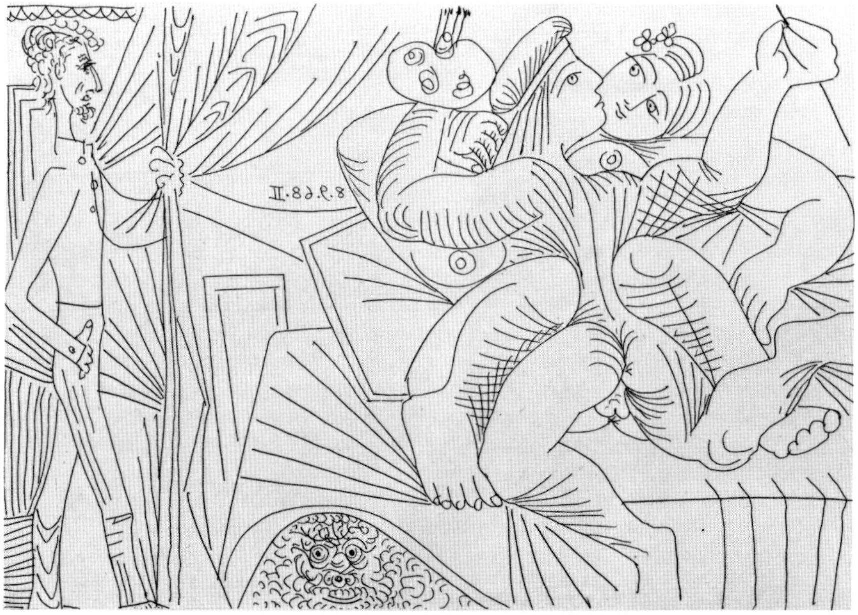

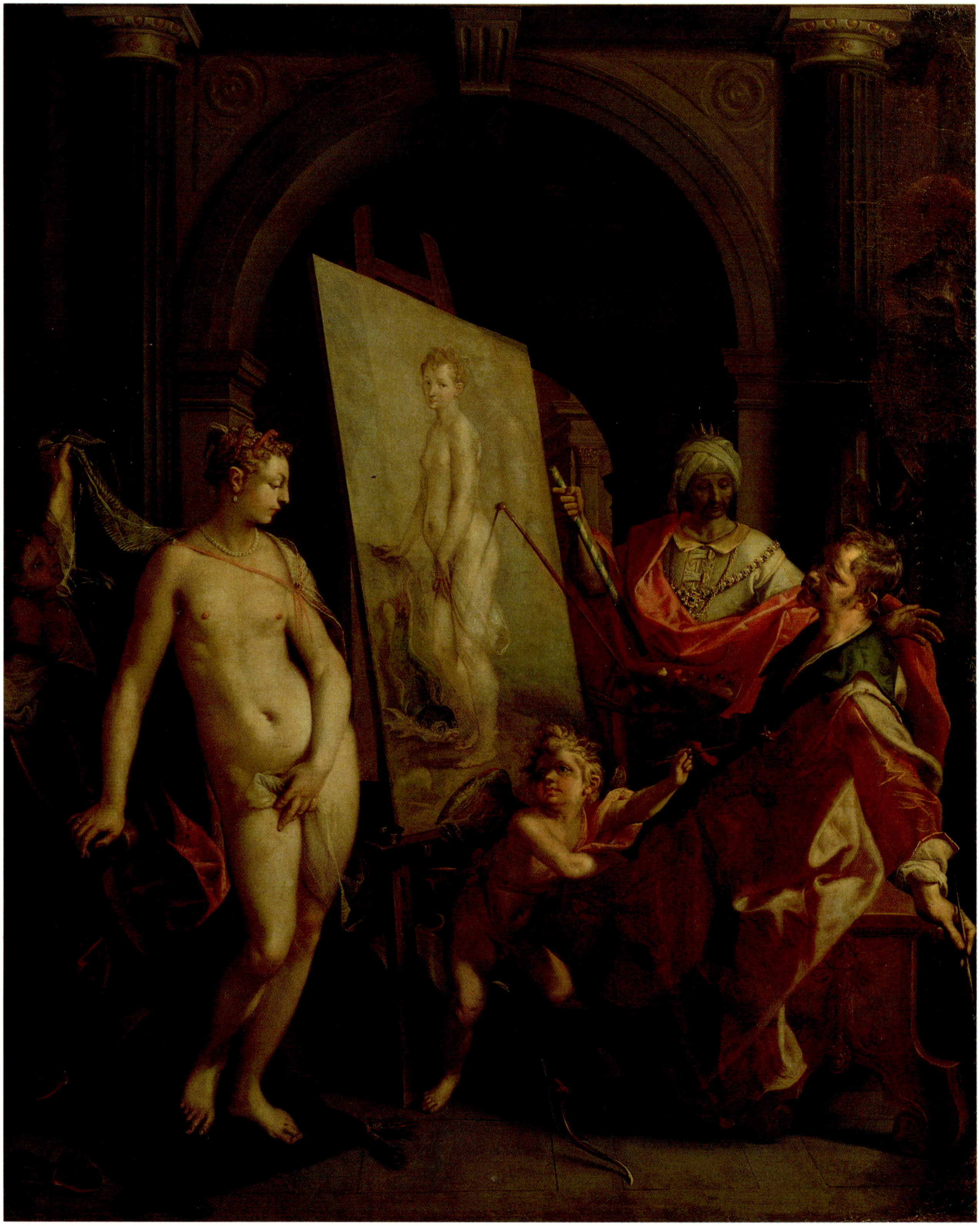

The studio and the cult of flesh

Jodocus van Winghe:
Apelles Painting Campaspe, c. 1600.

The workings of the studio revolve around the live model. The presence of the nude in the artist's studio as early as ancient Greece is attested by Pliny. The Roman historian recounts how Apelles, the official painter of Alexander the Great and the only artist permitted to represent his likeness, was asked by the king to portray in the nude the beautiful Campaspe, his favorite concubine. "Alexander gave a measure of the esteem which he had for Apelles by having him paint a nude portrait of the fairest and best-loved of his mistresses, Campaspe. As he worked, the artist fell in love with her, and so Alexander, who realized this, gave her to him. Great by his courage, he was greater still by his command over himself; such a deed honors him no less than a victory, for he conquered himself. He abandoned to the artist not only his pleasures, but also his affections, without letting himself be moved by his favorite's worries, who was passing from a king to a painter."[52]

Thus, the artist in question fell in love with a very special model whom circumstances made particularly untouchable; Alexander's great heart, however, his mastery of his passions, and his role as enlightened protector of the arts rendered him magnanimous. Unfortunately, no trace of Apelles' work has come down to us. Yet this episode is often mentioned. François I, an emulator of the great Macedonian ruler, had this scene represented by Primaticcio in the bedchamber of the Duchess of Etampes at Fontainebleau. Generally, the episode was highly regarded by the Renaissance.

In the studies of 17th century Flemish collectors the social significance of this story was prized, its theme taken as a glorification of painting and the painter for the greatest ruler of all time had honored a painter, had even judged him worthy enough to receive the favors of the royal concubine. Painting was thus ennobled, as when Charles V picked up Titian's fallen brush, or François I attended Leonardo da Vinci on his deathbed. Pliny's account emphasizes the power of Apelles, who was daring enough to put the king

Master L.D. *(after Primaticcio): Apelles Painting Alexander and Campaspe, c. 1545.*

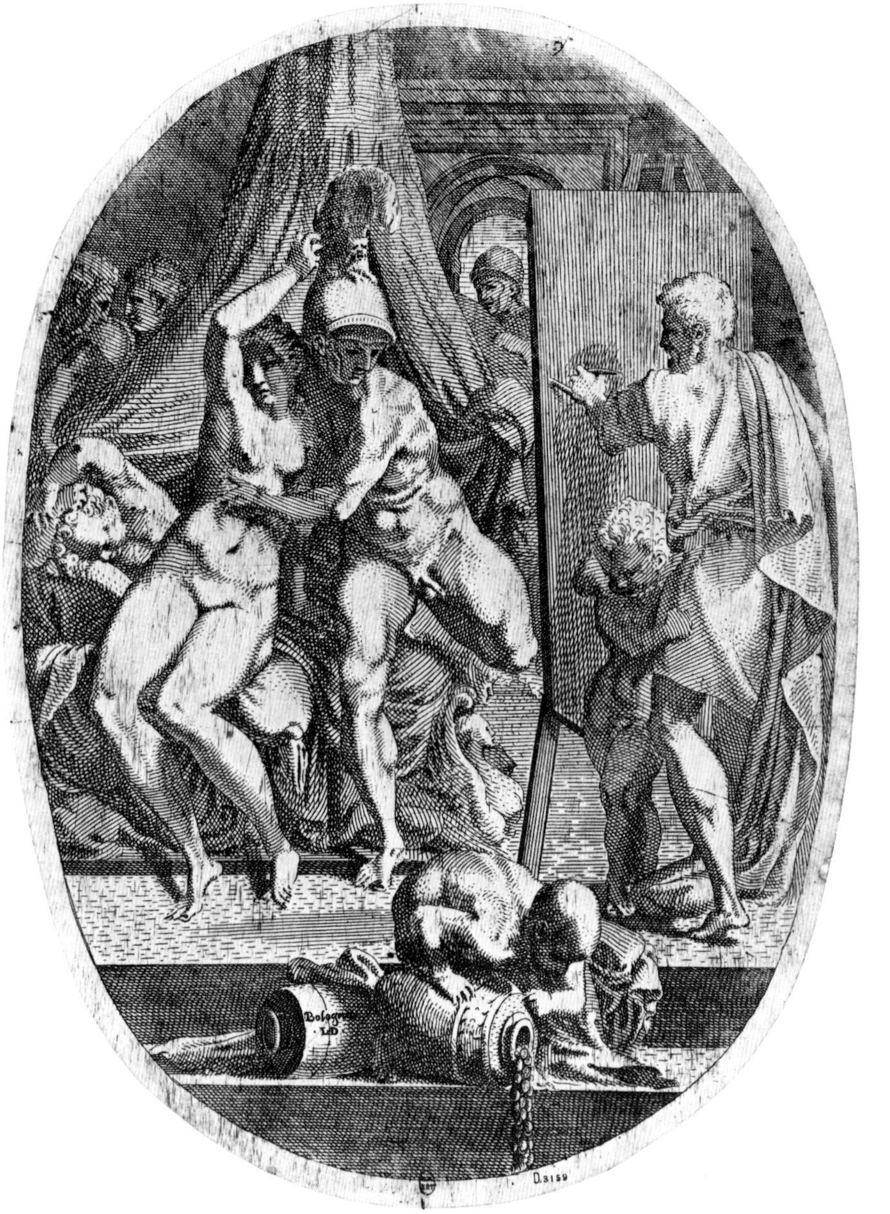

back in his place when he tried to occupy himself unduly with painting: "Apelles was very amenable in his manners, and for this he gained the favor of Alexander the Great. The king would often visit him in his studio—for, as we have said, he had issued a decree forbidding all other artists to paint his portrait. But one day, as Alexander was venturing too many opinions on the subject of painting, the painter gently asked him to be quiet, telling him that he was making a laughingstock of himself in front of the apprentices grinding his pigments. This shows the authority which his talent gave him over a king who was, moreover, known for his ease to anger."[53]

In the 19th century Apelles again appeared as the symbol of princely honors granted to painting. Since the Renaissance, the interpreters of this episode wondered in which spirit the artist had received his "gift." Was it with an attitude of pride, or on the contrary, one of humility? The only indication Pliny gives is to say that the mistress was being passed from a king to a painter, and that this did not trouble the king. Painting may have gained in prestige, but Campaspe hardly seems thrilled by the change.

To return to antiquity, we could indeed say that Apelles was bowing down before the embodiment of Beauty. All that Alexander did was to recognize a legitimate superiority. By treating this theme the descendants of Apelles, or those who claimed to be declared that beauty was their province, since only they could exalt its image through the sublimity of a work of art.

While antiquity occasionally resorted to the use of live models, the Middle Ages, until the Gothic period, remained suspicious of them. In the 13th century, Villard de Honnecourt seems to have called on the services of a cooperative mason willing to disrobe for his drawings. The cathedrals of Chartres, Reims, and Bourges especially, prove that the sculptors who worked there had a familiarity with muscles they could only have gained through the observation of nude models. Starting with the Quattrocento, however, flesh triumphed in a hymn to nudity as artists and anatomists began to combine their efforts. The Renaissance rediscovered the nudes of antiquity and used them liberally as justifications and pretexts for its own creations. Bronzino portrayed Cosimo de' Medici as Orpheus, Andrea Doria as Neptune, while Diane de Poitiers incarnated her Olympian namesake, and so on.

With the rise of individualism and the cult of genius, the relations between the artist and his model increased and took a special turn. In his *Autobiography*, the notorious Benvenuto Cellini

Jacques Louis David:
Apelles Painting Campaspe in front of Alexander, 1812-1813.

informs us as much about the general way in which models were used as about his own, very personal attitude toward them. An otherwise delicate goldsmith and sculptor, Cellini led a very eventful and roguish life: he seduced servant girls, had violent quarrels with the pope, and was known for his fierce jealousy and his thirst for revenge. An irrepressible ogre, he interrupted the sittings to debauch his models and give them a thrashing.

"Not satisfied with having made him take such a shameless little whore as his wife, as well as this—to round off my revenge—I used to send for her to make use of her as my model. Every day I gave her thirty soldi; and I made her pose in the nude. First, she wanted to be paid in advance, and then she wanted to make a good meal, and then I had my revenge by having intercourse with her, mocking at her and her husband for the various horns I was giving him. The fourth thing I did was to make her pose in great discomfort for hours at a stretch. And, in her discomfort, she was as much annoyed as I was delighted, since she was very beautifully mad and won me great honour."[54]

The sculptor finally sent the "saucy Caterina" away for good, but as a result he was sorely in need of a model to finish the Nymph for Fontainebleau. He hunted for a new model and found a poor girl of about fifteen whom he nicknamed "Scozzone"

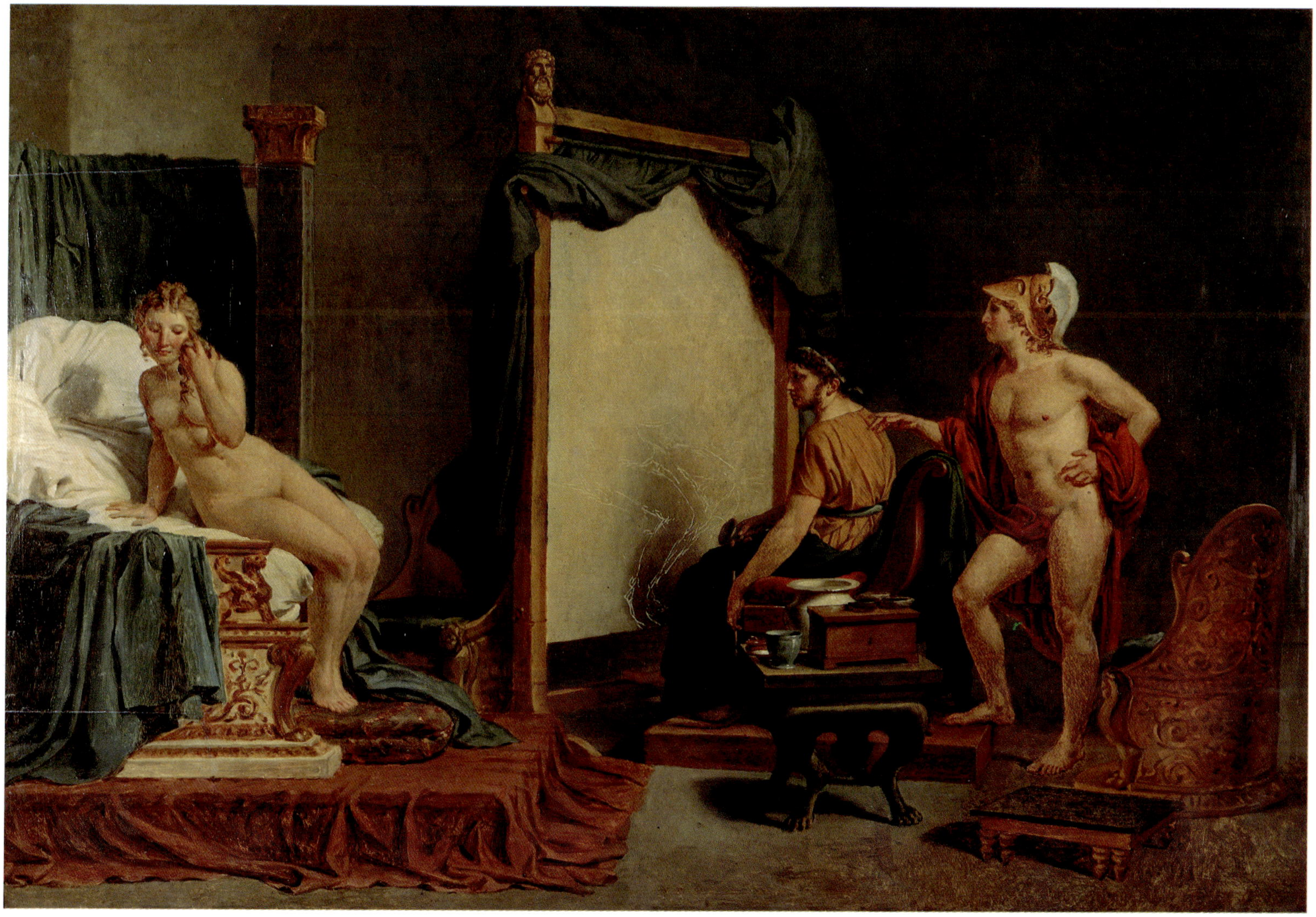

Jan Gossaert:
Neptune and Amphitrite, 1516.

("daredevil"), because of her taciturn temperament, vivacity and fierce gaze. Thanks to her he was able to finish the bronze *Nymph* of Fontainebleau and two Victories. A chaste virgin when he found her, he soon made her pregnant.

The escapades of the artists and the works that ensued may have amused the aristocrats, but they aroused indignation among the populace. As a precaution, Michelangelo's *David* was set up at night, yet even this did not prevent the statue from being lapidated, and the public authorities had to hide its nudity behind a garland of copper leaves. The wiser artists anticipated this censorship and took their own precautions. Benvenuto Cellini presented to François I a *Jupiter* with "delicate and gracious drapery to give it more majesty." Little good such self-censorship did him. Irritated by the Italian sculptor, the Duchess of Etampes suggested that Cellini had added this veil to dissimulate some imperfection in his work. The sculptor was outraged—violently so, one suspects—and the king had to intervene to temper the ill-humor of his mistress and the anger of his favorite artist.

The story of the *Last Judgment* in the Sistine Chapel is even more eloquent.[55] In 1536, Alexander Farnese, elected to the papacy with the name of Paul III, commissioned the "divine" Michelangelo to paint a *Last Judgment*. During a visit to the chapel to see the progress of the work, his master of ceremonies, Baggio, objected to the indecency of the composition and admonished the pope to this effect, but the latter took the artist's defense. To avenge himself, Michelangelo gave Baggio's likeness to the figure of Minos, the infernal judge, whom he represented as naked as a demon and with a snake appended to his member. Paul III, quite amused by the painter's prank, replied to Baggio's complaints by saying: "Lord Baggio, God has given me power over the earth and the heavens, but my authority does not extend as far as Hell; you will need some patience if I cannot deliver you from there."[56]

The Pope and the aristocracy defended the artist's work, but popular feeling was offended, and Aretino, the most libertine writer of the period, made himself the spokesman for this popular indignation—out of personal animosity toward Michelangelo. The fresco became the symbol of the fight against indecency. Thus, thirty years after its execution, the *Last Judgment* was "bowdlerized." Paul IV called on Daniele da Volterra, a friend of Michelangelo, to cover the offensive parts. Although he accomplished this task with great regret and parcimony, he was nonetheless given the nickname "Il Braghettone," which could loosely be translated as "The Underdrawer." These adventitious veils, however, did not satisfy those detractors who demanded the outright destruction of the frescoes. In his *Dialogue on the Errors of Painters*, Gilio da Fabriano launched a vehement attack on the *Last Judgment* and recommended the use of corrective measures. "Certain very worthy artifices have been perfected for the sake of preserving honesty, such as hiding the shameful parts of sacred figures with graceful veils."[57] The debate was revived under Clement VIII, who considered destroying the frescoes, but the entreaties of the Academy of Saint Luke dissuaded him from this extreme course of action. In the 18th century, Clement XIII had a few alterations effected, and rumor has it that as recently as 1936, Pius XI had a mind to adding even more drapery!

Another exemplary story features Veronese in Venice—an otherwise sensual city—being summoned before the Court of the Inquisition on charges of indecency. He had just decorated a Dominican convent and was reproached with having mixed religious subjects with dwarves, buffoons, drunken Germans, and other such "foolishness," and of having replaced an honest Magdalen with a dog. Veronese was found guilty and ordered to change his *Last Supper* into a *Feast in the House of Levi*. Warned and edified by reports of such reactions, a goodly number of artists henceforth prudishly draped their religious subjects. There was a time—not too long—when the Venetian Republic crusaded against the indecent exposure of saints.

The Renaissance was therefore divided into two currents: on the one hand, artists and aristocrats supported by high dignitaries of the Church who delighted in nudity; and on the other, the general public, which misguidedly applied the real-life criteria of propriety to artistic representations. This break made a clear distinction between sacred and profane art. There were those who looked askance at a Virgin giving the breast and who wanted to clothe the Child Jesus; while others, in more restrained circles, privately passed around prints depicting the sexual positions described by Aretino and engraved by Giulio Romano.

For centuries, prudes of all stripes made liberal use of fig, vine and laurel leaves. Maria Lesczynska, on the advice of her confessor, eclipsed the virility of the mythological heroes of Marly. Anatole France lampooned these do-gooders in the person of Monsieur Nicomède, President of the League of Decency, who boasted to Jérôme Coignard that he had affixed "six hundred vine or fig leaves to the statues of the King's gardens"! But, fig leaf or vine leaf?—the case for one or the other remained pending. In favor of the first there was the Bible, since in the Book of Genesis, Adam and Eve each adopted one after the Fall. Gustave Flaubert

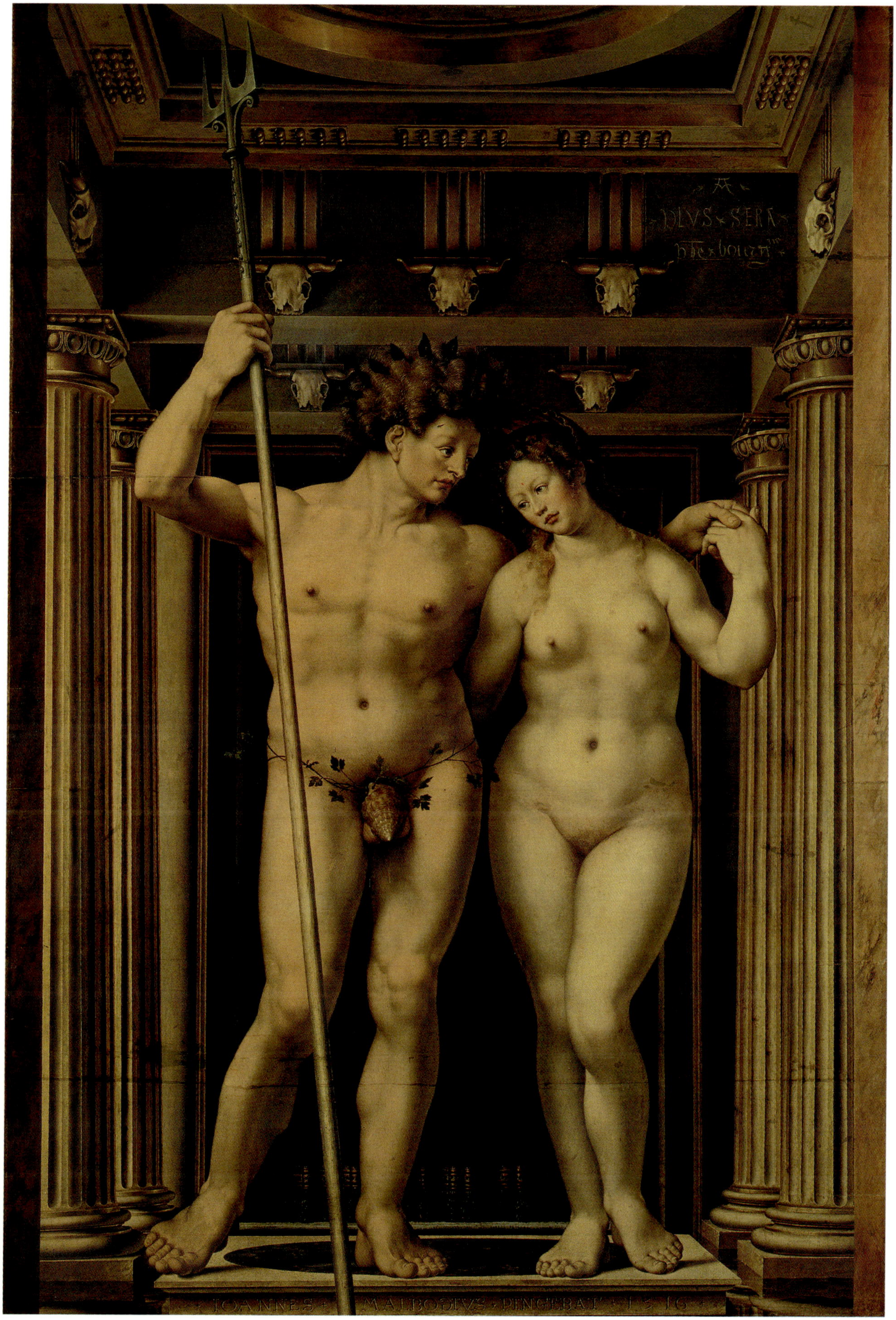

Jean-Michel Moreau, after Baudoin:
The Honest Model, beginning of the 18th century.

Anonymous:
The Model Disposed, 18th century.

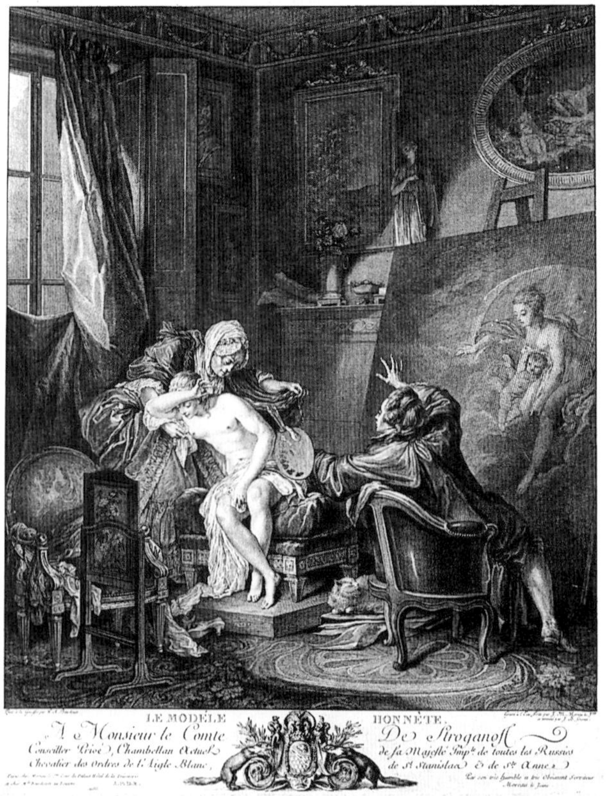

rebelled against the vine leaf after discovering the use to which it had been put in a provincial art museum. The writer would have given his fortune to "know the name, age, address, profession, and face of the gentleman who invented for the statues of the museum of Nantes those fig leaves made of tin that look like devices designed to discourage onanism. Casts of the *Apollo of Belvedere*, the *Discus Thrower* and a flute player have been outfitted with these shameful metal drawers that sparkle like pots and pans. One can see that this work was long premeditated and that it was executed with loving care; the edges are scalloped and they are affixed with screws to the members of these poor plaster figures now flaking away with pain. In these times of rampant folly, amid the common stupidity which surrounds us, what a joy it is to find, if only for the sake of diversion, at least one truly outstanding idiocy, one gigantic stupidity. In spite of all of my efforts, I have not been able to imagine a thing about the creator of these loathsomely prudish contrivances. I like to think that the entire township council took part in it, that the gentlemen of the Church lobbied for it, and that the ladies found them suitable."[58]

Among humorists, the aforementioned foremost forelimb leaf inspired as many puns and ribald allusions as they were supposed to discourage; who has not heard the one about leaves falling in autumn, or about the repentant satyr who wanted to turn over a new leaf? Yet artists generally fell into line and some even excelled in placing these appendages so that they appeared "natural." Drapery was extended to just the right spot, a bush would sprout in the exact place required by decorum, etc.

Be that as it may, academic training made systematic use of live models from the end of the 16th century on. The majority were male, but there were also female models, witness the drawings of the Rembrandt school in which we see the master and his students sketching a nude woman on a

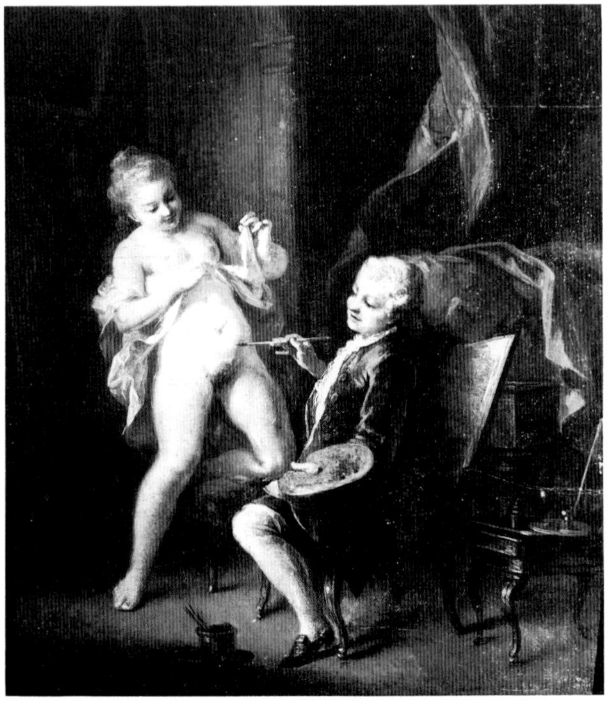

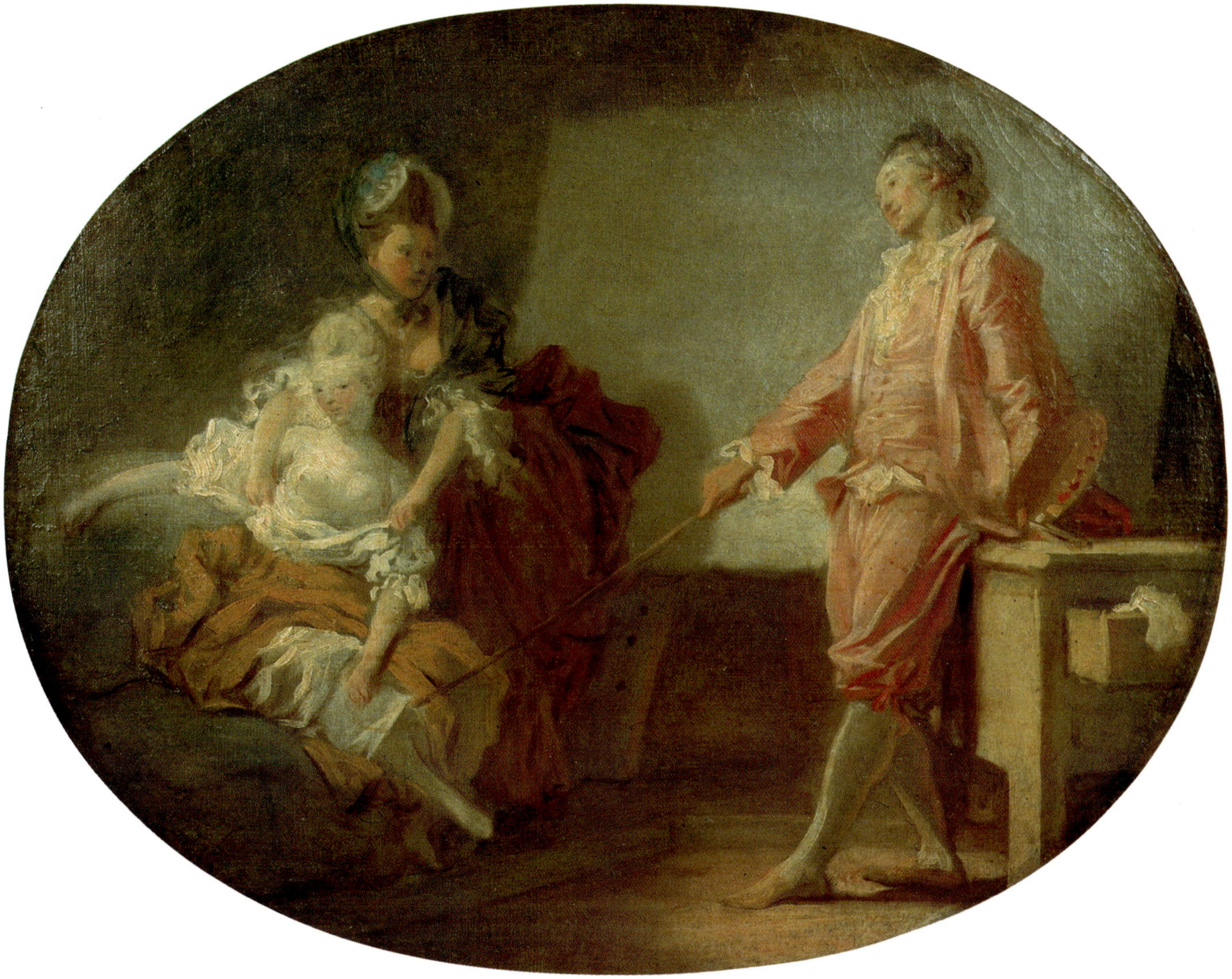

Jean-Honoré Fragonard:
The Model's Debut, undated.

podium set off at a distance, isolated and indifferent to the eyes focused upon her.[59] The master and his students are concentrating as they would in working on a still life, and without lechery—without apparent lechery in any case.

The posing sessions must have appeared suspect nonetheless, because it was not until the end of the 19th century that most of the official academies began to admit female models. For a long time only private academies provided access to the female nude. On the other hand, painters had recourse to more or less professional models in the privacy of their own studios. Puritanical souls could, alas, always be found to interfere. In an engraving after Baudouin, an old woman interrupts a posing session in order to cover the model with her coat, while the painter, making a great gesture in protest, perseveres. Baudouin, well known for his rather risqué subjects, wanted to establish a distance between his public persona and his work; a picturesque way of speaking about sublimation. Most beholders, however, did not catch on to these allusions and persuaded instead (rightly or wrongly) of the free *mores* enjoyed by artists had great fun matching such and such a type of woman represented by a painter with one or another of his mistresses. Honoré Fragonard subscribed to a libertine vision of sittings in his *The Model's Debut*, where he showed a matron undertaking to undress a timid novice, while the impatient painter lifts her skirt with his maulstick. Things are even more explicit in Frédéric Schall's *The Model Disposed*, in which the painter, like Picasso, embraces the model with his palette still in hand.

Diderot sharply criticized Boucher for the 18th century critic understood the erotic content of his paintings. "His debauchery probably attracts the attention of minor masters, women of low breeding, young people, the mundane, all those who are foreign to true taste, truth, right ideas, or severity in art; how could they resist Boucher's brio, his licentiousness, his glamour, his frills, his breasts, his bottoms, his epigrams?... The man takes up the brush only to show me bosoms and bottoms. I am delighted to see some, but I do not want them to be shown to me."[60] Is the nude acceptable then only if it is disincarnated?

Madame de Pompadour created a scandal when, succumbing to a craze for engraving and wishing to revive an antique tradition, she had herself portrayed in the altogether along with her royal lover disguised as Apollo in the act of crowning the genius of painting and sculpture. "This indecency made some wonder which royal guardsman or page had served as models; it turned out to be Messrs. de *** and de **; verses alluding to these events were written and passed around; they at least proved to the entire court that Madame de Pompadour had no idea of decorum in having the king engraved in the form of a nude Apollo."[61] Of course, it would have been unimaginable for Louis XV to pose nude in the salon of one of his mistress's residences.

Another telling anecdote involves a philosophical model: Voltaire. Some admirers decided to

François Boucher: Laure O'Murphy, 1751.

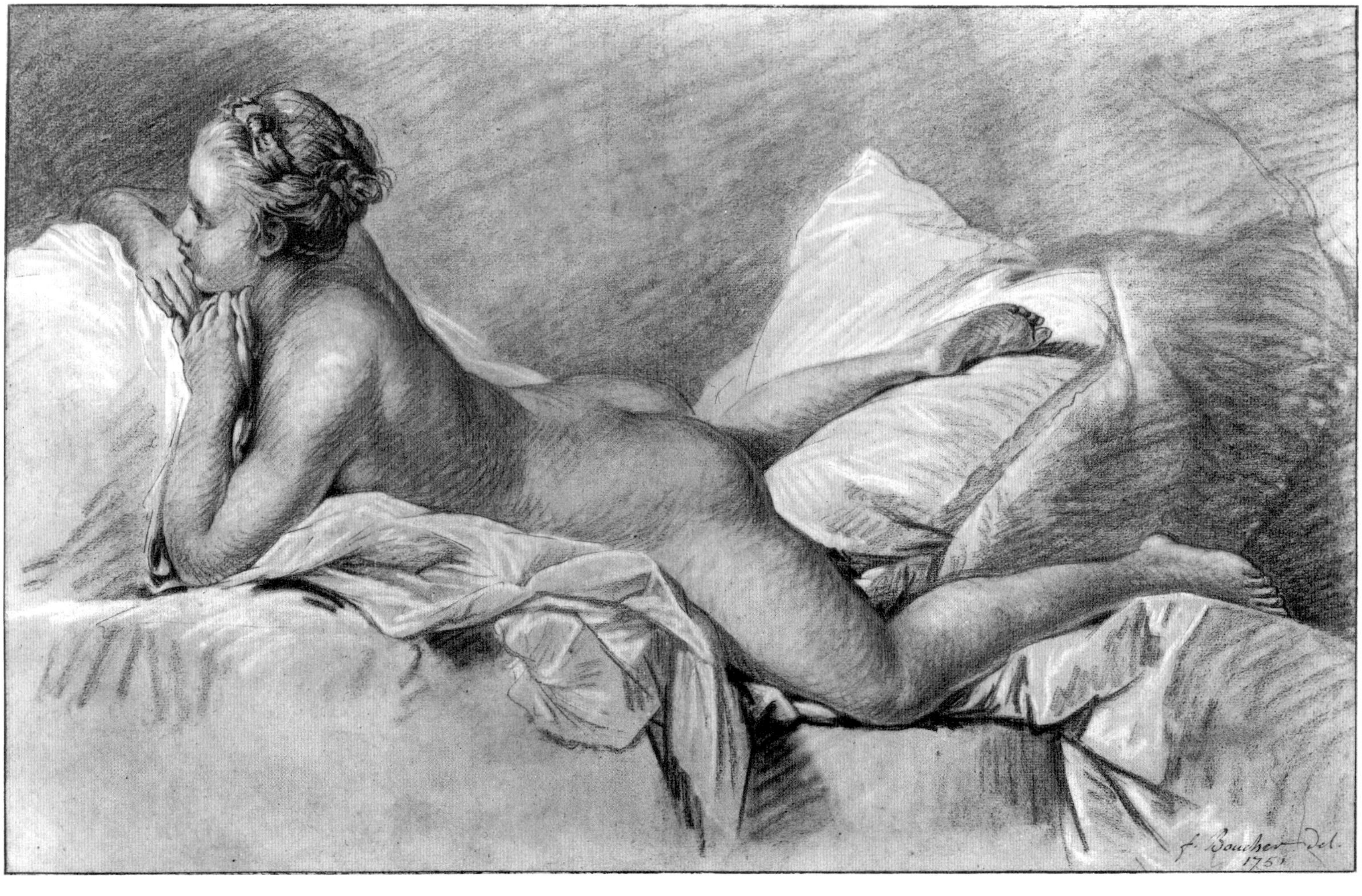

commission Pigalle to sculpt a statue in homage to the patriarch of Ferney. Pigalle's project to represent a nude philosopher in the antique tradition was greeted with enthusiasm, but Madame Necker suddenly realized that such a subject hardly suited a man in his seventies. She communicated her reservations to the philosopher himself: "I would like to have your opinion on Pigalle's caprice; he wants at all cost to depict you nude. We try to tell him that this would be indecent in the company of the nine Muses; that this statue should have neither wrinkles, nor muscles; that the old age of Voltaire is a portion of immortality; that drapery would suit this expressive face better; that we cannot clad ourselves in laurel leaves as before; that you have eaten too much of the tree of Science to be able to do without clothes; that we should use our imagination, which will perhaps give the head of the statue a winged or diaphanous body; that one does not undress to write, and scores of other excellent reasons, but that barbarian invariably replies that he, Pigalle, also wants to live in posterity, and he claims that his name will follow you through the centuries, that there is a place for everything under the sun, and that he wants to sculpt Voltaire. What are we to do, sir?" The old sage replied: "Nude or clothed, it does not matter much to me. In whatever way I am presented, I will surely inspire no dishonest thoughts among the ladies. M. Pigalle should be left absolute master of his statue. It is a crime in the fine arts to bridle genius."[62] Pigalle was therefore able to work in complete freedom, and people flocked to his studio to watch the progress on the "skeleton of M. Voltaire."

Yet, in that world supposedly so free of prejudices, it would have been morally inconceivable for the old man to pose in his birthday suit. Furthermore, and this is relatively secondary, the sittings for the face alone were a torment for Voltaire and Pigalle alike. The anatomy of the statue was provided by an old soldier, vigorous well-preserved veteran of the Seven Years' War. This made certain observers smile guessing that the practice of philosophy could not build up so many muscles! As it was, the statue was soon forgotten, relegated to a closet, and replaced by Houdon's portrait, which shows a philosopher in the antique style, amply draped.

In the 19th century the thorny subject of the model was approached fairly timidly, unless it was in the realm of erotic representation. It took the candor of a Courbet to conceive the juxtaposition of the painter and his unclad model in *The Studio*. This huge canvas, which Courbet subtitled "a real allegory determining a seven-year phase of my artistic life," is a sort of inventory of the contents of his studio. The artist represents himself in the act of

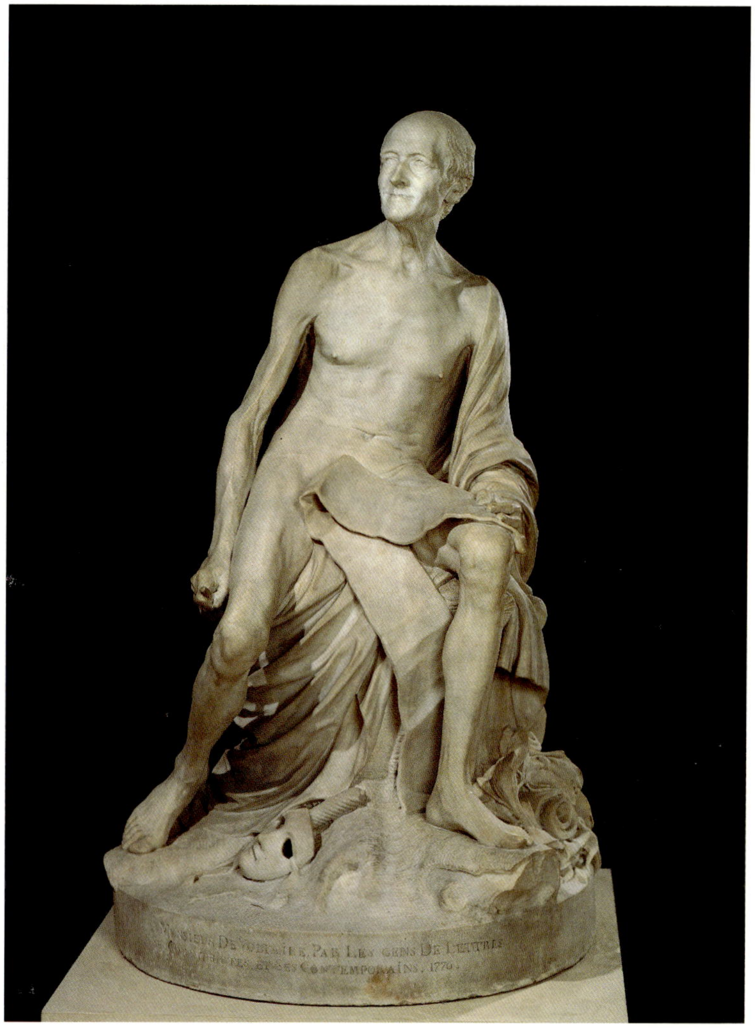

Jean-Baptiste Pigalle: Voltaire, 1770-1776.

painting a landscape of Franche-Comté under the gaze of a local shepherd boy. A nude woman standing behind the painter indulgently observes the artist at work. She is very present indeed given the fullness of her body. She is not posing (the painter is working on a landscape), but seems to be a partner to the work, a maternal presence almost, as though she incarnated the driving force of the studio even when she was not being directly used. It is manifestly she who brings light to the painting and gives it its center of gravity, the hub of what Courbet called "the moral and physical history of the studio." Foregrounded, she lords it, both predominant and primordial, over the host of other figures representing the "people who serve me and participate in my action," as the painter described them. These other figures, incidentally, form a rather cumbersome and fastidious catalogue of symbols.

This painting was rejected at the Salon of 1855, but Courbet was not deterred; at his own expense, he built a special pavilion, the "Pavillon du réalisme," adjacent to the grounds of the Exposition Universelle. The public as a whole proved indifferent, but no less of a master than Delacroix considered this composition as "one of the most singular works of our time"—which does not necessarily mean that he appreciated it! Curiously enough, *The Studio* did not unleash as strong a reaction as his *Bathers* had at the Salon of 1853. The Empress had then qualified these figures as "draught-horses," and Théophile Gautier thought that they looked like "obesities with poorly-distributed fat." The rustic Courbet had the latter critic wondering; "What did the painter have in mind in making a display of such astonishing anatomies? Did he want to protest in his own way against the white lies of Paros and Pentelikos? Was it hatred of the Venus de Milo that made this soiled body rise out of these dark waters?" Théophile Gautier nonetheless conceded that "this monstrous figure contains very finely toned and firmly modeled passages. The water has a deep transparency which is very simply rendered; the landscape is full of air and freshness, and this unfortunate canvas displays a great deal of misguided talent."[63]

Edmond About called the *Bathers* a "scandal of nudity." "It is less of a woman than a trunk of flesh, a body made of bark."[64] Yet after having heaped scorn upon this work, he invited future spectators to go to the Louvre and admire such a masterpiece next to the museum's Dürers and Jordaens! Mérimée pronounced an even more damning verdict: "M. Courbet may have wanted to give a lesson in morality; otherwise, I cannot understand why a man would have bothered copying from life an ungainly woman with her maid together taking an apparently much-needed bath in a pond... I confess that it is impossible to render a more living flesh; but it seems that M. Courbet does not mean to send his *Bathers* to New Zealand, where the merit of a captive is reckoned by the amount of meat she can provide for the dinner of her captors..."[65] Delacroix deplored the "uselessness of the idea." "A fat bourgeoise seen from the back, completely naked save for the shreds of a rag negligently covering the lower part of her bottom, rises out of a small patch of water that hardly seems deep enough to wash one's feet. She is making a gesture that expresses nothing while another woman, her servant we suppose, is shown seated on the ground in the process of pulling off her shoes. Stockings that one of them has just taken off are seen lying there. Between the two figures there is an exchange of thoughts that escapes comprehension."[66] However, Delacroix distinguishes subject and vigor. Prudhon, on the other hand, rebels straight out, "Right, there she is the fleshy well-to-do *bourgeoise*, deformed by sloth and luxury, whose flabbiness and bulk smother any ideal; who is fated to die of cowardice if she doesn't expire first in her own melted fat. There she is such as her stupidity, selfishness and cooking render her for us... Chubby and plump, brown and glistening—one will definitely not trade her for a Diane or a Hebe... She is a simple *bourgeoise*, whose husband, liberal under Louis-Philippe, reactionary under Republic, is at present one of the Emperor's most devoted subjects."

Decidedly, *The Studio* did not arouse such a verbal onslaught. True, the nude woman depicted there is clearly much less a "draught-horse," having become somewhat Parisianized, while the labored side of this large canvas, at first glance, may have beguiled the critics. The work was undoubtedly reduced due to its too ambitious exhaustivity. Courbet wanted to say too much and thus fell into mere description. Fortunately, the model emerges, generous, from the wave of drapery. "In Courbet's work," writes Pierre Mac Orlan, "naturally the extremity of the artist's fingers merges with his paintbrush. The paintbrush, better still the brush, is no object but a kind of apparent extension of the artist's entrails that obeys slight and secret reflexes. The paintbrush is one of the painter's organs."[67]

In *The Studio*, the painter soberly wields his brush, seemingly working under the silent dictation of the model, at rest as if she were whispering wise counsel. Could it be she who insiduously guides both his fingers and the brush? Woman, muse and model, the painter's constant preoccupation. "I realized," Courbet once said, "that I was going astray and that it was time I left the follies of love behind. I resolved to kill the woman who tormented my imagination. Stronger than Werther and Sterio put together, instead of turning to suicide I sacrificed her mercilessly in a great allegorical composition: 'Man delivered from Love by Death.' But soon the idea of the painting seemed false to me, and I asked myself: why hate woman? I should lay the blame on man's ignorance and egotism instead. Let her live! I began to understand the tolerance and freedom that are the principles of Realism... It is impossible to settle for only one woman if one wants to know woman in general..."[68] Where then to find the ideal model, both singular and plural?

In their studios painters and sculptors stalked and searched for her. Artists negotiated the prices of a pose. Around 1850 for example, models were paid four francs for a four-hour session, but very

Gustave Courbet:
The Painter's Studio, 1855.

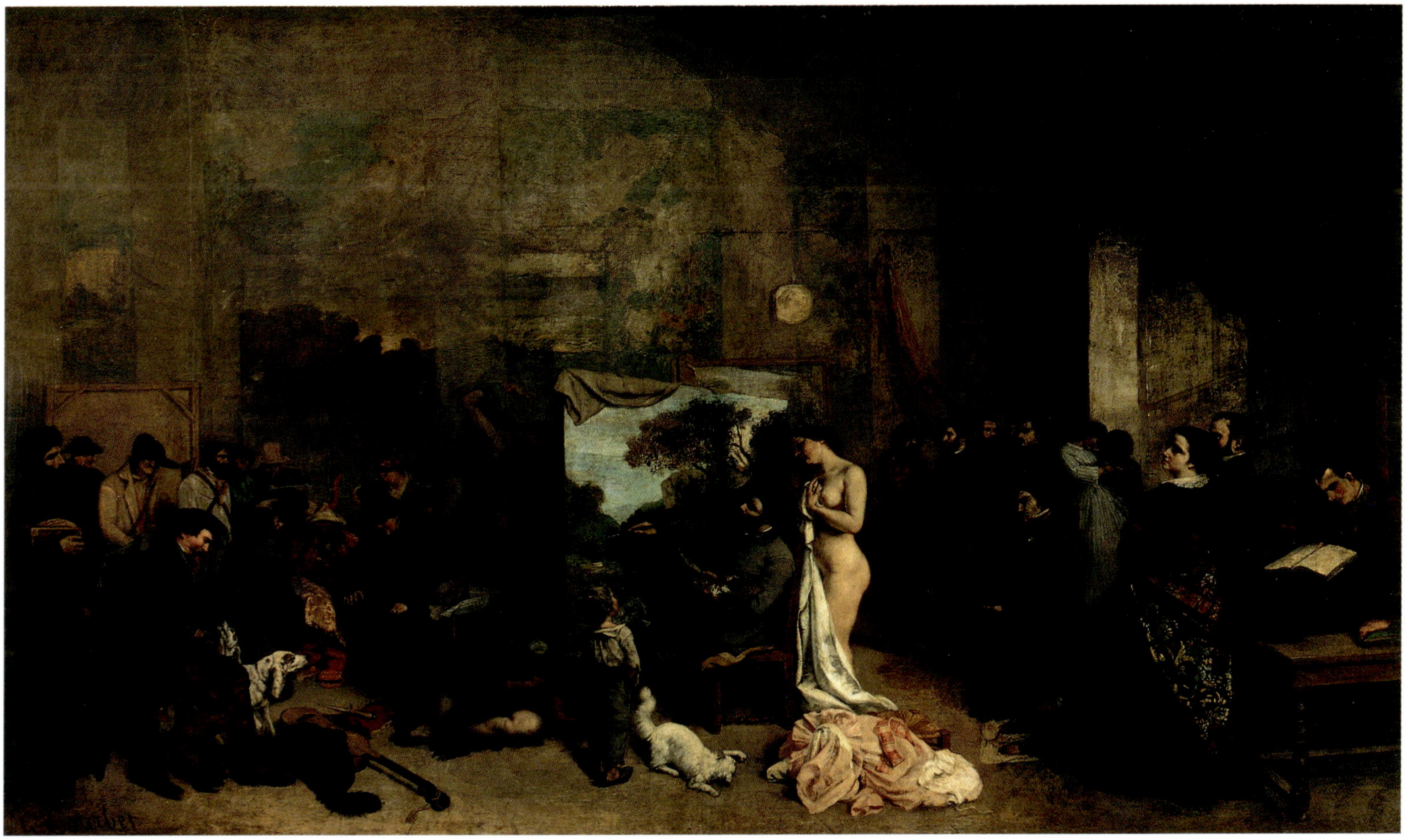

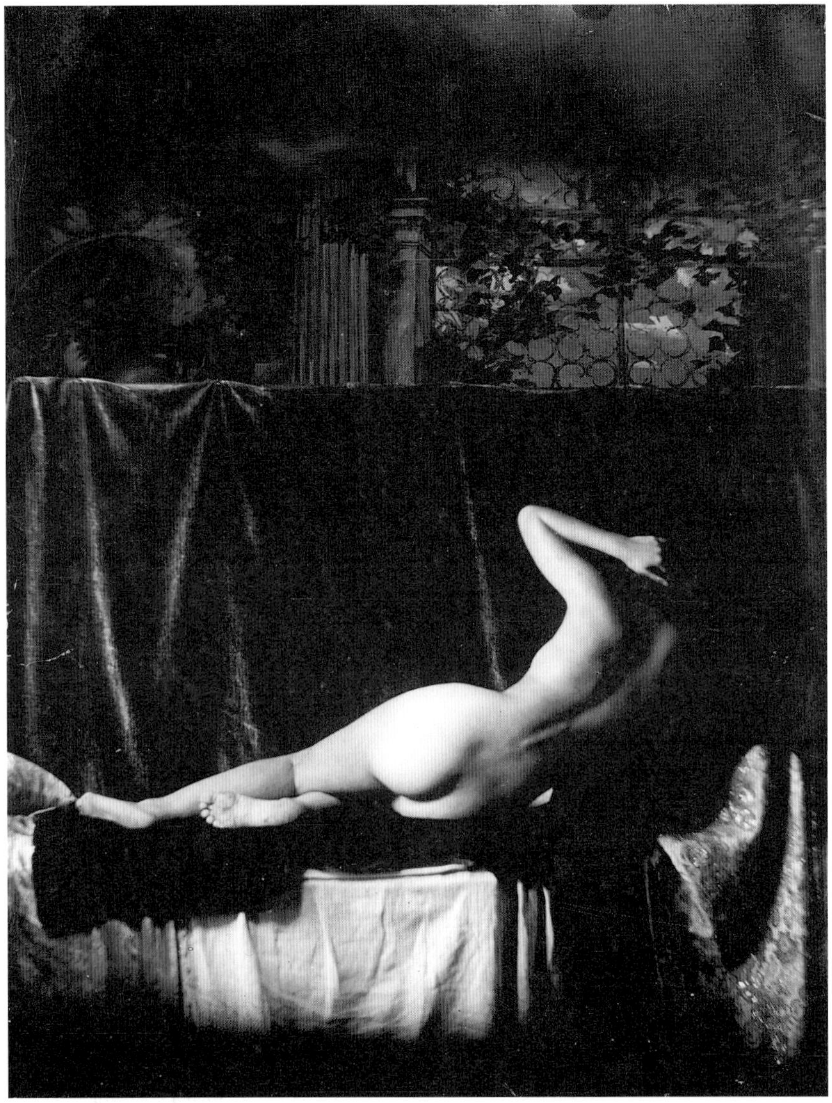

Mariano Fortuny: Model Posing, undated.

beautiful Jewish models, who were particularly prized, could fetch as much as six francs. In Paris, there were many Italians, fleshy Neapolitans, as well as working-class Parisian girls ready to reveal their charms, errand girls, milliners, laundresses, linen maids, young women rebelling against the bourgeois world. The cost of the pose varied and was higher for individual artists than for the academies. Place Pigalle formed a veritable marketplace for models. It was there that Puvis de Chavannes discovered Anna, whom he later passed on to Renoir.

In addition to the live models, photographs widely came into use. There were albums well stocked with hundreds of photographs of nudes, like Vignola's collection on the *Living Model*, illustrated with 225 pictures by Eugène Piron, which one ironic commentator described as an "artistic breviary for bearers of the seed which procreates eternal works." In this slew of documents several major themes of seduction regularly recur: women putting on their stockings, others manipulating their corsets. Many seem to chat with their mirror, some going so far as to kiss their image in a Psyche. Scenes of auto-eroticism and narcissism are at their height in satin decors. Frequently exoticism combines with eroticism in references to the Orient, North Africa and even "darkest" Africa, with native accessories to match, fans and bongo drums. Some catered to more bucolic tastes, and

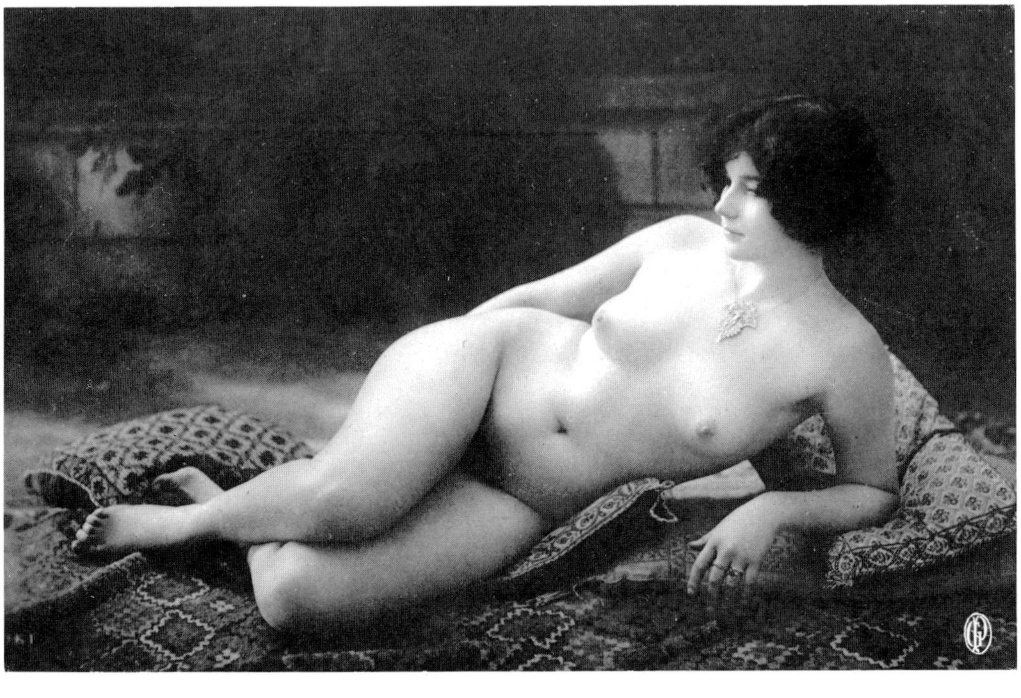

Anonymous: Nude (postcard), 1911.

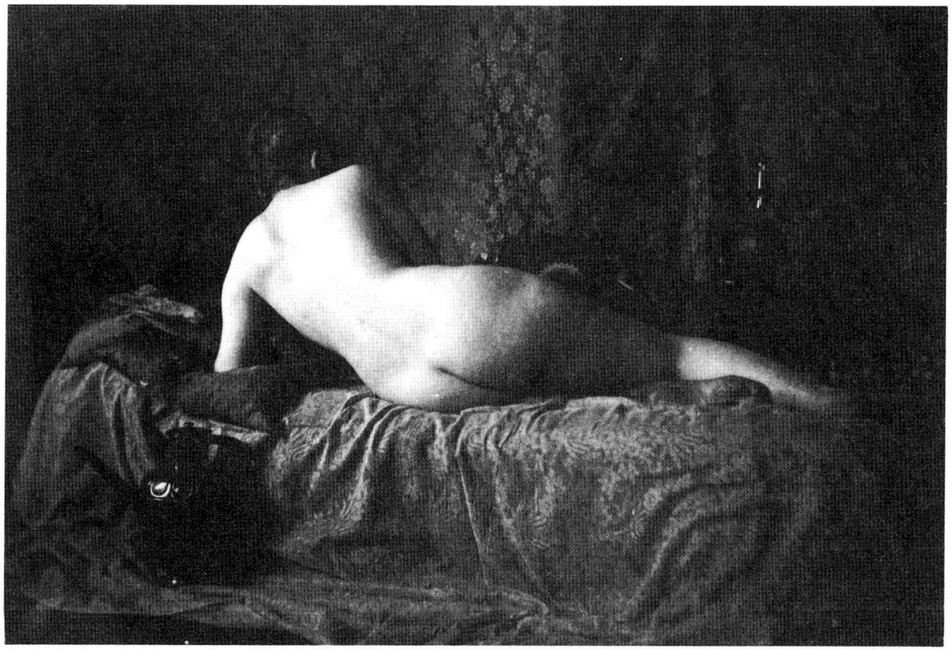

Thomas Eakins:
Reclining Nude, undated.

Eugène Durieu:
Nude, 1853-1854.

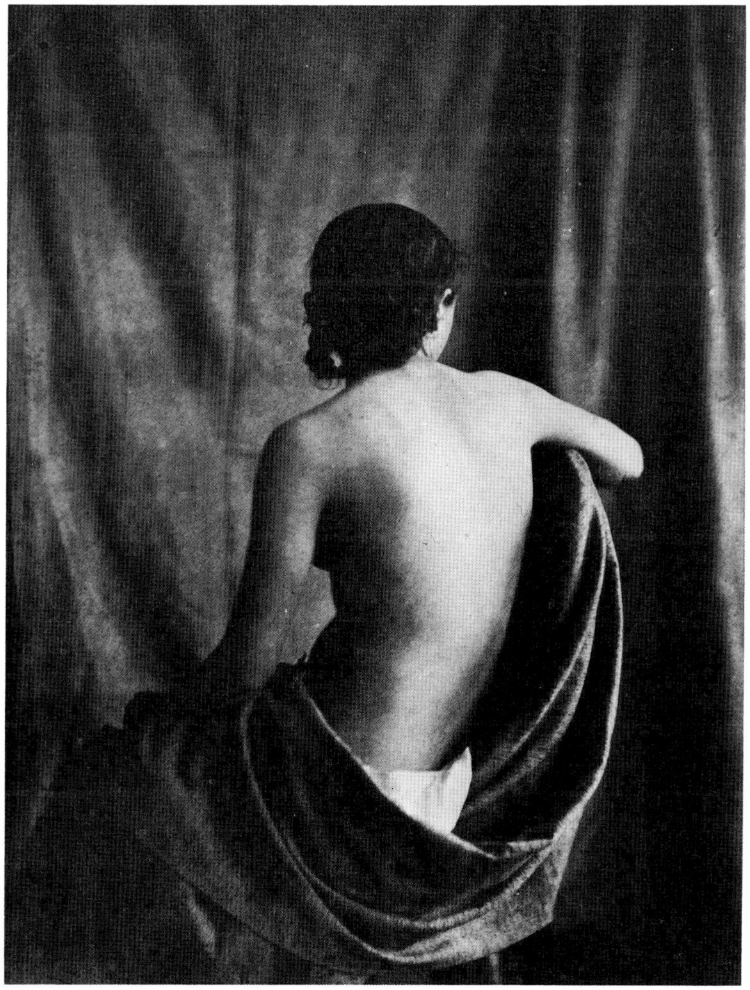

antique statuary inspired more than one pose as plump, fleshy women imitated the attitudes of marmoreal Venuses. In this kind of imagery, body hair was often expunged, camouflaged, by one device or another, shaved, or retouched on the prints. Was this oblitering, erasing motivated by a desire for idealization? Or did these tufts of hair lend a human, all too human, or even bestial touch to the subjects?

Artists plunged into this cut-rate iconography. Delacroix, Toulouse-Lautrec, Mucha, Munch, Bonnard, Khnopff and many others turned to photography. Some of these painters, filled with wonder and enthusiasm, practiced this young art. Others called on its services to the more prosaic end of reducing the length (and so the cost) of the sittings. Occasionally, photographers took pictures in the studios themselves, training their cameras on models installed on makeshift podiums, frozen in contrived and uncomfortable postures. The artist's studio, it should be said, was a place that exerted a certain fascination; no enlightened visitor to Rome would have missed an opportunity to visit the studios of Thorvaldsen or Canova. In Paris, Rodin's

Auguste Rodin:
Balzac Standing (sketch), 1891-1895.
Nude Study, 1892-1893.
Balzac Wearing a Dominican Gown, 1891-1892.

studio attracted curiosity for a variety of reasons. Photographers were unable to resist such subjects, and so we have Rodin posing next to his sculptures, cocking his ear to the life flowing in their stony hearts, or posing ostensibly next to an all-too-live model with breasts amply bared.

As a matter of fact, Rodin's working methods were rather unusual. One of his contemporaries was surprised to see that "in his studio, there are a number of nude models, both male and female, walking or just lounging around. Rodin pays them to provide him constantly with the image of nudity moving about with as much freedom as in ordinary life. He contemplates them incessantly and this is how he has long familiarized himself with the spectacle of muscles in motion. The nude, which for modern man is an exceptional revelation and, even for sculptors, is generally but an apparition limited to the length of the posing sessions, has become for Rodin a habitual sight. This familiar knowledge of the human body, which the ancient Greeks acquired by contemplating athletic exercises at the gymnasium—discus throwing, cestus boxing, the pancratium, and foot-racing—and which permitted their artists to speak the language of the nude naturally, the author of *The Thinker* acquired it through the continual presence of unclothed human beings moving to and fro under his gaze. In this way, he learned to decipher the expression of feelings in every part of the body."[69]

Thus, Rodin's models were recruited to pose without posing and present themselves naturally. While this must have occasioned some very comical scenes, Rodin had an eye for sensuality and beauty. When his biographer asked him if he thought that modern women were less beautiful than those in the days of Phidias, he replied: "Not at all, the artists of then had eyes to see them, while those of today are blind; that is all the difference. Greek women were beautiful, but their beauty resided above all in the minds of the sculptors who represented them."[70]

Rodin was a worshipper of the human body and nudity. "Art is a sort of religion... It is important to remember that the first commandment of this religion, for those who want to practice it, is to know how to model an arm, a torso or a thigh."[71] "If I am of the opinion that a sculptor can limit himself to representing real, living and breathing flesh without concerning himself with a subject, this does not mean that I exclude thought from his work; if I claim that he can do without symbols, this does not mean that I advocate an art which is devoid of a spiritual sense. But, if truth be told, all is idea, all is symbol. Thus, the forms and attitudes of human beings necessarily reveal the emotions of their soul. The body always expresses the spirit, which forms its

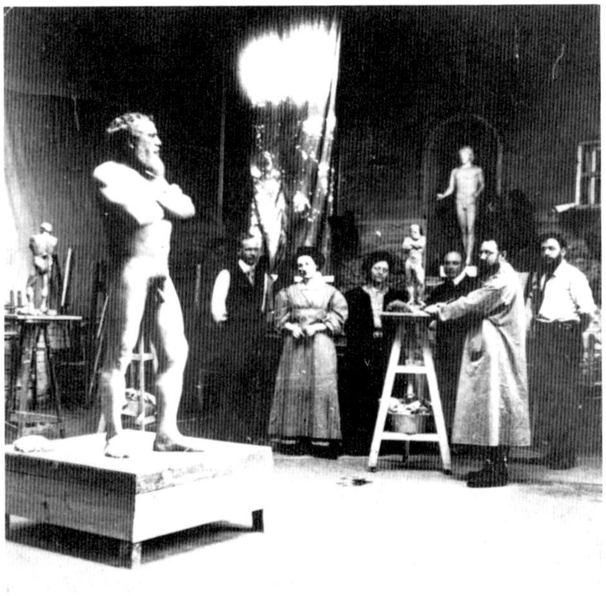

Matisse's Sculptor Studio in the Convent of Sacré-Coeur, Boulevard des Invalides, c. 1909.

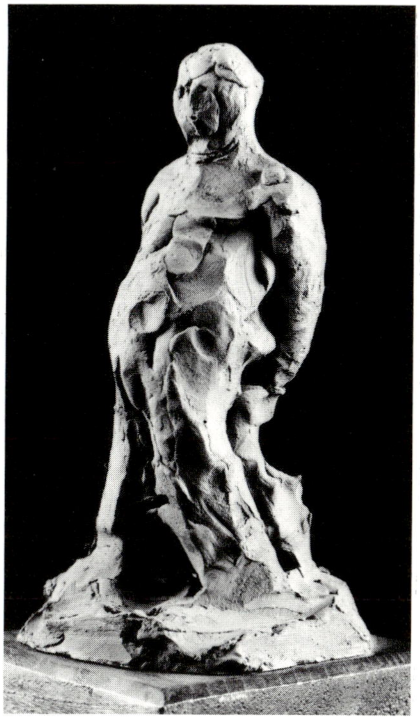
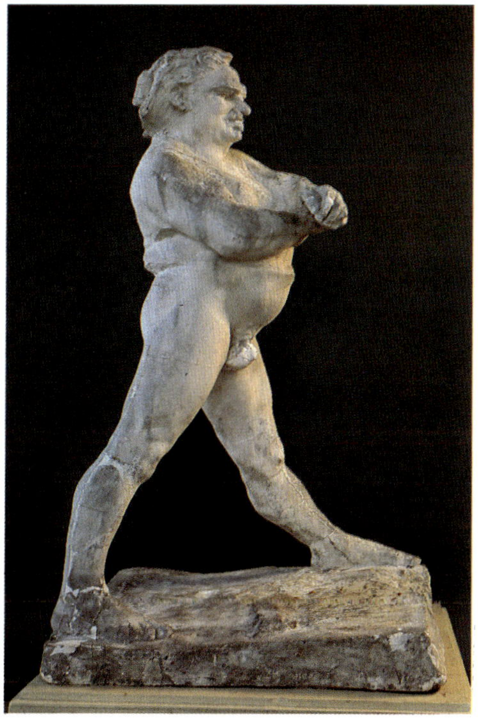
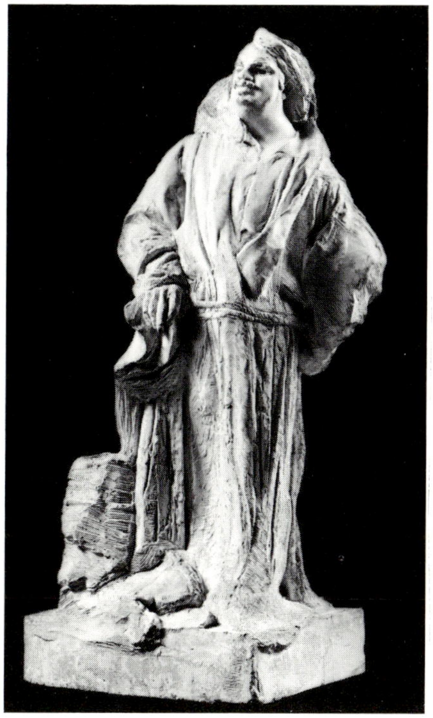

outer envelope. And for those who know how to see, nudity offers the richest significance."[72] To seize the essence of the model Rodin worked from life but freely exploited the resources of memory as well, using everything as grist for his mill. It is known that for the elaboration of his *Balzac,* he first used live models chosen with respect to the proportions observed on a daguerreotype by Nadar, from which he executed seven completely finished nudes in different poses. Afterwards, he returned to Lamartine's description of the writer and draped them in a greatcoat.

Rodin, wrote Rainer Maria Rilke of his friend, supposed "that imperceptible movements made by the models when they do not think themselves observed, if rapidly outlined, can contain a power of expression unimagined by us because we are not accustomed to giving them an active and sustained attention. Without taking his eyes off the model, letting his practiced and lively hand run freely over the paper, he drew a host of gestures never before seen, always offhand, and it was clear that the force of expression which emanated from them was tremendous; correspondences of movements that had never before been recognized and mastered in their entirety appeared, and they contained all the force and immediate warmth of an animal life, so to speak... And yet it seems that Rodin preferably experienced a woman's face as a part of his handsome body, as if he wanted his eyes to be the eyes of her body, and his mouth, the mouth of her body."[73]

"In front of the model, "Rodin explained, "I work with the same will to reproduce truth as if I were making a portrait, I do not correct nature, I incorporate myself into it; it directs me. I can only work with a model. The sight of human forms nourishes and comforts me. I have unbounded admiration for the nude, I worship it like a god. I tell you very simply that I haven't a single idea when I have nothing to copy; but when I see nature showing me various forms, I immediately find something worth saying, and even developing. There are times with a model when one thinks that there is nothing to find, and then, all of a sudden, a bit of nature shows itself, a strip of flesh appears, and this scrap of truth gives the whole truth and allows us to rise in one bound to the absolute principle of things."[74]

What an astounding declaration! Rodin nourished by the sight of the model. Rodin identifiying flesh with truth. Captivated by the model, Rodin had the feeling of incorporating himself with nature in its entirety. The nude connects man to the cosmos. The scultptor once exclaimed: "What a dazzling sight, a woman undressing, it is like seeing the sun pierce through clouds!"[75] The attractive ethic of sacred pleasure. With his chisel and brush, Rodin set out to discover the body, exploring it not like a geographer but like Michel Tournier's *Friday,* by uniting with mother earth.

The heights of intimacy are reached by fusion. Rodin insinuated his gaze into the most private recesses, returning to the origins of the universe and humanity; flesh was his willing accomplice. All of this gave him a very strong feeling of power. Wasn't it he who once told Rilke that on reading a religious book, he had amused himself by replacing the word God with that of sculpture, and it

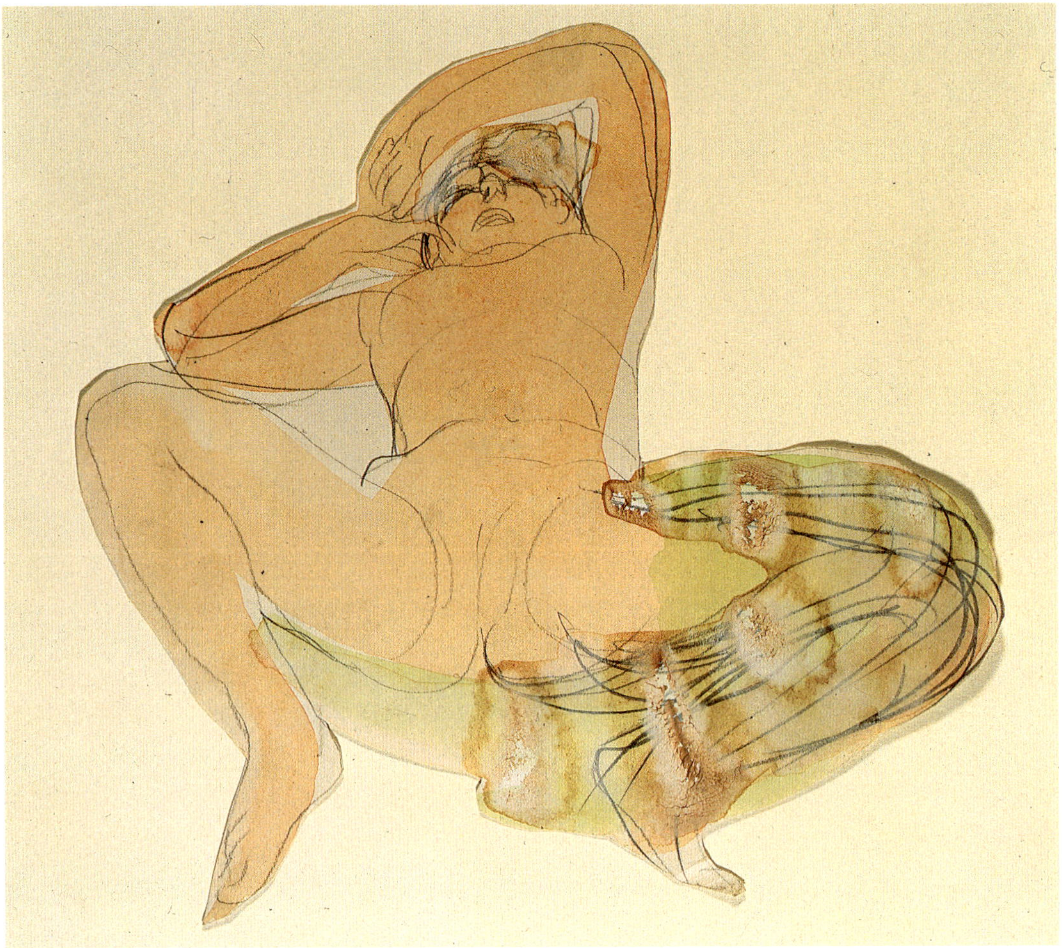

Auguste Rodin:
Reclining Nude with Legs Spread, undated.

worked "perfectly"? With the participation of the model, the artist makes the world anew, brings it once more into being.

In his erotic drawings, Rodin reveals a narcissistic, but nonetheless fundamental aspect of woman; woman as the "navel of the world"! Whether bacchante or courtesan, maenad or houri, dancer or sorceress, she engenders the whole world. How did Rodin manage to delve so far into the female body, to penetrate it so deeply, yet seeming only to brush it lightly with a gentle and lively audacity? Pleasure brings to life the eye and the image. Rodin was unequaled in laying women bare. He prompted them to touch themselves, to offer themselves. In exhibiting themselves, the models took pleasure in watching themselves take pleasure. Did they realize that they would probably be reborn as icons, even more beautiful, desiring still more, still more desirable?

Rodin was drunk with pleasure, voluptuous vision guided him. With dizzying speed, he captured the peak of sexual pleasure at various moments. One woman stretches herself out. Another, satisfied, curls up as if to hold in waves of pleasure. The pudendum is often shown in the foreground, retouched with very diluted "spots" of watercolor, like a juice the artist's eye drank in. Rarely has wetness been so overwhelming and fertile. His excited pencil scratches and gropes within the vulvas he portrays. The spot, a sublime stain, wets the pubis. Feeling flows. Rodin's line undulates, making these sensualists' bodies dance, minutely examining their ecstasy; it deflowers the paper by staining it , follows the cadence of the emotions, their pulsations. Water and pigment spurt, marking the climax. Immediate boarding for Cythera. The nude is rapture, and desire, the source of creation, of sensual abandon. The bodies tremble, unfold, arch in orgasm, defying the laws of gravity, the offered vagina quivers and gushes at the vertex of generously outspread legs.

Paroxysm and plenitude. Peaceful, brimming bodies, enveloped with caresses, fulfilled and relaxed, glowing, luminous, radiant, curled around themselves in sleep. Woman purring with satisfaction, a serene idol, sated by the beholder's penetrating gaze. Pliable and plant-like bayadere. Sumptuous Salammbô. Nereid bathed by the primordial waters, her face hidden by the waves. How was Rodin able to introduce himself so far into woman's intimacy? What passions, what love, what emotion animate his pencil and splashes of watercolor! Each can see in them, like Leonardo da Vinci's old walls, the most varied forms or, more exactly, the most varied sensations.

Rodin played on the "framing" and the "angle." Views from above, from below, close-up of a hand, one finger of which has slipped into the depths of the fleshy grotto. How the artist must have been close to his models, attentive to the most subtle vibrations of their beings, taking in their most secret scents! This is no longer observation, this is a complete proximity. How loving Rodin must have been for these women to surrender themselves so completely to his gaze, and with a generosity that escapes all notions of decency.

One Nereid floats, her vagina open, in a suggestive aquatic medium, oceanic boundlessness, warm and accommodating amniotic fluid. Woman is seashell, orchid, vulva. Born to be embraced, she gives herself to please and to be seen. Rodin's eye caresses her, explores her all over and floods her with liberally diluted pigments. In some instances, the sculptor-draughtsman took scissors to the paper and traced the outline of a foot, the arch of a back, the curve of a shoulder, in rapid, impassioned gestures, not bothering with excessive details or superfluous indications, swept by his momentum

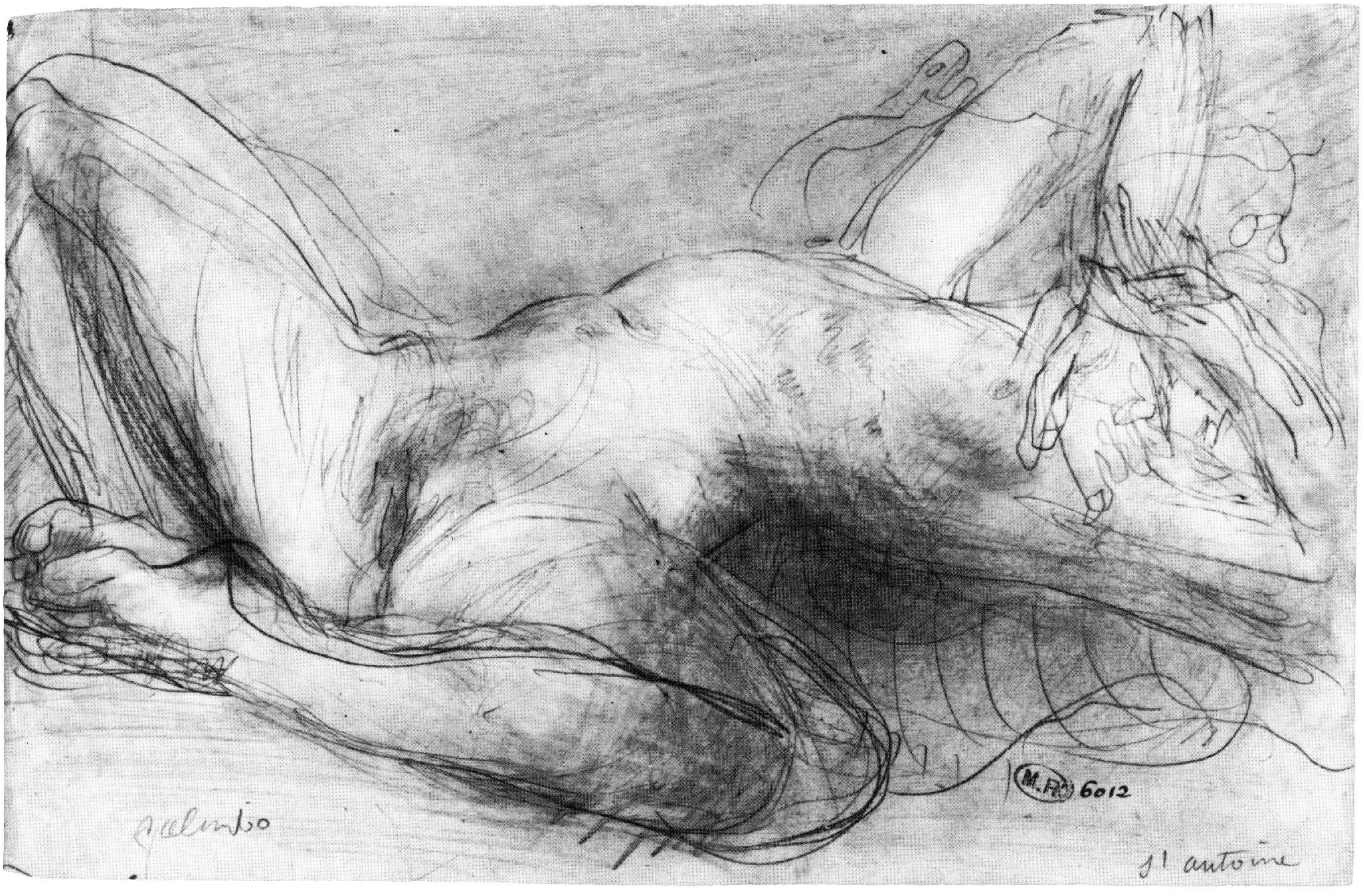

Auguste Rodin:
Salammbô, c. 1900.

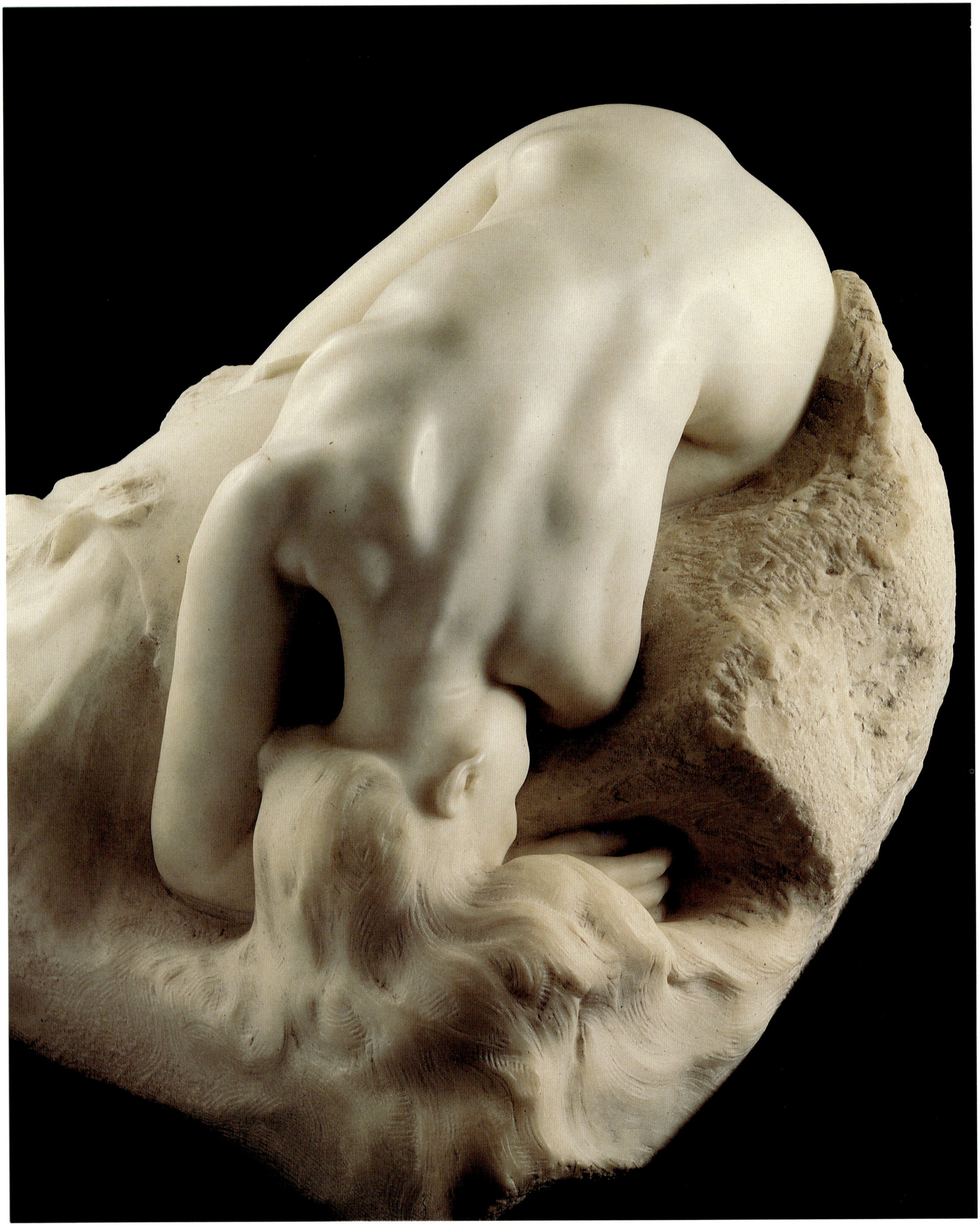

Auguste Rodin:
The Danaid, 1885.

along the silhouettes, trimming and skirting them in the heat of the action.

The integration of the model into the everyday life of the studio as Rodin advocated may be found—in another form, of course—in a recent novel by Patrick Grainville, *L'atelier du peintre* [The Painter's Studio]. The story, written in a superbly tooled language, features a painter nicknamed The Virginal (an allusion to sublimation?) who lives and works in Los Angeles with his students and models, male and female, in a communal arrangement. Relationships constantly form and dissolve between these characters "linked and separated by living wounds."[76] The studio functions like a microcosm organized around several elements: a skull, an *écorché*, a sphere representing the globe of the Earth, a mirror, Van Eyck's *Arnolfini Wedding*, reproductions fo Rembrandt's self-portraits, and a large nude. In the beginning was the nude, Adam and Eve, the painter's first models.

The studio is a "temple," a "mystic brothel," a "chapel of the eye," in which models are sacrificed, and poses are prayers. The painter and his students feed on this voluptuous, oceanic flesh. During the sittings, the Virginal merges with his model and no longer distinguishes his painting, nor himself from her. "I choose Ruth's right breast, outline it, add a coat of gouache, fill it in. It swells in my hand, poorly rounded, not too good, a bit odd, numb, bestial. I carefully work a very brown, very grainy, coagulated beauty mark in the skin. It sets, begins to develop... Flesh is plump... Let yourselves be fascinated, absorbed, become flesh yourself, black-skinned, fair of skin... Rubens... Renoir... between wheat, gold, leather and wild suede. To dwell in this flesh, to graft myself onto it, sew myself up alive in it, experience it and haunt it with my love."[77]

The cannibalistic artist incorporates himself into the model, finds there his own substance, or more exactly, the substance of his painting; he captures flesh tones through a singular initiation ritual over which death furtively hovers. "I like scars, seals, tatoos, the hallmarks of vice and crime. But all of it precise, very hard. I do not deny that there is a lyricism in putrefaction. I want my rot to take hold. The horror of decay. With me, decomposition is calculated. I never loosen my hold on the reins. I wanted to paint every degree of the body, every step of flesh, for flesh alone fascinates me... Flesh is what pursues me into the night, to the dizzying brink... I need to catch the body unawares as it bleeds, at fault... In that moment when flesh truly is made flesh, with all of its hollows, joints, recesses, where rise and fall are in the balance. I never take my eyes off it. I watch over it. And I am tempted."[78]

To respond to this obsession with flesh, this obsession with the color of flesh, the models must always be "on hand," available, at the mercy of his infernal and voracious eye. Perhaps because they are so indispensable, the sitters are often the object of a fierce and humiliating hatred. They are "a window display of flesh" that the Virginal violates, drowns in, and finds his fusional inspiration.[79]

This symbiosis reaches its climax during a posing session when, contrary to habit, the phallus of a model responds to the desire of one of the female students drawing him. "I know the ins and outs of flesh better, now that I have seen it bloom. Each parcel of the body, it seems to me, could be the seat of tropisms and turbulences. The great bodies stretch and distend. Their python rings move. Flesh suddenly proliferates before my eyes. Heavy, thick, coiling its deposits of precious metals. I plunge completely into this treasure, dwell in it, my colors knead fullness haunted by desire, veins swollen with lust. I love my two bodies, I make them mine to the limits of outrage. I am within. I am painting. My hands, my eyes are gouache. Several palettes loaded with living colors advance like galleons. I am blind. I do not know where I am going, what I am doing. Instinct alone guides me; but it is a lucid, faultless instinct. All I need to do is to dare these buttocks, these thighs, these torsos. I sculpt in matter that flows in profuse, heaving swells, oceans of flesh, eel, anaconda."[80]

Stunning and visionary homage to flesh in its sensual materiality; the omnipresence of nudity, as stimulating as it is perilous.

The contemplation of a naked woman
makes me think of her skeleton.

Gustave Flaubert

Antoine Wiertz:
Beautiful Rosine, 1843.

Beyond the nude or the anatomical passion

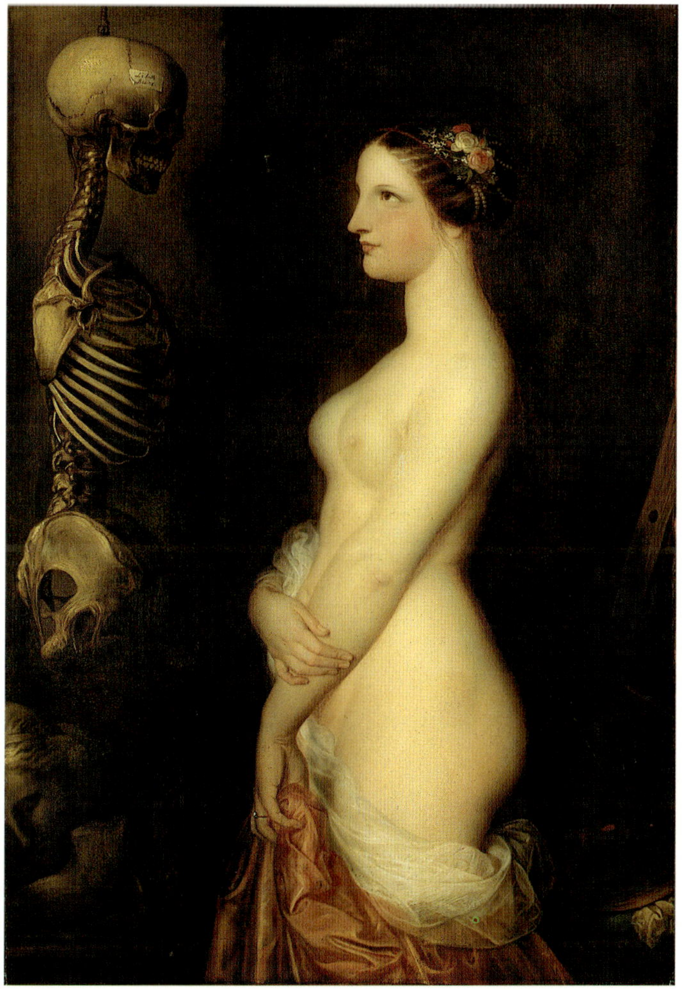

The delectation of *cadavres exquis*

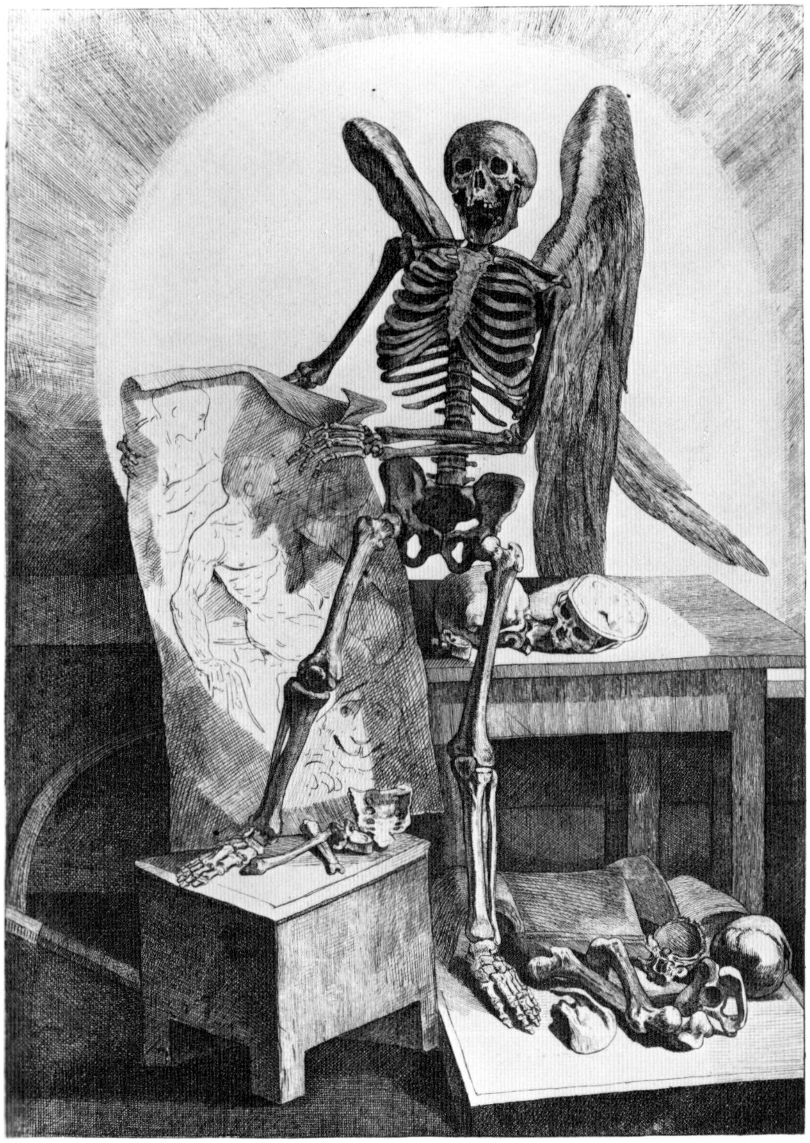

Jacques Gamelin:
The Skeleton Angel, 1779.

Art flirts with anatomy. Often in the studio, we can see side by side a live model and a skeleton, or plates of écorchés, not to mention still lifes—but that is another story. Leonardo da Vinci was perhaps the first to try to fuse art with knowledge of the inner workings of the human body. Not content to settle for what "meets the eye," he undertook to know more, to cut through appearances and observe what lies beyond visible data. This knowledge could be had through the surgeon's or the barber's scalpel, through wounds and incisions opening the way within. This indecorous intrusion and penetration into the forbidden recesses of privacy, long considered immoral, was authorized only by death. Da Vinci, Pontormo, Vesalius, and numerous others were considered mad to spend so much time rummaging around cadavers. Yet a diabolical curiosity led them to bear with the most frightful sights and odors. What *was* going on behind appearance, beneath the skin?

The écorché, they claimed, would help them to understand the human body better. Strange pretext. Before the unfathomable enigma of the body, both fair means and foul were permissable. Mystery stimulates knowledge. The artist thought he might find the answer on the other side of the epidermis. And so he dissected, flayed and emptied the body , wading through a world of putrefaction and nausea to reach the skeleton, that collection of bones hung dry and available in a corner of the studio. In his treatise *Della pittura*, Leone Battista Alberti discussed the difficulty of representing a dead body. Any artist who passed the test of depicting lifelessness he readily promoted to the rank of master. "Only a great creator knows how to represent the languor of the inert limbs and all of the aspects which death confers to the body."

For centuries, artists turned to anatomy, which served them as a frame of reference, and perhaps justified their existence. Flayed souls enthralled by flayed bodies. To elucidate the mystery of nudity, the flesh was stripped away. Flounces and furbelows having been confided to the cloakroom, in an ultimate strip-tease the skin itself, the last obstacle to the probing eye, was removed. Would these

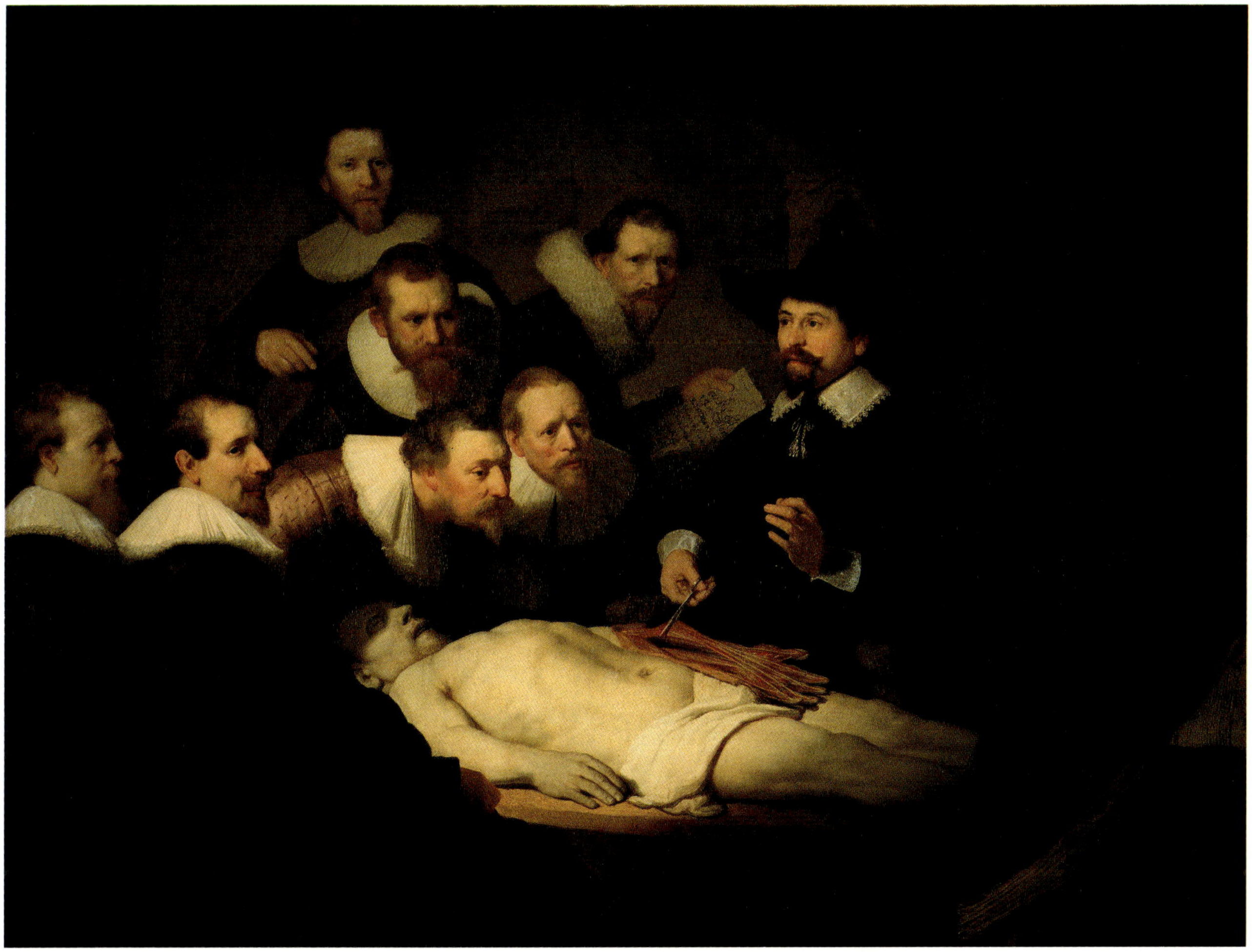

Rembrandt:
Professor Tulp's Anatomy Lesson, 1632.

exposed muscles and entrails tell of our beginning? For painters and sculptors, this investigation was justified. Inside, outside, with an indiscreet eye the artist examines the body, a devil of a voyeur. In his two *Anatomy Lessons*, that of Dr. Tulp and that of Dr. Deijman, Rembrandt immortalized the austere dignity of ordinary burghers who look as though they will never touch the corpse although armed with the most deadly instruments. The body, the raw material of analysis, lies exposed, not yet cold, blood-stained, at the mercy of the eye. Like a scalpel, the eye dissects, passes through the gaps among the body's fibers. What a imperative necessity!

The artist was not satisfied with the outside, the envelope; he wanted to know what it contains, to understand its joints, how the muscles are attached to one another. What does the skin hide then, what lies beneath that strong and fragile membrane pierced with orifices? What if the whole show—appearance and all the rest of it—were taking place inside? Wholeheartedly artists set to work and cut in. Art went the way of wounds and blood. Afterwards, illustrators invented light settings in order to pass the drama of dissection, erase or at least attenuate the crudeness of the anatomical plates. Some, moreover, are not without a certain humor and tragi-comical sense of association.

An écorché strolls with his skin draped around him like a stole, as if he were at an evening party. Another one strolls at the zoo. Yet another leafs

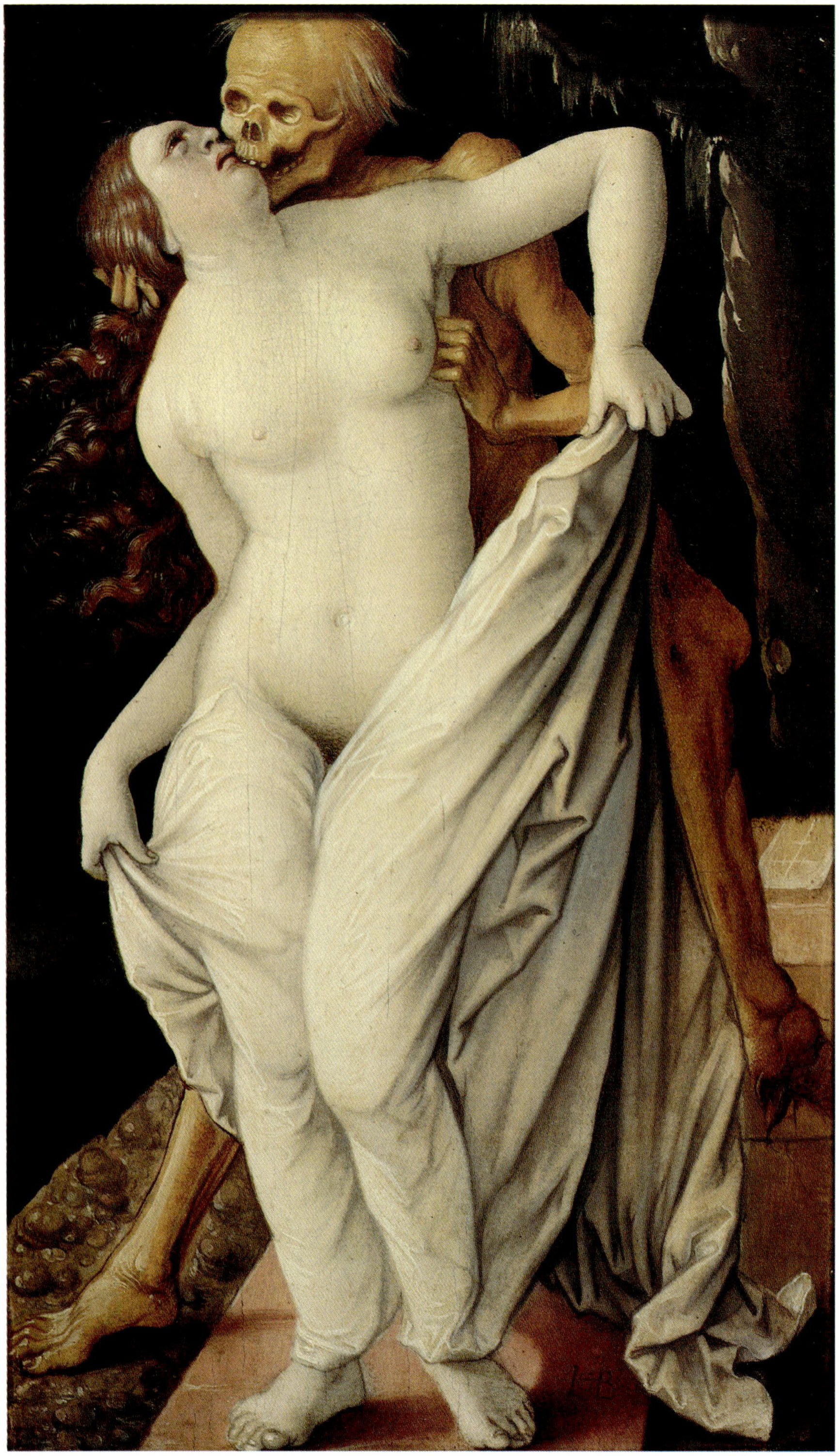

Hans Baldung Grien:
Death and the Maiden, 1517.

through a book. A touch of irony and cynicism renders the unbearable bearable: this final, extreme nakedness. Point of no return. The artists pretended to play with death, but theirs was not to be the last laugh, for death wins in every case. Lucas Cranach and Hans Baldung Grien never tired of representing youth, beauty and life at odds with death. The proud and sensual woman embraced by a putrescent cadaver and a grinning skeleton cannot long ignore vanity and melancholy. The hourglass is brandished with an intolerable arrogance. Always the same old song: "If you think little girl, little girl..."

Artists thirsting for immortality may have wanted to see death at close quarters, to touch it with their eyes. And so they made it their model, one as privileged as the live model. For some, like the great Leonardo, there were no favorites, there was no rivalry between the live and the dead model. Both were indispensable. When the live model did not suffice, the corpse was called in. When overexposure to the interior threatened, the artist turned once again to the smooth outer surfaces of life. This surprising shift back and forth was held to have certain didactic powers. Dead or alive,

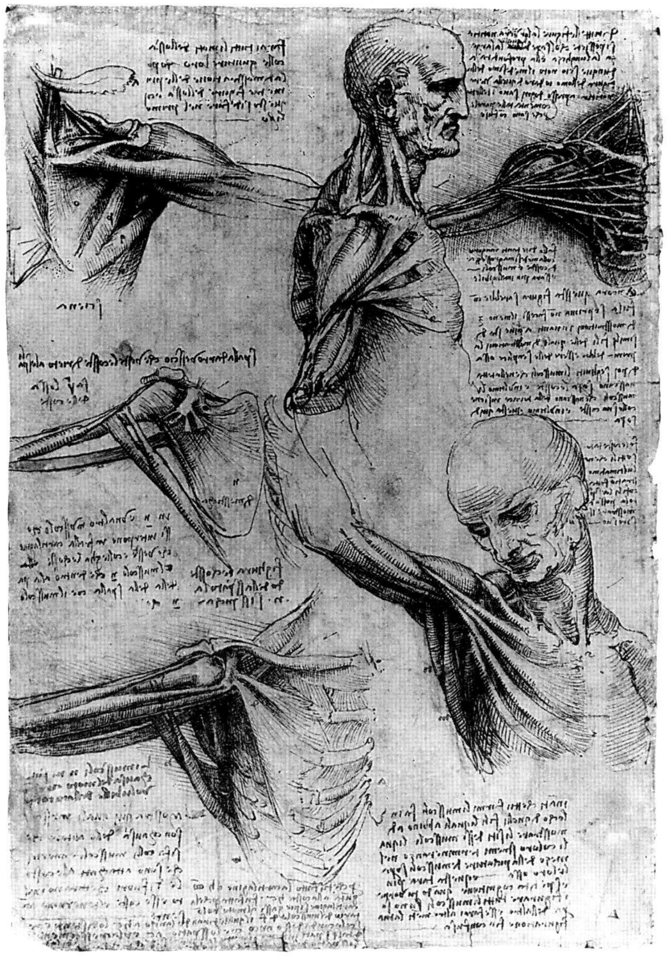

Leonardo da Vinci:
Muscles of the Shoulder (sheet with studies), c. 1510.

the body was a rich mine of information. And so artists stalked it throughout its transformations, into its last and least recesses.

Leonardo da Vinci was a pioneer in this field. He marveled at anatomy and had such a reverence for it that he was outraged by the thought that such an extraordinary machine could belong to both idiots and intelligent beings! "It seems to me that crude men of vile ways and lacking in spirit deserve neither so subtle an organism, nor such a great variety of works as men of great intelligence and rich in ideas; a simple sack into which their food would arrive at one end and leave at the other would suffice. In truth, they should be likened to feeding tubes, for they do not seem to me to have anything in common with the human species apart from language and the appearance; as for the rest, they are far inferior to beasts."[1]

With his mechanical eye, Leonardo da Vinci drew 228 anatomical plates: 27 of the thorax and abdomen; 50 of the heart; 31 of the genital organs; 30 of proportions; 32 of postures; 42 of the nerves and blood vessels; 16 of physiognomy. At the time, public baths and executions provided opportunities for gaining a familiarity with the nude and the corpse. In Florence during the Quattrocento, painters bought their pigments from apothecaries supervised by medical doctors, and so they mutually cultivated their relations.

Leonardo da Vinci eliminated the superfluous in his investigations and in his visual record of them. His plates are devoid of decorative motifs or scenographies that lend cadavers anecdotal roles derived from medieval "Triumph of Death" scenes: there is only an extreme rigor and methodic precision. The artist procured cadavers, attended public dissections, and even performed them himself on freshly-deceased bodies at the hospitals of Santa Maria Nuova and Santo Spirito in Rome. He was a precursor in many domains, even if at times he indistinctly mixes human and animal structures (Vesalius would do likewise). The organs of reproduction interested him especially, and while he was not very precise concerning the male member, he nevertheless explained erections as an influx of arterial blood (and not of air, as had been thought until then) by observing hanged criminals with post-mortem erections. Freud remarked that "His almost feminine sensitivity did not prevent him from following condemned prisoners to the gibbet in order to study their features decomposed by terror and to sketch them in his notebook."[2]

He juxtaposed the uterus of a woman with that of a cow, but was the first to give a good image of the position of the human foetus. Even more exceptional was the fact that he represented the act of intercourse, that filled him with both repulsion and fascination. "The act of copulation and the parts which it involves are of such hideousness that, were it not for the beauty of the faces, the adornment of the actors and their reserve, nature would have lost the human species!"[3] He depicted a profile view of a man with long and curly hair penetrating a faceless woman. In the margin, he scribbled notes about venereal ulcers known as the "Neapolitan sickness," which was very common then.

This engineer was attracted by all types of machinery, including that of the human body. He made—or made plans for—windmills, presses, levers, winches, gears, pumps, as well as automata, the most famous of which he built on the occasion of the King of France's visit to Milan: a roaring lion approached the ruler and, stopping only a few feet away, opened its chest to reveal a great expanse of lilies. An illusion of wild life.

The biographer Vasari was fascinated by Leonardo's protean genius and recorded much important information on the artist; he mentions in particular his relations with the anatomist Marcantonio della Torre of Pavia. Leonardo moved continually from the inside to the outside, of the body

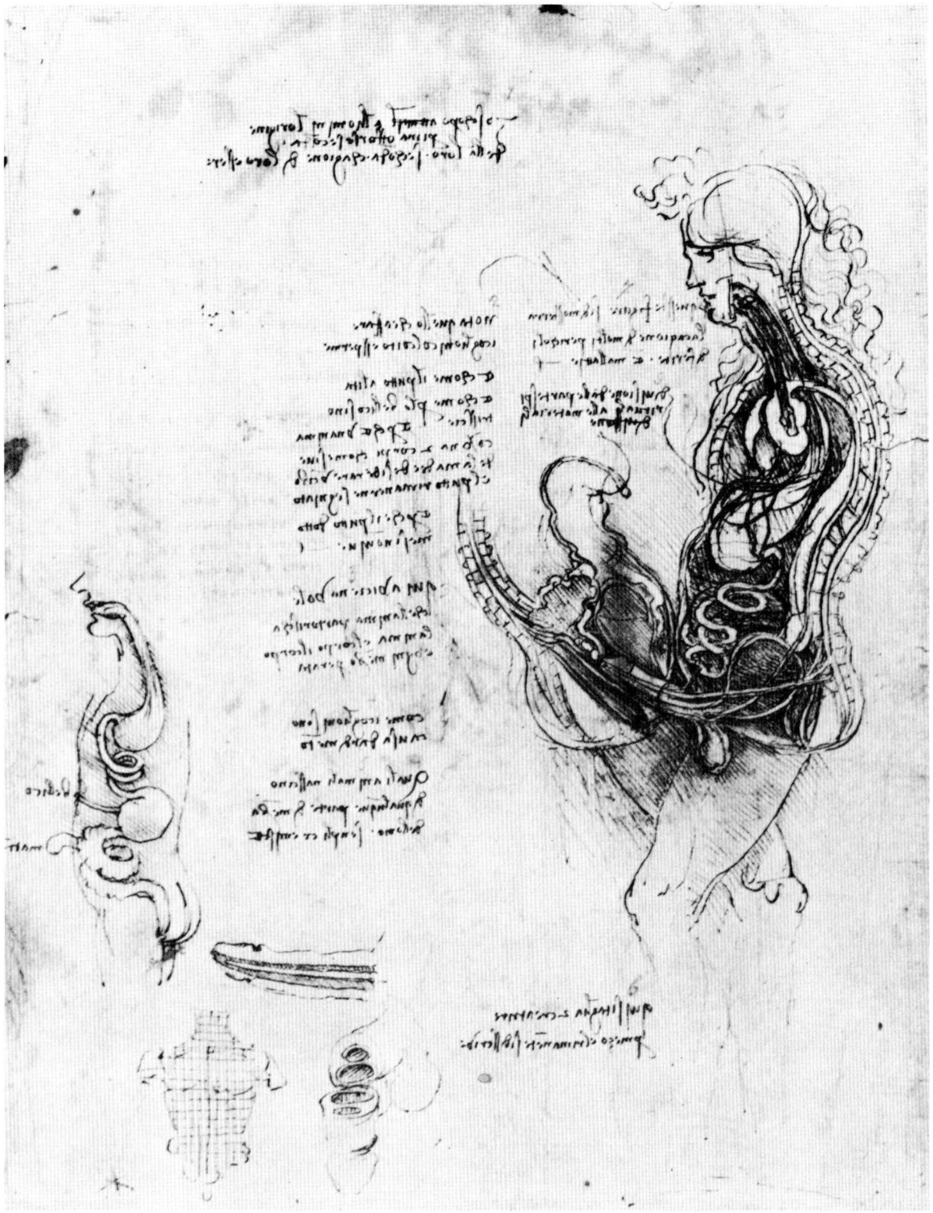

Leonardo da Vinci:
Copulation (sheet with studies), c. 1510.

from surface appearance to dissection in depth. For his famous portrait *Mona Lisa*, Vasari tells us that the artist had singers, musicians and buffoons come to the sittings in order to keep the beauty amused, thus avoiding the melancholic aspect which painting often gave to portraits. A practical application of the theory of the effects of inner emotions on the outer appearance.

Leonardo delighted in manipulating illusion, and even had a certain predilection for the grotesque. Vasari tells how he amused himself by making imaginary animals out of wax, or composing hybrid creatures by sticking wings, horns and a beard on a tame lizard! Leonardo the wag. He had the bowels of sheep de-fatted and cleaned to make them so thin that they could be held in the palm of the hand, then, attaching them to bellows he blew them up until they filled an entire room! The Florentine kept this curiosity about things mechanical to the end of his days. Even on his deathbed, he commented on his condition and the progress of his illness to François I.

The artist drew a particular pride from his anatomical experiments. He assessed the difficulties such experiments entailed, which he pointed out to students and potential readers in an imaginary dialogue: "You claim that it is better to see someone practice anatomy than to look at my drawings;

you would be right if you could see all of the details which my drawings show in a single figure, where, with all of your talent, you will see or recognize but a few veins. To acquire a proper and complete knowledge, I have dissected more than ten corpses, destroying all of the other elements, removing the least particles of flesh which surrounded these veins, without shedding any blood, except for the imperceptible bleeding of some capillaries. A single cadaver would not last very long, and so several had to be used in succession to gain a thorough knowledge. I did this twice to verify the differences. In spite of your love for research, you may be affected by nausea; and if that does not repulse you, then the fearful prospect of spending long hours at night in the company of these horrible, flayed and maimed cadavers might. And if this still does not repulse you, then you may lack the talent to draw the figures. And if you know how to draw, then you may be wanting in knowledge about perspective; and if you have such, then the aptitude for mathematical exposition and the method of calculating muscular force and energy; or you may lack patience, you may not be diligent enough. Whether or not I had all of these qualities, my hundred and twenty books will decide. I was hampered neither by avarice nor by negligence, only by time."[4]

Leonardo also dismissed the possible tendency to experience what this century designates as guilt feelings. "O investigator of our corporeal machine, do not be saddened if you reveal it thanks to the death of others; rejoice rather in the fact that the Creator, in His intelligence, conceived an instrument of such excellence."[5] This danger aside, there were others that menaced the painter in particular. For, after all, it should be remembered that Leonardo developed anatomy for the purpose of serving art. He therefore warned against an abusive application of anatomy to outrageous pictorial ends. "O anatomical painter... do not give to all of the muscles of the figure an exaggerated volume, because, even if they occupy a well-defined place, they do not protrude in so prominent a way, unless the member to which they belong is in a state of great force or extreme fatigue. If you proceed otherwise, you will succeed only in representing a sack of nuts and not a human figure."[6]

If anatomy is indispensable, it should be known sufficiently well not to be a slave to it, but rather used in moderation, so to speak; one should not be blinded by it to the point of forgetting the appearances above skin level. Again, this constant circulation between inside and out. Leonardo dissected and flayed his *cadavres exquis*, and then dressed them up again.

For centuries after Leonardo da Vinci countless anatomical plates, drawings and paintings were the point where art and medicine converged. It was said that Pontormo, "in a fit of melancholy and to make lifelike figures of the drowning victims of the Flood for the choir of San Lorenzo, kept corpses in water-filled troughs to make them become bloated, and stank up the entire neighborhood."[7] For his *Dead Christ*, Hans Holbein the Younger recovered the body of a Jew fished out of the Rhine and executed a painting that was completely at variance with conventional iconographic practice, representing the broken and forsaken body of a Christ laid out in state.[8] Rembrandt depicted the dead body opened in his presence by Professor Tulp with its livid color and the scandalous (from the Lat. "scandalum," trap, obstacle) incongruity of the figure's arm laid bare. Titian sketched the still-warm body of his dead daughter. Géricault schemed with his friends in hospitals to obtain fragments of fresh corpses.

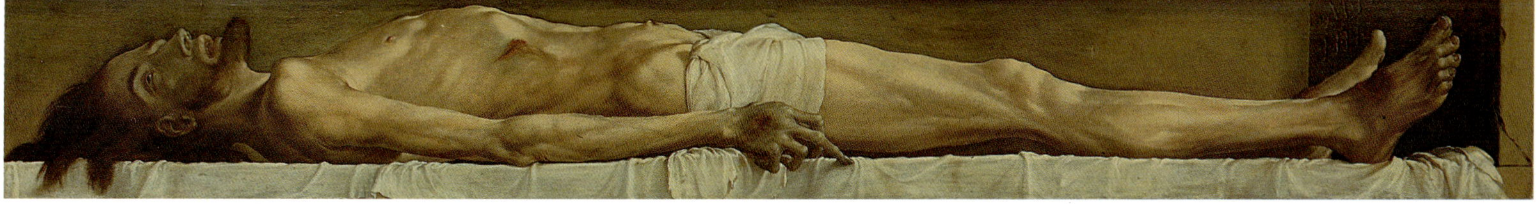

Hans Holbein:
The Dead Christ, 1521.

In praise of flayed souls

Andreas Vesalius:
Title page of the second edition of
De Humani Corporis Fabrica, *1555.*

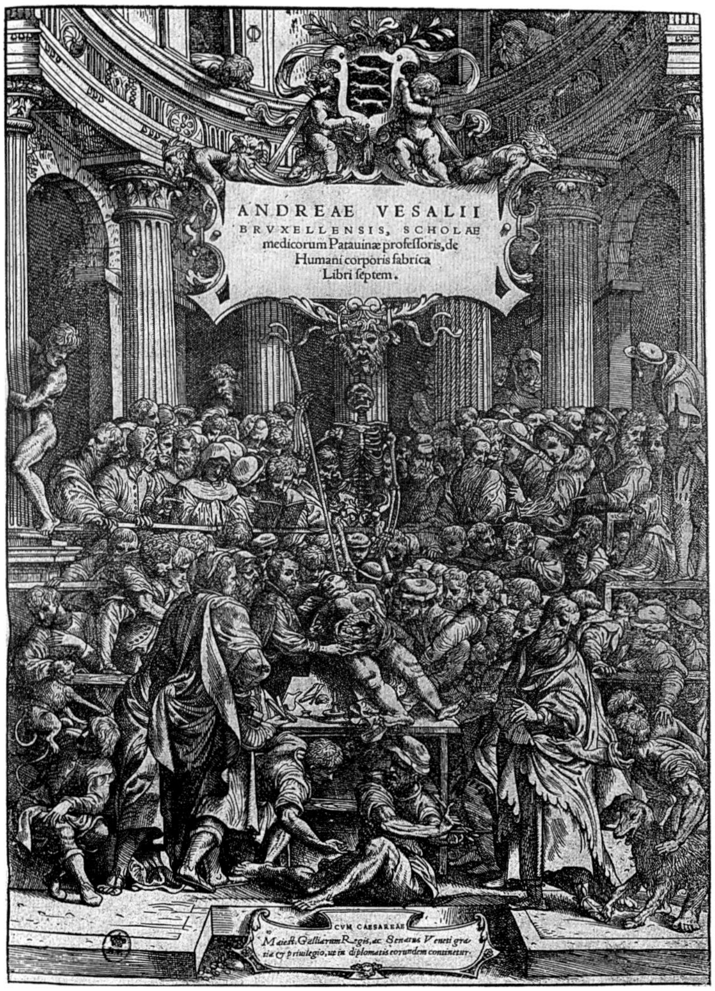

Exchanges between art and anatomy are continuous, and one of these is the anatomical plate. Physicians did not publish their own drawings but called upon the services of illustrators and engravers. It was long thought that Titian "illustrated" Vesalius. By their participation, other artists enriched these plates with a repertory of imagery linked to pathos and pain. The corpse was surrounded with atmosphere. Drawing was an act of gaining insight, as well as a source of macabre delight, precision and fantasy. The image sought to replace the autopsy. Knowledge was cannibalistic.

Vesalius remained ambiguous in his recourse to drawing, alternating, as he did, between satisfaction and dissatisfaction. In his preface to the *De humanis corporis fabrica* dedicated to Charles V, the twenty-eight-year-old anatomist wrote a veritable manifesto of the science of anatomy, "a science that is preserver of man's health, and by far the most useful one conceived by human genius, indispensable more than all the others, but difficult in the extreme and requiring painstaking labor... a subject of meditation also."[9] Vesalius hoped that His Majesty would be "charmed by the study of the organism" and "take pleasure in the attentive examination of that which is both the asylum and the instrument of our immortal soul, and which the Ancients, because of its many remarkable correspondences with the Universe, rightly called a microcosm."[10]

Vesalius took great care in the presentation of his treatise and included a portrait of himself holding an anonymous arm with dissected tendons, pen and paper to examine his observations lie at his disposal. The frontispiece illustrates his various intentions: the animals allude to comparative anatomy, a skeleton asserts the primacy of osteology, while above all a nude figure attached to a column attests to the importance of anatomical knowledge for drawing, a discipline whose resources Vesalius used with so much skill in his publications.

Whether Vesalius' illustrations were done by Titian (which nevertheless seems very unlikely), one of his students, or a talented unknown matters little, for the perspective and layout of shadows in these scenes were rendered with great skill. Scientific rigor seems to be in perfect accord with a certain extravagant fantasy that one would be less likely to imagine in a treatise on botany for example. When dealing with anatomy, the illustrator was particularly susceptible to the temptations of the imagination.

A skeleton calling the earth to witness leans on the handle of a hoe in the nonchalant pose of a gardener pausing for a rest. Roger Caillois said of this figure: "He looks as worried as any living being would when he thinks that only death will relieve him of his troubles."[11] Another, melancholic this time, props his head up with his left hand and rests his right hand on a separate skull, as in a *Vanitas* scene, all the while crossing his legs in a very debonair fashion. One flayed figure displays his pain against an eclectic architectural background graced with two obelisks. Another displays his musculature in profile while walking through ruins that look vaguely Roman. Yet another figure, looking very weary, unable to take another step, leans his back against an antique wall, arms dangling, head thrown back as if to catch his breath again. The écorché with his strips of flayed flesh is never alone on the page; the illustrator always gave him a setting, systematically framed him with a decor. Was this a way of attenuating or dressing up these intolerable visions? Pathos, however, was not the absolute rule. If one armless, stricken figure kneels on a pedestal adorned with a skull, others, on the contrary, seem to exude a certain optimism, especially when their backs are turned to the spectator, their arms slightly outstretched as if to indicate the background landscape enlivened with architectural ornaments.

"The skeletons meditate," Roger Caillois writes, "the écorchés stroll about. Their steadfast (and successfully maintained) determination not to pay any attention to a state that precisely forbids them to act as they do fools no one. Everyone knows that some of these figures, stripped almost entirely down to man's original clay, exist only in the form of an inert, dislocated framework, whereas others, who have lost only their outer wrappings, should be shrieking with pain. Who are they trying to

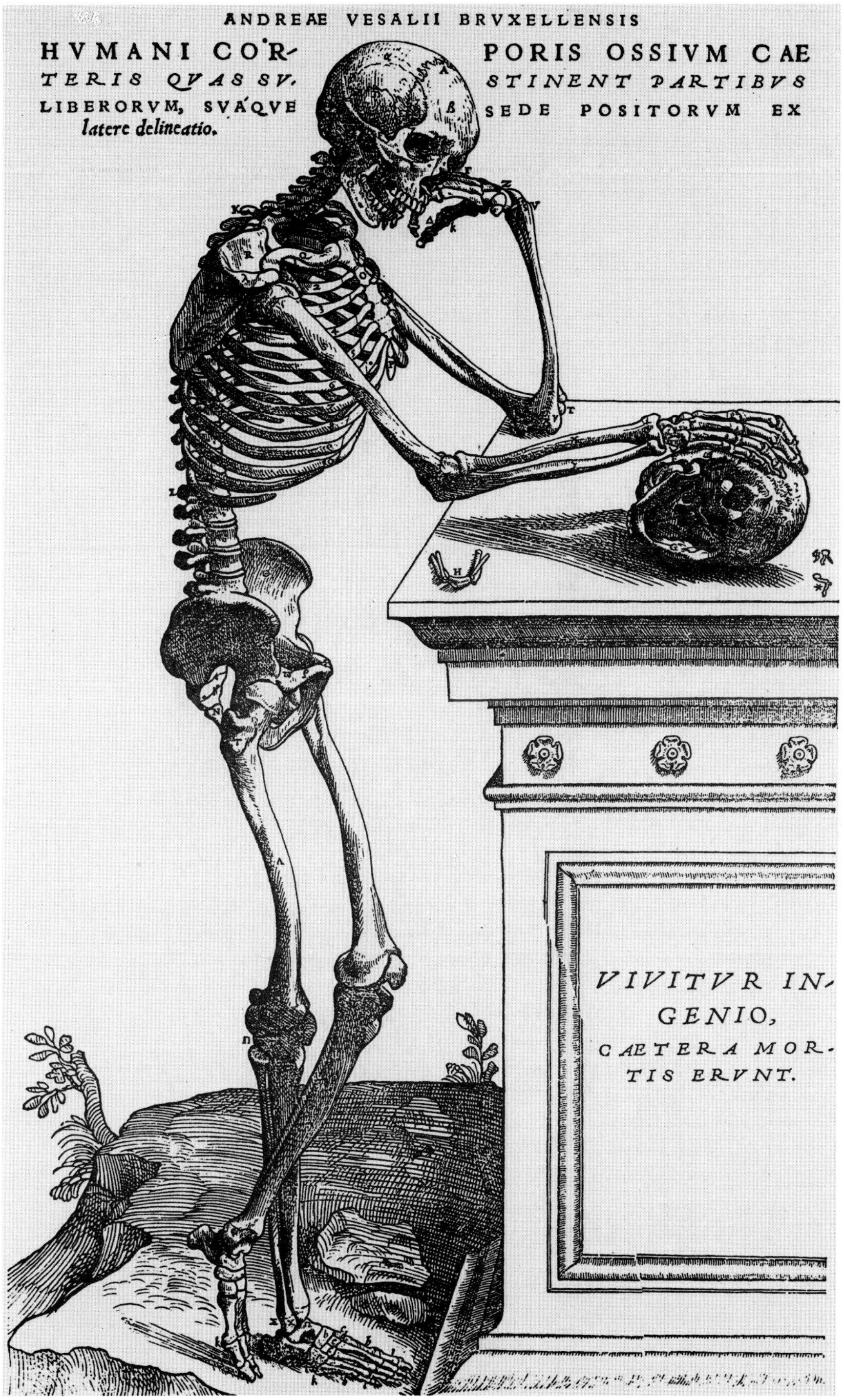

Andreas Vesalius:
Skeleton Meditating on a Skull, 1543.

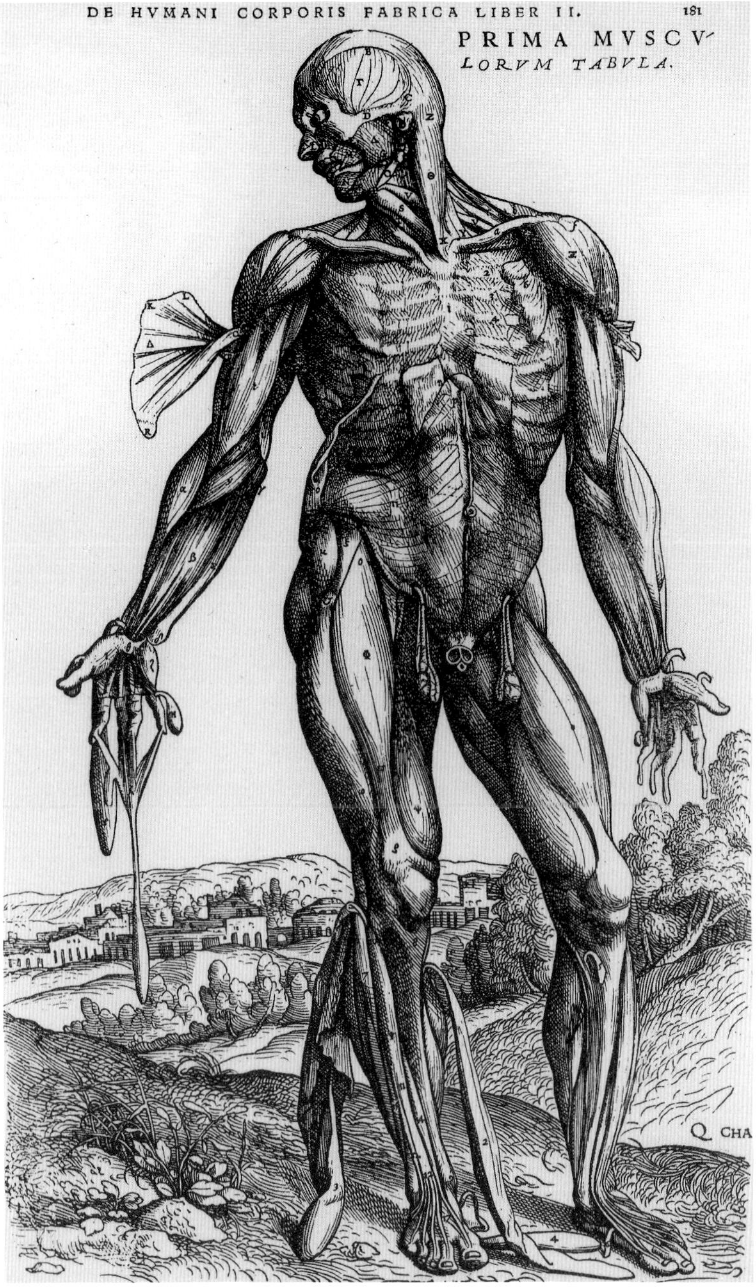

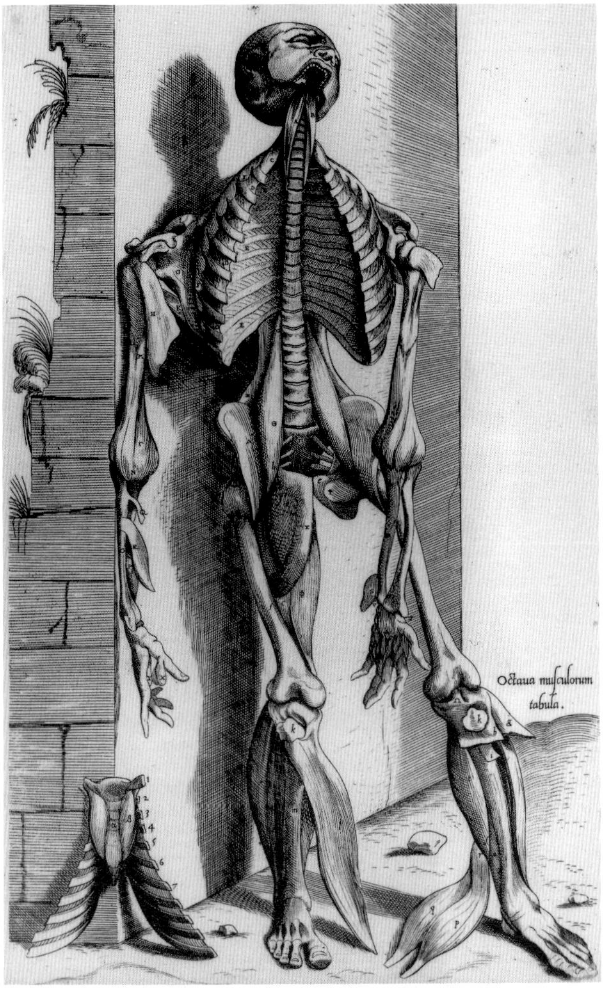

Andreas Vesalius:
Ecorché Leaning Against a Wall, 1543.

Andreas Vesalius:
Ecorché in a Landscape, 1543.

deceive, the former pretending to be engaged in an intelligent activity, and the latter displaying a scandalous nonchalance? In any event, they attempt to demonstrate the futility of death."[12]

In order to show the viscera, Vesalius and his artist used headless antique torsos, their limbs supposedly broken off by the passage of time; marmoreal fragments of Apollo and Venus of haughty gait, but filled with tangles of intestines. Fascinating and elegant contrasts in drawings that depict stone become flesh, and even more than flesh—entrails. All of this combined with great economy of time and space by leaving out the parts of the body unrelated to the immediate subject of study. A woman's bust has a lock of hair falling on her shoulder. The torso of a man with aged features reclines delicately on a convenient stone headrest.

To expose the contents of his cranium, one man kept his sideburns and moustache, while others preferred voluminous, curly beards. These light and tenuous touches were so many details meant to distract the attention from the essential horror, the dangerous revelation of the hidden and forbidden contents of the human body.

Vesalius exerted a fascination for centuries. His plates were reinterpreted scores of times and in all kinds of manners. Anatomists and artists were not the only ones drawn to the Brussels-born pioneer:

Charles Estienne:
Anatomical plate (Study of a Skull), 1546.

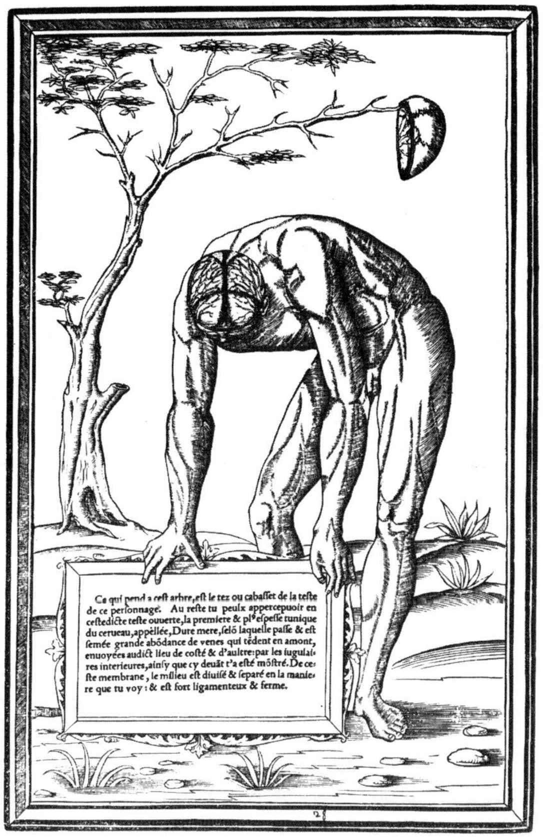

Vesalius also attracted writers. Petrus Borel, the Wolfman, devoted a fantastic short story to him in his *Immoral Tales.*[13] In Madrid, Vesalius, the "peeler" and "devourer of the dead" marries a young woman who soon proves adulterous; he murders her successive lovers and dissects them one after the other. Baudelaire took up the theme of the tilling skeleton in one of his poems. Marguerite Yourcenar made Vesalius one of the protagonists in her novel *L'Œuvre au noir*, etc. The anatomist became a figure of legend. The intrepid pioneer, frequenter of graveyards, scaffolds and hospitals, familiar companion of death, was he vampire or vulture? The story goes that he was regularly provided with prisoners whom he drugged with opium in order to perform vivisections.

In France, Charles Estienne, a contemporary of Vesalius, combined the talents of an anatomist, scholar, esthete and publisher. The plates in his books are full of references to the School of Fontainebleau: Rosso, Primaticcio, Perino del Vaga. Charles Estienne, who inaugurated the practice of public dissections in Paris, knew how to disseminate his ideas, and engraving provided him with the best means. He called on a number of artists, including Rosso in all probability, who had studied anatomy in Paris, and his student, Domenico Fiorentino. The artists drew their inspiration from mythology and the Bible. As in Vesalius, many skeletons are shown in landscapes embellished, in the foreground, with a few botanical details and altars, and in the background, with architectural elements displaying a pronounced taste for ruins.

The skeleton was often shown perched atop a pedestal. Certain écorchés brandish accessories like swords and staffs, while pointing a finger at sights unseen. One of them holds fast a piece of his flesh, another leans against a tree like a drunkard in a fit of melancholy. Some strike a coquettish pose, with a slight contrapposto, one hand on the hip, or in attitudes of great weariness. Others take on the pose of a Saint Sebastian. Many are very cooperative and do not hesitate to participate in their own martyrdom, pulling their wounds apart to give the spectator a better view. Their cooperation does not stop there, but requires them—regardless of their condition—to hold up the cartouche containing explanatory information.

One écorché with a vague gaze poses on a monumental edifice with small columns. A great number of these figures are ostensibly set outdoors. They exhibit their insides outside, in a natural setting, between blades of grass and Roman ruins. A skullcap, severed from its erstwhile owner, hangs from the branch of a tree. Passing references to antiquity abound. A figure with bulging muscles displaying his brains reclines like an ordinary river allegory. A Titian-style Venus displays her generous flesh interrupted for the sake of anatomical knowledge. Another woman turns her head to show a classic Greek profile, oblivious to the twins she carries in her womb.

In the interior (!) scenes, the atmosphere is fairly Venetian: plush cushions and ample drapery with a hint of the Oriental. The postures of the women revealing the innermost recesses of their wombs are fairly relaxed, and even lascivious at times. They spread their legs, one arm placed behind their heads. These ladies seem to be floating in languorous abandon, enjoying their pleasure, or more exactly the afterpleasure state. Georges Bataille, who was transfixed by the sight of photographs showing victims of Chinese executions, would certainly not have remained indifferent to these

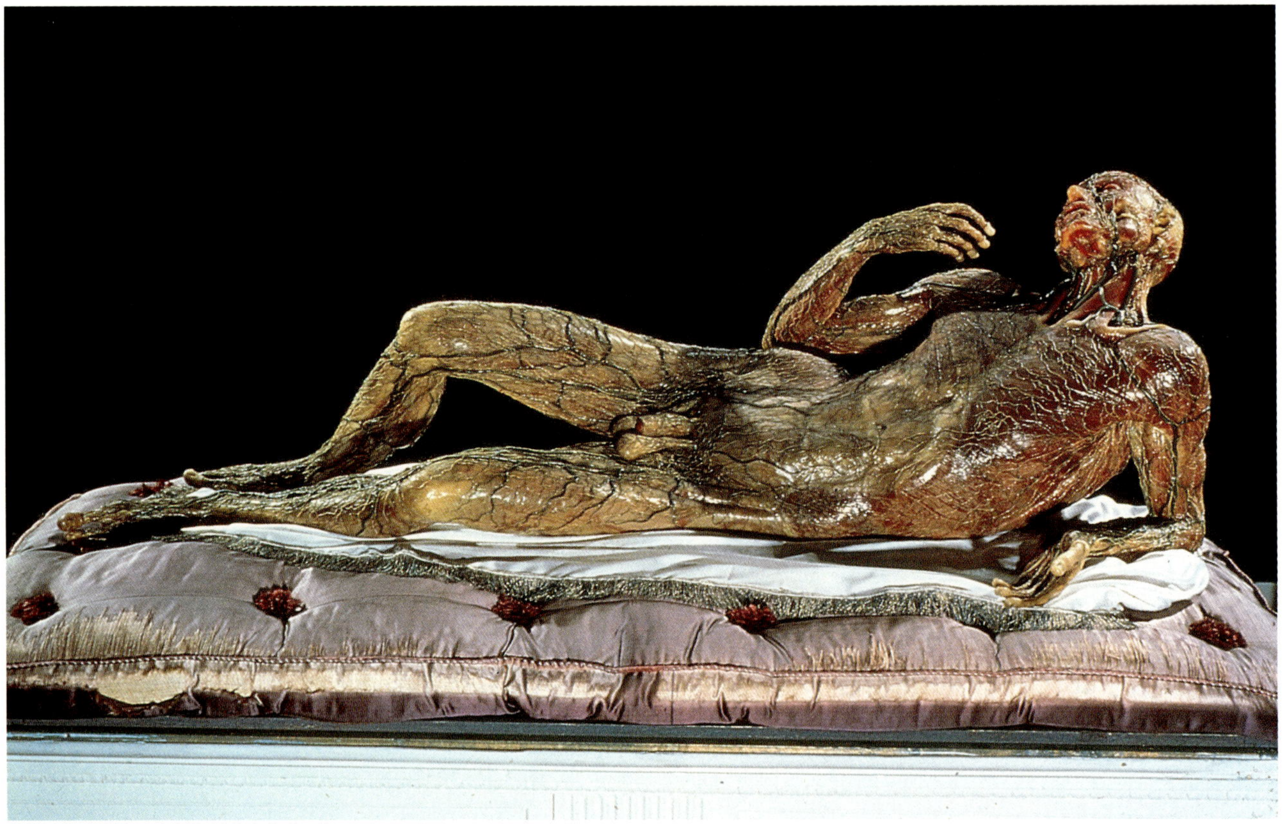

Anonymous:
Lifesize Wax Anatomy, c. 1785
(detail, page 172).

images of ecstasy, this strange Garden of Torments which Octave Mirbeau, who called women the "supreme artists of pain," would not have disowned.

Generally speaking, anatomical plates were born under the sign of ambiguity. They were the product of a dialogue between the surgeon and the illustrator, the latter's task being all the more daunting because he had to render tactile effects as well. Under Louis XIV, Charles Le Brun added anatomical subjects to his drawings and studies of physiognomy. In the North, Godfried Bidloo's book *Anatomi humani corporis* was illustrated with engravings made after the wash drawings of Gérard de Lairesse, who was known as the "Poussin of the North" because of his history drawings. A strange poetry emanates from these very elegant illustrations. The bodies are framed by drapery with delicately-shaded folds. A fly, traditional guest of trompe-l'œil painting, alights between flesh and tissue, and the flesh itself is rendered as a strange and precious lacework. Certain écorchés are all the more striking because they are only partially exposed. On the same figure we can see a flayed back next to nicely fleshed-out arms and wrists tied with thin strings. Haunting transitions treated with a delicate sensuality. Silent dramas. A rope holds the preparation, a pin stretches an aponeurosis, a sheet closes off the field. The textures are irresistibly rendered, a veritable inventory of tactile sensations: smooth, granular, fibrous, moiré, budding, silken, ligneous, flaccid, etc., all of this in a blend of realism and sensuality, rigor and theatricality.

In Rome, the director of the Academy of Painting and Sculpture commissioned the anatomist Bernardo Genga to compile an *Anatomia per uso e intelligenzia del disegno*. Genga prepared the cadavers especially for artistic instruction by placing the bones and muscles in attitudes of famous antique statues in Rome. The atmosphere is Baroque, agitated: angelic skeletons sport wings, others play ghost by wrapping themselves in sheets. Their poses are sometimes very lively, for they were drawn from life. Skeletons imitate the *Farnese Hercules*, the *Laöcoon*, the *Apollo Belvedere*, or the *Little Faun*. Gladiators in action show the play of their exposed muscles. The medical amphitheater and the antique theater became the antichambers of the artist's studio.

In the 17th century, in France and Holland, Vesalius was copied for the use of artists by eliminating from his work "all the difficulties and useless things which have been an obstacle for painters." One of these abridged and countlessly republished versions found its way into Cézanne's studio, as well as the studios of many other painters and sculptors. François Boucher, who paid close

Gérard de Lairesse:
Anatomical Plate, 1685.

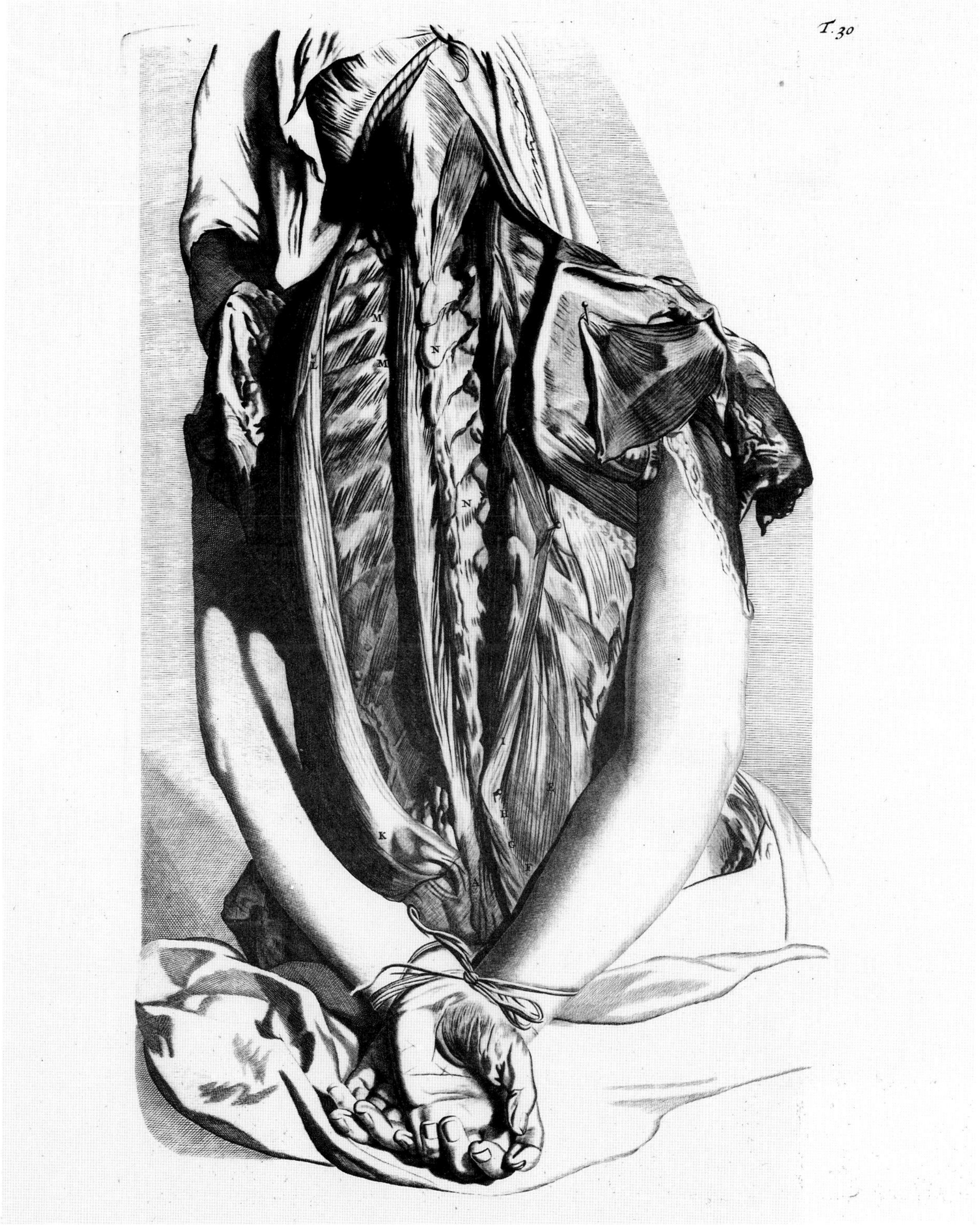

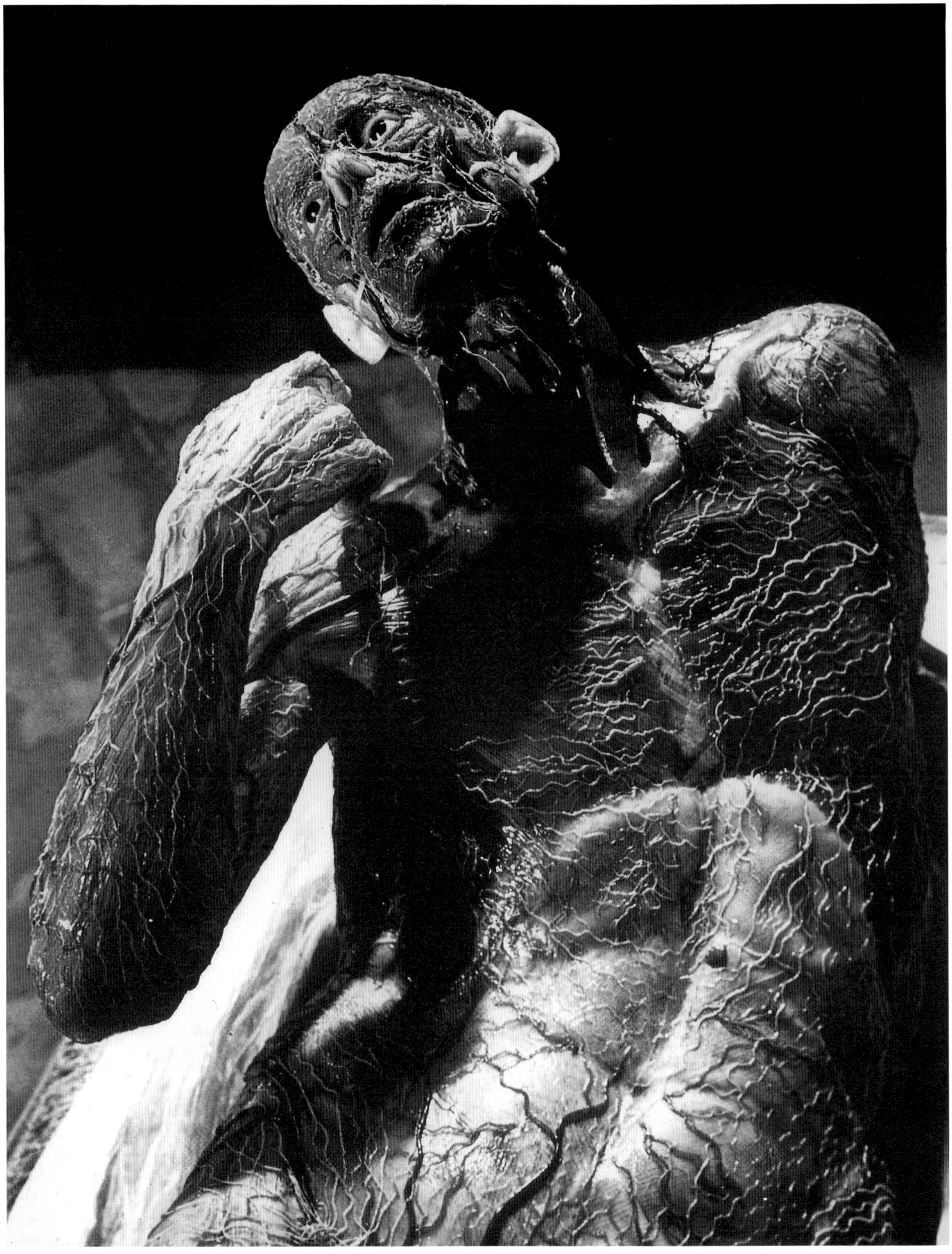

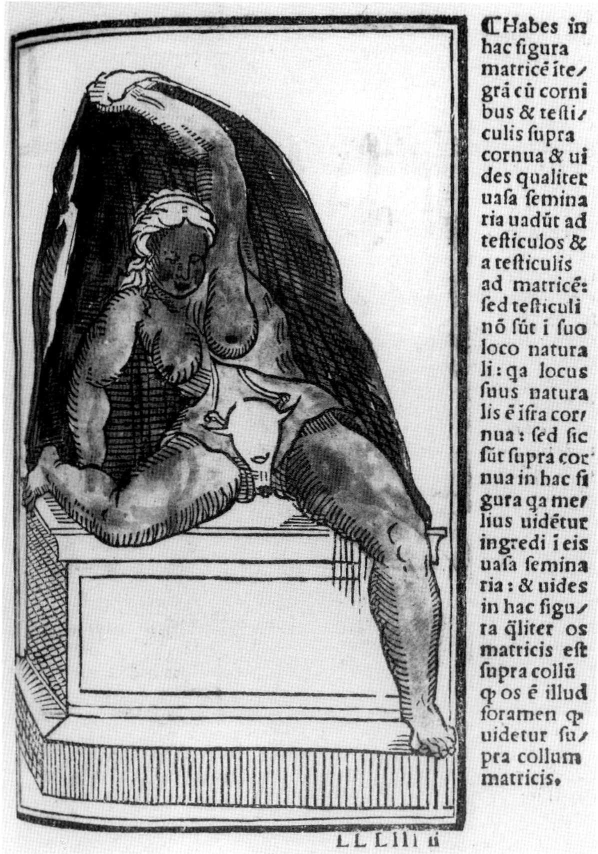

Giacomo Berengario da Carpi:
Woman Sitting on a Funeral Monument, 1521.

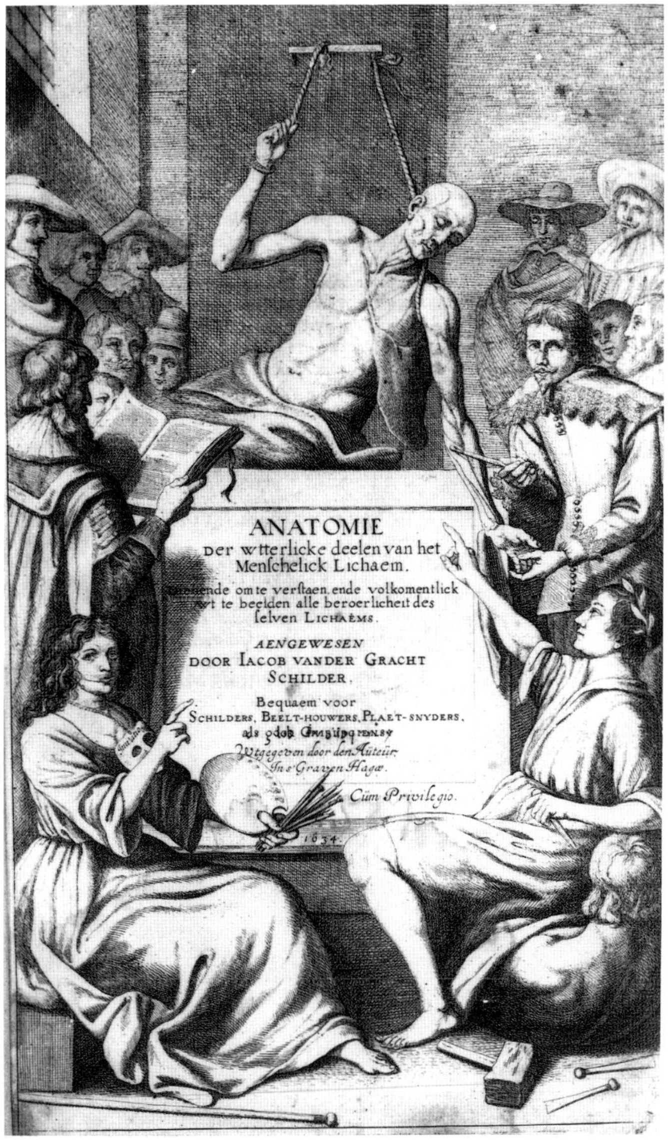

Jacob van der Gracht:
Title page of his work
Anatomie der witterlicke deelen*..., 1634.*

attention to anatomy, illustrated the frontispieces of various publications. The Baroque age was haunted by the revelation of the hidden forms of the body. Bernini's skeletons for the tomb of Urban VIII partake of the same obsession with death and mystery. Through anatomical plates, artists sought to approach the sources of the fantastic. The contents of these treatises are surprising: partial views accentuate the bizarre aspect of the figures. There is a sort of macabre humor also. An adult skeleton holds a small skeleton by the hand. Some skeletons seem to be waiting for God knows what, some betray boredom and impatience; others juxtapose the hourglass and the apple of the original sin; several display a sardonic smirk. One écorché walks with a measured step, while for the beholder's benefit one of his arms has been detached from the rest of his body. *Danses macabres* and picturesque parades.

Visual metaphors flourish: a woman with an open belly holds a gigantic eyeball, gaping like an exploded carnivorous plant. A man reclining lasciviously by a tree spreads his legs wide to reveal his sectioned member. A woman with her bowels in plain view strikes the pose of the *Venus Pudica*. At times the plates are overloaded and their layout is a bit chaotic. A sort of *horror vacui* makes the illustrator fill the page with haphazardly scattered details. An eye here, an ear there, a flying angel, Adam and Eve, a foetus, etc. Anatomical bazaar, pedantic bric-a-brac in an atmosphere of compassion. Often one sees hanging somewhere in the frame, at once pitiful and transcendental, the flayed skin of Saint Bartholomew.

On the frontispiece of an anatomical textbook intended for artists, prepared by Jacob Van der Gracht in Holland, and strongly impregnated with Vesalius and Michelangelo, a woman painter is shown wearing the mask of "imitatio" around her neck—a personification of painting. Nearby, a sculptor works on a statue, all the while keeping his eye on a corpse in the hands of a dissector.

Wandelaar's engravings were published in Leiden in 1747. The prints are given twice: the first time with an abondance of scientific information, the second for both the sake of verification and, it would seem, the pure esthetic delight the images afford. It is a surprising album, very sophisticated and refined, with elongated figures in mannered, aristocratic attitudes. Their surroundings, which betray an Italian influence, were delicately and carefully executed. A skeleton still endowed with his adductor muscles and diaphragm stands in the company of a hippopotamus. In one plate the skeleton and the great mammal are shown in frontal view. The former makes a theatrical gesture with his arm, while the latter feeds peacefully on grass. On the following plate the skeleton and river horse are turned around to show their respective posteriors. The hippopotamus raises its head and looks off, we know not where, with his ridiculous eyes. Roger Caillois expressed surprise at this unexpected pair: "The times were probably very keen on sensation... The skeleton is noble, proud, and even a bit fierce. He holds a protective arm over the inexplicable hippopotamus, which remains indifferent; the rough skin and tiny eyes of the one contrast with the impeccable bones and empty eye-sockets of the other."[14] There are other unexpected associations: a winged skeleton (or skeleton-angel?) stands in a relaxed pose, unrolling an academic drawing; at his feet, two bones form a cross. One kneeling bag of bones is completely absorbed in his reading. An écorché is crucified like Christ.

In the 18th century, courses in anatomy became part of the standard curriculum in the art academies, while in Paris, London, Amsterdam and Zurich, the publication of anatomy books intended for painters increased. The artists themselves decided what was necessary for their work. Charles Monnet, the court painter of Louis XVI, believed that the basics could be learned in six months thanks to his *Studies of Anatomy for Painters*, illustrated with 42 red-pencil plates (Géricault was to become well acquainted with these). The author gave instructions for the use of his manual: "Take each part separately, begin by learning the names of the bones, the origin and place of insertion of the muscles, their form at rest, then their function, which demonstrates the form they should have in action, and finally the skin, which imparts to all the rest that grace and nobility which is the fruit of long study... neglect not the head, the feet and the hands: I deemed it indispensable to give details of these."[15]

During this same period, which was so avid for sensation, Jacques Gautier d'Agoty put color at the service of his already exemplary concern for scientific accuracy. He wanted the plates to be of the same scale as the parts they described, and so he published large formats which required specially assembled plates to save space. Dissections

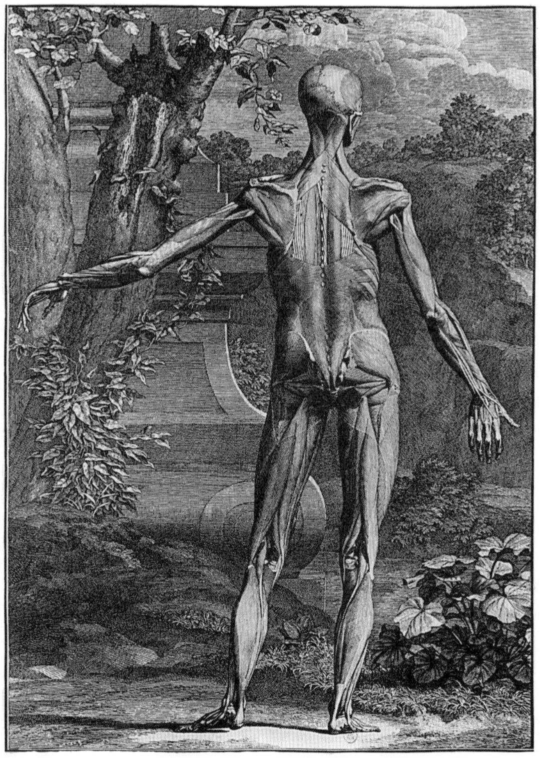

Jan Wandelaar:
Ecorché back view, 1747.

Jan Wandelaar:
Skeleton With Hippopotamus, 1747.

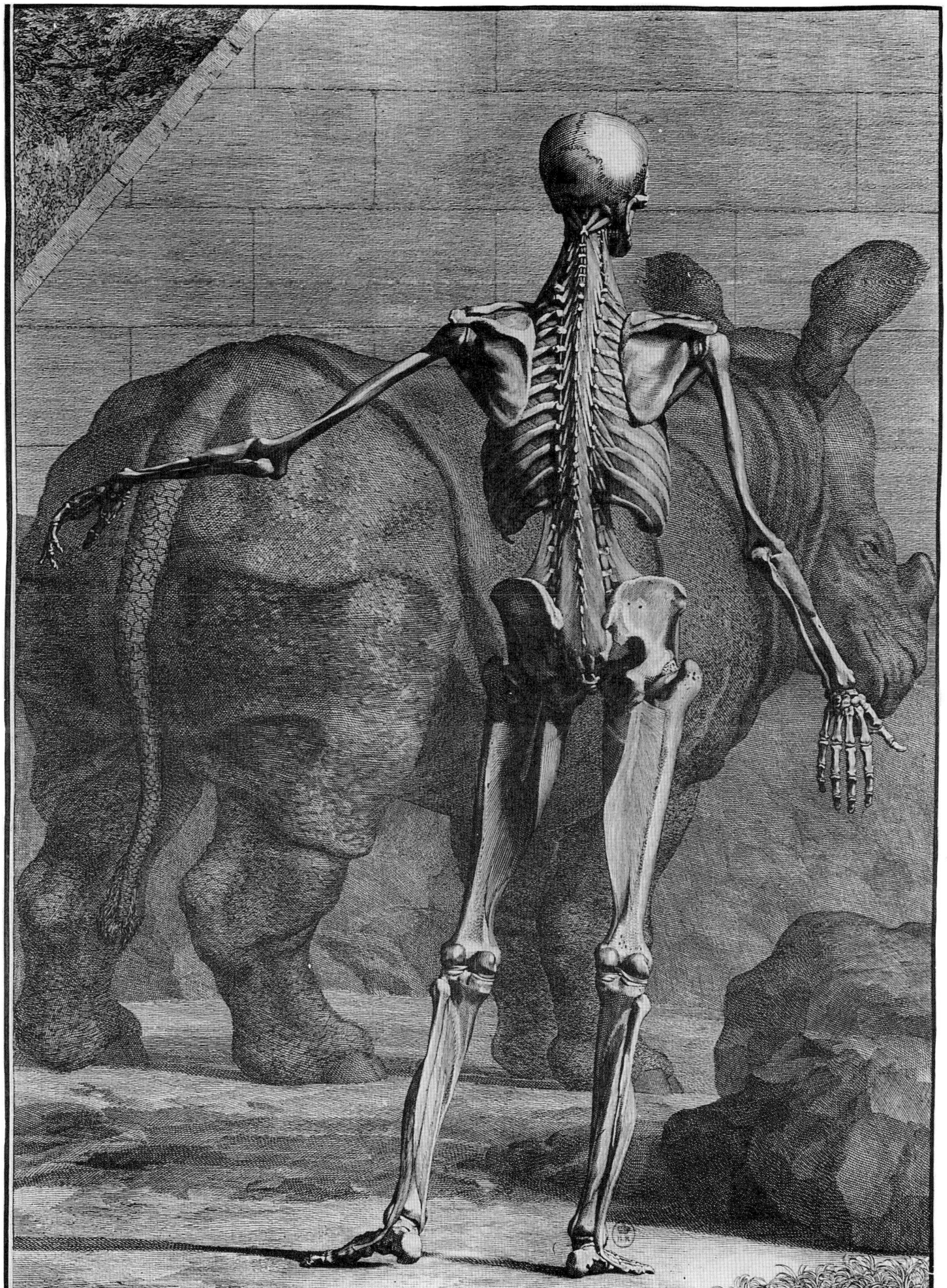

Jacques Gautier d'Agoty: The Anatomical Angel, 1746.

were often only partially represented, so as to leave part of the body "untouched for the pleasure of the eye." A most praiseworthy scruple! At first his assistants were anatomists of the King's Garden who had been trained at the Academy of Surgery. But gradually Gautier d'Agoty did without their services, called himself anatomist, no longer respected the lifesize format. Art began to predominate. In some ways a prelude to Romanticism was Gautier d'Agoty's treatment of a subject that was then very much under discussion, human reproduction. His plates show embryos nestled in the wombs of disheveled women. The painter-illustrator-printer-anatomist then fell prey to the bizarre and morbid, not hesitating to represent a splendid hermaphrodite in his *Anatomical exposition of venereal illnesses.*

One woman (who later became the "anatomical angel" of the Surrealists) exhibits her flayed back whose raised muscles give her an extremely beautiful pair of wings. The remainder of the body is intact, and the face, shown in profile, has a slightly melancholic expression. "For the dissection of the muscles demonstrated in this plate, we used a female cadaver, for the muscles there are more delicate and take up less space, thanks to which we were able to show more of the figure; we left the head for what pleasure it might afford."[16] Sensuality approaches paroxysm here. This woman gives herself in her ultimate nudity.

Another woman, shown frontally, reveals her contents, or a portion thereof. The face, an arm, a breast, and the greater part of the bust are still untouched and covered with an attractive, soft, honey-colored skin. One breast and arm have been carefully shorn of their protective covering. The belly is wide open, but this does not seem to have any more of an effect on its owner than to add a tinge of melancholy to her gaze. "Truth is naked," wrote Valéry, "but beneath the nakedness, there is the flayed flesh."

The animate and the inanimate combine, and, paradoxically enough, this is made to seem almost "natural"! There is so much grace in these images that Jacques Gautier d'Agoty must surely have fallen under the spell of the écorché, male or female. The private is made public, openly offered to the delight of the eye. The *cadavre exquis* begins to give signs of life in its red-lined coat. Gautier d'Agoty's woman is standing, confident in her beauty, and in the more than full fullness of her open and closed flesh. Nothing is said of the parchment-like rigidity of the cadaver or of putrefaction. Grief is sublimated, idealized. The horror is sublime, flexible, elegant; the death-agony, esthetic. The edges of the incision are soft openings, tender décolletés that greet the eye, arousing a tactile vision.

Sectioned and undone, the body presents itself without inspiring repulsion, or rather, inspires a repulsion dressed up in precious distinction. The menace of death takes on wordly airs, "After you, my dear Sir!" As if the life of the flesh were not in the balance. The graceful corpses of Gautier d'Agoty, which have no unpleasant odors, belong more to the plant and mineral realms; their flourishes are as delicately tooled as those of a piece of marquetry or goldwork decorated with gemstones. This elegance exorcizes the carcass with a scandalous, a scandalously intimate beauty. Entrails amplified by fantasy, blood as appealing and luxurious as the red velvet of opera seats, undulating garlands of veins.

No shroud hides the post-mortem wounds of the scalpel. The rich colors and the attractive lines make death a delightful spectacle. The écorché, killed twice-over, the second time by the instruments of the surgeon or barber, nonetheless retains its particular distinction.

Never again did artist attain the shimmering esthetic quality of Gautier d'Agoty. In the 19th century, anatomy was used regularly, but there were no more spectacular innovations in its pictorial presentation (which does not mean that this was the case for the use artists made of it). There was still an interest in anatomy, but it became

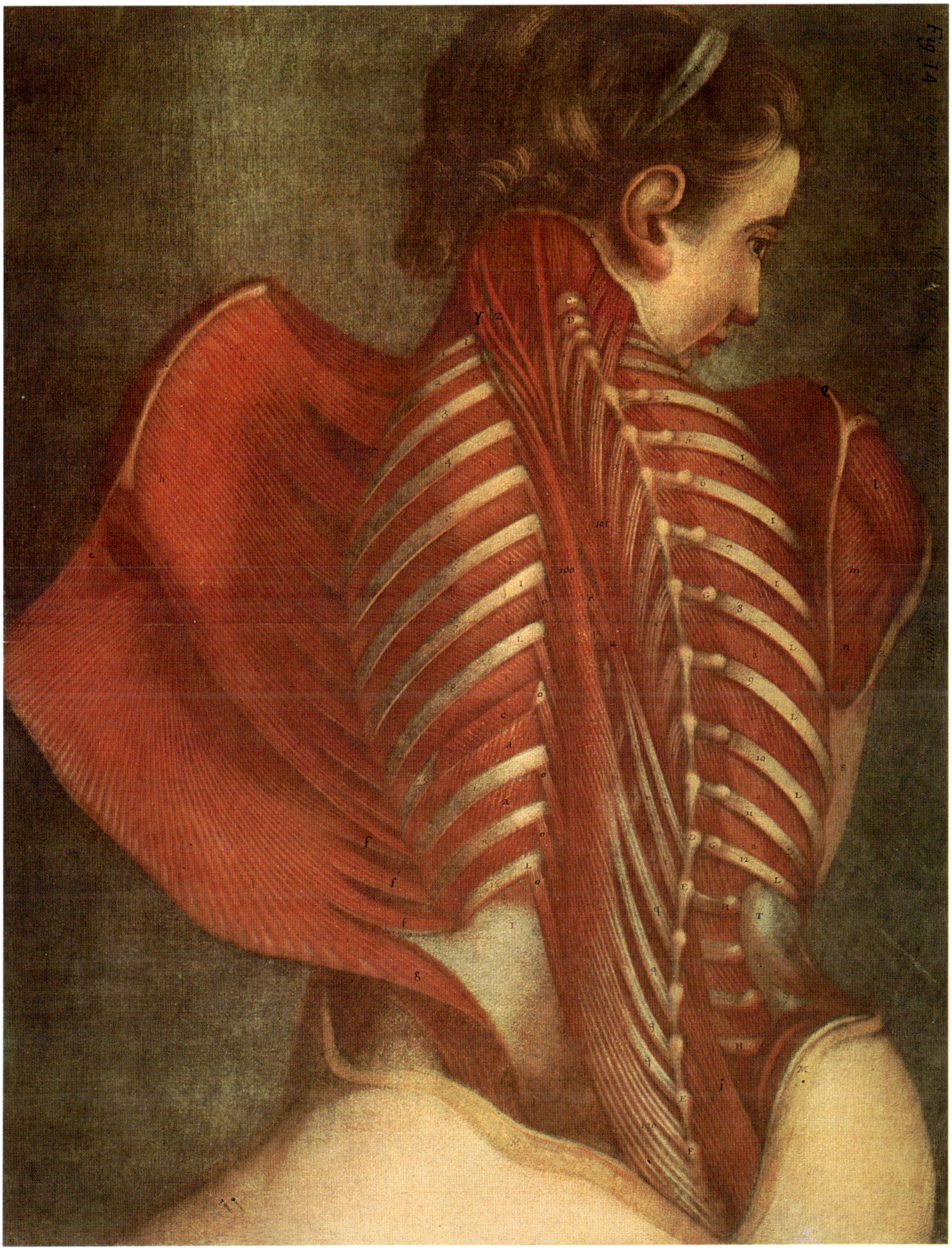

Théodore Géricault:
Anatomical Fragments, c. 1818-1820.

instrumentalized to the detriment of fantastic dramatization.

During the 19th and 20th centuries, many of the great classics of anatomy were republished. In 1829 Montalembert, a history painter, devoted no less than one entire volume to anatomy in his treatise on painting. Artists relied officially and deliberately on this science. At the library of the Ecole nationale des Beaux-Arts, Géricault studiously copied Giuseppe del Medico's *Anatomia per uso dei pittori e scultori*, published in Rome in 1811. These efforts later helped him in his work on *the Raft of the Medusa*. To work on this great composition he intentionally set up his studio near the Hôpital Beaujon. "He rented a very spacious studio in the quartier of Saint-Philippe-du-Roule; he was thus only a few steps away from the Hôpital Beaujon. He had arranged with the interns and nurses to provide him with bodies and severed limbs. It was at this time that he painted the head of a thief from Bicêtre he had been given; he kept the model for fifteen days on his roof and used the study, turned around, for the figure lying down on the left in the painting. He also painted that magnificent study representing two legs seen from the feet with an arm on the collarbone... which was probably the finest piece of painting he ever did. For a few months, his studio was a sort of morgue; they say that he kept corpses until they were half-decomposed; he worked obstinately in this charnelhouse which even his most devoted and intrepid friends ventured to enter only with the greatest difficulty and without lingering."[17] Géricault would also eventually make the acquaintance of Savigny, a doctor and survivor of the Medusa, and Georget, a head doctor at the Salpêtrière. The painter of the *Raft of the Medusa* sought life through a knowledge of death. He also tried to depict the intermediary state, the death agony, and worked on écorchés of both human beings and horses.

Throughout the 19th century, and as Charles Le Brun had done in the previous century, anatomy was related to the discipline of physiognomy. In London, for example, Charles Bell published an *Essay on the Anatomy and Philosophy of Expression*. He combined clinical studies of anatomy in the tradition of Da Vinci, Dürer and Le Brun, with his own observations on the field of battle at Waterloo. "Horror is full of energy," he wrote and to add to the naturalism he noted next to one of the plates, "On the evening I drew this figure, that same day, I saw three men die in this way."[18] According to the particular theories of the times, it was thought that each emotion—horror, despair, doubt, admiration, joy, suspicion, etc.—could be described in anatomical terms; each emotion had its own geography of nerves and muscles.

At the same time, in Paris, Pierre Nicolas Gerdy rewrote anatomy for painters and sculptors in terms of "external forms." For each region of the body he established a topography of "hills and vales" and compared his findings with one hundred and fifty works in the Louvre. This research led to passages such as these: "The sterno-cleido-mastoid fascicule ends at the collarbone... This is well rendered in the *Resting Hercules*, the *Follower of Bacchus*, and Guido's *Jesus and The Woman from Samaria*; it is extremely well represented in a *Saint Peter*, with joined hands by Lanfranc; it is ungainly in Géricault's *Seated Young Man*, in the *Head* formerly called a Demosthenes, and it is perhaps outside in the *Hadrian*, in the *Dancing Faun*, the *Farnese Hercules*... These observations show that, as the free, ardent and often audacious imagination of the ancients could not submit to the yoke of truth, they neglected the observation of nature and abandoned themselves to the conceptions of their own spirits. Poets, philosophers and artists of all kinds prefer inventing the world to discovering it."[19]

The conclusion is that art takes liberties with nature—and that is what makes it art. Ingres did not hesitate to add a vertebra to the neck of his *Grande Odalisque*! Europe analyzed its masterpieces in order to find a recipe, dimly realizing nonetheless that there was no absolute formula. Antique statuary and Michelangelo's sculptures were reconstructed as écorchés. Academic teachings exploited the resources of anatomy as a complement to the model, and occasionally as a palliative too. It was believed that there were some muscular contractions that could not be demonstrated in a sustained manner on the body of the model. In a sense, through the intermediary of the corpse anatomy awarded the artist time. Mathias Duval, professor at the Ecole des Beaux-Arts in Paris and member of the Academy of Medicine, explained: "When the model poses, no matter how carefully we try to make him reproduce the impression of movement, by the very fact that he must hold the pose for a lengthy time, a sort of balance establishes itself between the activity of the different muscular masses; this means that we no longer see the detail of such and such a muscle necessary for the accomplishment of one of the phases of the movement, but, as this movement is simulated only through the fixation of one of its phases, the muscular actions so produced are not very energetic, and are spread uniformly throughout the whole of the body so as to maintain the subject in that particular attitude. We think that we have a movement in front of our eyes, whereas the most we have is a more or less eccentric form of stability, so eccentric at times that we have to give supports

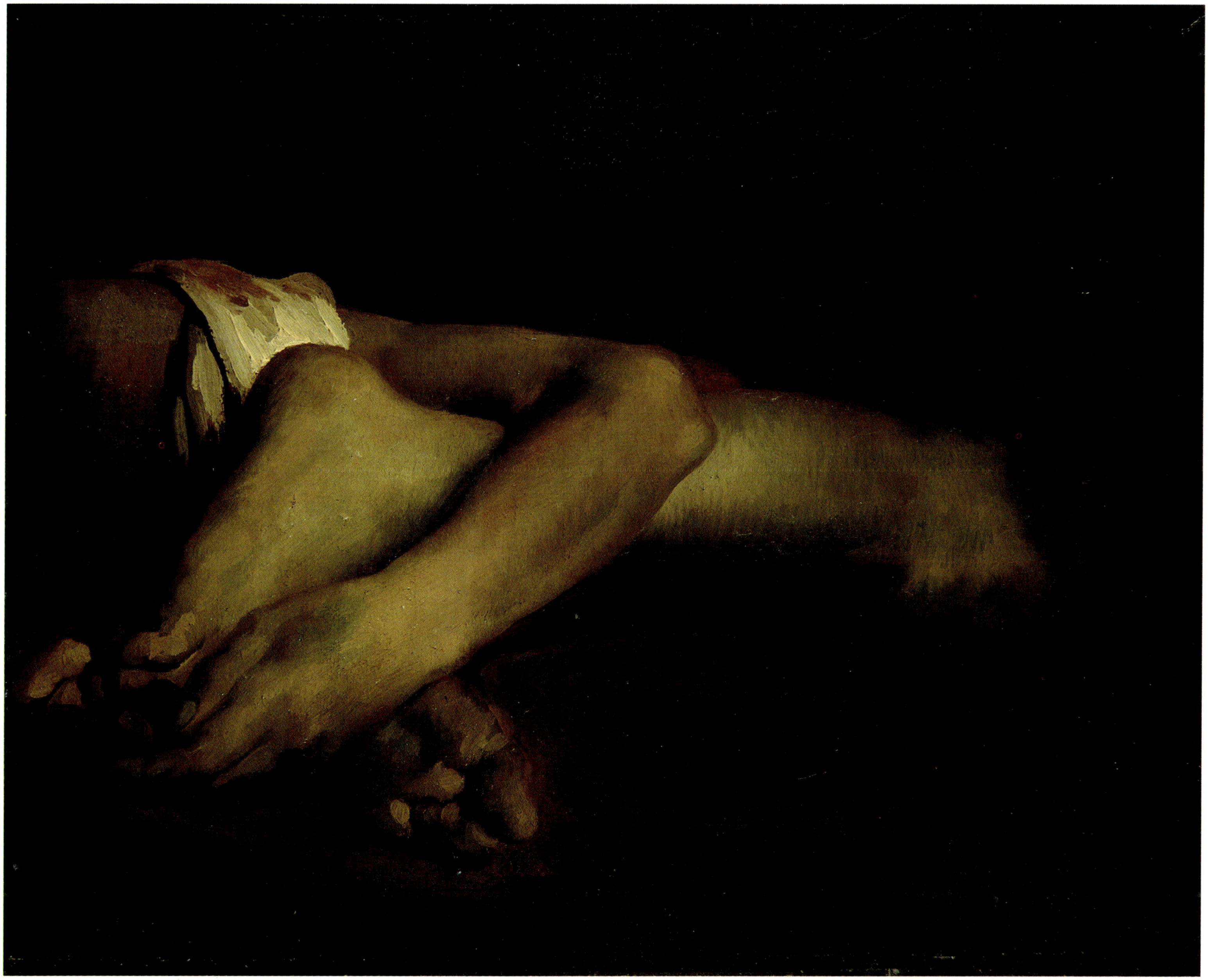

other than the natural ones to help the model hold himself, either by resting on a staff or leaning on a rope hung from the ceiling. Under such conditions, most anatomical details disappear; they can be recovered if one has learned to recognize their level and features by previous anatomical examination; but one cannot hope to obtain this knowledge through the inspection of the model alone."[20]

Mathias Duval also justified the necessity of anatomy by the fact that in his day, unlike antiquity according to the physician-professor, there were no longer any athletes with the necessary strong and supple musculature, and that the models were just ordinary human beings. Thus, one further connection between art and anatomy, but more a matter of application than innovation in this case. The point of exhaustion had been reached. The sculptor Jean-Marie-Bienaimé Bonnasieux, a resident of the Villa Médicis and the official sculptor of the proper French society in Rome, tells in his diary how he shared subjects with Docteur Terasse, each paying half of the "three or four francs" charged. "He takes the torso and I the limbs; he studies life on death, while I myself, following the muscle down to the bone to which it was attached, study not only the movement that it produced and the limit of this movement, but also, and especially, the projections and depressions which this made on the outside."[21] These worthy efforts produced no noteworthy results. A certain type of anatomy was no longer needed as such. Which hardly means that anatomy does not continue to haunt the pathways of creation. It is simply at another level that it exerts its fascination on writers and artists.

Francis Bacon:
Three Studies for a Crucifixion (right panel), 1962.

The anatomical sensation

If artists, beginning with Leonardo da Vinci, entered the human body by way of a pretext (the study of anatomy), in the 20th century they venture into it by way of sensation. The painter par excellence to build his entire work on the outpouring of the contents of the body is of course Francis Bacon. Before him, painters captivated by anatomy transgressed the frontiers of the skin and colored their descriptions of the visceral world with their fantasies. Francis Bacon, perhaps for the first time in the history of painting, eliminated description for the sake of sensation alone. The bodies represented by Bacon are alive, alive to the point of paroxysm, to a hysterical degree; living and howling, living beyond the reach of language. Flayed bodies, contorted bodies, blobs of seething, howling, purple-tinted flesh.

It is orgasm, the anatomical struggle. The raw flesh is no longer protected against the surrounding cold, ascepticized space caught in the web of deceptive perspectives. The flesh bubbles, tightens into a knot or explodes into fragments, putrefies, bleeds like butcher's meat in a refrigerated display window. It is no loger a question of nudity, and the term of wound is too weak for these tragic athletes and their inexorable fates. The cirme is repeated in canvas after canvas, and one would be tempted to say, tautology aside, that each body painted is assassinated in its proper life.

The paroxysm of life clashes with the paroxysm of death. Death violates life at the instant of its utmost exacerbation, scattering burning and squirming entrails. At times, the carcass of a butchered ox (reminiscences of Rembrandt and Soutine) is juxtaposed with that of a man. The condition of animals is as intolerable as that of man, with their common torsions, contorsions and distorsions. The body is evoked at the limits of its biological contingencies; it leaps out of itself, gushes, vomits, shits in the form of spurts of paint. Bacon crucifies it several times in the three phases of his triptych. Each pictorial act is a torture and a murder; not the deliberately organized torments of Octave Mirbeau in the *Jardin des supplices* or of Kafka in *The Penal Colony*, but a much more "barbarian" torture in which the painter captures—through the frenzy of the pictorial gesture—the instant which immediately precedes death. Not one of his figures has any future whatsoever.

Contrary to the anatomical plates, these are not animated corpses, but living beings about to pass away at any moment. It is a praise of the death agony in the accelerated time of emergency. It is the grand finale of life, the last explosion before the onset of decay, before the lowering of the curtain and the complete encroachment of night. Death is here, an imminent menace ready to abolish everything in the spasm of a last cry.

Although "figurative" then, Bacon's painting escapes description; it tells no story, but depicts this ultimate and spasmodic instant. The pictorial space, which is cold and defined by illusory cues, is a field of operations which frames and holds a solitary figure caught in a movement that imprisons it forever in an irreversible destiny. With its last bit of strength, the body what we might call the energy of despair, tries one more time to escape itself; it pours out from its own orifices. By the time the curtain is completely down, not a drop of blood will remain.

Anchored in its bestiality, the body's last impulse is propelled by animal forces that are beyond words. The flesh explodes, fixed in a splendid tension from which sometimes emerges a piece of carcass, of bone structure, usually a section of the spine. The organs are displaced, the "official" structure of the body is overturned. Flesh composes and decomposes itself in a ferocious anatomy of sensation. Suffering and lacerations change its geography. Bacon crucifies, and the distinction between man and animal becomes imperceptible. The mouth that howls and through which the body escapes itself no longer really belongs to the human species. "The face is undone as from an acid that consumes the body," writes Gilles Deleuze[22].

In this "state," the painting works directly on the level of sensation; it is strictly no longer possible just to look at it, to obsere and analyze it. On seeing these écorchés, the spectator is referred to his own wounds. No representation, but the brutal transmission of an experience, body to body, flesh to flesh, in a fatal cry which is communicated by sympathy, in the etymological sense of the word, that is a corespondence of pathos.

Bacon's flayed bodies are in such a paroxystic state that it becomes unbearable; it leads to a theater of cruelty in which organs are mixed without distinction. Mouths and sphincters emerge everywhere. The anatomy falls apart. The orifices become polyvalent or indefinite (which is the same

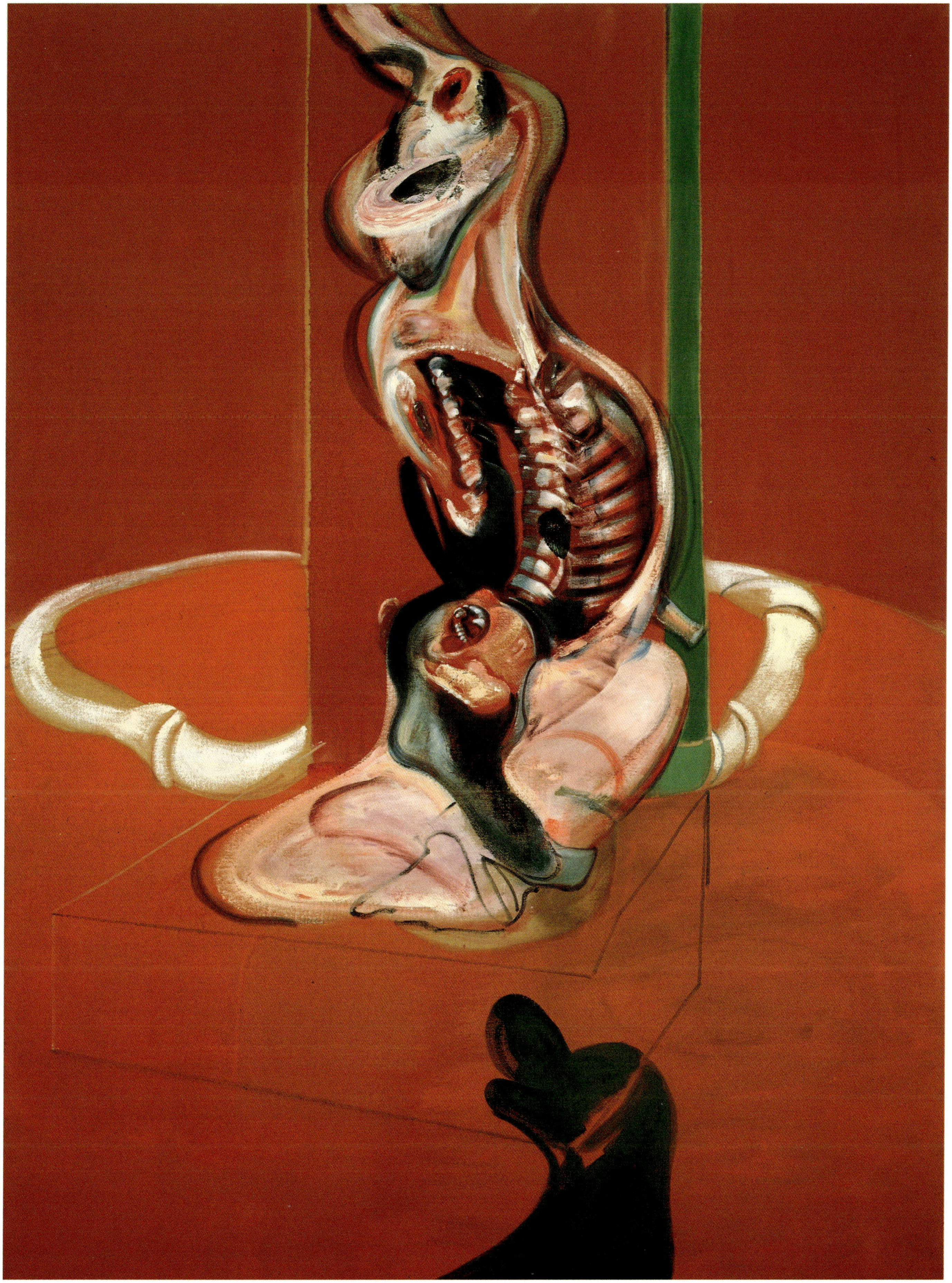

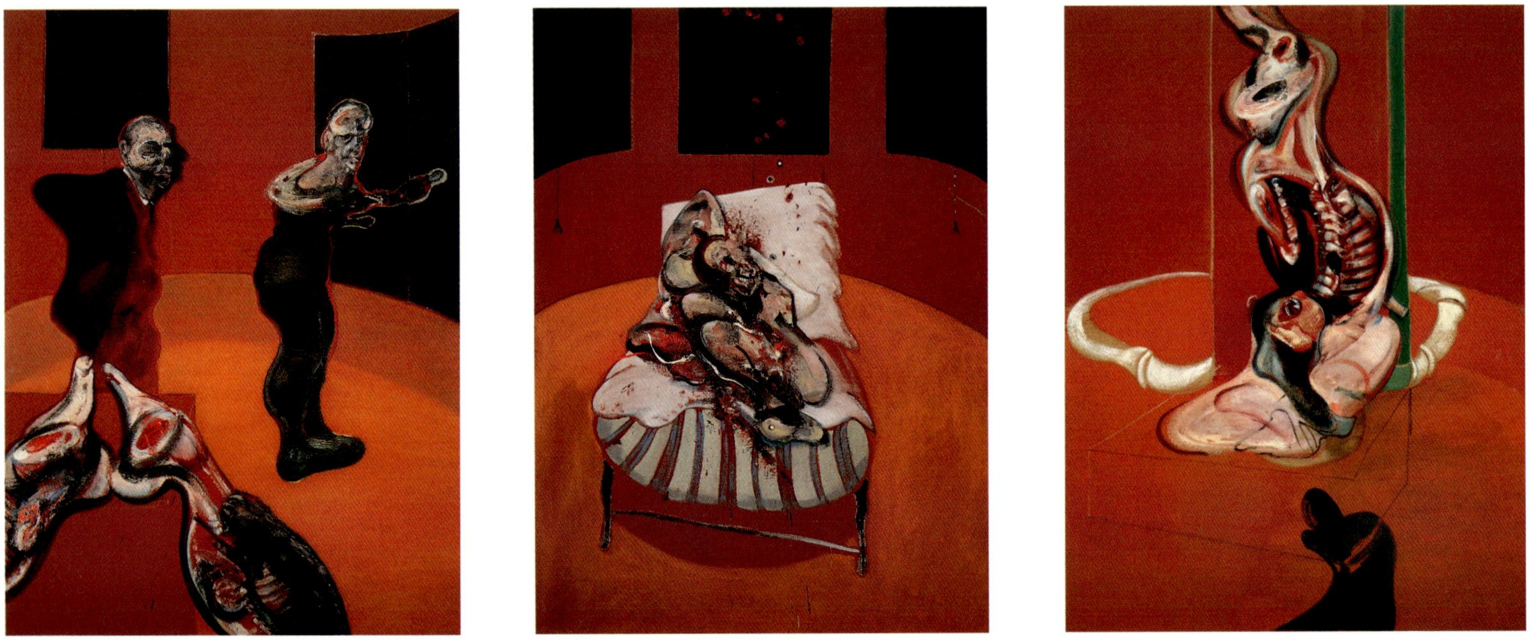

Francis Bacon:
Three Studies for a Crucifixion (general view), 1962.

thing). Infernal rhythms shake the body or overwhelm its structures, overturning its semblance of organization, "as in hysteria," notes Deleuze.

Contractions, paralysis, hyperesthesia, anesthesia criculate on the level of the nervous system. The hysterical patient feels himself in his head, in his stomach, in his liver. By a phenomenon of autoscopy, he sees himself not from the outside, but from the inside of his own organs. An imaginary anatomy is built up by perception, erasing this or that other part of the body, accentuating such and such another part, or displacing yet another. It is the great anatomical chaos, the bazaar of organs. Each part has an intolerable presence, so excessive that it becomes obscene (from "obscenus," evil portent), off-scene.

The body empties itself of its existence. It cannot contain such excess of life. "Life is frightful," Cézanne often said, all the while trying to breathe it into his bathers, apples and victorious mountains. In Bacon's work, life overflows, and this overflow has no other outlet than death. After the cry there is—nothing. The point of no return. The figures howl for their lives. The Irish artist does not like to paint the dead, however, or people he does not know as if they were wanting in flesh. Nor does he like to work with his models present either (too much flesh then?). He prefers to rely on recent memory or on a photograph, even though he refuses to give the least esthetic value to photography. He is interested in the photographs because of the "slight discrepancy with respect to the fact" which they introduce, thus referring that much more violently to the fact itself. "Thanks to the photographic image," the painter explains, "it happens that I begin to roam in the image and discover what seems to me to be its reality, much more so than when I look at the thing itself. And the photographs are not just points or reference; they often stimulate ideas as well."[23] For Bacon, photography is a sort of "dictionary" that enables him to "review the memory."

"Even in the case of friends who would come and sit, I have photographs taken for their portrait, because I much prefer to work from the photographs than from them. It is true that I would not paint from a photograph the portrait of someone I did not know. But if I know them and also have photographs of them, I find it easier to work in this way than when they are actually present in the room. I think that if the image were there, present, I would not be able to wander as freely as with the photographic image. This is probably just because of my own nervous disposition, but I find it less inhibiting to work on them from memory and from their photographs than to have them right there, sitting in front of me... It inhibits me because, if I like them, I cannot do the things which I inflict on them in my work. I prefer to make it privately, this attack which enables me to record their reality more clearly."[24] A bizarre union with a present-absent model; present in its discrepancy, absent in its immediate physical reality.

Bacon also uses photography by association. When he took David Sylvester as a model, the latter was surprised to see him constantly looking at pictures of wild animals. Bacon later explained: "A picture can be profoundly suggestive by its relation to another picture. At that particular time, I had the idea that textures should be thicker, and so, for example, that the skin of a rhinoceros would help me to reflect on the texture of human skin."[25]

By passing constantly among different degrees of the model's reality, the artist tracks down the mystery of appearance. "What I would like to do now, personally, is, for example, to paint portraits that would be portraits but would come from things having nothing to do with what are called the illustrative facts of the picture; they would be done in another way, and yet they would show the appearance. For me, the mystery of painting today is in the manner in which appearance can be rendered. I know it can be illustrated, I know it can be photographed. But how can this thing be rendered in such a way that the mystery of appearance is captured in the mystery of the brushwork? It is by an illogical working method, an illogical way of trying to arrive at what—one hopes—will be a logical result, in the sense that one hopes to be able to render the thing suddenly present in a completely illogical way, but in a completely real way, so that, in the case of a portrait, the person will be recognizable."[26]

In these appearances beyond appearance, what predominates is the presence of flesh and meat. "I have always been very moved by pictures of slaughterhouses and meat, and for me they are closely associated with what the Crucifixion is all about. There are extraordinary pictures of animals taken as they were being led to the slaughter. And the smell of death... We know nothing about it, of course, but these photographs show that they are so aware of what is about to happen to them that they will do anything to try to escape."[27] This attraction to flesh in pain, be it divine, human or animal, follows the pathways of identification.

"For sure, we are meat, we are potential carcasses. If I go to the butcher's, I am always surprised not to be there in the animal's place. But treating meat in this particular way is perhaps like the way in which we can treat the spine, since we see pictures of the human body in X-rays all the time, and this evidently changes the ways in which we can treat the body. You must know that fine pastel by Degas in the National Gallery that represents a woman sponging her back. You will find, all the way at the top of the spine, that it almost juts out of the skin. And this grips and twists her so much that we are more conscious of the vulnerability of the rest of the body than if Degas had drawn the spine running naturally up to the neck. He breaks it up so that it seems to come out of the skin. Whether Degas did this intentionally or not, it gives much more grandeur to the picture because we are suddenly as conscious of the spine as of the skin, which he usually painted so that it covered the bones. As far as I am concerned, such things were certainly influenced by X-ray photographs."[28] A new modality of the relationship between the artist and medicine.

For Bacon, meat has a great "beauty"; with its infinite range of colors, it is the quintessential subject matter of the painter. He focuses his powers as a colorist on the mouth, that mucous membrane which acts as a passage between the inside and the outside. He was fascinated by an old textbook with colored photographs of mouth diseases that he had found in a bookshop. "I guess you could say that I like the shininess and the color inside the mouth and, in a sense, I have always hoped to be able to paint a mouth in the same way that Monet painted a sunset."[29] This correspondence between the scarlet of fire and the scarlet of blood is not surprising in an artist who wanted to create pictures that "coagulated" sensations.

This "optimist completely without hope," as he has defined himself, wants to reconstruct on the sidelines of death his own special anatomy—"pools of flesh"—and he hopes "to be able to make figures emerging from their own flesh with their bowlers and umbrellas and to make these figures as poignant as a crucifixion."[30] And so, through this recurring theme of the crucifixion, emerges the self-portrait: intimate, "poignant," "accidental" (words often used by Bacon), and bloody, with the blood which condenses life and death in its course.

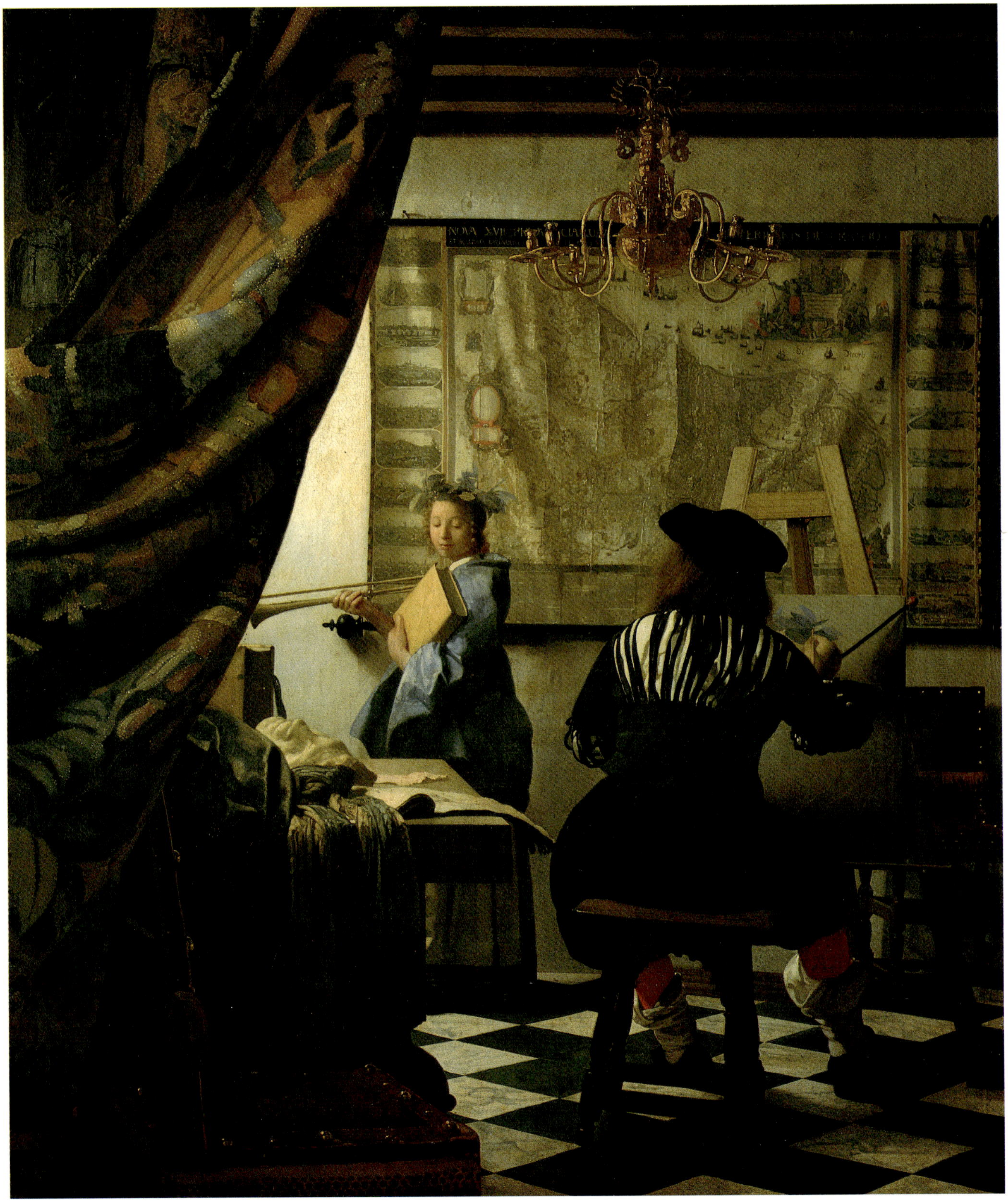

From the pose to the pause, in lieu of a brief epilogue

The multifaceted and labyrinthine relationship between the artist and his model is played out in an infinity of variations. A man and a woman (usually) welded by the gaze. A poser who shows perhaps more of herself than she imagines, and yet less than the artist would like to see.

The model stands at the heart of the studio, in its center of gravity, radiant in her grandiose nudity, which seems to be the very foundation of painting, and raises to an extreme power the existence of the body. Woman in all her guises is the object and subject of creation: femme fatale and saint, maiden and mother, whore and goddess. On her flesh antipodes converge and focus.

Flesh—pure and tainted, holy and outraged—dictates interdictions, invites transgressions, highlights the paradoxical workings of art. On this flesh, the creator tries to fix his wanderings, but it leads him to the brink of the abyss, to the perilous and uncertain zone in which the work is done and undone, on a tightrope above the abyss.

Eros interferes between the artist and the model armed with all of his arrows. The posing session is a lesson in love, even if the artist does not hesitate to torment the model in order to come as close as possible to what he is seeking.

All ways and means are good. The model is the very apprenticeship of art. Fantasies and painstaking tasks gravitate around her. The magic ritual is highly codified in order to neutralize the bewitching power of the model, to appropriate her power and inject it into the weave of the canvas or the veins of the marble.

Jan Vermeer:
The Painter's Studio, c. 1672-1673.

Neutralization, appropriation, and also hypnosis. The artist always returns to the model, at times in spite of himself, and despite his need for independence. It is as if, inevitably, he had to extract the very substance of the body offered to his scrutiny; a knowing, fusional and carnivorous scrutiny.

That essential couple, the artist and his model, engender each other, prey on each other, establish a relationship that involves offering and withholding, fecundation and destruction, frustration and satisfaction.

The artist is not just a voyeur, for he is in a state of hypnosis, active hypnosis. He is active, sketching, testing flesh-tones, modifying the pose. Assisted by proportions, measurements, theories of all kinds, canons of beauty and other illusions, he tries to tame that ungraspable nudity.

He toys with chemistry in order to find the tints which most approximate flesh; he toys with medicine and becomes an anatomist in order to find out what happens under the skin. His curiosity is motivated by an enigma which constantly eludes him. The model mobilizes him, helps him to avoid stagnation. Through her, he renews and nourishes himself (by a strange etymological coincidence, the French speak of "croquer un nu," literally, to crunch a nude). He pursues his posers: shades of passion, jealousy, impatience, etc., all of the ingredients of love are brought together.

This passion for the model endows the painter or sculptor with feelings of power and powerlessness. Confronted with his theoretical paraphernalia, the body maintains its opacity. The artist realizes the limits of his participation, at times to the point of dereliction. But he experiences at times the feeling of a superhuman power, a power which authorizes him to create illusion, that superior and open double of reality, the abode of dreams and fantasies.

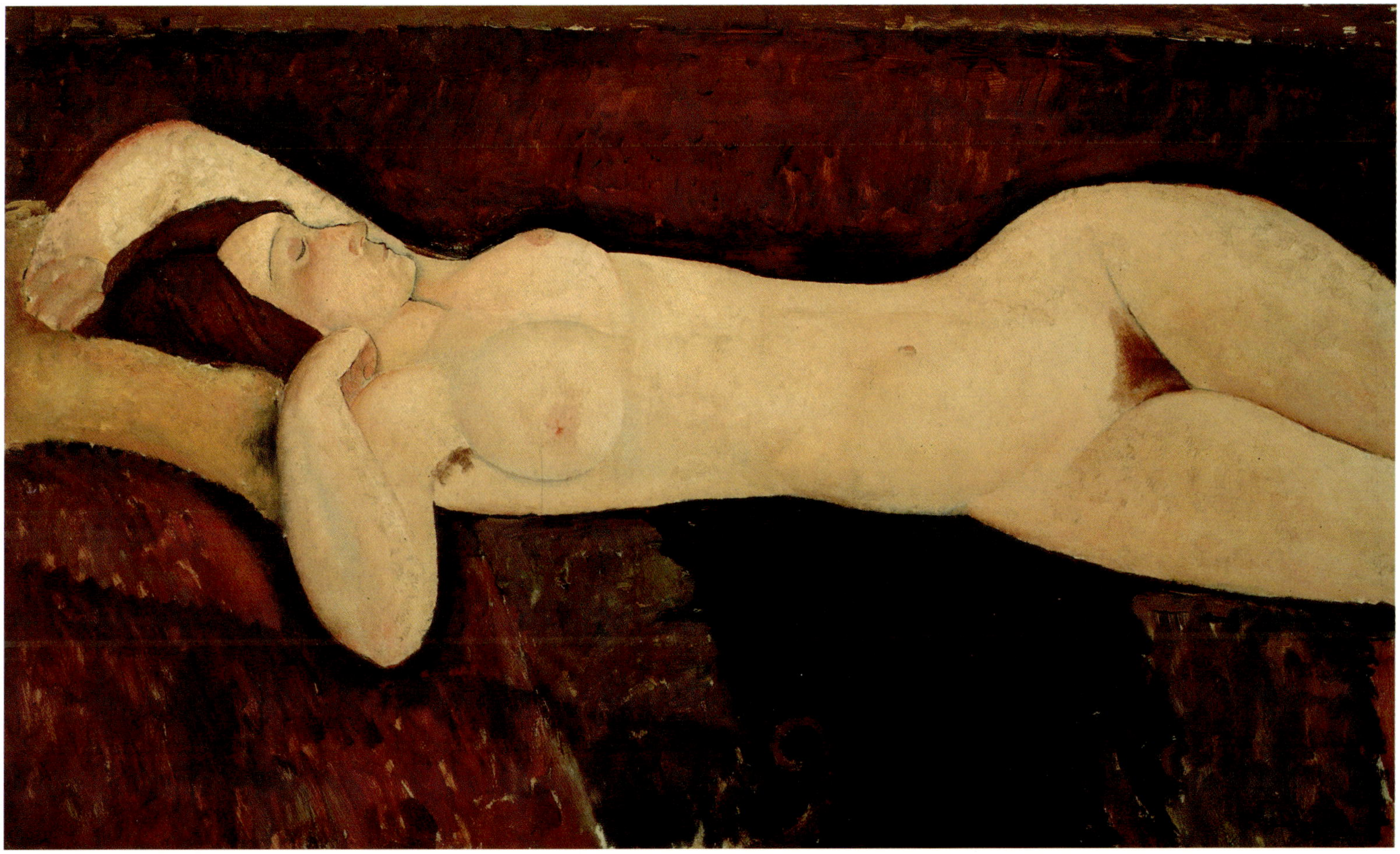

Amedeo Modigliani:
Reclining Nude, c. 1919.

Notes

Notes to Chapter One

[1] J.-P. Sartre, *Qu'est-ce que la littérature?*, Paris, Gallimard, 1985, p. 20.

[2] R. Barthes, *Roland Barthes par lui-même*, Paris, Seuil, 1975, p. 93.

[3] *Ibid.*, p. 72.

[4] M. Merleau-Ponty, *Le visible et l'invisible*, Paris, Gallimard, 1964.

[5] D. Anzieu, *Le corps de l'œuvre*, Paris, Gallimard, 1981, p. 44.

[6] *Ibid.*, p. 72.

[7] The concept *moi-peau* (the ego-skin) developed by the psychoanalyst Didier Anzieu could be applied to the creation of a work of art, be it pictorial or sculptural. See D. Anzieu, *Le moi-peau*, Paris, Dunod, 1985.

[8] J. Guillaumin, "La peau du centaure," in *Corps-création*, Presses universitaires de Lyon, Lyons, 1980, pp. 227-269.

[9] M. Loreau, *La peinture à l'œuvre et l'énigme du style*, Paris, Gallimard, 1980, p. 22.

[10] G. de Maupassant, *Le Horla*, Paris, Gallimard, 1986, p. 51.

[11] O. Rank has pointed out this characteristic. See *Don Juan et le double*, Paris, Payot, 1973, with a great number of examples.

[12] F. M. Dostoyevsky, "The Double", in *Notes from the Underground*, London, Penguin Books, 1972.

[13] Pliny, *Natural History*, Book XXXV, 151, The Loeb Classical Library, London, William Heinemann Ltd, 1959.

[14] See, for example, A. Breton, *Nadja*, Paris, Gallimard, 1964.

[15] G. Vasari, *Lives of the Most Eminent Painters, Sculptors and Architects,* translated by J. Foster, London, G. Bell, 1885-1890.

[16] Quoted in the catalog *La peinture dans la peinture*, Musée des Beaux-Arts de Dijon, 18 December 1982 - 28 February 1983.

[17] *Ibid.*, p. 91.

[18] R. Barthes, *La chambre claire*, Paris, Gallimard-Seuil, 1980.

[19] O. Wilde, *The Picture of Dorian Gray*, edited by Peter Ackroyd, Penguin Books, London, 1985, p. 27.

[20] *Ibid.*, p. 144.

[21] *Ibid.*, p. 50.

[22] *Ibid.*, p. 120.

[23] *Ibid.*, p. 208.

[24] *Le Portrait de Dorian Gray*, Paris, Stock, 1983, Preface, p. 6.

[25] In the short story of the same name. See other examples in E. A. Poe, *Tales of Mystery and Imagination*, Everyman's Library, J. M. Dent and Sons, London, 1984.

[26] E. A. Poe, *op. cit.*, p. 205.

[27] P. L. Assoun, "Des effets pervers du narcissisme, le portrait de Dorian Gray," *Cahiers de psychologie de l'art et de la culture*, 2, 1985, pp. 75-92.

[28] This phantasm of being dispossessed is found in a number of other tales, particularly in M. Tournier's work, *La goutte d'or*, Paris, Gallimard, 1985. It is shown there in relation to the theft of an individual's self through his photographic image in Muslim culture.

[29] Ovid, *Metamorphoses*, Book III, The Loeb Classical Library, London, Heinemann Ltd, 1960.

[30] Quoted in "Narcisses," *Nouvelle revue de psychanalyse*, 13, Spring 1976, p. 313.

[31] L. B. Alberti, *Della pittura*, London, C. Grayson, II, p. 62.

[32] S. Freud, *Leonardo da Vinci and a Memory of His Childhood* (1910), *The Standard Edition of the Complete Psychological Works of Sigmund Freud*, London, Hogarth Press, vol. XI, 1957.

[33] S. Freud, *The Moses of Michelangelo* (1914), The Standard Edition, vol. XIII, 1953.

[34] S. Kofman, *L'enfance de l'art*, Paris, Galilée, 1985; Kofman reviews all of Freud's texts dealing with artistic production.

[35] S. Freud, *Totem and Taboo*, The Standard Edition, vol. XIII, p. 90.

[36] S. Freud, *ibid.*

[37] Quoted in S. Kofman, *op. cit.*, p. 189.

[38] A. Ehrenzweig, *L'ordre caché de l'art*, Paris, Gallimard, 1974, p. 141 *seq.*

[39] L. Andréas Salomé, *L'amour du narcissisme*, Paris, Gallimard, 1980, p. 116.

[40] *Ibid.*

Notes to Chapter Two

[1] See P. Bonafoux, *Les peintres et l'autoportrait*, Geneva, Skira, 1984.

[2] *Ibid.*, p. 5.

[3] Van Gogh, *Correspondance*, Paris, Grasset, 1960.

[4] Brassaï, *Conversations avec Picasso*, Paris, Gallimard, 1964, p. 147.

[5] P. Bonafoux, *op. cit.*, p. 142.

[6] *L'autoportrait à l'âge de la photographie*, Musée cantonal des beaux-arts de Lausanne, January-March 1985.

[7] H. Matisse, *Ecrits*, Paris, Hermann, 1972, p. 35.

[8] *Ibid.*, p. 69.

[9] *Ibid.*, p. 99.

[10] *Ibid.*, p. 163.

[11] *Ibid.*, p. 162.

[12] *Ibid.*, p. 196.

[13] *Ibid.*, p. 65.

[14] *Ibid.*, p. 85.

[15] *Ibid.*, p. 72.

[16] P. Strieder, *Dürer*, Anvers, Fonds Mercator, 1982, pp. 22-24.

[17] "Le journal de Pontormo," *Macula*, 5-6, 1979, pp. 5-44.

[18] Wallace Collection, London.

[19] 1938-1945, Beaubourg.

[20] 1931, Beaubourg.

[21] Ovide, *op. cit.*, Book X.

[22] Michelangelo, *Poésies*, Paris, Didier et Cie, 1875, p. 88.

[23] *Ibid.*, p. 171.

[24] *Ibid.*, p. 191.

[25] *Ibid.*, p. 237.

[26] *Ibid.*, p. 87.

[27] *Ibid.*, p. 219.

[28] *Ibid.*, p. 216.

[29] E. Zola, *L'Œuvre*, Paris, Fasquelle, 1966, p. 17.

[30] *Ibid.*, p. 70.
[31] *Ibid.*, p. 330.
[32] *Ibid.*, p. 337.
[33] R. Kipling, *The Light That Failed*, London, Penguin Classics, 1988, p. 136.
[34] J. Cary, *The Horse's Mouth*, Penguin Books, London, 1969, p. 97.
[35] *Ibid.*, p. 57.

Notes to Chapter Three

[1] *La peinture dans la peinture*, *op. cit.*, p. 84.
[2] This representation is due to an interpretation of a term used by Cicero, *simulacrum*, that is, image.
[3] A. Vollard, *Renoir*, Paris, Georges Gres, 1920.
[4] T. Gautier, *Mademoiselle de Maupin*, Paris, R.P., undated, p. 87.
[5] H. de Balzac, *The Unknown Masterpiece*, translated by A. Rudolf, The Menard Press, London, 1988, pp. 11-12.
[6] *Ibid.*, p. 14.
[7] *Ibid.*, p. 21.
[8] *Ibid.*, p. 18.
[9] *Ibid.*, p. 20.
[10] *Ibid.*, pp. 25-26.
[11] A. Vollard, *Paul Cézanne*, Paris, Georges Gres, 1919, p. 102.
[12] Quoted in R. Jean, *Cézanne, la vie, l'espace*, Paris, Seuil, 1986, p. 73.
[13] *Ibid.*, p. 96.
[14] *Ibid.*, p. 96.
[15] *Ibid.*, p. 309.
[16] L. Brion-Guerry, *Cézanne et l'expression de l'espace*, Paris, Albin Michel, 1966, p. 186.
[17] A. Vollard, *op. cit.*, p. 124.
[18] J. Lord, *Un portrait par Giacometti*, Paris, Mazarine, 1981.
[19] *Ibid.*, p. 30.
[20] *Ibid.*, p. 48.
[21] *Ibid.*, p. 56.
[22] *Ibid.*, p. 108.
[23] J. Genet, *L'atelier d'Alberto Giacometti*, L'arbalète, 1963.
[24] *Ibid.*
[25] Quoted in G. Didi-Huberman, *La peinture incarnée*, Paris, Minuit, 1985, p. 12.
[26] *Ibid.*, p. 26.
[27] William Hogarth, *The Analysis of Beauty*, ed. Joseph Burke, Oxford, The Clarendon Press, 1955, p. 95.
[28] *Ibid.*, pp. 125-126.
[29] *Ibid.*, pp. 178-179.
[30] *Ibid.*, pp. 74-75.
[31] E. Delacroix, *Journal*, Paris, Plon, 1932, vol. 2, p. 195.
[32] *Ibid.*, p. 157.
[33] *Ibid.*, p. 147.
[34] *Ibid.*, vol. 1, p. 113.
[35] *Ibid.*, vol. 2, p. 125.
[36] *Ibid.*, vol. 3, p. 317.
[37] *Ibid.*, p. 320.
[38] *Ibid.*, vol. 2, p. 399.
[39] *Ibid.*, vol. 1, p. 459.
[40] Quoted in P. Bonafoux, *op. cit.*, p. 125.
[41] M. Serres, *Les cinq sens*, Paris, Grasset, 1985, p. 32.
[42] *Ibid.*, p. 33.
[43] A. Vollard, *Renoir*, *op. cit.*, p. 19.
[44] *Ibid.*, p. 116.
[45] *Ibid.*, p. 80.
[46] *Ibid.*, p. 160.
[47] *Ibid.*, p. 238.
[48] Quoted in J.-L. Vaudoyer, *Le nu féminin*, Paris, Flammarion, undated, p. 6.
[49] *Ibid.*, p. 57.
[50] *Ibid.*, p. 35.
[51] *Ibid.*, p. 20.
[52] E. Panofsky, *Meaning in the Visual Arts*, Doubleday and Company, Garden City, N.Y., 1955, pp. 55-107.
[53] Leonardo da Vinci, *Les carnets*, Paris, Gallimard, 1942, p. 191.
[54] *Ibid.*, p. 233.
[55] Cf. *infra.*
[56] Dürer, *Lettres et écrits théoriques*, Paris, Hermann, 1964, p. 15.
[57] *Ibid.*, p. 187.
[58] *Ibid.*, p. 187.
[59] *Ibid.*, p. 162.
[60] *Ibid.*, p. 198.
[61] L. Sacher-Masoch, *L'esthétique de la laideur*, Paris, Buchet-Chastel, 1967, p. 65.
[62] *Ibid.*, p. 106.
[63] H. Delaborde, *Ingres*, Paris, Plon, 1870, p. 114.
[64] C. Baudelaire, *The Flowers of Evil*, "Beauty."
[65] A. Breton, *L'amour fou*, Paris, Gallimard, 1937, p. 26.
[66] *Ibid.*, p. 21.
[67] E. Delacroix, *op. cit.*, vol. 1, p. 394.
[68] J. Baudrillard, *De la séduction*, Paris, Galilée, 1979, p. 17.
[69] A. Walter, *Les relations d'incertitude*, Arles, Actes-Sud, 1987, p. 24.
[70] Cf. *supra.*
[71] J. Baudrillard, *op. cit.*, p. 107.
[72] *Ibid.*, p. 107.
[73] *Ibid.*, p. 115.
[74] J. Foucart, *Rembrandt*, Paris, Flammarion, 1971, p. 12.
[75] O. Wilde, *Intentions*, in *The Complete Works of Oscar Wilde*, Collins, London, 1948, p. 970.
[76] *Ibid.*, p. 970.
[77] *Ibid.*, p. 982.
[78] *Ibid.*, p. 989.

Notes to Chapter Four

[1] That is, a low class prostitute such as were found around the rue Bréda in Batignolles.
[2] Articles quoted in *Manet*, Grand Palais, 22 April - 1 August 1983, p. 165.

[3] *Ibid.*, p. 172.
[4] *Ibid.*, p. 179.
[5] *Ibid.*, p. 172.
[6] Quoted in *Le dernier Picasso*, Centre Georges Pompidou, 17 February - 16 May 1988, p. 34.
[7] E. Zola, *Œuvres complètes*, Paris, Tchou, 1969, vol. 12, p. 838.
[8] *Ibid.*, p. 839.
[9] P. Valéry, *Œuvres complètes*, Paris, Gallimard, 1960, vol. 2, p. 1329.
[10] *Manet*, Grand Palais, *op. cit.*, p. 181.
[11] Quoted in G. Bataille, *Œuvres complètes*, Paris, Gallimard, 1979, vol. 9, p. 139.
[12] Quoted in *Manet*, Grand Palais, *op. cit.*, p. 180.
[13] G. Bataille, *op. cit.*, p. 130.
[14] *Ibid.*, p. 126.
[15] *Ibid.*, p. 147.
[16] *Ibid.*, p. 159.
[17] Quoted in P. Lafond, *Degas*, Paris, Floury, undated, p. 26.
[18] *Ibid.*, p. 23.
[19] Quoted in *Degas*, Grand Palais, 9 February - 6 May 1988, p. 443.
[20] *Ibid.*, p. 446.
[21] Quoted in P.-A. Lemoisne, *Degas*, Paris, Librairie centrale des Beaux-Arts, undated, pp. 106-107.
[22] *Degas*, Grand Palais, *op. cit.*, p. 445.
[23] Quoted in C. Rich, *Degas*, Nouvelles éditions françaises, undated, p. 10.
[24] Quoted in P. Lafond, *op. cit.*, p. 18.
[25] Quoted in *Degas*, Grand Palais, *op. cit.*, p. 414.
[26] P. Valéry, *Degas-danse-dessin*, Paris, Gallimard, 1938, p. 128.
[27] *Ibid.*, p. 30.
[28] Quoted in *Elles*, Paris, Quatre chemins, 1952, p. 12.
[29] P. Huismans, M.-G. Dortu, *Lautrec par Lautrec*, Paris-Lausanne, Bibliothèque des arts – Edita, 1964, p. 139.
[30] A. Malraux, *La tête d'obsidienne*, Paris, Gallimard, 1974, p. 117.
[31] Quoted in *Les demoiselles d'Avignon*, Musée Picasso, 26 January - 18 April 1988, p. 378.
[32] *Ibid.*, p. 392.
[33] Brassaï, *Conversations avec Picasso*, Paris, Gallimard, 1964, p. 230.
[34] *Ibid.*, p. 470.
[35] A. Malraux, *op. cit.*, p. 108.
[36] *Ibid.*, p. 50.
[37] *Le dernier Picasso*, Centre Georges Pompidou, *op. cit.*, pp. 100-123.
[38] M. Leiris, *Le peintre et son modèle*, Montpellier, Fata Morgana, 1980.
[39] H. Parmelin, *Le peintre et son modèle*, Paris, Cercle d'art, 1965.
[40] *Ibid.*, p. 112.
[41] *Le dernier Picasso*, *op. cit.*, p. 18.
[42] H. Parmelin, *op. cit.*, p. 118.
[43] *Ibid.*, p. 120.
[44] *Ibid.*, p. 92.
[45] *Le dernier Picasso*, *op. cit.*, p. 25.
[46] Brassaï, *op. cit.*, p. 65.
[47] H. Parmelin, *Les dames de Mougins, secrets d'alcôve d'un atelier*, Paris, Cercle d'art, 1954.
[48] *Le dernier Picasso*, *op. cit.*, p. 42.
[49] *Ibid.*, p. 71.
[50] *Ibid.*, p. 48.
[51] *Ibid.*, p. 52.
[52] Pliny, *op. cit.*, XXXV, 86.
[53] *Ibid.*
[54] B. Cellini, *Mémoires*, Paris, Société littéraire de France, 1919, vol. 2, p. 72.
[55] See J.-C. Bologne, *Histoire de la pudeur*, Paris, O. Orban, 1986.
[56] *Ibid.*, p. 196.
[57] *Ibid.*, p. 198.
[58] G. Flaubert, *Voyages*, Paris, Les Belles Lettres, 1958, vol. 1, p. 203.
[59] *La peinture dans la peinture*, *op. cit.*, p. 197.
[60] Quoted in J.-C. Bologne, *op. cit.*, p. 209.
[61] *Ibid.*, p. 210.
[62] *Ibid.*, p. 211.
[63] Quoted in L. Bénédite, *Courbet*, Paris, Renaissance du livre, undated, p. 46.
[64] *Ibid.*, p. 46.
[65] Quoted in P. Mac Orlan, *Courbet*, Paris, Editions du Dimanche, 1951.
[66] Quoted in L. Bénédite, *op. cit.*, p. 50.
[67] *Courbet*, Mac Orlan, *op. cit.*, p. 7.
[68] Quoted in P. Mac Orlan, *op. cit.*
[69] A. Rodin, *L'art*, interviews collected by P. Gsell, Paris, Gallimard, 1967, p. 14.
[70] *Ibid.*, p. 92.
[71] *Ibid.*, p. 162.
[72] *Ibid.*, p. 137.
[73] R. M. Rilke, *Auguste Rodin*, Paris, Emile-Paul Frères, 1928.
[74] Quoted in P. du Colombier, *Les plus beaux écrits des grands artistes*, Paris, La Colombe, 1946, p. 375.
[75] Quoted in P. Sollers, A. Kirili, *Rodin, dessins érotiques*, Paris, Gallimard, 1987, p. 21.
[76] P. Grainville, *L'atelier du peintre*, Paris, Seuil, 1988, p. 23.
[77] *Ibid.*, p. 214.
[78] *Ibid.*, p. 246.
[79] *Ibid.*, p. 298.
[80] *Ibid.*, p. 306.

Notes to Chapter Five

[1] L. da Vinci, *Les Carnets*, Paris, Gallimard, 1942, p. 128.
[2] S. Freud, *Leonardo da Vinci and a Memory of his Childhood*, The Standard Edition, *op. cit.*, vol. XI.
[3] L. da Vinci, *Les Carnets*, *op. cit.*, p. 95.
[4] L. da Vinci, *Traité de la peinture*, Paris, Berger-Levrault, 1987, p. 224.
[5] *Ibid.*, p. 225.
[6] *Ibid.*, p. 226.

[7] "Le journal de Pontormo," *Macula*, 5-6, p. 47.

[8] See J. Kristeva, *Soleil noir, dépression et mélancolie*, Paris, Gallimard, 1987, pp. 117-150.

[9] A. Vesalius, *De humani corporis fabrica libri VII*, Basileae, per Ioannem Oporinum (1555). Vesalius' remarkable work has been made available to modern readers in a recent French edition: *La fabrique du corps humain*, Arles, Actes-Sud, 1987, p. 19.

[10] *Ibid.*, p. 49.

[11] R. Caillois, *Au cœur du fantastique*, Paris, Gallimard, 1965, p. 147.

[12] *Ibid.*, p. 146.

[13] P. Borel, *Champavert, Contes immoraux*, Paris, Editions des autres, 1979, pp. 110-130.

[14] R. Caillois, *op. cit.*, p. 159.

[15] Quoted in J.-L. Binet, P. Descargues, *Dessins et traités d'anatomie*, Paris, Chêne, 1980, p. 92.

[16] *Ibid.*, p. 120.

[17] C. Clément, *Géricault, étude biographique et critique avec le catalogue raisonné de l'œuvre du maître*, Paris, 1879.

[18] Quoted in J.-L. Binet, P. Descargues, *op. cit.*, p. 215.

[19] *Ibid.*, p. 216.

[20] M. Duval, *op. cit.*, p. 14.

[21] Quoted in *La sculpture française au XIXe siècle*, Grand Palais, 10 April - 28 July 1986, p. 29.

[22] G. Deleuze, *Francis Bacon, logique de la sensation*, Paris, La différence, 1981, p. 23.

[23] F. Bacon, *L'art de l'impossible, entretiens avec David Sylvester*, Geneva, Skira, 1976, vol. 1, p. 69.

[24] *Ibid.*, p. 80.

[25] *Ibid.*, p. 71.

[26] *Ibid.*, vol. 2, p. 74.

[27] *Ibid.*, vol. 1, p. 55.

[28] *Ibid.*, p. 92.

[29] *Ibid.*, p. 98.

[30] *Ibid.*, vol. 2, p. 36.

Bibliography

ALBERTI L. B., *Della pittura*, London, C.Crayson, undated, book II.

ANDRÉAS SALOMÉ L., *L'amour du narcissisme*, Paris, Gallimard, 1980.

ANZIEU D., *Le corps de l'œuvre*, Paris, Gallimard, 1981.

ASSOUN P. L., "Des effets pervers du narcissisme, le portrait de Dorian Gray", *Cahiers de psychologie de l'art et de la culture*, No. 11, autumn 1985, pp. 75-92.

BACON F., *L'art de l'impossible, entretiens avec David Sylvester*, Geneva, Skira, 1976.

BALTRUSAITIS J., *Le miroir*, P. Elmayan-Le Seuil, 1978.

BALZAC H. DE, *The Unknown Masterpiece*, London, Menard Press, 1988.

BARTHES R., *La chambre claire*, Paris, Gallimard-Seuil, 1980.

Roland Barthes par lui-même, Paris, Seuil, 1975.

BATAILLE G., *Œuvres complètes*, Paris, Gallimard, 1979.

BAUDELAIRE C., *Œuvres complètes*, Paris, Gallimard, 1976.

BAUDRILLARD J., *De la séduction*, Paris, Galilée, 1979.

BELLMER H., *L'anatomie de l'image*, in "Bellmer," *Obliques*, undated.

BÉNÉDITE L., *Courbet*, Paris, Renaissance du livre, undated.

BILLETER E., *L'autoportrait à l'âge de la photographie*, Musée cantonal des beaux-arts de Lausanne, January/March 1985.

BINET J.-L., DESCARGUES P., *Dessins et traités d'anatomie*, Paris, Chêne, 1980.

BOLOGNE J.-C., *Histoire de la pudeur*, Paris, Olivier Orban, 1986.

BONAFOUX P., *Portraits of the Artists*, Geneva, Skira, 1985.

BOREL P., *Champavert, Contes immoraux*, Paris, Editions des autres, 1979.

BRASSAÏ, *Conversations avec Picasso*, Paris, Gallimard, 1964.

BRETON A., *L'amour fou*, Paris, Gallimard, 1937.

Nadja, Paris, Gallimard, 1964.

BRION-GUERRY L., *Cézanne et l'expression de l'espace*, Paris, Albin Michel, 1966.

CAILLOIS R., *Au cœur du fantastique*, Paris, Gallimard, 1965.

CARY J., *The Horse's Mouth*, London, Penguin, 1969.

CELLINI B., *Mémoires*, Paris, Société littéraire de France, 1919.

CLÉMENT C., *Géricault, étude biographique et critique avec le catalogue raisonné de l'œuvre du maître*, Paris, 1879.

DELABORDE H., *Ingres*, Paris, Plon, 1870.

DELACROIX E., *Journal*, Paris, Plon, 1932.

DELEUZE G., *Francis Bacon, logique de la sensation*, Paris, La différence, 1981.

DIDI-HUBERMAN G., *La peinture incarnée*, Paris, Minuit, 1985.

DOSTOYEVSKY F. M., *"The Double," in Notes from the Underground*, London, Penguin, 1972.

DU COLOMBIER P., *Les plus beaux écrits des grands artistes*, Paris, La Colombe, 1946.

DUVAL M., CUYER E., *Histoire de l'anatomie plastique*, Paris, Alcide Picard et Kaan, 1898.

DÜRER A., *Lettres et écrits théoriques*, Paris, Hermann, 1964.

EHRENZWEIG A., *L'ordre caché de l'art*, Paris, Gallimard, 1974.

ELLES, Paris, Quatre chemins, 1952.

FLAUBERT G., *Voyages*, Paris, Les Belles Lettres, 1958.

FOUCART J., *Rembrandt*, Paris, Flammarion, 1971.

FREUD S., *The Standard Edition of the Complete Psychological Works of Sigmund Freud*, London, Hogarth Press, 1953-1974.

Delusions and Dreams in Jensen's Gradiva (1907), vol. IX.

Leonardo da Vinci and a Memory of His Childhood (1910), vol. XI.

The Moses of Michelangelo (1914), vol. XIII.

Totem and Taboo (1913), vol. XIII.

GAUTIER T., *Mademoiselle de Maupin*, Paris, R.P., undated.

GENET J., *L'atelier d'Alberto Giacometti*, L'arbalète, 1963.

GRAINVILLE P., *L'atelier du peintre*, Paris, Seuil, 1988.

GUILLAUMIN J., *La peau du centaure, in* "Corps-création", Presses universitaires de Lyon, 1980, pp. 227-269.

HOGARTH W., *The Analysis of Beauty*, Oxford, Clarendon Press, 1955.

HUISMANS P., DORTU M.-G., *Lautrec par Lautrec*, Paris-Lausanne, Bibliothèque des arts-Edita, 1964.

JEAN R., *Cézanne, la vie, l'espace*, Paris, Seuil, 1986.

KIPLING R., *The Light That Failed*, London, Penguin, 1988.

KOFMAN S., *L'enfance de l'art*, Paris, Galilée, 1985.

KRISTEVA J., *Soleil noir, dépression et mélancolie*, Paris, Gallimard, 1987.

LAFOND P., *Degas*, Paris, Floury, undated.

LEIRIS M., *Le peintre et son modèle*, Montpellier, Fata Morgana, 1980.

LEMOISNE P.-A., *Degas*, Paris, Librairie centrale des Beaux-Arts, undated.

LORD J., *Un portrait par Giacometti*, Paris, Mazarine, 1981.

LOREAU M., *La peinture à l'œuvre et l'énigme du style*, Paris, Gallimard, 1980.

MAC ORLAN P., *Courbet*, Paris, Editions du Dimanche, 1951.

MALRAUX A., *La tête d'obsidienne*, Paris, Gallimard, 1974.

MATISSE H., *Ecrits*, Paris, Hermann, 1972.

MAUPASSANT G. DE, *Le Horla*, Paris, Gallimard, 1986.

MERLEAU-PONTY M., *Le visible et l'invisible*, Paris, Gallimard, 1964.

MICHELANGELO, *Poésies*, Paris, Didier et Cie, 1875.

NARCISSES, *Nouvelle revue de psychanalyse*, No. 13, spring 1976.

OVID, *Metamorphoses*, London, Loeb Classical Library, 1960.

PANOFSKY E., *Meaning in the Visual Arts*, New York, Doubleday, 1955.

PARMELIN H., *Le peintre et son modèle*, Paris, Cercle d'art, 1965.
Les dames de Mougins, secrets d'alcôve d'un atelier, Paris, Cercle d'art, 1954.
PLINY, *Natural History*, London, Loeb Classical Library, 1959.
POE E. A., *Tales of Mystery and Imagination*, London, Everyman's Library, 1984.
PONTORMO, *Journal, in* "Macula," No. 5-6, 1979.
PRÉVERT J., *Imaginaires*, Geneva, Skira, 1970.

RANK O., *Don Juan et le double*, Paris, Payot, 1973.
REINACH A., *Recueil Millet*, Paris, Klincksieck, 1921.
RICH C., *Degas*, Paris, Nouvelles éditions françaises, undated.
RILKE R. M., *Auguste Rodin*, Paris, Emile-Paul Frères, 1928.
RODIN A., *L'art*, entretiens réunis par P. Gsell, Paris, Gallimard, 1967.

SACHER-MASOCH L., *L'esthétique de la laideur*, Paris, Buchet-Chastel, 1967.
SARTRE J.-P., *Qu'est-ce que la littérature?*, Paris, Gallimard, 1985.
SERRES M., *Les cinq sens*, Paris, Grasset, 1985.
SOLLERS P., KIRILI A., *Rodin, dessins érotiques*, Paris, Gallimard, 1987.
STRIEDER P., *Dürer*, Anvers, Fonds Mercator, 1982.

VALÉRY P., *Degas - danse - dessin*, Paris, Gallimard, 1938.
Œuvres complètes, Paris, Gallimard, 1960.
VAN GOGH V., *Correspondance*, Paris, Grasset, 1960.
VASARI G., *Lives of the Most Eminent Painters, Sculptors and Architects*, London, G. Bell, 1885-1890.
VAUDOYER J.-L., *Le nu féminin*, Paris, Flammarion, undated.
VESALIUS A., *De humani corporis fabrica libri VII*, Basel, 1555.
VINCI L. DE, *Les carnets*, Paris, Gallimard, 1942.
Traité de la peinture, Paris, Berger-Levrault, 1987.
VOLLARD A., *Paul Cézanne*, Paris, G. Gres, 1919.
Renoir, Paris, G. Gres, 1920.

WALTER A., *Les relations d'incertitude*, Arles, Actes-Sud, 1987.
WILDE O., *Intentions, The Complete Works*, London, Collins, 1948.
The Portrait of Dorian Gray, London, Penguin, 1985.

ZOLA E., *Œuvres complètes*, Paris, Tchou, 1969.

Exhibition catalogues

Degas, Grand Palais, 9 February - 16 May 1988.
La peinture dans la peinture, Musée des Beaux-Arts de Dijon, 18 December 1982 - 28 February 1983.
La sculpture française au XIXe siècle, Grand Palais,10 April - 28 July 1986.
Le dernier Picasso, Centre Georges Pompidou, 17 February - 16 May 1988.
Manet, Grand Palais, 22 April - 1 August1983.
Les demoiselles d'Avignon, Musée Picasso, 26 January -18 April 1988.

List of Illustrations

PHOTOGRAPHS

SKIRA

Text and plates printed by
IRL Imprimeries Réunies Lausanne s.a.

Binding by
Mayer & Soutter S.A., Renens-Lausanne

Printed in Switzerland